HISTORY

OF THE

SUPPRESSION OF INFANTICIDE

HISTORY

OF THE

SUPPRESSION OF INFANTICIDE

IN

WESTERN INDIA

UNDER THE GOVERNMENT OF BOMBAY:

INCLUDING

NOTICES OF THE PROVINCES AND TRIBES IN WHICH THE PRACTICE HAS PREVAILED.

JOHN WILSON, D. D., F.R.S.

GYAN

Published by

Gyan Publishing House
5, Ansari Road
Daryaganj, New Delhi-110002
Phone: 011-47034999, 9811692060
E-mail: books@gyanbooks.com

Distribution Network
gyanbooks.com
India, USA, Canada, UK, Australia, France

ISBN: 978-81-212-8828-6 (PB)
First Published, 1855

2nd Impression 2023

Printed at: Gyan Press, Delhi.

HISTORY OF THE SUPPRESSION OF INFANTICIDE
Author: John Wilson

SUPPRESSION OF INFANTICIDE
IN WESTERN INDIA.

HISTORY

OF THE

SUPPRESSION OF INFANTICIDE

IN

WESTERN INDIA

UNDER THE GOVERNMENT OF BOMBAY:

INCLUDING

NOTICES OF THE PROVINCES AND TRIBES IN WHICH THE PRACTICE HAS PREVAILED.

BY JOHN WILSON, D.D., F.R.S.,

HONORARY PRESIDENT OF THE BOMBAY BRANCH OF THE ROYAL ASIATIC SOCIETY, AND MISSIONARY OF THE FREE CHURCH OF SCOTLAND, ETC.

BOMBAY

SMITH, TAYLOR AND CO.

LONDON: SMITH, ELDER AND CO., 65, CORNHILL.

M.DCCC.LV.

TO

JOHN POLLARD WILLOUGHBY, ESQ.,

FORMERLY OF THE BOMBAY CIVIL SERVICE,

AND NOW ONE OF THE DIRECTORS OF THE EAST INDIA COMPANY, ETC.

MY DEAR SIR,

IN the History of the Suppression of Infanticide in Western India, a goodly number of the sons of Britain are associated with devisings and deeds of benevolence, well worthy of remembrance and commemoration by their grateful countrymen. Among them the names of DUNCAN, WALKER, and WILLOUGHBY stand conspicuous:—of DUNCAN, who discovered the existence of the horrid systematic child-murder of the Jáḍejás of Káṭhiáwáḍ and Kachh, and wisely directed and encouraged the first movements towards its discountenance and abolition; of WALKER, who with much ingenuity and ability negociated the first engagement for its abandonment; and of WILLOUGHBY, who ultimately suggested or adjusted the practical measures of inquiry, registration, review, reward, and punishment which through the divine blessing have effected its extinguishment as a custom. To you, as the survivor of these "first three heroes" in this honorable field of

> Peace with her victories
> No less renowned than war,

I inscribe this volume, in which the origin, progress, and issue of this great work of Christian philanthropy are fully, though simply, recorded. This I do in all sincerity, and with the respect and deference which are due to the ability, prudence, zeal, and perseverance, which as assistant-resident at the Court of Baroda, political agent in Káṭhiáwáḍ, chief secretary in Bombay, and a member of the government of the western presidency of India, you brought to bear on the cause for upwards of a quarter of a century, during which it made great demands on your observation, vigilance, judgment, and administrative capacity. To the public functionaries who have been united with you in this labour of love and duty, I trust that the following pages will also be acceptable, more especially as in framing them I have conscientiously sought to be guided by the maxim of equity, *suum cuique tribue;* and because I have made each of them in his turn, as far as possible, his own historian, seeking only to introduce to the reader the subject under report, and to evolve the analysis, maintain the connexion, and furnish the illustrations and applications which the narrative has seemed to require. Among these distinguished fellow-workers, in late years, specially worthy of their country's approbation, are COLONEL LANG, in Káṭhiáwáḍ and the Máhíkanṭhá; SIR HENRY POTTINGER, COLONEL MELVILL, MR. LUMSDEN, and MR. RAIKES, in Kachh; COLONEL JACOB, and Mr. MALET, in Káṭhiáwáḍ and Kachh; Major WALLACE in the Máhikanṭhá; and His HIGHNESS THE RA'O OF KACHH, who has been as zealous in the cause as any of his European counsellors. The BOMBAY GOVERNMENT has not failed to mark and encourage their efforts and those of the other meritorious officials mentioned in these pages, as well as those of yourself, for the support and countenance and review of which, from first to last, and under all its governors, it is entitled to the highest credit. Nor has the Honorable the Court of Directors of the East India Company been less observant. It early expressed its high commendation of the proceedings of the first movers in the cause. It has watched over those of their successors with undiminished attention and interest. In 1815, it enjoined, in the most serious and earnest manner, its representatives in Bombay "to be unremitting in their endeavours to accomplish the humane object," of the abolition of infanticide "wherever the British influence can be felt or exerted." It has continued to maintain its anti-infanticide establishments in India at great expence of money and labour. It has shown a wise discrimination in the instructions which it has issued on the subject, and in its distinct approbation, in particular, of the measures with the origination and pursuit of which you have have been so intimately connected. Writing to the Government of India on the 16th May 1838, it thus expressed itself:— "We think it desirable that you should obtain from the Bombay Government and circulate among your political functionaries, a clear, and succinct statement of the system which has now been practised for some years with considerable success by that Government for the suppression of Infanticide in Káṭhiáwáḍ, and which conforms in all respects to our conception of the most efficacious means of obtaining the desired result."

The reader of the following pages will be at no loss to discover the sources of the narrative which they contain. It is derived principally from the official records of the Bombay Government. To a portion of these documents on the subject of infanticide, the public has access in the volumes of Major Edward Moor and the Rev. Dr. Cormack, in which the proceedings of Governor Duncan and Colonel Walker are fully detailed, and more especially in the Parliamentary Papers ordered to be printed on the 17th June 1824, 25th June 1828, and 21st June 1843. For those of a later date, I have been directly indebted to the Bombay Government itself, which, on the kind proposal of LORD FALKLAND, for which I beg to express my best thanks, has, under both the administration of his Lordship and that of his successor LORD ELPHINSTONE, furnished me with copies of them, or given me the use of the originals. For the facility with which I have found access to them individually, I have been much indebted to Mr. R. HUGHES THOMAS, of whose practical familiarity with the numerous and multifarious documents in the political department of the secretariate you need not to be informed. I should have been glad to have included in my work a detail of the measures adopted for the suppression of Infanticide in Rajputáná properly so called and Central India, under the Supreme Government; in the North-West Provinces, under the Government of Agra; and on the banks of the affluents of the Indus, under the Administration of the Panjáb. But I have felt that till these measures, so promising at the present time, are more advanced, the treatment of them would have interfered with the unity of this work, and made demands upon me for illustrations of peoples and provinces to which I am an entire stranger, except as an humble student of the general ethnography of this great country. Even in regard to the provinces under the Bombay Government actually treated of in these pages, I should certainly have declined to deal with them, had I not personally traversed them all in their length and breadth, and that in the case of most of them more than once, mingling freely with their inhabitants of all classes, literally from the prince on the throne to the beggar on the hill of ashes; had I not, in the exigencies of my own professional duties, diligently investigated their manners and customs and the religious and historical foundations on which they rest; and had I not enjoyed the acquaintance and friendship of most of their British functionaries, from Colonel Walker downwards to those who now hold office within their borders.

Exterior to India, there is a general belief that the measures of Duncan and Walker for the suppression of infanticide in Káṭhiáwáḍ and Kachh met with a speedy and complete success. This, it will be seen, was far from being the case. The diabolical monster against which these earnest philanthropists contended did not receive from them his fatal blow. They pointed out his existence; they declared that the influence of Britain must be applied for his taming; they succeeded in soothing him into the promise that he would never again go forth on his career of destruction. But they did nothing more. Events soon showed that as little dependence was to be placed on Rajput honour and veracity as on Rajput humanity. The monster revived and returned to his deeds of blood and pollution. Anew he had to be treated with British skill and determination. He had to be bound by the cords and meshes of political restriction and restraint. The hand of punishment had to descend upon his back in strokes which he could feel, and the foot of power had to rest upon his head with such pressure as induced him, like the Káliya of Hindu fable before Krishna, to murmur out, "Behold I am without strength, without poison." The struggle with him has lasted for nearly half a century; and even now it is scarcely ended. The eye of British vigilance will probably never be safely withdrawn from Rajput sovereignty and society, till those moral influences are felt throughout the provinces of India which shall introduce the blessed day in which "the sucking child shall play on the hole of the asp, and the weaned child shall put his hand on the cockatrice den." But, still, as matters at present stand, great and good have been the results of the political wisdom and Christian philanthropy which have been brought to bear on the Rajput states of Western India. The blood of five hundred Jáḍejá female infants yearly shed by the unnatural parental hand in Káṭhiáwáḍ and Kachh, and of at least a hundred more in the districts of Pálanpur, the Máhíkáṇṭha, and Ahmadábád, no longer defiles these territories, acting within them as a moral pestilence, and crying loud for the vengeance of Heaven. The humanizing influences of the arrangements which have been made, and which are still in operation, have been widely felt. The British Government has obtained credit among millions of people for mercy and disinterestedness; and the general confidence in the advantages of its administration has been greatly encreased. The anti-infanticide history of Western India, while in many respects it is of a painful character, is both interesting and instructive to the student of human nature and of the religious systems and practices of the East. One fact connected with it is well worthy of special notice. While Hinduism has really sought to prevent infanticide by express legislation, it has in reality given great encouragement to its origination and continuance, by the status which it has assigned to the female sex and by many of its general ordinances. It is only divine revelation which proves itself adequate to the preservation of the equilibrium of perfect morality.

I have only to observe in conclusion that, in the representation of the numerous oriental names of persons and places occuring in this work, I have, excluding one or two slight inadvertences caused by the imperfection of my authorities, rigidly followed, as in other publications, the system of Sir William Jones with the few modifications of it which have been adopted by the Royal Asiatic and Royal Geographical Societies, the advantages of which are now becoming every day more widely recognized. Had it not been for the purpose of illustrating the claims of the *Jáḍejás* for descent from the *Yádavas* of the Mahábhárat and the *Jáḍá* of Sindh, and other etymological reasons, I should have been content to write of them under their common English designation of *Jarejahs* and of their present countries as *Kattywar* and *Kutch*, instead of *Káṭhiáwáḍ* and *Kachh*, which accuracy demands.

Begging you to excuse all the imperfections of this work, in the subject of which you are so deeply interested, I am,

My dear Mr. Willoughby,

Yours with much esteem and respect,

JOHN WILSON.

BOMBAY, APRIL, 1855.

CONTENTS.

CHAPTER. I.

CHAPTER III.

CHAPTER III.

CHAPTER IV.

CHAPTER V.

CHAPTER VI.

CHAPTER VII.

CHAPTER VIII.

CHAPTER IX.

CHAPTER X.

CHAPTER XI.

CHAPTER XII.

CHAPTER XIII.

CHAPTER XIV.

CHAPTER XV.

CHAPTER XVI.

CHAPTER XVII.

SUPPRESSION OF INFANTICIDE.

CHAPTER I.

ORIGIN AND PREVALENCE OF INFANTICIDE—CIRCUMSTANCES UNFAVOURABLE AND FAVOURABLE TO ITS PRACTICE IN INDIA.

MURDER is the first specific crime brought to our notice after the fall of man from his state of innocence and righteousness; and in its form of INFANTICIDE it has been more or less practised and approved, from motives of corrupted religion and mistaken social economy, by almost all the tribes and nations of the world.

When the grand objects of sacrifice the earliest prescribed rite of religion,—the acknowledgement by the worshipper of a guilt deserving suffering and death and the foreshadowing of the offering of the promised Substitute and Saviour,—were forgotten or obscurely remembered, the maxim that the "fruit of the body should be given for the sin of the soul" obtained a wide currency in the human family. Speedily the character of the Divinity was mistaken for that of a Demon; and in the conceptions formed by man of God, a malevolence thirsting for blood was substituted for a love of holiness seeking to impress on the intelligent creation the dread of sin by pointing to the great redemption needed for its absolution. Children of tender age became the most manageable, as well as most precious, of victims. They were not only destroyed to deprecate and avert apprehended evil, but offered up as the price and purchase of desired good. To a few only of the many examples of their disposal for these objects can we advert.

The *Phœnicians* and *Canaanites* made their children "pass through the fire to Moloch" or Baal,—for the meaning of the names is the same,—the "lord" or sun, of whom fire was the symbol and servitor; and so firmly had they established this cruel rite in the countries of their sojourn that even the *Israelites* who were commissioned by God to supplant the Canaanites because of their abandonment to wickedness, and who were themselves forbidden to give their seed to this false god on the penalty of death,* were frequently tempted to become their imitators in this horrid iniquity. Even Solomon, the wisest of men, did not escape its contamination,

> First, Moloch, horrid king besmear'd with blood
> Of human sacrifice, and parents' tears
> Though for the noise of drums and timbrels loud
> Their children's cries unheard, that pass'd through fire
> To this grim idol. Him the Ammonite
> Worshipped in Rabba and her watery plain,
> In Argob and in Basan, to the stream
> Of utmost Arnon. Nor content with such
> Audacious neighbourhood, the wisest heart
> Of Solomon he led by fraud to build
> His temple right against the temple of God
> On that opprobrious hill; and made his grove
> The pleasant valley of Hinnom, Tophet thence
> And black Genhenna call'd, the type of hell.

Manasseh actually sacrificed his son to Moloch.† Even after the good king Josiah had defiled Tophet in order to put a stop to the infantile sacrifices there practised,‡ the crime was revived, and called forth the solemn denunciations of the prophets.§

* Lev. xx. 1; Deut. xviii. 10—12.

† 2 Kings xxi. 6.

‡ 2 Kings xxiii. 10.

§ Jer. xix. 5; xxxii. 35; Ezek. xvi. 20, 21; xxiii. 37, 39.

The *Carthaginians*, who were a colony of the Phœnicians, carried with them to the shores of the Mediterranean, the religion of the mother country. In all emergencies of state, and at all seasons of public calamity, they presented their own offspring to their wrathful God. They had their special festivals, too, for their infantile sacrifices. They selected their victims from the most noble and respectable families. "If a person," says Bryant, who has well collected the testimony of antiquity respecting their offerings of blood, "had only one child it was the more liable to be put to death, as being esteemed more acceptable to the deity, and more efficacious of the general good! Those who were sacrificed to Kronus [the analogue, according to the Greeks, of Moloch] were thrown into the arms of a molten idol, which stood in the midst of a large fire, and was red with heat. The arms of it were stretched out, with the hands turned upwards, as it were to receive them, yet sloping downwards, so that they dropt into a glowing furnace below. To other gods they were otherwise slaughtered, and as it is implied, by the very hands of their parents." "Justin describes this unnatural custom very pathetically. Such was their blind zeal, that this was continually practised; and so much natural affection was still left unextinguished, as to render the scene ten times more shocking from the tenderness which they seemed to express. They embraced their children with great fondness, and encouraged them in the gentlest terms, that they might not be appalled at the sight of the hellish process; begging them to submit with cheerfulness to this fearful operation. If there was any appearance of a tear rising, or a cry unawares escaping, the mother smothered it with her kisses, that there might not be any shew of backwardness or constraint, but that the whole might be a freewill offering! These cruel endearments over, they stabbed them to the heart, or otherwise opened the sluices of life, and with the blood, warm as it ran, besmeared the altar and the grim visage of the idol."

"Would it not," says Plutarch with reference to these very atrocities, "have been more eligible for the Carthaginians to have had the atheist Critias, or Diagoras, for their lawgiver at the commencement of their polity, and to have been taught that there was neither god nor demon, than to have sacrified as they were wont to the god which they adored." "These people used knowingly and willingly to go through this bloody work, and slaughter their own offspring. Even they who were childless would not be exempted from this tribute, but purchased children, and put them to death. The mother who sacrificed her child stood by, without any seeming sense of what she was losing, and without uttering a groan. If a sigh did by chance escape, she lost all the honour which she proposed to herself in the offering, and the child was notwithstanding slain. All the time of this celebrity while the children were murdered there was a noise of clarions and tambours sounding before the idol, that the cries and shrieks of the victims might not be heard. 'Tell me now,' said Plutarch, 'if the monsters of old, the Typhons and the Giants, were to expel the gods, and to rule the world in their stead, could they require a service more horrid than these infernal rites and sacrifices."*

Though the details of sacrificial infanticide practised by other ancient nations may not be so shocking as those now mentioned, to the eye and ear of that sensibility which has been begotten and nourished among those whose "lines have fallen in the pleasant places," this, it is to be feared, is only because they have not been recorded with so great minuteness. They are still of a most painful and heart-rending character. The *Pelasgi*, whose wanderings and settlements are known to have been so extensive in Asia and Europe, vowed in a time of scarcity that they would present the tenth of all that should be born to them for a sacrifice. The *Greeks*,

* Bryant in Annual Register, 1767.

both of the peninsula and archipelago and of the adjoining coasts, had their human sacrifices, from which children were not excluded; and of them the *Spartans* whipped their children with such severity before the altar of Diana Orthia that they frequently expired under the torture. The *Sabines* on one occasion during a famine vowed to sacrifice everything born during the succeeding spring, provided it were averted.* The *Romans* were scarcely behind the Greeks in atrocities of this kind; and Caius Marius, according to Clemens, offered up his own daughter to obtain success in a battle with the *Cimbri*. The worship of the *Gauls*, and *Celts*, and *Germans*, and *Northerns* was peculiarly dark and cruel, both as far as youth and age, of both ruling and subject families, were concerned. The *Persians* were not guiltless of shedding innocent infant blood in the name of religion. Herodotus directly charges them with burying children alive, and mentions the case of fourteen children so disposed of by the orders of Amestris the wife of Xerxes.† The destruction of illegitimate children by procuring abortion seems to be warranted by the Zandávastá.‡ The *Arabs* sacrificed children and buried them under their altars, even when they had no idols. Among the *Israelites* alone, sacrificial Infanticide seems to have been absolutely forbidden.§

* Smith's Rom. Antiq. quoted in Beck's Medical Jurisprudence, vol. i. p. 378.

† Herod. Hist. Polymnia, v.

‡ See author's work on Pársí Religion, pp. 79-82.

§ The tentative command given to Abraham to offer his son Isaac as a "burnt-offering," was issued directly by the Lord of life and death as a simple test of obedience, and not for the purpose of either establishing or supporting a religious ceremony; and its object was to prove whether Abraham would, in the view of it and his determination to obey it, still believe that the promise of offspring through Isaac would be fulfilled. "By faith Abraham when he was tried, offered up Isaac: and he that had received the promises offered up his only-begotten Son, of whom it was said that in Isaac shall thy seed be called: accounting that God was able to raise him up; from whence also he received him in a figure." Heb. xi. 17-19.

The murder of children from particular views of social economy has not been less extensive and horrid than that in the name of religion. Of this fact many striking and impressive illustrations have been collected by Malthus in his well-known work on Population, and by Dr. Miller of Glasgow in his treatise on the Origin of Ranks; and referred to by Dr. Cormack in his excellent work on Infanticide, and by several writers on Medical Jurisprudence. "The motives," says Dr. Cormack, "which led to this crime among different tribes, will be found to vary with circumstances; but that which gave power and prevalence to any motives whatever, must necessarily be admitted to have been the want of natural affection."*

On the cases, so frequently noticed, amongst *barbarous or semi-barbarous nations*, it is not necessary particularly to dwell. Among them the feeling of obligation to rear their offspring has varied much with the possession or removal of the means of their care and support. Difficulties in procuring sustenance, the approach or apprehension of famine, the loss of a mother, distress in war, inconvenience in family arrangements, obstacles to marriage, and other trials and inconveniences, have been too often viewed as reasons for the neglect, desertion, or destruction of their offspring. "In *China*," which has made more progress in modern times in economic civilization than any other heathen country, it is said, "religion and interest concur in favouring the rearing of children; for the happiness of deceased ancestors is supposed to be increased by the honor done them by their descendants; and the law requires that children shall maintain their parents in indigent old age. Yet in the great cities of Pekin and Canton, in particular, Sir George Staunton found the exposure of children to be very common. Among the Chinese, however, it is to be ascribed to the extreme poverty, which is so frequently

* Cormack on Infanticide, p. 42.

occasioned, in that vast empire, by a redundant population, which, even in years of plenty, presses close to the means of subsistence."*

Of the crime of Infanticide, even the most *civilized*

* Cormack on Infanticide, pp. 43-4. Late documents shew that in regard to China this statement is not altogether correct, for they accuse the rich, as well as the poor, of the crime, which the Chinese government now seriously seeks to prevent, as appears from the following interesting proclamation of Le, the late Lieut. Governor of the province of Canton, dated 19th February 1838, which we take from the Chinese Repository.

"Lieut. Governor Le hereby promulgates his instructions. Whereas heaven and earth display their benevolent power in giving existence, and fathers and mothers exhibit their tender affection in loving their offspring, it is therefore incumbent on you, inhabitants of the land, to nurse and rear all your little infants, whether male or female. On inquiry, I find that in the province of Canton the drowning of female children is common, and that both rich and poor run into this practice. The causes of infanticide are manifestly these; the poor suppose, that because they have not the means of support, it is unfitting they should nourish a commodity (female infants) which will become only an increasing source of expenditure; while the rich affirm, that such slender tenants of the nursery can never be raised to any important posts in the household. Surely you forget, that your mothers and wives about you were once female children. Had there been no mothers, whence would you have obtained your own bodies? If you have no wives where will be your posterity? Being yourselves the offspring of those who were once female children, why cast your own into the field of death? Reflect! Consider what you are doing! The destruction of female infants, is nothing less than the slaughter of human beings. That those who kill, shall themselves be killed, is the sure retribution of omniscient heaven.

"Should the widowed mother ever be left without a son, on whom she can be dependent for maintenance, the husband of a daughter may become the support and solace of her old age: is this a benefit lightly to be esteemed? Moreover, that just conduct ensures happiness, and that its opposite leads to misery—are two principles of retribution most firmly supported by reason. The crying, weeping babe, the moment it comes into being, is entangled in the net of death! To do this, requires the disposition of a pirate—the utter extinction of every generous feeling! To such the hope of numerous posterity, a long line of descendants—celestial reason will never grant.

"Recently an essay on Infanticide has been written by Hwang Wan, a literary gentleman belonging to the district of Yingtih. Therein I *nations* of antiquity, including those of *Greece* and *Rome* their highest type, have not been guiltless. "It is probable," says Malthus, "that the practice of infanticide had prevailed from the earliest ages in Greece."* "And when Solon permitted the exposing of children, it is probable that he only gave the sanction of law to a custom already prevalent,"† The Spartan lawgiver, indeed, ordered every child to be examined by the elders of the tribe, and when weak or deformed to be thrown into a cavern at the base of Mount Taygetus, "concluding," as mentioned by Plutarch, "that its life could be of no advantage either to itself or the public, since nature had not given it at first any strength or goodness of constitution"‡ "The source of the crime with individual perpetrators," says Dr. Cormack, who has notic-

perceive that the reciprocal influences between heaven and man, the basis of success and misfortune, of weal and woe,—are delineated with force and light sufficient to unstop the ears of the deaf and to open the eyes of the blind. Copies of this essay I have caused to be sent into all the departments and districts of the province, with admonitions and instructions, that the practice of infanticide may everywhere be examined into and forbidden. I also issue this proclamation for the instruction of all the inhabitants of the province, both civil and military. Henceforth it becomes the duty of each and all of you to revere the benevolent power of heaven and earth; to exercise in their fullest extent those kind feelings which fathers and mothers owe their offspring; and when you have sons and daughters born to you and your hearts are inclined to this most foul and cruel practice of infanticide, then break from your slumbers, repent and turn from your former misdeeds. And you, elders and gentry, chief among the people, ought likewise continually to endeavour by your exhortations, your support, and your kindness, to prevent the destruction of human life. Hereafter, if any dare to oppose and act in opposition to these instructions, it shall be the duty of the elders and gentry to report them to the local magistrates, that they may be seized, examined, and punished. Assuredly no clemency will be shown to such offenders. Therefore give good heed to these instructions. A special proclamation."

* Malthus on Population, 6th ed. vol. i. p. 233. † Ib. p. 234.

‡ Plut. Lives, by Langhorne, vol. i. p. 12.

ed the facts with a high tone of moral feeling "was, no doubt apathy and convenience, whilst the object of the state was to check a redundant and unproductive population. Of all the states of Greece, the Thebans are mentioned by Ælian, as the only exception to the general practice of exposing infants at the will of their parents. Schefferus, in his annotations on the passage of Ælian, remarks, that 'this conduct of the Thebans was contrary both to the law and the practice of the rest of the Greeks, and particularly of the Athenians.' By the other states of Greece, infanticide was sanctioned and regulated by law. Some legal provisions, indeed, for the regulation of this practice, seem to have been thought requisite by the most profound and able philosophers of Greece. In the republics of Plato and Aristotle, accordingly, we find very special enactments suggested on the subject; and with as much apparent apathy as if parental feeling and natural effection were unworthy of man. The period of marriage was to be fixed in regard of either sex; the children of poorer citizens were to be destroyed at their birth; and the children of parents of whatever rank, who had attained a certain age, were never to be allowed to appear. These two philosophers agreed in one principle, which appears to have been the great political maxim with Greek legislators, that there should be kept up an effective population, proportioned to the wants and resources of the state; and to this object were to be sacrificed every feeling of humanity, and every thing that renders man worthy of his nature and his name.* In this respect the Romans were not superior to the Greeks. It may be proper here to quote the words of Dr. Miller, who will not be suspected of prejudice against that celebrated people. 'By a law of Romulus,' says he, 'parents are said to have been obliged to maintain their

[* Even the Greek poets allude to the prevalent custom without abhorrence, as Euripides in his Ion and Sophocles in his Ædipus Tyrannus.]

male children, and the eldest female, unless when a child was, by two of the neighbours, called for the purpose, declared to be a monster. A regulation of the same nature is mentioned among the laws of the twelve tables; but there is ground to believe that little regard was paid to it; and even under the emperors, the exposing of new-born children, of either sex, appears to have been exceedingly common.'* It is well known also, that, according to the laws and customs of the Romans, the father had anciently an unlimited power of putting his children to death, after they were grown up, and even officially employed by the state, and likewise of selling them for slaves. To allude, even slightly, to the practices of the Romans, on this point, would fill the reader with disgust and horror, and satisfy him that the picture of them drawn by St. Paul is, by no means overloaded. 'Vicious habits of every possible kind, preventive of population,' says Malthus, 'seem to have been so generally prevalent, at this period,' that of the Emperors, 'that no corrective laws could have any considerable influence.'† From these statements it appears that infanticide, in one way or other, has prevailed, not in barbarous nations alone, but generally speaking over all the heathen world; and that so far was it from being prevented by the boasted wisdom, civilization, and refinement of Greece and Rome, these very qualities were employed in cherishing, regulating,

* Miller on Ranks, 4th edit. pp. 131—2.

† Malthus, 6th edit. i. p. 247. In a note in the preceding page, he says, "How completely the laws relating to the encouragement of marriage and of children were despised, appears from a speech of Minucius Felix, in Octavio, cap. 30. *Vos enim video procreatos filios nunc feris et avibus exponere, nunc ad strangulatos misero mortes genere elidere sunt quæ in ipsis visceribus medicaminibus epotis originem futuri hominis extinguant, et parricidium faciant antequam pariant.*" "This crime," adds he, "had grown so much into a custom in Rome, that even Pliny attempts to excuse it:" "Quoniam aliquarum fecunditas plena liberis tuli veniâ indiget," lib. xxix. c. 4.

and perpetuating the crime. The conclusion, which seems to be warranted by these facts, is, that we have little security against infanticide, or any other crime against nature, where Christianity is unknown."* It is remarkable that the laws of Moses do not specifically mention the crime in connexion with any social custom, a sufficient intimation that the people to whom they were primarily addressed were not addicted to its commission in this relation. Even Tacitus mentions their peculiar preservation of their offspring.† A similar humanity has been claimed for the ancient Egyptians; but we can never overlook their cruel order to murder all the male children of the Israelites. It is only before the direct or indirect influences of the Bible, as in the well-known cases connected with the South Sea Islands, and those in India, which it is our purpose to narrate in the following pages, that Infanticide has given way. It was Christianity and not philosophy, indeed, that first lifted up its voice against the crime of Infanticide as practised by the Romans. "By Constantine the Great two decrees were issued—one for Italy in the year 315, A. D.;—the other for Africa, in the year 322. By these it was ordained that, in order to prevent the exposure, sale, or murder of new-born children, those who were too poor to rear them should receive assistance from the public treasury, in the way of food, clothing and other necessaries. At the same time, he ordered a severe punishment to be inflicted on a cruel father. These edicts are supposed to have been issued under the advice of the celebrated Lactantius."‡

* Cormack on Infanticide, pp. 44–49.

† Nam et necare quemquam ex agnatis, nefas. Hist. lib. v. 5.

‡ Of the early feelings of Christians in reference to Infanticide, the following illustrations are given in Beck's Medical Jurisprudence.

Justin Martyr says, "But we who are truly Christins, are so far from maintaining any unjust or ungodly opinions, that exposing of infants, which is so much in practice among you, we teach to be a very wicked

India, when considered from certain points of view, is a country in which the prevalence of Infanticide, and especially Female Infanticide, could scarcely be expected. Though the system of bloody sacrifices is not repugnant to the *Védas*, and especially their latter or preceptive portion, the Bráhmaṇas, — which have been shown by professor H. H. Wilson to sanction even human sacrifice,—it is not very reconcilable with the metaphysical tenet, early held and promulgated in the progress of the religious development of the *A'ryá* set-

practice; first because we see that such children, both girls and boys, are generally all trained up for the service of lust, for as the ancients bred up those foundlings to feed cows, or goats, or sheeps, or grass horses, so now adays such boys are brought up only to be abused against nature; and accordingly you have a herd of these women and effeminate men, standing prostitute in every nation; . . . . and another reason against exposing infants, is that we are afraid they should perish for want of being taken up, and so bring us under the guilt of murder."

Tertullian, in his Apology, thus expresses himself, "How many of you," (addressing himself to the Roman people, and to the governors of cities and provinces) "might I deservedly charge with infant murder; and not only so, but among the different kinds of death, for choosing some of the cruelest for their own children, such as drowning or starving with cold or hunger, or exposing to the mercy of dogs; dying by the sword being too sweet a death for children, and such as a man would choose to fall by, sooner than by any other ways of violence. But Christians now are so far from homicide, that with them it is utterly unlawful to make away a child in the womb, when nature is in deliberation about the man; for, to kill a child before it is born, is to commit murder by way of advance; and there is no difference, whether you destroy a child in its formation, or after it is formed and delivered; for we Christians look upon him as a man who is one in embryo; for he is a being like the fruit in blossom, and in a little time would have been a perfect man, had nature met with no disturbance."

To the same effect is the testimony of Minucius Felix. "I see you exposing your infants to wild beasts and birds, or strangling them after the most miserable manner. Nay, some of you will not give them the liberty to be born, but by cruel potions procure abortions, and smother the hopeful beginnings of what would come to be a man, in his mother's womb." "And these forsooth are the lessons which you learn from your gods; for Saturn exposed not his children, but he ate them."—Vol. i. pp. 380—381.

tlers in India from whom the Bráhman priesthood originated, that all life whether in its vegetable or animal, irrational or rational, human or divine, forms, is essentially the same essence and substance. In the Institutes of Manu, which in their more ancient portions are held to be prior to the era of Buddha, A. C. 543, this tenet is distinctly announced; and great tenderness to animal life is professed. Animals and vegetables, according to this authority, have "external consciousness and are sensible of pleasure and pain." "All transmigrations recorded [in sacred books] from the state of Brahmá, to that of plants happen continually."* "Liberality alone" is the prevailing virtue of the *Kali*, or present age, while sacrifice was that of the *Dwápára*, or preceding age.† Bloody sacrifices, which were nevertheless tolerated by Manu, under certain regulations, were entirely forbidden by *Shákya Muni*, or *Buddha*. Though the followers of this sage, who long formed the vast majority of the people of India, were viewed as heretics by those esteeming themselves the orthodox Hindus, yet when Bráhmanism was reproduced in its present *Pauránik* or legendary form, after the defeat of the Buddhists about the commencement of the seventh century after Christ, the tenderness to animal life which had been inculcated by the Buddhists was still maintained, and remains to this day a characteristic of their religious and civil practice. Infanticide seems to be specifically forbidden in the Puránas under its proper designations. The following passages bearing on this subject have been adduced from them by Bháu Dájí, Esq., now a licensed medical practitioner in Bombay, whose excellent Essay on Infanticide will afterwards fall to be noticed.

स एष जीवन् खलु संपरेतो वर्त्तेत यो ऽत्यंतनृशंसितेन ॥ देहे मृते तंमनुजाः शपंति गंता तमों ऽधंतनुमानिनोध्रुवं ॥‡

* Manu, i. 49, 50. † Manu, i. 86.

‡ Bhágavata Purána, Skanda, x. 2.

बालहत्यां प्रकुर्वंति नराः पापेन मोहिताः ॥ ते यांति नरकं घोरं तामिस्राख्यं महत्तमं ॥*

स्त्रीबालविप्रगोहंता सर्वकर्मबहिष्कृतः ॥ स याति नरकान् घोरन् याव दिंद्राश्चतुर्दश ॥†

स्वकर्मवशगान् घोरान् नरकान् प्रतिपद्यते ॥ भ्रूणहा विप्रहा चैव तत्तत्कर्मफलप्रदान् ॥‡

स्त्री बाल गोद्विजघ्नानां सर्वेषां च द्विजन्मनां ॥ इहलोके परे वा पि नगतिर्विद्यते क्वचित् ॥§

अंतर्जले त्रिरावर्त्यं गायत्रीं प्रयतोजपेत् ॥ मुच्यते पातकैः सर्वैर्यदिन भ्रूणहा भवेत् ॥||

पावयन् सकलान् विप्रान् दशकोटीमुनीश्वराः ॥ ब्रह्मघ्नं च सुरापं च यदि न भ्रूणहा भवेत् ॥¶

मत्तं प्रमत्त मुन्मत्तं सुप्तं बालं जडं स्त्रियं ॥ प्रपन्नं विरथं भीतं न रिपुं हंति धर्मवित् ॥**

स्त्रियाः स्वसुर्गुरुमत्या वधोयं यशः श्रियं हंत्यनु काल मायुः ॥††

स्त्रीहत्या दुःखदा वीर कीर्तिघ्नी पाप कृत्तमा ॥ ‡‡

विषाग्नि दामपतिगुरून् निजापत्यप्रमापणिम्

विकर्ण करनासोष्टीं कृत्वा गोभिः प्रमापयेत्·§§

"Listen to what our sacred laws say.

"The man, who commits a heinous action, is as the dead while living, and men always speak reproachfully of him, and when he dies he is condemned to the hell called Támisra."

"He who takes pleasure in sin and commits infanticide falls into the great hell called Támisra."

In the Varáha Purána Naráyana says to Nárad;

"The man, who destroys female infants,|||| bráhmans and cows, has transgressed all law and is condemned to dark hells, as long as the fourteen Indras exist.

* Padma Purána. † Varáha Purána.

‡ Náradíya Purána, Narka Mahátmya. § Brahma Vaivartha Purána.

|| Agni Purána, Gáyatrí Mahátmya.

¶ Gáyatrí Pancháng, Gáyatrí Mahátmya.

** Bhágavata, Skanda i. 7. †† Bhágavata, Skanda x. 2.

‡‡ Deví Bhágavata. §§ Yádnyawalkya Smriti, chap. ii.

|||| [In the original infants only are mentioned.]

"He, who murders an infant or a bráhman, is condemned to those hells which are due punishments to such crimes."

"He who is the destroyer of women, infants, [cows], or bráhmans, cannot attain bliss either in this world or the next."

"He who standing in water repeats regularly the Gáyatrí, may be freed from all other sins, but not from Infanticide."

"By repeating ten crores of Gáyatrís a man may be freed from the guilt of killing a bráhman, or of drinking liquor, but never from that of Infanticide."

"The man who knows his duty, will not kill one who is intoxicated, nor one who is suffering from disease, nor one who is insane, nor one who is asleep, nor an infant, nor one who is inactive, nor one of the female sex, nor one who begs for mercy, nor an enemy deprived of his chariot, nor one who is struck with terror."

"Of the female sex, he who murders his sister, his daughter,* or a pregnant woman, his success, his prosperity, and his life-time pass away."

"The murder of a female inflicts misery both in this world and the next."†

"Those women, who, by administering poison murder their husband, father or offspring, should be seized by the king, and have their ears, nose and lips cut off, and should be trampled to death by bullocks."

"Infanticide is reckoned one of the great sins, and is punished by condemnation to the hell Támisra, which is described in the Garuḍa Purána to be a copper sheet eight thousand miles square, below which fire is kindled and above fall the piercing rays of the sun."

Too much, however, is not to be made of these facts and authorities as inimical to Infanticide in India. They must be considered in connexion with the whole genius of Hinduism, and the general constitution of Indian society. The worship of demons and ghosts by bloody sacrifices and rites has from the very beginning been a characteristic of the Cushite, or Scythian or Turanian immigration into India, which preceded that of the A'ryás; and with this worship Bráhmanism has made, and is still making, many compromises, as in the demon-worship of the Dakhan and Malabar. Several of the gods and goddesses of the Hindu Pantheon, particularly *Shiva* in some of his forms, and *Devi* or *Káli*, are ima-

* [The words "his daughter" here are an interpolation.]

† [Or rather, The murder of a female is a source of pain, and a destroyer of renown, and most wicked.

gined to be of the most blood-thirsty character.* In one of the groups of figures in the caves of Elephanta, Shiva, in the form of *Bhairava*, is actually represented, as about to sacrifice a child. This child he holds in one hand, while he has a bare sword to strike the fatal blow in another, a bell to intimate the appointed moment in a third, and a vessel to receive the blood in a fourth, there being altogether eight hands to the monster.† The recognition of the spirit of man as essentially of the same nature as the life of the brutes, while it elevates the brutes debases man. Much of the favour shown to woman by the Hindu Shástras,—when indeed they do show her favour,—is founded on the low idea that she is the property of man, as his ox or ass. It is on this understanding, and that she may bear to him a son, without whom, natural or adopted, he can have no salvation, that her life is to be preserved, and that she is to have that degree of comfort which may be allotted to her. Her general debasement, according to the Hindu Shástras, is extreme. This is a subject, bearing so directly on the estimate which must be ultimately formed of the value of female life in India, that it may be proper for us to enter into particulars respecting it.

Of the original constitution of woman, as distinguished from that of man, the Hindu sages and legislators, the authors of the Hindu sacred books, have thus written:—"Falsehood, cruelty, bewitchery, folly, covetousness, impurity, and unmercifulness are woman's inseparable faults." "Woman's sin is greater than that of man," and cannot be removed by the atonements which destroy his. "Women are they who have an aversion to

* See translation of the Rudhirádhyáya of the Káliká Purána, in Asiat. Res. Vol. v.

† Dr. Stevenson, in an interesting paper, interprets this group as representing the destruction of the sacrifice of *Daksha* by Shiva; but this, with an oversight of some of the figures. Mr. Erskine has correctly noticed the group in the Bombay Transactions, vol. i. p. 230.

good works." "Women have hunger two-fold more than men; intelligence (cunning), four-fold; violence, six-fold; and evil desires, eight-fold."* "Through their evil desires, their want of settled affection, and their perverse nature, let them be guarded in this world ever so well, they soon become alienated from their husbands. Manu allotted to such women a love of their bed, of their seat, and of ornaments, impure appetites, wrath, weak flexibility, desire of mischief and bad conduct. Women have no business with the text of the Védas. This is the law fully settled. Having therefore no evidence of law, and no knowledge of expiatory texts, sinful women must be as foul as falsehood itself, and this is a fixed rule. To this effect, many texts which may shew their true disposition are chaunted in the Védas." † It will be observed that it is the *sex*, and not the *race*, that is here condemned. The idea that woman is a "help-meet" for man, seems never to have entered into the minds of the Hindu sages. They uniformly treat her as a necessary evil, and a most dangerous character. Her position according to them, is that of a continuous slavery and dependence. "By a girl," they enjoin, "or by a young woman or by a woman advanced in years, nothing must be done, even in her own dwelling-place, according to her mere pleasure: in childhood must a female be dependent on (or subject to) her father; in youth, on her husband; her lord being dead, on her sons: a woman must never seek independence."‡

The Hindu Shástras have made no provision of affection and regard for a *daughter*. She is viewed by them, as far as her parents are concerned, merely as an object to be "*given away*," and that as soon as possible. She is declared by them to be marriageable, even in her infancy, to a person of any age, and of course without

* The original Sanskrit of these and other passages will be given in the second edition of the author's Exposures of Hinduism.

† Manu ix. 18, 19. ‡ Manu, v. 158.

2

her own choice, or intelligent consent. The most trivial circumstances, such as the possession of reddish hair, are stated to be obstacles to her marriage. The candidate for union with her is thus directed:—"Let him choose for his wife one [a girl whose form has no defect] who has an agreeable name; who walks like the adjutant bird, or like a young elephant; whose hair and teeth are moderate respectively in quantity and size, [whose body has exquisite softness."] * According to the letter of the law, the parents are not to sell their daughter, but they may receive valuable gifts, the equivalent of a price, in her behalf.† Marriages of a character which should be peculiarly disreputable, and which cannot here be particularised, have the sanction, though not the preference, of the *Shástra.*‡

The Hindu *wife* is placed under the absolute will of her lord, without any reference to moral distinctions; and even in religious matters he intervenes between her conscience and her god. "A husband," says Manu, "must constantly be revered as a god by a virtuous wife. No sacrifice is allowed to women apart from their husbands, no religious rite, no fasting: as far only as a wife honours her lord, so far is she exalted in heaven."§ "Let a wife," it is said in the Skanda Purána, "who wishes to perform sacred ablution, wash the feet of her lord, and drink the water; for a husband is to a wife greater than Shankar or Vishnu. The husband is her god, and priest, and religion; wherefore abandoning everything else she ought chiefly to worship her husband." The husband is actually cautioned against allowing his affections to rest upon her in the degree that is lawful in the case of others of his kindred. "Let not a woman be much loved," it is enjoined; "let her have only that degree of affection which is necessary. Let

* Manu, iii. 10. The words within parentheses are from the comment.

† Manu, iii. 51. ‡ Manu, iii. 20-34. § Manu, v.

the fulness of affection be reserved for brothers and other similar connexions." When kindness to the woman is urged, it is recommended principally as calculated to promote the husband's benefit.* A rope and a rod are expressly mentioned as the ordinary supports of a husband's authority.† With the husband the wife is not to have communion and fellowship in eating or travelling, except in particular circumstances. On trivial grounds, even for an unkind word, she may be superseded or divorced.‡ For polygamy and licentiousness on the part of the husband, there can be pleaded not only certain laxities of legislation, according to which they appear as matters comparatively trivial, but even the alleged example of the gods themselves.

The dishonour of a *father* and the dishonour of a *mother*, according to the Hindu Shástras stand in different categories, though both of them are forbidden. "By honouring his mother, he (the son) gains this world; by honouring his father, the intermediate (or ethereal), and, by assiduous attention to his preceptor, even the (celestial) world of Brahmá."§ One of the prescribed methods of dishonouring his mother, is that, in certain circumstances, of igniting the funeral pile by which the living, as well as the dead parent is to be consumed, and by which he is to be made an orphan in a double sense. Another is by exercising absolute control over her when she is spared after her husband's death.

The injunctions laid down in the Hindu "sacred books" respecting the treatment of a *widow*, are many of them of a harsh and inequitable character. In no circumstances is she permitted to remarry, as a widower may do, though she may have been espoused in merest infancy and never once have been under her husband's roof.‖ Throughout life she must live deprived of many

* See the case of her ornaments, Manu, iii. 61. † Manu, viii. 299.

‡ See Manu, ix. 81. § Manu, ii. 233.

‖ Manu, v. 158, compared with 168.

lawful comforts and harmless enjoyments. According to the Shástras, she must be divested of ornaments, and submit even to the mortification of never sleeping on a couch.

These statutory injunctions and representations of the Hindu Shástras, are in direct antithesis to the claims of humanity as far as the female sex is concerned. They have not yet become obsolete or ineffective among the Hindu people. They influence the spirit and habits of the whole of Hindu society. They overpower the special legislation for the preservation of woman's life. How few Hindu female children, in consequence of them, receive on their birth a cordial welcome into this world! How many of them, instead of being reared with care and tenderness, are consigned to neglect, issuing in death! How averse is the community to all female education directed to the culture of the mind and the regulation of the moral affections! How numerous are the premature and foolish and unsuitable marriages, especially on the female side! How many spouses are treated as prisoners by the higher classes, and by the lower, as slaves! How incapable are mothers of devoting themselves with intelligence and prudence to the intellectual and spiritual training of their offspring and of winning it to the love, acknowledgement, and practice of what is good! How destitute are widows of that sympathy and support which their bereavement requires, even when they escape the *Satí*, or method of purity, which the Shástras require when they recommend the bereaved wife to surrender herself to consumption on the funeral pile of her husband! The recommendation of Satí alone may account for the practice of Infanticide. If to preserve a widow's chastity, she may be burned, a daughter, of whose marriage in the line of caste and dignity of family there is but little prospect, may be destroyed.

Farther than this we have still to go in discovering the responsibility of Hinduism for the Infanticide which exists. Poverty and hunger, according to Manu, authorize the breaking of the general law as to filial life: "*Ajígartta*, dying with hunger, was going to destroy his own son (*Shunahshépha*); yet he was guilty of no crime since he only sought a remedy against famishing."* None of the moral precepts of the Hindus are absolute. Even truth, the pillar of the universe, may be violated with impunity. "A giver of false evidence from a pious motive, even though he knew the truth, shall not lose a seat in heaven: such evidence men call divine speech." "In the cause of courtezans, of marriages, of food eaten by cows, of fuel for a sacrifice, of benefit or protection accruing to a Bráhman, there is no sin in an oath."† While such licenses as these are given, where, it may be asked, is there any absolute moral security in the land?

* Manu, x. 105. Sir William Jones, after the words "destroy his own son," adds on the authority of the commentator, the clause "*by selling him for some cattle;*" but this interpretation is not warranted either by the original, or by the story of Shunahshe'pa, which has been lately investigated by professor H. H. Wilson.

† Manu, viii. 103, 42. For further explanations of the moral licentiousness of Hinduism, see author's "Exposures of Hinduism."

CHAPTER II.

DISCOVERY OF INFANTICIDE IN INDIA AMONG THE RÁJKUMÁRS NEAR BENARES AND THE JÁḌEJÁ'S OF KAṬHIÁWÁḌ AND KACHH BY THE HON. JONATHAN DUNCAN.

Sir John Shore, afterwards Lord Teignmouth,—a name famous alike for the maintenance of peace in India during his administration as Governor General, and for the dissemination throughout the world of the Bible, the grand source of peace, and of national as well as personal reformation, after his retirement and settlement in Britain,—writes as follows:—"That the practice of Infanticide should ever be so general as to become a custom with any sect or race of people requires the most unexceptionable evidence to gain belief: and I am sorry to say, that the general practice, as far as regards female infants, is fully substantiated with respect to a particular tribe in the frontiers of Juánpur, a district of the province of Benares, adjoining to the country of Oude (*Audh*). A race of Hindus called Rájkumárs, reside here; and it was discovered in 1789 only, that the custom of putting to death their female offspring by causing the mothers to starve them, had long subsisted, and did actually then very generally prevail amongst them; the Resident at Benares, in a circuit which he made through the country where the Rájkumárs dwell, had an opportunity of authenticating the existence of the custom from their own confessions; he conversed with several; all unequivocally admitted it, but all did not fully acknowledge its atrocity; and the only reason which they assigned for the inhuman practice, was the great expence of procuring suitable matches for their daughters, if they allowed them to grow up."* The Resident of Benares, here referred to, was Jonathan Duncan, of the Bengal Civil Service, a singularly shrewd Scotch gentleman, well acquainted with the Hindustání, the popular language of the province, and the Persian, long the language of the Indian courts, who for the effective discharge of his official duties made the native customs and character his study, even before the curiosity of Britain in the East was awakened by the disquisitions and researches of a Jones and a Colebrooke. When reporting on the Cessions to the East India Company in the neighbourhood of the "holy city" of the Hindus, he gave what was called, "not an absolutely flattering, but a certain degree of favourable description of the general state of the country;" and, in the spirit of accuracy and fidelity which he cultivated through life, he failed not to "describe the principal exceptions" which he found in the district now mentioned. Of that district the most consequential inhabitants were the Rájkumárs—originally denominated *Rajputs*, for the names are synonymous,—supposed to be about 40,000 in number, and claiming royal lineage and direct descent from Rájá Pithaurá, the last of the Chohán dynasty of Delhí. They were represented as exceeding their connexions in Rájputáná,—the great seat of the Rajputs,—in the "wildness of their notions and peculiarity of their manners," being insubordinate and revengeful, though not without their "point of honour" in adhering to such engagements as they were "pleased to enter into." In a latter communication† it was stated of them, that it was "no unfrequent practice among them" "to put their daughters as born to them to death, by immediately causing their

* Asiatic Researches 8vo. edit., vol. iv. pp. 338, 339.

† Dated 21st October 1789.

mothers to starve them," and that consequently, from necessity, they married into other Rajput tribes. So generally was this inhuman custom prevalent among them, that the only exception which could be brought to notice was this, "that now and then the more wealthy Rájkumárs, will sometimes spare and bring up their female issue, especially when they happen to have none of the male line." "This horrid custom," it was added, "is said to exist also among some other tribes, more especially in the Wazír's dominions,*and is thought to be founded in the Rájkumár tribe on the inherent extravagant desire of independency entertained by this race of men, joined, perhaps, to the necessity of procuring a suitable settlement in marriage for these devoted females, were they allowed to grow up; and the disgrace which would ensue from any omission in that respect. Nor is this species of atrocity of a novel institution, for a similar principle as existing among the Indians, was known by the ancient Greeks and Romans, and is still to be found noticed in their relations of this quarter of the world:" This information, which at the time it was conveyed to the authorities must have been very startling, was afterwards found to be substantially accurate. Infanticide *was* practised to a great extent at this time, by other tribes besides that of the Rájkumárs,—by the Rajput tribes in general, forming all the chivalry so-called of India. The notice of the crime by the Greeks and Romans, however, as existing in India, rested only on the authority of Captain Wilford, more remarkable for the wildness and ingenuity of his conjectures than the patience and accuracy of his historical deductions.

Mr. Jonathan Duncan was a man of action as well as of observation. A few months after his discovery of the general prevalence of the horrid crime of Infanticide among the Rájkumárs, he was able to say that he had brought those of them who were under British authority

[* Those of the king of Oude *(Audh)*, the nominal Wazír of the Great Moghal.]

to enter into a covenant for its abolition. Of the kind, or measure, of persuasion by which he effected this happy arrangement, he has given us no information. It was brought about by him after he made a tour in the districts in which Infanticide prevailed, and after he had found that the Rájkumárs had, in palliation of their crime, "only to plead the great expence of procuring suitable matches for their daughters, if they allowed them to grow up."

The form of Agreement according to which the Rájkumárs pledged themselves to abandon Infanticide, was dated the 17th December 1789, and ran in the following terms:—

"Whereas it hath become known to the Government of the Honourable English East India Company, that we of the tribe of Rájkumárs do not suffer our female children to live, and whereas this is a great crime, as mentioned in the Bretino Bywunt Pooran, (*Brahmá Vaivartta Purána*) where it is said, that killing even a fœtus was as criminal as killing a bráhman; and that for killing a female or woman, the punishment is to suffer in the nerk (*narka*) or hell called Kal Sooter, (*Kála-Sutra**) for as many years as there are hairs of that female's body; and that afterwards that person shall be born again, and successively become a leper, and be afflicted with the *zakham:* and whereas the British Government in India, whose subjects we are, have an utter detestation of such murderous practices, and we do ourselves acknowledge that, although customary among us, it is highly sinful, we do therefore hereby agree not to commit any longer such detestable acts; and any among us who (which God forbid) shall be hereafter guilty thereof, or shall not bring up and get our daughters married, to the best of our abilities, among those of our cast, shall be expelled from our tribe, and we shall neither eat nor keep society with such person or persons, besides suffering hereafter

[* The hell of heated and burning copper, one of the twenty-one hells of the Hindus.]

the punishments denounced in the above purána and shástra."

This agreement, as far as the prevention of Infanticide is concerned, is thoroughly satisfactory; and its reference to the sinfulness and inhumanity of the crime is appropriate. It is to be regretted, however, that, as proposed by a Christian and British functionary, it should lay the gravamen of the charge against that horrid practice on the supposed violation of the *Shástra*, however interpreted. The greatest caution is required in the use of arguments *ex concessu* in dealing with the living false systems of religious faith. The resolution to visit offenders with exclusion from caste, must appear to all acquainted with the peculiarities of that institution, which has more to do with the ceremonial than the moral, to have been impracticable and nugatory.

Mr. Duncan's success with the Rájkumárs led him to direct his best attention also to the *Raghuvanshas*,—another sub-division of Rajputs,—inhabiting Chandwaj and Mográ; but the result of his correspondence with them is not mentioned in the government papers. The Governor-General approved of what he had done in reference to the Rájkumárs, who were British subjects; and by various Regulations made the offenders among them in cases of Infanticide amenable to the Company's Court for murder, under the penalty of its highest punishment. Mr. Duncan's name, in consideration of his benevolent exertions in the case, was deservedly enrolled in the list of distinguished British philanthropists; and for several years it was imagined, that in consequence of the express covenant which had been made, and the fear of punishment, the crime had altogether disappeared among the Rájkumárs. The melancholy truth, however, was by and bye discovered, that though somewhat concealed, it was still perpetrated to a large extent. On information by Messrs. Fortescue, Smith, and Shakespeare, local officials, the Governor-General in Council expressed the sad truth, on the 30th August 1816, that the measures of Mr.

Duncan and the Regulations of government, had "failed to prevent the inhuman practice," and "that although a greater degree of precaution was observed to prevent detection, there was too much reason to fear that the crime itself had not in any degree diminished." At this period, the general demoralizing effect of the crime was apparent to the British authorities in the provinces. In alluding to the insubordination, and violence, and savage cruelty of the parties among whom it prevailed, Mr. Fortescue, rightly observed, that "the jealous and hasty pride which induces them to become the murderers of their own female offspring has probably a considerable effect in blunting their feelings against a sympathetic sense of the pains they inflict on one another on the smallest pretence of right or offence, and in rendering the dread of public justice of light or no collective influence." Yet, in the absence of moral enlightenment, this dread of public justice, was the principal motive, in the first instance, on which the government could rest for enforcing from the Rájkumárs obedience to their own engagements and the authority under which they were placed. This view of matters was taken by the Superintendent of Police in the Western Provinces in 1819. In referring to a letter of Mr. Cracroft, the magistrate of Juánpur,—who proposed various economical arrangements which might be subsidiary to the exertion of the civil power in dealing with Infanticide,—he thus wrote:—"The practice being declared to be a crime, it is the duty of the magistrate to do his utmost to convict those who still persist in it." It was the long neglect of this principle, as we shall afterwards see, which was the cause, in several provinces of India, of the continued shedding of innocent blood warm from the womb. It was its adoption, which, in late years, has so much tended to the suppression of Infanticide not only in the Juánpur districts but in the Rajput states in general.

But these notices of the attempts to suppress Infanticide near Benares we cannot extend.* We have referred to them at present, only because it was the discovery of Infanticide at Benares which led to the discovery of its existence in the important provinces under the political superintendence of Bombay, where it had been long practised to a fearful extent.

Mr. Jonathan Duncan, on the appointment of the East India Company, which had formed a high idea of his talents and probity, was transferred from Bengal, to the office of Governor of Bombay in 1795. His habits of mind and his former experience led him, when he came to the Western Presidency, to indulge the inquisitiveness which was natural to him, and which he had elsewhere cultivated with so much advantage to himself and the people placed under his authority. He was not only accessible to the natives; but, with due restrictions, he systematically sought to maintain with them regular intercourse. He personally conversed and corresponded with them, whenever he found them capable of giving him useful and practical information. When he was on his first visit to Surat in 1800, he asked Kṛipá Ráma, the minister of the Nawáb of that city, whether any traces of Infanticide were found in his locality, so contiguous to Baroch, the ancient Barygaza, where Captain Wilford had imagined it to exist in the days of the Greeks. The reply which he received was this:—"Heretofore I have heard people say that among the tribe of Rajput, and especially among the Rájás of that class, the birth of a daughter in their houses was considered as disgraceful; on which account their women refused to let their newly-born daughters have access to their milk, and put them in any way to death; but this practice is not general through all the sub-divisions of their tribe, though in several places they do thus stony-heartedly kill them."

Mr. Duncan,—to abridge his own narrative which

* See Parliamentary Papers on Hindu Infanticide: 1789-1820.

here commences,—returned to Bombay in July 1800. He had no farther opportunity of prosecuting his inquiries into what foundation there might be for believing the practice of female Infanticide to obtain in any places of the West of India, till the fact was again incidentally brought to his notice, between two and three years afterwards, by a native lady,—her name is worthy of remembrance,—Gajrá Báí, a descendant of one of the Gáikawáḍ Rájás of Gujarát, who had repaired to Bombay on political grounds.

"In view to the farther investigation of the grounds of Gajrá Báí's information, Mr. Duncan entered into a correspondence on the subject with Captain Seton, then on a political mission at Mándaví, the chief port of the country of Kachh, a territory situated to the north-west of the province of Gujarát, the gulf of the same name intervening, and constituting the line of division between the two states."*

Mr. Duncan, writing to Captain Seton on the 8th January 1804, says, "I send you a memorandum from Gajrá Báí (the daughter of Fatteh Singh, one of the Gáikawáḍ princes in Gujarát) or rather the result of what she related to-day in conversation; and request you will make every inquiry in your power into so curious a subject, as the alleged custom of your Kachh friends killing their female infants. I have heard Captain Wilford of Benares, say, that in some old Greek author in his possession, he has read of the same thing being a practice in his time in that quarter of India."

Captain Seton's reply to this communication, which was dated the 23rd March, 1804, corroborated the mournful information which Mr. Duncan had previously received, and brought additional facts and surmises to light.

"The custom mentioned in Gajrá Báí's relation is in force to this day; every female infant born in the Rájá's

* Moor's Hindu Infanticide, pp. 18-19.

family, of a Rání or lawful wife, is immediately dropped into a hole dug in the earth and filled with milk, where it is drowned.

"Dhan-kuwar Bái, who is now alive at Bhuj, the capital of Kachh, is the daughter of Ráo Lakhpat, by a *pátar* or Gujarat *kánchaní* (strolling dancing-girl) sister to Ráo Goḍ, the last Rájá and aunt of Ráo Ráydhan, the present Rájá. The latter has a son and a daughter by a slave of one of the Ránís, now ten or eleven years of age; the custom in question not extending to them, but only to the Rájá's children by his Ránís, or consorts. Neither does it necessarily extend to the Jáḍejás, or collateral descendants of the Rájá's family, though most of them, through choice, adopt it, there being but two men of this cast of any note who have brought up their daughters; and these are Vṛidrají and Náthjí, who will be again noticed. Vṛidrají Jáḍeja's daughter is married to the son of the Bháwanagar Rájá.

"This custom of drowning female infants is not peculiar to Kachh, but is common among the heads of the *Khatri* or Rajput tribes.* It is practised in the family of the Jám of Nagar, in the peninsula of Gujarát; and in that of the Miázah, or Kaloris of Sindh, and in others. The Rajputs of Kachh are originally from Sindh, and are called Sindh Sammá, and Sindh Sumra. They fell back on Kachh before the Muhammadans, driving out the Káṭhis, who had before driven out the *Sát Sinhas* or Seven Lions.† Those that remained in Sindh were converted to Muhammadism, and have been since driven out by the Tálpuris. Part of them here (in Kachh) form the cast of Jamádárs, mentioned in my official correspondence as forming the third party in this government. They marry Rajputs' daughters, but do not give their

* The Rajput tribes in general claim descent from the ancient *Kshattriya*, or warrior caste.

† This popular allusion to the dynasty of the *Sinhas* in Gujarát, which will be afterwards referred to, is worthy of notice.

own, it being contrary to the Muhammadan religion. The Rajputs eat what is dressed by Muhammadans, but not from the same dish or plate, and of every thing except beef and fowls, which latter are, in a manner, forbidden; as none in whose family a *Deva* (or incarnation) has been are allowed to eat them; and as they all pretend to this honor, it would be an affront to make them such an offer. Game is preferred to tame animals. They drink spirits, but this does not imply an impurity of caste, neither does the license extend to the women; who in every respect, live as the highest caste of Bráhmans. The Rájás of Kachh and Nagar are descended of two brothers; the elder, of Kachh, named Maha-Ráo, the younger Maha-Ráj.* The Murvi chieftain, within the peninsula of Gujarát, is of the same family; and the history of all is contained in the History of Khengár and Ráéb the two brothers above alluded to, which I shall get and translate. The next great man in their history is Rájá Bhárá, who was driven from Sindh, and the most powerful in Sindh was Rájá Unaḍ.

"I have already intimated that the Jaḍejás destroy their daughters; and though Vṛidráji and Náthji had, from the fear of having no sons, and thereby wanting heirs of any sex, saved theirs, it is by no means a general practice. The Jamádárs, whose origin has been before adverted to, take in marriage the daughters of the Soḍha Rajputs,† who rear their female children for sale, and also destroy their infant female progeny. The expense, and difficulty of procuring suitable husbands, is the excuse usually made; the Rájá's pretext is that he considers it beneath him to match his daughter with any man."

On a subsequent occasion, in the same year, Captain Seton added, "The family of the Jám, adverted to in my preceding letter, also take their wives from the tribe

* The Soḍha Rajputs reside in Párkar, north of the Great Raṇ.

† The Kachh family is commonly held to be of the younger branch.

of Sodha, who are at present living between Sindh, Multán, and Jaudpur. It might be supposed that the women would be averse to the destruction of their daughters; but from all accounts it is the reverse, as they do not only assist in destroying them, but when the Musalman prejudices occasionally preserve them, they hold these daughters in the greatest contempt, calling them *Mahájan*, thereby insinuating that their fathers have derogated from their military cast, and become pedlars."

The information communicated by Captain Seton was in the main confirmed by Mirzá Mortizá, a descendant of the stationary Moghal officers of revenue for the province of Gujarát; by the inquiries of Mr. S. Halliday, the superintendent of Police in Bombay; and by Sundarjí Sivají, a respectable native employed in the purchase of horses in Kachh and Káthiáwád for the British Army in India. The last mentioned informant verbally mentioned to Mr. Duncan, in a conference held with him in April or May 1805, "That throughout all the country of Kachh, there may be six or eight houses wherein the Jádéjá masters of families bring up their daughters; but otherwise the practice of killing them is general: and, besides what happens within the limits of that country, the Jádéjá chieftains of Murví, Gondal, and Jámnagar in the peninsula of Gujarát do also kill their female infants."

Possessed of this information the Bombay Government, at the zealous instigation of Mr. Duncan, resolved to use its best endeavours for the suppression of the barbarous crime to which its attention had been directed, even though the states in which it was practised were not under its immediate jurisdiction. On the 27th of May 1805, it issued its instructions to Major Alexander Walker, the Resident of the Court of the Gáikawád in Gujarát, to whom, and the Peshwa of Puná, the territory of Káthiáwád was tributary, to communicate with Shivají Sundarjí then on his way from Bombay to Baroda, and "to endeavour to prevail on him to take an active part as the agent of the British Government for effecting the abrogation in that quarter of a system so revolting and detestable." This movement, considering its benevolent and disinterested object, and the circumstances in which it originated, was in the highest degree creditable to the Bombay Government. Major Walker, an officer of great ability and experience and knowledge of native character, at once discerned its importance; but on intimating the receipt of the communication which had been addressed to him respecting it, he plainly declared that difficulties of no ordinary kind lay in the way of a favourable issue. "I fear," he said, "the humane attempt of the Honourable the Governor in Council will not be successful, to any great extent, in restraining the superstitious and religious prejudices of a tribe so far removed from the authority of the British Government, and so little acquainted with the principles of improved society.* In Mr. Duncan he had a prompter and counsellor who could not be easily discouraged.

* Letter of Major Walker to F. Warden, Esq., Secy. to B. Govt. 1st Sept. 1805.

CHAPTER III.

GENERAL DESCRIPTION, WITH HISTORICAL NOTICES, OF KÁṬHIÁWÁḌ AND KACHH—BRITISH CONNEXION WITH THESE PROVINCES — MAJOR WALKER'S SETTLEMENT OF THE TRIBUTE OF KAṬHIÁWÁḌ—HIS REPORT ON THE EXISTENCE OF INFANTICIDE—HIS EFFORTS FOR ITS SUPPRESSION.

THE provinces of Káṭhiáwáḍ and Kachh, in which the existence, to a large extent, of systematic Female Infanticide had been certified to the Bombay Government, are both marked and distinct in their character, and of great interest in a geographical and historical point of view. Both of them are peninsular, and separated from one another by the small Gulf of Kachh; and in the rainy season they are almost insular.

Káṭhiáwáḍ, or the Peninsular Gujarát, is bounded on the north by the Gulf of Kachh, and the *Raṇ*, or desert of mud and sand with brackish water, which forms the continuation of that Gulf; on the east, by the Gulf of Cambay and a line drawn from its northern extremity to the eastern corner of the *Raṇ;* and on the south and west by the Indian Ocean. It lies between 20° 40′ and 23° 10′, north latitude; and 69° 2′ and 72° 25′, east longitude. It is, when cut diagonally, about 160 miles from west to east, and about the same extent from north to south. It has been roughly estimated by Major LeGrand Jacob, who has published an able and valuable geographical and statistical paper respecting it in the Transactions of the Bombay Geographical Society,* at 22,000 square miles.

* Trans. of Bombay Geo. Society, vol. vii. pp. 1-96.

Its larger portion is of a level and undulating character, not greatly elevated above the sea, and sloping to the coasts; but it has a few remarkable elevations and clusters and ranges of hills and mountains, from which descend, in all directions, numerous rivers, or rather rivulets, to the sea. The larger and central portion of it is of the trap or basaltic formation, overlaid in some places with freshwater sandstone. Its western margin is of oolite, and its eastern of newer sandstone. Its highest elevations, which are in the Girnár cluster of mountains, are of primitive formation. Its soil is in general admirably adapted for pasturage, and grain; and much of it is suitable for cotton. Its wildest parts, naturally and socially, lie to the south, the habitat alike of the beasts of prey and semi-barbarous men. Exclusive of the eastern portion, which has been placed under the British Ahmadábád Collectorate since the British conquest of the Peshwa in 1818, it contains the following ten provinces, the number of the inhabitants of which we give on the authority of Major Jacob.

	Inhabitants.
Okha'manḍal, the district of *Okha'*, forming the north-west corner of the peninsula, now under the Gáikawáḍ	12,500
Hala'ḍ, principally the property of the *Ja'ḍeja's*, and named from Jám Halá, of Kachh, the third from Ráydhan, the first mentioned by name in connexion with that province.	358,560
Machu-Ka'nta', on the banks of the *Machu* (fish) river, principally, like the preceding, the property of the Jáḍejás.	28,749
Jha'la'wa'ḍ, so named from the present principal proprietors of its soil, the *Jha'la'* Rajputs	240,325
Barda', in which the *Jaitwa'* Rajputs are settled	46,980
Ka'ṭhia'wa'ḍ, the province of the *Ka'ṭhi's* properly so-called.	189,840
Sorath, in which we have the remains of the name *Saura'shtra*, anciently applied to the whole peninsula..........	320,820
Gohilwa'ḍ, in which the *Gohil* Rajputs are settled	427,980
Und Sarwaiya, imbedded in the preceding	11,373
Ba'bria'wa'ḍ and *Ja'fara'ba'd*, the country of the *Ba'bria's*, and the district of the town of *Ja'fara'ba'd*...........	18,468
Total Population......	1,475,685

Colonel Walker, says Major Jacob, "estimated the population, not including Bábriáwáḍ, Jáfarábád, and Okhámanḍal, at 1,975,900 souls. In 1831, Mr. Blane's census, [the details of which, with much valuable information by its director, are in the office of the political agent at Rájkoṭ] exclusive of the two last districts, gave an estimate of 1,759,277, and of 4030 towns and villages. My inquiries have produced a lower result, viz 1,475,685 for the whole of the peninsula under the political agency, inhabiting 3794 towns and villages." To this population of 1,475,685, however, we have to add 90,536 for the district of Dhandaká, and 60,361 for that of Goghá,* both belonging to the English Government and under the Collectorate of Ahmadábád, making a grand total of 1,626,582 for the peninsula.

The population of this province is of a very varied character. "For diversity of races, exotic and indigenous," says Colonel Tod, "there is no region in India to be compared with Saurâshtra, where they may be seen of all shades, from the fair, and sometimes blue-eyed Káṭhí, erect and independent as when his fathers opposed the Macedonian at Multán, to the swarthy Bhíl, with keen look, the offspring of the forest." † Though its multifarious immigrations from early times cannot be minutely narrated, various traces of them and of the dynasties to which they were subjected can yet be found. Hindu tradition, or rather invention, has hallowed the land by associating with its western shores many legends of Hanumán, the monkey-assistant of Ráma, and of the exploits of Krishna after his flight from Mathurá to the west; but this it has done without any countenance from the Rámáyana or Mahábhárata, the ancient epics of the Hindus, inventing, in violation of their geography, its cities of Sudhámapur identified

* Fawcett's Report on Collectorate of Ahmadábád, in Bombay Govt. Records, No. V. New Series, p. 1.

† Tod's Travels in Western India, p. 257.

with Porbandar, and Dwáraká now thus denominated, to promote a gainful and delusive pilgrimage. The Buddhist edicts of the great emperor *Ashoka*, of the third century preceding the Christian era, however, are engraved with an iron pen on the granite rock of Girnár near Junágaḍ. In juxtaposition with the same commemorative tablets, are notices of the charitable deeds of succeeding kings. The *Sáh* or *Sinha** kings of *Sauráshtra*,—probably the revivors of a more ancient dynasty of the same designation, who perhaps gave that name to the country, which is found in Ptolemy's Geography and which it would have been most convenient to retain,—possessed it as the seat of their sovereignty from about the Christian era, or the century following, their capital in all probability being Sihor, anciently Sinhapur, now the second town in Gohilwáḍ.† The *Walabhí* dynasty, the era of which dates from the overthrow of the preceding dynasty, A. D. 318, to A. D. 524, according to Col. Tod, or according to a Chinese traveller rather more than a century later,‡ was formed by the declaration of inde-

* Professor H. H. Wilson derives *sa'h* from *sa'dhu'*, a saint; but the learned natives of Western India, as Vishnu Sháštrí, with more probability, get it from *sinha*, a lion. Mr. Thomas, too, who has written a valuable essay on its coins in the Journal of the Royal Asiatic Society, gives it this origin also.

† "About two stages to the southward of *Walabhi'* lies the town of *Sihor*, also mentioned as a place of great antiquity by Col. Tod. Our visit to it convinced us that the Colonel has not formed a mistaken judgment respecting it. The ancient name of the place was *Sinhapur*, from which the modern name is obviously derived. We are disposed to consider it the capital of the *Sinhas* who made the first *Aryan* invasion of Ceylon—from which it, perhaps, received the name of *Sinhaldwip*,—and the seat of whose authority, we concur with Professor Lassen in thinking, must have been in Gujarát. We make another conjecture respecting it. It was probably the capital of the *Sa'h* kings. (*Sinha*, as Mr. E. Thomas supposes) of *Soura'shtra*."—Author's Second Memoir on the Cave-Temples and other Antiquities of Western India, in Journal of B. B. R. A. Society, Jan. 1853.

‡ See prof. Wilson's Ariana Antiqua, p. 408.

pendence of Vijaya Séna, one of the Sáh commanders-in-chief, and had its capital at the now ruined town of Walá, formerly Walabhípur in the modern Gohilwáḍ; and its members, though followers of Shiva, were the patrons of the Jainas, or Buddhist Seceders, yet numerous in the province, two of whose most renowned high-places, with wondrous temples and religious structures, are at Girnár, the highest mountain of the peninsula rising 3,500 feet above the level of the sea, and Pálitáná about six marches from Walá and half that distance from Sihor. The *Kulis*, whose denominations are numerous, are probably the Aborigines of the country. The *Ahirs* of the peninsula are a pastoral tribe, the *Abhirs* of the ancient Hindu writings, originally inhabitants of the country about the mouths of the Indus, denominated in Ptolemy's Geography, *Abiria*. Among the earliest so-called "Rajput" inhabitants of the country are the *Jaitwás*, who notwithstanding their claims of kindred with the monkey god, are probably a branch of the Scythian *Getæ*, now occupying the north-western portion of the province, and who, as will be afterwards seen, have to a considerable extent practised Infanticide; the *Chorásámás*, whom we agree with Major Jacob in supposing to have proceeded from the *Cháwaḍás* who long reigned at Anhílwáḍá, or Píran Pattan; the *Solankis* who are supposed by Colonel Tod to have succeeded the Cháwaḍás at Anhílwáḍá* about A. D. 931; the *Jhálás*, whom we take to be a branch of the *Makwáná* Kulís converted to Bráhmanism;† the *Wálás*, probably reputed descendants of the Walabhí princes; the

* In a copper-plate charter lately presented to the Bombay Branch of the Royal Asiatic Society by Mr. W. E. Frere, C.S., and now before me, this town is denominated *Anhi'lpa'ṭak*. This charter, granting a piece of land to a Bráhman, bears the date of *Samvat* 1086, or A. D. 1029. It is that of *Ra'ja' Bhi'mde'va*, of the *Solanki* Dynasty, which succeeded the *Cha'waḍa'*.

† So we have heard the *Makwa'na's* declare them to be; while we have found some of the *Jha'la's* admit the relationship.

Surwaiyas, and *Rázádás* obscure representatives of the *Sauryas* or *Sinhas*, and the kindred of the Ráo of Junágaḍ conquered by Mahmud Sháh Bégaḍa about A. D. 1472; and the *Gohils*, who entered the country on their expulsion from Márwáḍ about the end of the twelfth century. The *Pramárs*, a detachment from the *Agnikula* tribes of mount Abu,—like the others under the same denomination,—are probably descendants of Kulís. The *Muhammaḍans* are principally the offspring of invaders of the province, from the time of Mahmud of Ghazní, A. D. 1024 to that of Mahmud Begaḍa, A. D. 1472, as now mentioned, and of subsequent adventurers.* The *Káṭhís*,—from whom, in consequence of the terror which they inspired in the predatory Maráthás when they first visited the province, the whole peninsula has in late times been denominated,—are undoubtedly of Scythian origin, as indicated both by their name and physiognomy.† They entered the country from the banks of the Indus, but at what time cannot be definitely ascertained. The *Jats* found also in various parts contiguous to the Indus are admitted to be also Scythians, corresponding with the *Getæ*, with whom we have already connected the *Jaitwás*. The *Jaḍejás*, with whom these pages have most to do, entered the country from Kachh. They are the descendants of the Rajputs of Sindh, and allege that they are the representatives of the *Yâdavas* of the Mahábhárata. The accounts which are current of their entrance into Kachh and Káṭhiáwáḍ are very contradictory; but the following statement, founded on various ma-

* See Major Jacob's Report, pp. 17, 18, for a notice of the Muhammadan movements in the province of Gujarát posterior to Mahmud. Its northern and western shores were occasionally visited by the Arabs during their early invasions of Sindh. See the "Appendix to the Arabs in Sindh," vol. iii. part i. by Sir Henry Elliot.

† The Káthí horse is exactly the type of what we see on the Indo-Scythic coins. The Káṭhís are mentioned in connexion with the force of Siláh-ed-Dín who seized Tatta in 1520. Erskine's Hist. of India, vol. i. p. 368.

nuscripts which we have examined and inquiries which we have pursued with intelligent natives, and on European tables of chronology, may be received as an approximation to historical precision. Sindh was first seriously invaded by the Muhammadans about the year of Christ 711. It was a possession of the Ummyad Khalifs in 750. In 1025 it was conquered by Mahmud of Ghazní. The *Súmrás*, a native tribe, converted to Muhammadism, attained to power within its boundaries about 1054; and they in their turn were overthrown in 1340* by the *Sammás*, another native tribe also converted to Muhammadism. Some of the Sammás, probably before this time, had spread into the adjoining territory of Kachh, where they partly maintained their Muhammadism, and partly returned to Hinduism, which their forefathers had been driven by violence to embrace. The Sammás in Sindh were overcome by Sháh Beg Arghun in 1521; and numbers of them, after that event, fled to and settled with their brethren in Kachh. Of these fugitive Sammás and the elder Sammá settlers in Kachh, the Jádejás are the descendants. Their chief had the title of *Jám*, formerly borne by the head of the tribe in Sindh. He seems to have been descended from the earlier Sammá settlers; for, in the genealogical tables, we find Ráydhan, the first Jám in Kachh, mentioned as being there A. D. 1464. The thirteenth Jám after this Ráydhan, through his eldest son Gajanjí settled at Vinján,—the younger being Udojí, from whom the Ráo of Kachh is descended,—passed into the peninsula of Gujarát, and established himself at Nawánagar or Jámnagar in Haláḍ, and conquered that, and the neighbouring territory, in Samvat 1596, or A. D. 1539. This was the origin of the establishment of the

* This is the date given by Mr. Erskine in his History of India vol. i. p. 358 Mr. Postans in his Personal Observations in Sindh (see Dry Leaves from Young Egypt, p. 378) gives it as 1351. On the Sindhian dates, see the work of Sir Henry Elliot already referred to. Sir Henry thinks that the Su'mrás were not Moslems during the early period of their sway. See p. 186.

Jáḍejás in Káṭhiáwáḍ. The Jáḍejás got wives principally from the *Soḍhá* rajputs of Párkar on the borders of the Raṇ or desert of Kachh ; and most of them returned to Hinduism. Most incorrect estimates have at various times been made of their numbers in that locality. Their male population, according to a careful census of Colonel Lang, amounted in 1849 to 7353. According to religion they are still Hindus, rendering special homage to Vishnu, to the Sun, to Shiva, and to Déví or Mátá, whom they sometimes denominate *Hingláj* and *A'shápurí*, and reverencing all the legends of the Puránas, and giving them an absurd local application. They occasionally practise bloody sacrifices. Many of them do not scruple to drink spirits and other intoxicants ; and they use considerable liberty in the matter of food. They have *Ráj-gurs*, or Rájgors, or royal family priests, distinct from the ordinary Bráhmans ; and they have great respect for *Bháṭs* or *Bhárats*, and *Chárans** their family bards and chroniclers. Of their connexion with Persia, as alleged by Walker and Moore, there is no evidence, though the word *Jám* may have some relation to the Zand *Yimo*, or *Jamshíd*—*Yimo-Kshaito*.

The sovereignty of Káṭhiáwáḍ is greatly divided and impaired. At present, even after many encroachments of the Maráthás, there are within the province nominally 224 separate jurisdictions, which are actually divided, in the case of the minor Rajput and Káṭhí States, into many other "sovereignties" so-called.† The province is tributary to the Gáikawáḍ and British Governments, the latter of which now maintains within it the rights of the Peshwa as well as collects the whole of the tribute. On various portions of it, the Muhammadan chief of Junágaḍ has claims for *Zortalabí*, or compromise for

* *Bha'ṭa*, related to the Sanskrit, *bhaṭṭa* or *bhaṭṭas*, suggests the Latin *vates*. The *Cha'rans* are so denominated from their secular occupation of graziers, united with their poetical engagements.

† See Jacob, p. 21, 22.

black mail. Education, even in its simplest elements, is but little diffused in the province; and the principles of civil and criminal law are but slightly understood by its people, the country, till lately, having been quite remarkable for its turbulence and violence. Generally speaking, its people are not more immoral than those of other parts of India. They are distinguished for their hospitality especially to Hindu and Jaina pilgrims, who swarm through the province. The Bráhmans have but little influence in the land; and the most important portion of them, the *Nágars*, are completely secularized as managers and clerks to the native Rájás. The *Chárans* and *Bháṭs* are sacred characters and genealogists, the bards of the chiefs, occupying themselves, too, in the rearing of cattle. They are sometimes Rájgurs, family priests, to the chiefs, as well as the Bráhmans, professing to bear the sins of their representatives. The *Jainas*, to whom most of the merchants and money-lenders belong, are haughty and intolerant to the full extent of their power, which is not inconsiderable, as they contrive to bring most of the chiefs into their debt. To most, or all, of the tribes now mentioned, references are made in the subsequent progress of this narrative.

KACHH (Cutch) is in many respects similar to Kaṭhiáwáḍ. It is a narrow neck of land, bounded on the north by a small frith into which formerly the Korí, or most eastern embochure of the Indus, emptied itself, and by the northern division of the *Raṇ*, a large portion of which is covered with brackish water during the rainy season. It is separated from Kaṭhiáwáḍ on the south by the Gulf of Kachh, which is not above thirty miles in its greatest breadth. The curve formed by the peninsula is a hundred and fifty miles in length. Its greatest breadth is about fifty miles. It is principally of sandstone, and nummulite limestone, elevated by marine volcanoes. Its soil is of a light character, its most fertile portion being that of the district of Abráshiá. Its population amounts to about half a million. Its highest tribe is the *Jáḍejá*, the chief of whom, and the first ruler of the province, is His Highness the Ráo, at his capital Bhuj. The other Jáḍejás with himself form the *Bháiyád* or brotherhood of that community. The Jáḍejás of Kachh, the male population of which ranges between six and seven thousand, and those of Káṭhiáwáḍ as we have just seen, have the same origin, and are intimately connected with one another, though separated by the Gulf now mentioned. Bráhmans are numerous in Kachh; but they have no great influence in the province. Its merchants, like those of Káṭhiáwáḍ, are famous throughout India. Its agriculturists are remarkable for their skill and industry. A good many of its people follow pastoral pursuits. Kachh, like Káṭhiáwáḍ, is sadly in want of educational appliances, though the present Ráo in point of information and culture is far superior to his predecessors.* He is the descendant of Udojí, the son of Ráydhan already mentioned. Hamírji, the seventh from Udojí, had four sons, Khengár, Sáhib, Ráéb, and Aliájí. Khengár, who had for some time been resident with his mother near Ahmadábád, as a fugitive from one of his brothers, having there attracted the notice of Ahmad Sháh, received from him military assistance; and returning to Kachh, took Bhuj, since made the capital, in Samvat 1594, or A. D. 1537, and founded the present dynasty.†

At the time of the discovery of Infanticide in Káṭhiáwáḍ, the relations to it of the British Government were of a very limited and remote character, and such as ren-

* For a general classification of the population of Kachh, see Oriental Christian Spectator, 1835.

† The succession from Ráydhan, according to the principal *Wansha'vali* which we have used is the following:—Bhármalji, Samvat 1642; Ráo Bhoj, 1688; Ráo Khengárji, 1702; Ráo Shrí Megh, 1711; Ráo Raydhanjí, 1722; Ráo Prágjí, 1754; Ráo Godjí, 1772; Ráo De'saljí, 1775; Ráo Lakhpat, 1808; Ráo Godjí, 1817; Ráo Ráydhan, 1835; Ráo Bhármaljí, 1870; Ráo De'saljí, the present Ráo, 1875. By subtracting 57 from each of these dates, the Christian year is ascertained.

dered it extremely difficult, for British officials, however disinterested and humane in their motives, to deal with the atrocious crime in an effective manner. The claims of the paramount power in India to international interference with the inferior states, were then but partially realized. The province was merely tributary to the Gáikawáḍ of Baroda and the Peshwa of Puná, two of our Maráthá allies, whose independent sovereignty we duly admitted. Kachh was even more remote from our influence, as the connexion of the Maráthás with that province was of the slightest character; and it did not even touch on our own territory.

The first inroad of the Maráthás into Gujarát, it is here proper to observe, took place under Shivají the founder of their empire, and was as entirely unprovoked and unjustifiable as any of their other movements exterior to their own country. Its issue was the subjection of a part of that territory to the tribute of the *chauth*, or portion of the fourth, which was levied under the pretence of a protection which was neither needed nor desired. Trimbak Ráo, Dhábáḍí, the *Sénâpati*, or commander-in-chief of the Maráthá Forces, was in his day, the instrument of further aggression in Gujarát. About the year 1724, he quarrelled with the Peshwa Bájíráo, who had usurped the principal power of the Maráthás from the nominal Rájá in the succession of Shivají; and taking the field he was defeated. His widow Ambá Báí remained at Taḷégáum, the family seat, while her son Yéshwant Ráo fled to the Muhammadans. Pilájí Gáikawáḍ, was a general in the service of the Dábáḍí; and in 1726 he led an army in the name of Ambá Báí into Gujarát, then governed for the Moghal by Shujáít Khán. He conquered a large portion of the province, the half of which, on the continental side, was ceded by the Muhammadans, and reverted to himself on his adoption by Ambá Báí, on the loss of her own sons. His title to its sovereignty having been confirmed by Sháhu Rájá of Sátárá, the nominal head of the Maráthá empire, he became the founder of the Gáikáwáḍ dynasty. Continuing his successes, he took Baroda in 1731; and dying in the following year, he was succeeded by his son Dámají, who, actuated merely by motives of self-aggrandizement, carried his arms into the peninsula of Káṭhiáwáḍ, a small part of which he subjected to his own sway, and the larger portion to tribute. He even entered the province of Kachh, where at Bhuj, he received as an addition to his haram, a daughter of Ráo Lakhpat, the chief Jáḍejá of that province, by one of his concubines. About 1748, the Peshwa, having effected a rupture with him, and caught him, forced him to cede to him about half the revenues of his country, as the price of his liberty, and to keep a large contingent, said to be of 10,000 horse, for the use of the Maráthá state. Dámají died in 1768. Four sons, Sayájí, Fatteh Singh, Govind Ráo, and Manájí survived him. Of these the two first-mentioned were the eldest, Sayájí being blind and incapacitated from rule; but Govind Ráo was by a superior wife. Fatteh Singh, after large contributions to the Peshwa Mádhavaráo, got *Sanads* or Warrants for Gujarát; but others, in favour of Govind Ráo, and in consideration also of large bribes, were afterwards issued by Rághobá, the brother of Mádhaváráo who had usurped the Peshwaship, after the murder of his nephew and ward Náráyan Ráo, the rightful heir. Rághobá, when forced to leave Puná,—in consequence of the righteous indignation of his countrymen, who called for the posthumous child of Náráyan, Mádhava Ráo, to occupy the *Gadí* of that state,—went from Bombay to Gujarát, expecting Govindráo to make common cause with him. Náná Farnavís, the noble minister of the youthful Peshwa Mádhavaráo, however, was more than a match for them both; and by the treaty of Purandar he got the English to concur in the recognition of Fatteh Singh as the chief of Gujarát, who reigned at Baroda till 1789, when he died and was succeeded by Manájí his half-brother, who by his decease made way for Govind Ráo, who on his death in 1800 was succeeded by his son Anandráo, with whom the British Government entered into special alliance in 1802.*

A word on the origin of the British relations with Kachh is here necessary. Ráo Ráydhan who squatted himself on the cushion of that province in 1778, through his own licentiousness and cruelty brought on madness; made a show of conversion to Muhammadism; and greatly oppressed his subjects, principally through means of Africans and foreigners employed by him as slaves and servants. When the long-suffering patience of his people was exhausted, and they had seized him and put him into confinement, his brother Bháíjí, his lawful successor in the conduct of affairs,—for he had no legal son,—was unable to manage them on account of his minority; and the direction of the State fell into the hands of twelve Musalmáns, commanders of mercenary troops, of whom Dosal Vén was the acknowledged head till 1792, when he was expelled from office by Fatteh Muhammad, another of their number, a native of Sindh, possessed of considerable administrative ability, which he continued to exercise after Bháíjí became of age. The rival of Fatteh Muhammad was a Hindu, named Hansráj, the governor of Mandaví, the chief seaport of Kachh, whose partizans gave him possession of Bháíjí, *alias* Prathiráj, who was carried off from Bhuj during the temporary absence of Fatteh Singh. Hansráj, to bring the dissensions between himself and the other functionary to a close, proposed to the Bombay Government in 1801-2, to cede Kachh to its management, on condition that Bhuj, the capital, should be reserved for the Ráo. Bháíjí died in 1802; and a similar proposal was made in 1804 both by Fatteh Muhammad who had charge of the person,—of the Ráo Ráydhan at Bhuj and also command of An-

* The names and dates here are given from a comparison of documents both native and European, and from a memorandum of Mr. Jonathan Duncan.

jár the second seaport of the province,—and by Hansráj, now restricting his administration to Mándaví. The Bombay Government, however, declined to form at this time a closer alliance with Kachh than what was required for the protection of its own subjects and allies; and rested satisfied with securing, in 1809, an agreement from Kachh for the suppression of piracy, very abundant near Kachh, and the confinement of its troops to its own territories; with warning the Sindhians against the invasion of Kachh; and with promising to aid the *darbár*, or court of Bhuj, in the settlement of some of its claims on the Jám of Nawánagar. The Kachh government did not fulfil its stipulations. Piracy by sea, and plunder by land, continued to exist on the borders of Kachh. This called for the interference of the Bombay Government through Captain MacMurdo, its agent in that province. His measures were for some time retarded through the death of Fatteh Muhammad, of Hansráj, and of the insane Ráo Ráydhan, and the disputes which followed about the succession. When Ráo Bhármaljí,—a son of Ráydhan by a slave-girl,—ultimately called to power, sat down on the royal cushion, he was only eighteen years of age; and by factions prevalent both among Hindus and Musalmans, he was greatly restricted in his administration. The greatest disorder, confusion, and cruelty prevailed throughout the province and its borders. Bhármaljí ere long sympathized with the disturbers of the peace, and sought to profit by their plunder. His government became very unpopular, particularly among the Jáḍejás forming his own *bháíyád*, to whom he was under great obligations. He placed himself even in indirect hostility to the British Government; for, when a British and Gáikawáḍ force was reducing Juriá in Kaṭhiawáḍ, his minister Shivaráj, the son of Hansráj, supplied the rebels at that place with ammunition and other assistance. On the fall of Juriá, he made a show, from fear, of putting down robbery in his own district of Wágar, parties from which had committed great depradations in Káṭhiáwáḍ; but he soon returned to Bhuj with his troops. The robbery and plunder in Káṭhiáwáḍ were again resumed without effective resistance on his part; and the British and Gáikawáḍ Governments, which had been put to an expence, from first to last, of about ten lakhs of rupees for their suppression, made a requisition on Bhármaljí for reimbursement and a guarantee against future incursions. Bhármaljí having permitted the time allowed for his answer to pass unimproved, the British troops entered his territories, took Anjár and Tuná, and advanced on his capital, when he was obliged to comply with the demands made upon him, now raised to twenty lakhs of rupees; to furnish an yearly tribute of two lakhs of korís,—less than two-thirds of a lakh of rupees,—and to enter into a general treaty of peace and alliance. This brings us to 1816, much in advance of our general narrative, which, however, would be unintelligible without these notices.* No one who sees the quiet and order of Kachh at the present day, can imagine what it was in the past generation, or understand the difficulties encountered in dealing with it in questions of political expediency and philanthropic interest.

But to return to Káṭhiáwáḍ. The usual method of realizing the tribute exacted from the peninsula in behalf of the Gáikawáḍ and Peshwa, was by periodical circuits enforced by military array. One of the ameliorations proposed under the alliance now referred to, "was," to use the words of Mr. Duncan, "to avoid the necessity for the ever-recurring and coercive progress, by inducing the dependent local rulers in Káṭhiáwáḍ, chiefly through an appeal to their own interests, to accede to an equitable permanent accommodation; ascertaining the amount of their future pecuniary acknowledgments, without the concurrence of force for their

* On the history of the British connexion with Kachh, see Sketch of the History of Kachh, appended to Dr. Burnes's interesting narrative of his Visit to the Court of Sindh.

realization. Toward the attainment of these salutary ends, it was deemed expedient that one general circuit should be made through the peninsula assisted by the appearance of a detachment from the British subsidiary force; and it was thought a duty of humanity to aim also, on this occasion, at the suppression of female Infanticide." The plans of the Bombay Government in reference to these matters were approved of by the Supreme Government of India, though in a somewhat cautious form as far as the attempt to suppress Infanticide was concerned.

"We cannot but contemplate with approbation," it was intimated by that government, "the considerations of humanity which have induced you to combine with the proposed expedition, the project of suppressing the barbarous custom of female Infanticide. But the speculative success even of that benevolent project, cannot be considered to justify the prosecution of measures which may expose to hazard the essential interests of the state; although as a collateral object, the pursuit of it would be worthy of the benevolence and humanity of the British Government."*

The proposed expedition to Káṭhiáwáḍ was committed to Major Alexander Walker, the Resident at the Court of the Gáikawáḍ, an officer highly fitted by his character and talents for the efficient discharge of its delicate and important duties. It was commenced by him in 1807; and he held both its political and military command. He was successful in accomplishing the revenue settlement of the province on a basis which has been but little disturbed since his day; in collecting and arranging an immense quantity of curious and valuable information connected with its diversified tribes; in suggesting many measures calculated to secure its peace and tranquillity; and above all, after no long interval, in inducing its Jáḍejá nobles to enter into engagements for

* Letter dated 31st July 1806.

the total supression of the crime of Infanticide, the systematic commission of which had for so long a period constituted their sin, and shame, reducing them in matters of humanity below the level of the most barbarous tribes. His various reports on Káṭhiáwáḍ, presented to the Bombay Government, are among the most able and interesting documents which the British administration in India, greatly less appreciated than it should be for its talent and industry, can furnish. That which narrated his endeavours for the suppression of Infanticide is dated the 15th March 1808. Though it is somewhat discursive, and contains not a few unnecessary digressions, and repetitions, not to say misapprehensions, it is possessed of extreme interest both in a literary and philanthropic point of view. We shall either extract its most important portions, subjoining to them such remarks as may be necessary for the elucidation of our narrative, or make such an abridgement of it, with additional notices, as is required by the subject of which it treats.

On the *origin* of Infanticide Major Walker thus writes:—"The Jáḍejás relate, that a powerful Rájá of their caste, who had a daughter of singular beauty and accomplishments, desired his Rájgur, or family Bráhman, to affiance her to a prince of desert and rank equal to her own. The Rájgur travelled over many countries, without discovering a chief who possessed the requisite qualities; for where wealth and power were combined, personal accomplishments and virtue were defective; and in like manner, where the advantages of the mind and body were united, those of fortune and rank were wanting. The Rájgur returned, and reported to the prince that his mission had not proved successful. This intelligence gave the royal mind much affliction and concern, as the Hindus reckon it to be the first duty of parents to provide suitable husbands for their daughters; and it is reproachful that they should pass the age of puberty without having been affianced, and be under the necessity of living in a state of celibacy. The Rájá, however, rejected, and strongly reprobated every match for his daughter, which he conceived inferior to her high rank and perfections. In this dilemma, the Rájá consulted his Rájgur; and the Bráhman advised him to avoid the censure and disgrace which would attend the princess remaining unmarried, by having recourse to the desperate expedient of putting her to death. The Rájá was long averse to this expedient, and remonstrated against the murder of a woman, which, enormous as it is represented in the Shástra, would be aggravated when committed on his own offspring. The Rájgur at length removed the Rájá's scruples, by consenting to load himself with the guilt, and to become in his own person responsible for all the consequences of the sin. Accordingly the princess was put to death; and female Infanticide was from that time practised by the Jáḍejás."* This is obviously an *ex post facto* explanation of the origin of the Jáḍejá Infanticide. "It resembles," says Major Walker himself, "the tales of infancy, rather than the grave history of a transaction, involving the fate of a numerous portion of the human race." He adds, "Whatever may have been the motives that led the Jaḍejás to embrace the extraordinary practice of destroying their daughters, conveniency and policy have contributed to continue and extend it. The scruples of religion were lulled and quieted, by the ideal security of another race being responsible for the crime. Opinions and habits, from which at first we have an aversion, as they grow familiar rise into consideration and establish their ascendency. The superstition of the Jáḍejás easily reconciled them to the expedient proposed by the Rájgur; which freed them from the fear and consequences of sin and undermined their compassion and affection for their offspring. The sentiments of nature and humanity were supplanted by the passions of avarice and pride; for the right of destroying their daughters

* Walker's Report, paragraphs, 9-16.

grew into a privilege, which they regarded as a distinction and honor peculiar to their caste. The Hindu precepts and customs concerning marriage are full of family distinctions, exact so many observances and impose so many restraints, that a military tribe, like the Jáḍejás, might not be reluctant to receive a dispensation. These restraints, when their operation is strictly enforced, occasion many inconveniences, and in some situations they may prove insurmountable. All these difficulties are felt more in the cases of women than of men; and the expense attending their marriage is an obligation which the Jáḍejás consider it for their interest and advantage to be exempted from." To the conquest of Sindh by the Muhammadans, too, Major Walker refers, as explanatory of the origin of Infanticide among the Hindus who wandered from that province. "The Jáḍejás, finding themselves surrounded by tribes who had embraced a new faith, and precluded thereby from marrying their daughters to those among them among whom they were formerly accustomed to contract matrimonial engagements may, under such circumstances, have preferred the expedient suggested, and encouraged by superstition, of destroying their female offspring." On the consideration here adverted to, much stress is to be laid, though it be a fact that other Rajput tribes less oppressed by the Muhammadans than the Jáḍejás have fallen into the habitual commission of the same crime.

On the *continuance* of the practice of Infanticide by the Jáḍejás after their emigration from Sindh to the south, Major Walker thus comments. "We know that the Jáḍejás maintained their independence in Sindh for a long period, and resisted their invaders with spirit and fortitude." "In subsequent times, when the emigration of the Jáḍejás into Kachh and Gujarát, inhabited by Rajputs, offered abundance of husbands for their daughters, and removed the plea for their destrution, the custom had been established, and was considered as one of their inalienable rights. The Jáḍejás had also conceived many barbarous notions of their own superiority, and they undervalued or despised the tribes amongst whom they had obtained a compulsory settlement. The circumstance of conquest, under which they settled in Kachh and Gujarát, confirmed this sentiment of superiority." These explanations are probably to a good extent correct. Still, Major Walker, formed a right judgement, when he added, "The great cause for their destroying their children is avarice, and that they may not be exposed to the cares and expence attending their establishment in life." "Considerable weight must be given to the apathy and indifference with which it has ever been received by the rest of the Rajput families and the Bráhmans, who are numerous in this country. It does not appear that any effort has been made for the general suppression of this crime, for which they possessed a simple and effectual remedy by refusing to affiance their daughters to the Jáḍejás, unless on the condition of rearing their female offspring. Such an idea never seems to have occurred to the other Rajputs; on the contrary they appear to have countenanced the practice of Infanticide not only by intermarrying their daughters with the Jáḍejás, but by allowing them to become the instruments of murdering their own offspring. These Rajputs were led to this unnatural compliance from the ease and facility with which their acquiescence enabled them to marry their daughters. To this interested motive they appear to have sacrificed the sentiments of religion and humanity without any repugnance. They excused, however, to me, and endeavoured to palliate their want of sensibility by pleading the immediate usages of caste, and the impropriety of interfering in those of the Jáḍejás."

About the *methods* of the destruction of their infant daughters by the Jáḍejás, Major Walker's inquiries were probably as successful as could have been expected. They were reluctant to speak on the *díkrí márawání chál*,—"the custom of killing daughters,"—remarking that it was an "affair of the women." It was well ascertained, however, that it was especially "an affair of the men;" as it was according to their hints or orders that the crime was perpetrated by the women. They appeared, it was found, to have had several methods of destroying the infant; but two were commonly prevalent. Immediately after the birth they put into the mouth of the infant some opium, or drew the umbilical cord over its face to prevent respiration. The destruction of such tender objects was not difficult. In some instances death followed neglect, without violence. The mother was said to be the usual executioner in Káṭhiáwáḍ, and the female Rájgur in Kachh. When an inquisitive person asked a Jáḍejá, the result of the pregnancy of his wife, he would, if it were a female, answer "NOTHING," an expression in the idiom of the country sufficiently significant, and used with the utmost levity. Only a few instances were known of any of the Jáḍejás of Káṭhiáwáḍ having preserved their daughters; but by doing so, they rather lost than gained repute. Most of the Jáḍejás in Kachh who had become proselytes to Muhammadanism saved the lives of their daughters. "I endeavoured," says Major Walker, "to ascertain the motives of the Jáḍejás who preserved their daughters; and by their own confession this act of humanity did not proceed from parental feelings. It appeared to be inspired, not by motives of affection for the object so much as by personal considerations, arising from the ideas of the metempsychosis, which are so universally and rigidly observed by the Shrávak baniás, who are the followers of Jina. These people consider it a sin to deprive any being or creature, however, mean or noxious of life; and their doctrines are said to have made an impression on a few of the Jáḍejás."* Any argument against Infanticide

* In another portion of his report Major Walker notices all the instances which had been brought to his notice of Jáḍejás who had saved their daughters. Makájí of A'nandagaḍ, who had embraced the eclectic views of the Hindu reformer Kabír, renounced for a time intercourse with his wife, lest any daughters should be born to him, whom, as a Jáḍejá, he

which might be supposed to be derived from the doctrine of the metempsychosis, is available in reason equally in the case of a Bráhmanist as in that of a Jaina. Yet it is a fact that the Jainas in the peninsula of Gujarát are the most ostentatious in their professed regard for the preservation of life, especially that of the brutes, which, they say, are incapable of asking the aid of man whose fellows they may have been in former births. To the preservation of life, however, the doctrine of the metempsychosis is *not*, logically speaking, favourable. As every creature has a certain number of births to go through before absorption in the case of the Bráhmanists,* and before liberation or extinction in the case of the Jainas, death would appear rather to hasten than delay these grand results. It is a feeling of simple brotherhood, as far as life is concerned, with the unfortunate brutes which makes the Jainas so tenderly preserve them. For the life of man, this feeling is by no means so strong among them as for the life of the brutes. While the slaughter of a cow in one of their towns would well-nigh produce rebellion, the slaughter of a helpless infant would scarcely excite among them a feeble dissatisfaction.

Major Walker's inquiries into the *statistics* of Infant-

would have been required to put to death. When by the commands of his chief, and to avoid scandal, he returned to his wife, and four daughters were born to him in succession, he allowed his religious principles to triumph over the prejudices of his tribe. The chief of Karsorá preserved a daughter, ultimately married to the Rájá of Bháwanagar, the highest chief of the peninsula,—in deference to the offer of an Arab Jamádár to remit his arrears of pay, on condition that he saved her life. Dádájí, the brother of the Thákur, or Baron, of Rájkoṭ, preserved a daughter from natural affection. Hutájí, a professed robber, saved two daughters, it was thought from the same motive, but probably as an "atonement" for his numerous crimes. These girls he dressed and habited like boys; and to Major Walker they denied their sex. The chief of Máliá reared one daughter in deference to the entreaties of his wife.—Report, 117-140.

* The number of births, according to the Shástra, which must precede absorption is 8,400,000.

icide were not much to be depended on. One account which he received, he was aware, had the appearance of exaggeration. It estimated the Jáḍejás in Kachh and Káṭhiáwáḍ at 125,000, and the number of female infants annually destroyed at 20,000. Another estimated the yearly infanticides in the latter province at 5,000, and those in Kachh, making allowance for the families which, it was supposed, had discontinued the practice, at 25,000, being in all 30,000 infantile murders in the space of twelve months. A third, which he considered as much below the truth as the preceding was above it, gave the annual infanticides south of the gulf of Kachh as ranging between 1,000 and 1,100, and those north of that gulf at about 2,000. Even this last estimate, to the credit of human nature be it said, was greatly in excess of the reality. It is evident from the statistical tables, now carefully prepared, that the annual number of ascertained female births among the Jáḍejás in Káṭhiáwáḍ may be stated at about 250, and in Kachh at about 225. The infanticides among the Jáḍejás alone, then, did not fall much short of 500 annually. Taking them at this estimate,—for we must make some allowance for births still concealed—how horrid does the practice appear. Five hundred murders a year among the princes and nobles of a community of no great extent! How provocative of the indignation of God this fearful shedding of innocent blood! How hardening to the hearts of all concerned in its perpetration or connivance! How destructive of all tender and gentle feeling in families, must the total absence of a sisterhood have been in their education and training!

Of the existence of the practice of Infanticide *in another Rajput tribe* in the peninsula of Gujarát, Major Walker received certain information. It was that of the *Jaitwás* of the province of Bardá, the capital of which is the considerable town of Porbandar on the western coast. They neither avowed nor defended the practice when it was laid to their charge; but the fact that their

Ránás, or chiefs, had no grown-up daughters for more than a hundred years was decisive evidence against them.*

The practice of Infanticide could never have been established among the Jádejás had the neighbouring Rajputs refused to give them their daughters in mar-

* Of the existence of Infanticide among *more remote tribes of Ra'jputs*, too, Major Walker was well aware. "The practice of female Infanticide prevails with the *Ráj Kumárs*, and other tribes in *Bengal;* where it has been [as was then supposed] happily abolished. The custom of putting their infant daughters to death, has also been discovered to exist with the *Rátoḍ Rajputs* of *Jaypur* and *Jaudpur*, but this fact when reported to *Europe* was doubted and denied to be possible. It is confirmed, however, by every intelligent and well-informed native of that country; nor does there appear any grounds whatever for questioning its existence. The existence of the custom is traced to other tribes of *Hindustán*, and in particular to the *Játs* and *Mewáts*; which latter are a sect of *Musalmans*. I am indebted for this information to Nizám-ud-dín Husain ; and the following is the translation of a memorandum which he gave me on the subject. 'The *Ját* chiefs of *Bhartpur* are stiled *Sensuiwal? (sic);* those people, or the *Sensuiwals*, are in the habit of putting to death their daughters at the moment of their birth, by opium, or by strangling. The cause of their doing so proceeds from a supposition which they entertain, that it is a great disgrace to give their daughters, even in marriage, to any person. And many *Mewáts* who are *Muhammadans*, but who are known under the appellation of *Mewáti*, whose country is near that of the *Játs*, kill their daughters from the same cause. I suppose the governors of *Hatras* and *Mursán* follow the same practice. These people are all of the Ját caste.' I have learnt from other sources of information on which I rely, that some of the *Ratoḍ*, the *Hari* of *Bundi Kotá*, the *Waish* in the *Purab*, the *Játs* in *Hindustan*, and some of the *Kaçhhwás* of *Jaypur*, and other *Rajput* tribes kill their daughters. The *Jáḍejás* are aware that the custom of Infanticide is practised by many other tribes besides their own; but although it is probable that they have a common origin, I could not discover the traditionary motive that had led to the introduction of Infanticide amongst so many people of Hindustán. The practice, however, appears to be maintained among them by the same causes which operated with the *Jáḍejás*. Pride, avarice, the cares of a family, the disgrace that would attend the misconduct of their women, the difficulty of establishing them in life, and apprehension of exposing their daughters to ill-treatment, were assigned in variably by every person acquainted with this subject as the cause that induced these tribes to commit Infanticide."—Report, 197-203.

riage. No such virtue, however, was found among them. "They marry apparently," wrote Major Walker, "into any of the Rajput tribes." The *Jhálás*, *Wághélás*, *Gohils*, *Chorásámas*, *Pramárs*, *Soḍhas*, *Sarwaiyas*, *Jaitwás*, *Wálás*, *Wáḍáls*, were ever ready to furnish them with wives, for the usual considerations of money and family alliances, even though they knew that their female offspring must be destroyed. Instances were not wanting of Jáḍejá chiefs living even in a state of polygamy and concubinage with women of various castes and creeds, who alleged that they were too poor to rear a single daughter. Their female children by their concubines they did not generally destroy, sparing them "rather from a contemptuous opinion of their inferiority, than from humanity." Their concubines or *rákhelís* they encouraged to burn themselves on their funeral piles, even though they held that their wives might spare themselves from the right of Satí. The exemption in favour of the latter, it was thought, originated in the custom of the lowest castes of the people to burn themselves with their husbands, to the detriment of the feasibility of the rite itself.

It is due to the memory of Major Walker, to give in detail his own narrative of his ingenious *efforts for the abolition* of the practice of Infanticide, with the extent and nature of which the reader has now been made acquainted, principally on his own authority.

"I entered on this undertaking," he says, "with sanguine expectations of success, but which were, for a long time, disappointed; and I must own that the natives had formed much more just opinions on the subject, when they foretold the difficulties that would attend the attempt; which few of them thought could be overcome, but by the Company making a conquest of the country. I conceived that reason and feeling would effect the relinquishment of a barbarous custom unconnected with the principles of society; and which all the passions of the human mind, and all the forms and maxims of religion, were combined to destroy. As it was evident also that the most disinterested humanity had led the Honourable Company to interfere for the abolition of female Infanticide, I conceived that this reflection, and the respect due to their mediation, would have disposed the Jáḍejás to comply with a request, which it was scarcely to be supposed could be at variance with their own sentiments. But sentiments of nature and humanity have no influence with the *Jáḍejás;* and I was soon, however reluctantly, obliged to relinquish the favourable expectation I had formed of success. The difficulties were many and formidable. I had been for several years in habits of friendly correspondence with Jéhájí, the chief of Murví, and he had continually expressed a strong desire to cultivate the favour of the English Government. The artifices of this chief, and his *vakíl* (agent), who resided in my camp, deceived and amused me for some time with promises, which proved fallacious. I availed myself of the agency and influence of Sundarjí Shivají * after his arrival in camp, but with no better success. At last Jéhájí transmitted a paper, in which he offered to accede to my wishes by preserving his daughters, provided I would reduce *Málía*, and restore the village of *Karálá*, of which he had been deprived by the Gaikáwáḍ Government. The possession of this paper I considered of importance, as it discovered the selfish and mercenary motives, that attached the Jáḍejás to Infanticide. I preserved it as a testimony which refuted their pretences of the inviolability of the practice, as a custom of the *caste;* and destroyed every argument which they attempted to found on principle. When Jéhájí perceived the disadvantage which attended the possession of this paper, he made several applications to induce me to restore it, with which I did not comply. As my intercourse and knowledge of the Jáḍejás increased, every circumstance

* [See above, p. 48.]

tended to shew that they followed Infanticide from mean and interested motives only. It was also evident that it would be very difficult to awaken their natural feelings; and that the same motives of conveniency and interest, would have more influence in inducing them to relinquish the practice, than any arguments derived from humanity, morality, or religion. It appeared likewise from the communications of Jehájí and others, that the reproach and odium of being the first to renounce an ancient practice operated as a considerable motive. The weight and authority of this example could not be complete, unless it was set by a chief of acknowledged rank and superiority. The *Ráo* of *Kachh* seemed to possess these qualifications, from his family, and extent of territory. I was induced, therefore, to select this chieftain; but addressed myself principally to Fatteh Muhammad, whose authority is paramount in that country, and from whom as a zealous *Muhammadan*, I was led to expect the exertion of his influence for suppressing a crime against nature and religion. The answer however of Fatteh Muhammad destroyed every hope of success from that quarter.* This *Jamádár*, who rose from

* The letter here now referred to by Colonel Walker was without date, but received on the 21st October, 1807. As it is of a very curious character, it may be here inserted.

(After compliments). "It is notorious that since the Avatára of Shrí Krishna the people, the Jádejás, who are descended from the Jadus, (Yádavas) have, during a period of 4900 years, been in the habit of killing their daughters; and it has no doubt reached your knowledge, that all of God's creation, even the mighty Emperors of Hindustán, Sháh Jehán, Aurangzíb, and Akbár, who have successively reigned in Hindustán; those of Khorásan, and Irán, and the Rájás of the four quarters of Hindustán; besides all others the conductors of the affairs of this world, who have existed from time to time, have always preserved friendship with this Court, and never acted in this respect, female Infanticide, unreasonably.

"Even the King of the world, who is protected by God, the King of Rum [the New Rome or Constantinople], descended from a long line of illustrious ancestors who have reigned over that country from the earliest times and in whose dominions is situated the inestimable and the humble station of a goatherd, and is extremely illiterate, had the sentiments of his letter probably dictated to him; and by the hand of his writer, transmitted, in an inflated and ostentatious style, an elaborate defence of the practice of Infanticide; such as could be expected to proceed only from an infuriated and bigoted Jaḍejá. It may not be unworthy of remark that this defence of Infanticide was written and composed by a *Nágar Bráhman*, and promulgated in the name of a *Muhammadan* whose religion inspires them with horror against these murders. In the meanwhile every effort and endeavour was continued to prevail on the *Murví* chief to abandon Infanticide, which the long detention

glorious Mecca, never once thought of putting a stop to the custom which prevails among the Jáḍejás of killing their daughters, but on the contrary has preserved friendship at all times with this *darbár*: and merchants possessing lakhs of wealth belonging to his country reside here, and people of equal wealth of this country reside there, but he never once uttered any thing on the subject. But you, who follow the paths of the King, and who are an *amír* (noble) of the great Sirkár, the Honourable Company, having written me on the subject, I have derived much uneasiness, for it does not accord with your good character.

"You should reflect, that though the authority of many kings and rájás, the King of Rum excepted, has decayed, or passed into the hands of others, still the Government of this country has remained unmoved from the period of the avatára of Krishna unto this day, and this country contains so many brothers of one heart, descended from a common parent, as is not to be found in any other quarter; but they have not to this day departed from the habit of female Infanticide; they have however approved of two good customs. First, in this country neither birds nor animals are killed, goats excepted; and but few even eat them. Secondly, charitable places for fakirs [religious beggars] going and coming from Mecca, and Hindus performing pilgrimages, are so strongly planted that the pilgrims suffer no annoyance.

"This *darbár* has always maintained friendship beyond bounds with the Sirkár of the Honourable Company; and notwithstanding this, you have acted so unreasonably in this respect, that I am much distressed. God is the giver, and God is the taker away; if any one's affairs go to ruin he must attribute his fortune to God. No one has until this day wantonly quarrelled with this Darbár who has not in the end suffered loss. This *Darbár* wishes no one ill, nor has ever wantonly quarrelled with any one. Every thing that may happen is from God. I bow obedient. Do not again address me on this subject."

of the detachment in the vicinity of that city afforded. It was the daily subject of letters, messages, and conferences. The humanity and tenderness congenial to the sex induced me to expect the assistance of the women of Jéháji's family. The preservation of their offspring appeared naturally and peculiarly their business. I conceived that my appeal to wives and mothers, and to women who came from tribes that rejected Infanticide, would be attended with every advantage. I was farther led to entertain great hopes from this plan, on account of the high character of the mother of the chief of *Murví*, for prudence, propriety of conduct, and a benevolent disposition. As this lady possesses considerable influence over her son, I expected that she would exert it in favour of a measure, agreeable to her own feelings. The embarrassed state of Jéháji's affairs, and the countenance which he stood in need of from me for retrieving them, were circumstances which I conceived would occur to the discretion of his mother; and urge her to obtain from her son a concession which might give the family a claim to my support. My overtures to this lady were at first received with the feelings natural to her sex; and she seemed disposed, with the rest of the women, who held several consultations together on the subject, to unite their influence for the abolition of Infanticide. But these ebullitions were of short duration:—the Jáḍejás were alarmed, and the women contended for the ancient privilege of the *caste;* they were led away from the path of nature and humanity by the example and influence of their husbands. The mother of the chief of *Murví* requested that she might be excused soliciting her son on this head, and referred me for any farther information to Jéháji. At this period my prospect of success was very obscure and distant:—but although these efforts had failed of their desired effect, they were notwithstanding, useful; and paved the way for success, by turning the attention of the country to a subject, which, it would appear, had never before attracted any public notice. By discussing the subject frequently in the public *Kachéri*, and exposing the enormity of the practice, as contrary to the precepts of religion and the dictates of nature, every *caste* came to express an abhorrence of Infanticide; and the obstinate prejudices of the Jáḍejás began to be shaken. The maxims and passions which favoured Infanticide, were probably for the first time canvassed, and censured with freedom. The progress of this system was slow, but it was insensibly spreading its influence, and became a subject of universal conversation. The novelty of the attempt, and the extraordinary nature of the subject, also attracted general attention. But whatever influence these circumstances might produce, as Jéháji was the first chieftain that I had addressed on the subject, it was of the utmost importance to make some impression on him. I bent every exertion, therefore, and tried various expedients to reclaim this chief, who had already destroyed two of his daughters, from the practice of Infanticide. At last I obtained from Jéhájí a conditional writing to the following effect:—'From motives of friendship the Honourable Company have urged me to preserve my daughters; to this I consent, if the chiefs of *Nawânagar* and *Gondal* agree.' This was the first considerable step towards the attainment of this great object; and the writing appeared to reduce the question to a kind of point of honour, or respect for antiquity, in setting the example of sanctioning an innovation on a general habit. From the character and behaviour of the *Jám*, I could have no hopes that he would set this example; but as the family of Déwají of *Gondal* had already preserved several of their daughters, I was led to entertain the most favourable expectations from the general disposition of this chief, and his reputation for humanity. It may be proper to mention, that Jéhájí first proposed to insert the names of the *Ráo* of *Kachh* and *Jám* of *Nawânagar* in his writing; but I positively refused to receive the paper unless it comprised Déwají of Gondal. The compliance of Jéhájí with this request, it may be but fair to consider as a favourable indication of his sentiments; and that he was secretly not extremely averse to agree to the abolishing of Infanticide. It may be presumed he was acquainted with the disposition of Déwají, and of the general opinion that this chief, when pressed, would renounce the practice of killing his daughters. From Dosájí of *Máliá* I obtained a similar writing to that received from the chief of *Murví*. I had conceived great expectations from Dosájí, who had preserved a daughter, and had by his *vakíl* (agent) afforded repeated assurances that he was ready to renounce Infanticide; but it is remarkable that this chief used every evasion and delay to avoid executing a formal deed in renunciation of the practice. It is necessary to notice here, that there were several petty *Jáḍejá* chiefs in my camp, whose distressed and dependant circumstances rendered them obsequious to any measure proposed by Government; and they were ready to bind themselves by any engagement to renounce Infanticide: but I conceived that their early formal acquiescence would not have the force of example with any of the superior chiefs, and would rather prejudice the cause. Under these ideas, I declined for the present entering into engagements with the petty chiefs who followed the camp. The narrative must now accompany the operations of the Detachment, which traversed the country of Jám and arrived at *Kandorérá*. I employed this time, as often as circumstances and opportunity permitted, in favour of the design for abolishing Infanticide. Wasanjí Ishwarjí, the *vakíl* of the *Gondal* chief, residing in camp, enabled me frequently to converse with him on the subject; and this sensible and respectable *Bráhman* was easily persuaded to unite his influence with mine, to prevail on his master to enter into a formal obligation for discontinuing Infanticide. During these events, Wasanjí had occasion to proceed to *Gondal* on some revenue affairs; and before his departure he privately gave me such assurances, as I conceived might be confided in, that he would, on his return, obtain authority from Déwají, to enter into any engagements which might be required, for preserving the daughters of the Jáḍejás, residing in that part of the country. In this, and every endeavour for suppressing Infanticide, it is with great pleasure that I mention the cordial and zealous assistance of Viṭhalráo Diwánjí, the commander of the Gáikawáḍ army. This officer, with the peculiar ardour of his character, embraced every occasion of exposing the enormity of the crime, and of promoting, by his arguments and influence, a detestation of the practice. The mission of Wasanjí Ishwarjí was entirely successful; and on his return to camp, after expressing the reluctance of his master to set an example which might bring on him the reproach of his caste, a deed of the most solemn, effectual, and binding nature was executed, renouncing for ever the practice of Infanticide.

"The following is a translation of this instrument:—'Whereas the Honourable English Company and *A'nandráo Gáikawáḍ Sená Kḥáskḥél Shamsher Bahádur*, having set forth to us the dictates of the Shástras and the true faith of the Hindus; as well as, that the *Brahmá-Vaivarttaka Purána* declares the killing of children to be a heinous sin; it being written that it is as great an offence to kill an embryo as a Bráhman; that to kill one woman is as great a sin as a hundred Bráhmans; that to put one child to death is as great a transgression against the divine laws, as to kill a hundred women; and that the perpetrators of this sin shall be damned to the Hell *Kála Sútra*, where, he shall be infested with as many maggots as he may have hairs on his body; be born again a leper, and debilitated in all his members: We Jáḍejá Déwají and Kuér Nathu, Zamindárs of Gondal, (the custom of female Infanticide having long prevailed in our caste) do hereby agree for ourselves, and for our offspring; as also we bind ourselves in behalf of our relations, and their offspring, for ever, for the sake of our own prosperity, and for the credit of the Hindu faith; that we shall from this day renounce this practice; and in default of this, that we acknowledge ourselves offenders against the Sirkárs.* Moreover, should any one in future commit this offence, we shall expel him from our caste, and he shall be punished according to the pleasure of the two governments, and the rule of the Shástras. The above writing is duly executed."

This form of engagement, it will be seen, is similar to that into which the Rájkumárs entered under Mr. Jonathan Duncan, on which we have already remarked,† that while it is perfectly satisfactory as far as the interdiction of Infanticide is concerned, it makes the English Government the patron and teacher and avenger of the Hindu faith. At the time it was prepared little comparatively was thought, even by the wisest and best of our countrymen residing in India, of the moral relations of the measures of our administration, on which the greatest stress is ever to be laid. The great ambition of our politicals was too often to please and gratify, even by religious concession and flattery. It is with painful feelings that we now read such an exordium as we find in one of Major Walker's letters written about this time to Shivají Sundarjí on the great theme of humanity which was so near his heart:—"I have received your letter, and I understand its contents; but to-day being *Vitípát*,‡ which is an unlucky day, I therefore am unable to write a particular answer until to-morrow; I beg you to wait." Even though the inability here referred to may have originated in the absence, from superstitious reasons, of a principal clerk, it should not have been announced in a manner seemingly deferential to superstition.

* The British and Gáikawáḍ Governments. † See above, p. 42.

‡ Sanskrit *vyatípát*, the seventeenth day of the *Yogas*, considered by the Hindus particularly unlucky.

"With the exception of the Jám every Jáḍejá chief readily and without offering a single objection, subscribed to a counterpart of this instrument." Every other Jáḍejá possessed of the least authority or influence in the country did the same. The Jám, who was the first in rank of the Jáḍejás of Káṭhiáwáḍ, opposed it by every art and subterfuge as long as he could. He attempted to prevent Déwají of Gondal from signing it, but fortunately ineffectually. He requested, with reference to his own family, that neither he nor his own offspring should be included in the engagement, but that he should only bind himself for his other relations and their offspring. No exception, however, could be made in his favour. "It is sufficient, to expose the unworthy motives of this chief," wrote Major Walker, "to mention that after he had agreed to the engagement for renouncing Infanticide, he had the effrontery and meanness to solicit an abatement of his revenue, in order to re-imburse the expence, which, as he alleged, he would in future be liable to in consequence of bringing up his daughters." If the truth had been fully known, it would have been found that not another Jáḍejá who signed the engagement was actuated at the time by nobler or more disinterested motives. It was deference to the will of the English Sirkár, and not to the will of God or the voice of humanity, which led them to its adoption. It was received to get rid of a disagreeable importunity, and doubtless in the hope that it might be violated with comparative impunity, as the Jáḍejás themselves were to be the executors of its highest penalty,—that of expulsion from caste,—and as additional punishment was rather obscurely prescribed, to be inflicted "according to the pleasure of the two governments [the British and Gaikawáḍ] and the [indefinite] rule of the Shástras." Still, as a primary measure, it had very high importance.

Major Walker's estimate of the advantages of the engagement was doubtless formed in all sincerity. It was thus expressed. "The instruments ascertain with precision what the parties have stipulated to perform; and besides inflicting the penalties derived from caste and religion, those deeds confer on the Company and the Gáikáwáḍ, a clear and legal right of punishing the offenders. It seems to be incontrovertible, that, whatever may have been its origin, the Jáḍejás continued Infanticide from motives of interest or convenience; and the same motives are now brought into operation to counterbalance their former prejudice;—for if they were to relapse, and again kill their daughters, they would be liable to the disgrace of expulsion from their families, and to arbitrary punishment; exposing themselves evidently to much greater disadvantages and vexations, than can possibly arise from preserving their children. The illiterate condition of the Jáḍejás, the confined state of their information, and the acquiescence of successive generations, had shut their eyes to the atrocity of Infanticide; but it is not too much to expect, that the instruction and lights they have lately received, may produce a beneficial change in their sentiments. The crime of Infanticide has been exposed to the community; and many men who never reflected upon it before, will now, under the impression of its enormity, insensibly impart their sentiments to the Jáḍejás who live amongst them. The intercourse of life, and the equal state in some points of the members of their society, afford abundance of opportunity for this communication; and it will produce that influence which is generally the consequence of a free exchange of correct opinions. Among the causes also which are likely to maintain the observance of these engagements, superstition may be mentioned, which was before acting in favour of Infanticide. The Jáḍejás now understand the punishment denounced by the Shástras for the crime; and the same spirit of religion which transferred the sin to the Rájgur will be equally disposed, by a kind of retributive justice, in consequence of their own voluntary deed, to make them in future answerable for every violation of their contract. Even a temporary disuse of Infanticide would assist towards its entire abolition, by allowing reason and natural feelings to recover their ascendancy. The great satisfaction of the country, and the general contentment of the Jáḍejás themselves, after they had signed the instruments for abolishing Infanticide, whatever repugnance they had before expressed to the measure, appeared to me to afford strong grounds for believing that the engagements would be permanent. The efficacy, however, of these engagements, and the entire suppression of this vice, must be maintained by the vigilance and vigour of the Company's and the Gáikáwáḍ Government. Their power or influence must be exerted to punish the first instance of transgression. It may appear to have been desirable, but it was not easily practicable, to have defined the nature of the punishment to be inflicted on future offenders. The great inequality in the power and rank of the Jáḍejás, rendered it difficult to fix with any advantageous precision, on a common standard of punishment." To this it may be added, also in the words of Major Walker, "It is remarkable that none of the Governments [except that of Jehángír on a particular occasion*] who have acquired an ascendancy in India have ever been induced to attempt the abolition of Infanticide; and that a custom so repugnant to every principle of reason and natural affection should have been permitted to exist and be tolerated, even at the very walls of the capitals of the Muhammadan sovereigns of Delhí and Gujarát, without an attempt to abolish it." The honour of the suppression of all the great inhuman rites of India has been reserved for a Christian nation.

With his distinguished success in Káṭhiáwáḍ, Major Walker was quickened in his endeavours in behalf of

* This interpolation we insert on the authority of the Akbál-Námah, as quoted by Colonel Walker himself on the 27th August, 1819.

the province of Kachh. These endeavours, however, were at this time wholly unsuccessful. His renewed appeal to Fatteh Muhammad, the minister of the Ráo, merely called forth a second defence of Infanticide, with the declaration that it was improper for him to say more to the Jáḍejás on the subject. The fact was, that this wily Jamádár feared the subversion of his own power by the Jáḍejá brotherhood, and did not like to offend that body. Major Walker came to the conclusion, which was unhappily proved to be a sound one, that no strong hope could be entertained that Infanticide would be *soon* abolished in Kachh.

CHAPTER IV.

RESULTS OF COLONEL WALKER'S ARRANGEMENTS FOR THE SUPPRESSION OF INFANTICIDE—EFFORTS OF CAPTAIN CARNAC IN THE SAME CAUSE.

Major Walker's success in negotiating the agreement with the Jáḍejá chiefs of Káṭhiáwáḍ for the suppression of Infanticide met, as it well merited, with the cordial approbation of the Bombay Government, the minute of which on the occasion, on account of the important counsels and suggestions which it contained, is well worthy of being recorded in full.

"In acknowledgment of the letter above recorded from Major Walker, and of its several accompaniments, he is to be advised, in addition to the approbation already expressed under date the 8th of March, on the success of his exertions in putting, (it is hoped) an effectual end to the horrid practice of Infanticide in and throughout the Peninsula of Gujarát, that Government have perused, with the interest arising out of the extraordinary nature and great importance of the subject, the more particular details furnished by his present address, of the probable rise and progress, and the too certain prevalence of this nefarious system amongst the Jáḍejás; and, in one instance at least, among Jaitwá Rajputs; and whilst we cannot sufficiently commend that solicitude, perseverance, and ability, to which is to be ascribed the procuring of the obligations entered into by all the chieftains to abandon it, we are sensible that it must require the vigilant and concurrent attention of both the government of the Gáikawáḍ, and of the Honourable Company to ensure, especially during the first years, the faithful adherence of the several parties to the salutary stipulations to which they have thus been brought to subscribe. But we rely on the zeal of the Resident, who will not fail to stimulate the native administration of Baroda, and through it, their officers in Kaṭhiáwáḍ, to attend to and make periodical reports of the new system thus happily introduced; which if allowed to operate, must soon become manifest in the number of female children which every Jáḍejá house may soon be known to contain; while on the other hand the want of such indication will constitute proof sufficient of the influence of the old prejudice, and of that disregard to engagements, which, in the present instance, ought not to be treated with much indulgence, but rather punished by a moderate fine, to be always imposed with the privity of the British Government through the Resident; and the amount of which to be applied to the relief of those among the more indigent classes of the Jáḍejás who shall be known to fulfil and adhere to the letter and spirit of their engagements; or, therwise, by the infliction of such other penalty as the local authorities may deem the most impressive, and likely to ensure the attainment of an object so highly salutary and indispensable in all respects, as is the extirpation of the baneful practice of Infanticide from all the districts of Káṭhiáwáḍ, with an ultimate view to the same humane object in Kachh.

"It is accordingly desired that the Resident will concert with the Gáikawáḍ Government the best means for obtaining periodical notices of the obligations; making it also a rule to submit (exclusive of such intermediate reports as may become necessary) one general statement on the last day of each year, how far the amended system has been acted on and observed, what deviations are known or suspected to have been made from its rules, and what measures pursued for their enforcement; the whole to be accompanied with an estimate of the number of lives that may, under the blessing of Divine Providence, be thus ultimately saved to the community."

The Court of Directors of the East India Company were not less hearty in their approbation of the proceedings of Colonel Walker, as shown by their dispatches of the 30th August 1809 and 29th August 1810, in the latter of which they acknowledged that his perseverance was entitled to their "highest commendation."

The first intimation of the practical working of the Engagement of the Járejás, was conveyed in an official letter from Colonel Walker dated from the Residency of Baroda, 16th December 1808. It certified, on the authority of the native agents of the Gáikáwáḍ in Káṭhiáwáḍ, the preservation of the lives of *twenty* Járejá females, the natural death of *two*, and the murder of *three*, one of whom was the granddaughter of the Gondal chief, of whom, however, no person would act as the public accuser. Among the parties who had saved a daughter was an individual of the Dharol *Bháiyád*, who had been formerly instrumental in the death of three of his daughters in succession. Colonel Walker esteemed these results of great importance; and doubtless they had this character. They were shown by a very limited portion of the Járejá territory; and other districts, it was thought, would furnish similar evidence of the respect shown to the Engagement. The inference drawn from them was that "the practice is decreasing, or that public opinion now views it in a different light than formerly." The general results, however, it is to be noticed, had only been partially ascertained. Had more strict and extended inquiry been made, it would have been found that the instances of the evasion of the Engagement, even at first, were more numerous than those of compliance with its requisitions. With no adequate arrangements for the supervision of the Járejás, it was scarcely to be expected, in the view of their former habits, that they would all at once prove true to the dictates of humanity which they had so long set at defiance. It was dangerous, indeed, to allow a treaty, deliberately formed between national governments, to depend principally on the influence of "public opinion," for its execution, especially when that "public opinion" had never formerly been instrumental in preventing in a single instance the crime which it was designed to suppress.

A "moderate fine," it will have been noticed, was the specific punishment, recommended by the Bombay Government to be applied in the case of offenders; and with this punishment Colonel Walker requested the Gáikawáḍ Government to visit the parties who, it had been ascertained, had actually violated their engagements. It was a punishment which required a firm hand for its infliction; but of the use of such an instrument for its application we have but little evidence. On the expulsion from caste, the most formidable penalty adverted to in the Engagement, nothing was said. Such a punishment as that, in fact, in connexion with which the British Government could not properly interfere, ought never to have been one of the stipulations.

In 1809, Káṭhiáwáḍ was revisited by Colonel Walker. On his return to Baroda, he addressed the following letter to the Bombay Government. It is dated the 29th December 1809, and takes a more sanguine view of the progress of the cause which he had so deeply at heart than was warranted by the facts of the case; though the incidents to which it adverts were of the most gratifying nature.

"During the recent expedition into Káṭhiáwáḍ I was not unmindful of inquiring into the success of the humane arrangements introduced under the influence of the Honorable Company's Government, for the abolishment of female Infanticide among the Jáḍejá Rajputs; and I am happy to report that this reform has completely taken root.

"I have the honor to enclose a list of those Jáḍejás [32 in number] who have preserved their female children, which fell under my own direct observance. On my halt at Dharol, I had all those in the immediate neighbourhood who were capable of attending brought to my tent; and many were too young to be brought from any distance. It was extremely gratifying, on this occasion, to observe the triumph of nature, feeling, and parental affection, over prejudice and horrid superstition; and those who, but a short period before, would, as many of them had done, have doomed their infants to destruction without compunction, should now glory in their preservation, and doat on them with fondness.

"The whole of the instances submitted in the accompanying list have occurred since the execution of the engagements renouncing the practice of Infanticide. Among these the Honourable the Governor in Council will observe the name of the Rájá of Murví, Kuér Dádájí of Rájḳot, and Kuér Wakájí of Dharol, and of several other men of rank and influence, whose example must have a most beneficial effect.

"The list of lives which have been saved to the community by the humane interference of the Company's Government might be very considerably increased by extending the inquiry into the Jáḍejá villages; but this will be sufficient to show that the preservation of female children has now become general. There is no reason to doubt of the final abolishment of this inhuman practice. When once the natural emotions of parental affection have resumed their sway, it may reasonably be expected that this cruel and barbarous prejudice will be condemned by those who formerly most strongly supported it.

"I respectfully beg leave to submit to the consideration of the Honourable the Governor in Council, a memorandum of a disbursement made in presents to those Jáḍejás who had preserved their daughters, and who visited me at Dharol. The fund whence this disbursement is to be defrayed is from the *nazaráná*, exacted from the chieftain of Gondal, and which the Honourable the Governor in Council is already apprized, included an amercement for the destruction of the female infant of that chieftain's son. This arrangement is in conformity to the instructions of the Honourable the Governor in Council, and I respectfully trust it will be honoured with their approval and sanction."

This, we believe, was the last communication addressed to Government by Colonel Walker, on the subject of Infanticide during his residence in India. How with his ideas of the number of Jáḍejás in Káṭhiáwáḍ, and with the means of information which he possessed as the adviser of the Gáikawáḍ's Government and the head of an expedition to that province, he could be satisfied with the meagre list of parties who had saved their female children which he forwarded to the Bombay Government, it is difficult to see, unless we suppose that he was really trusting more to public opinion, to time, and to example for the suppression of Infanticide than to the Engagement which he had laboured with so much zeal and ability to procure.

The benevolent feelings of Colonel Walker must have been highly gratified by the presentation to him in Káṭhiáwáḍ of some of the individuals who had actually been spared from destruction in consequence of his own endeavours. How affecting it must have been for him to hear, as he actually did at Dharol, the tender Rajput daughter rescued from the murderous hand of the parental destroyer, exclaim with infantile voice, COLONEL WALKER SAVED ME! This must have been more precious to his generous heart than the approbation of his country, which he afterwards cordially received, especially after the publication of the narratives of Moor and Cormack. Encouraged by what he witnessed, he divided the sum of Rs. 1,400 as presents among seven of the daughters of the Jáḍejás who were presented to him. Though liberality of this kind is in fact a rebuke of the parents into whose hands it would come, it was wisely administered. The uncivilized and uninstructed mind, like that of a child, must be wooed to good by reward, as well as deterred from evil by punishment.

Captain James Rivett Carnac, formerly the assistant, was the successor of Colonel Walker, as Resident at Baroda. His first communication to the Bombay Government on the subject of Infanticide was dated the 24th November 1811. He was then in Káṭhiáwáḍ, heading an expedition against the Jám Jasají of Nawánagar, against whom he had four days previously urged the following complaints from his camp.

"Previous to my departure from Baroda, I communicated with you on some particular points, to which I received no satisfactory answer; and though your conduct on this occasion has not been becoming your situation, I shall at present dispense with your oversight, and apprize you of the reasons which have made me come to this quarter.

"The first is to require from you the discharge of the just demands of the Government of Ráo Ráydhan [of Kachh]; and on this head I suppose you will conform to what justice may dictate.

"The second object of my journey is to require from you the persons who committed the barbarous act of wantonly wounding an English gentleman, convinced that if reason guides your conduct, and you regard your character, no difficulty will be experienced on this score.

"Lastly, the infringement of your engagement respecting Infanticide will be fully investigated. It was the hope of the British Government that your rank and situation in this country would have impelled you to be foremost in showing a good example, as well in the strict performance of your public obligations, as in renouncing a practice hostile to humanity, and contrary to the tenets of the sacred shástra.

"On this point I shall expect particular satisfaction

from you ; and the instances of misconduct to the Gáikawáḍ Government will be made known to you by the orders of the Máhárájá, Futteh Singh.

"In order to discuss these several points I beg you will send with despatch Mukhtiár Wakíls (authorized agents) to this camp."

Before this communication reached Bombay, Mr. Duncan had ceased to be the head of its Government, having died on the 11th August 1811. His successor, pro tempore, was Mr. George Brown. He did not approve of this early reference in the negociations with the Jám to the affair of Infanticide. Of that reference, however, Captain Carnac gave most satisfactory explanations. "The abolition of this inhuman practice in this country could not be accomplished until Lieutenant Colonel Walker, became enabled to obtain the assent of Jám Jasájí, whose example was declared indispensable by the other Jáḍejá chiefs, for their concurrence. On these grounds it appeared to me of some importance that the earliest notice should be taken of the acts of the Nagar chief in violation of his engagement. It was consistent with the prompt measures adopted by Lieutenant Colonel Walker, with the Gondal chief in 1809; but the recognition of this deviation in the instance of the Jám was not required, exclusively, as it affected the act itself, but principally to deter others from imitating it, either from the belief that we had deserted an object so strongly supported by every consideration of common humanity, or that we were unwilling to insist on the fulfilment of the stipulations with the most powerful chief in the country. It also occurred to me that the introduction of any subjects for discussion at a more advanced period of my negotiation might create distrust in the mind of Jám Jasájí, (notoriously suspicious in his disposition) as to the limits of our demands. In submitting, however, this explanation, I am aware that the subsequent exposition of the hostility of Jám Jasájí to each of the demands contained in my address to him of the 21st November renders it superfluous, except in justification of my measures." These explanations appear to have been viewed as satisfactory. "The Governor in Council," it was afterwards officially stated in a letter to Captain Carnac, "is extremely solicitous to persevere in the efforts already made for the attainment of the humane and beneficial object of extirpating the horrid practice of Female Infanticide from Káṭhiáwáḍ. The disavowal of Jám Jasájí of his engagements for that, and for the other purposes for which he had afforded security, is an indisputable indication of the unprincipled character of that chieftain, as described in the following emphatic terms by Colonel Walker. 'The character of this chief exhibits an extraordinary contrast of great arrogance and extreme submission, of insolence and timidity; and the treachery and cruelty of Jám, are only restrained by the cowardice of his disposition.'"

The issue of Captain Carnac's prompt interference with the Jám on this occasion was, that he demanded and obtained from him a fine of 5,000 rupees, paid in two instalments, for his breach of his Infanticide Engagement, and induced him to sign a new engagement dated the 25th February 1812, the tenor of which was as follows:—

"It has been a practice among the Jáḍejás of my caste not to permit any female infants to live. The two Sirkárs [the English and Baroda] have pointed out to me the true Hindu religion, and that the Brahmá Waiwartta Purána declared it to be a horrid crime, and that killing an infant is the same as killing a Bráhman and also that the murder of a woman is equal to that of 100 Bráhmans.

"In this case both the murder of an infant and woman occur, for which crime the perpetrator will receive as many punishments as there are hairs on the woman's body, and will be born a decrepit leper in the next transmigration. The Sirkár in the year 1864, (A. D. 1807) having explained this to me, I agreed not to commit this crime, or to allow it in my *bháiyád*, and passed a writing to that effect.

"I did not give proper information to the Sirkár's mehtá, (clerk) who came to inquire into the business, on which account I again engage to Government that neither myself, descendants, nor bháiyád, will commit this act; and if we should, we are guilty before the Sirkár. If I know of any of my caste having committed this act, I will turn him out of the caste, and answer to Government as they may choose.

"I also give Bhárot Méru, mehtá of Viramgáum, and Bhárot Rámdás Nathu of Jalsan, as securities for the above.—Já'm Jasá'jí'."

Nothing further was heard from Captain Carnac on the subject, till a letter dated the 18th July 1816 was received by the Bombay Government. It contained the following statements.

"I should have been happy to announce that female Infanticide was entirely eradicated from the Peninsula of Káṭhiáwáḍ. Although there has lately been no evidence afforded to me, either by my assistant, or the Gáikáwáḍ local authority, of any Jáḍejá having destroyed his offspring since the accession to the engagements by the means of Colonel Walker, I have been disappointed in the result of the statement of those children who have been reported as preserved. The accompanying letter from Captain Ballantine [one of Captain Carnac's assistants] seems to vouch only for *fifteen*, the disparity of which number is very great according to the ordinary progress of population. I am persuaded, however, that there could have been no want of exertion in the public officers in Káṭhiáwáḍ for ascertaining those persons who may have departed from their engagements. The difficulty of discovery, by the interspersed state of the Jáḍejás over a considerable tract of country, and the pervading principle among these people not to destroy the practice which their own prejudices approved, will account for the continuance of female Infanticide in defiance of any public obligations for its suppression.

"It is important that our humane endeavours have preserved some victims, and that the act [of preserving daughters] is not now considered disgraceful to the families which have given this laudable example. The general adoption of the practice among the Jáḍejás extenuated the crime, and apologized for this violent perversion of the instinctive feelings of human nature; but as children are now preserved, it is natural to believe that the Jáḍejás must gradually return to the influence of those natural feelings which are the best security for the success of our interference.

"Among those who have given the example, the Right Honourable the Governor in Council is aware that the Rájá of Murví is included. He has now two daughters, who will shortly be offered in marriage; and I submit, with great deference, that nothing would better conduce to the suppression of Infanticide in this part of India, or be considered a more honourable proof of the regard of the British Government to the Rájá, than the nuptials of his daughters being conducted at the public expense.

"With a view of relieving us from the charge, I would propose that Captain Ballantine should be sedulous in his inquiries after those Jáḍejás who may have sacrificed their female children subsequent to their engagements, and that he exact a pecuniary fine, conformably to the penalty prescribed when those engagements were contracted. I would also propose that the means to be given to the Rájá of Murví should not be delayed until we have realized the fines from the delinquent Jáḍejás, but that he is apprized immediately of the intention of the Company's Government to perform at its own expense the nuptials of his daughters, in a manner consistent with the honour of the family."

It is apparent from these representations, that the cause of the abolition of Infanticide in Káṭhiáwáḍ had actually made no progress since the departure from

India of Colonel Walker; and that even the progress made towards its suppression in the time of Walker, had been much over-estimated. Only fifteen Jáḍejá females, after an interval of eight years from the ratification of the Engagement, are as yet known to have been saved! The anarchy and confusion which had existed in Káṭhiáwáḍ from the feeble efforts of the Gáikawáḍ and Peshwa governments to follow up the general settlements made by Colonel Walker for the pacification of its tributaries there, afforded some explanation, but no justification, of this lamentable fact.

The Bombay Government of the time did not see fit to comply with the specific recommendations of Captain Carnac, which had been suggested to him by Captain Ballantine his deputy in Káṭhiáwáḍ. It passed the following Resolution:

"The Governor in Council does not approve of Capt. Carnac's entertaining an establishment for the purpose of suppressing female Infanticide, which, even admitting its formation to be essential to effecting that desirable object, we are not at liberty to sanction without the authority of the Honourable Court; nor does it appear advisable to adopt the other proposition, of defraying the expenses of the marriage of the children of a Jáḍejá.

"Captain Carnac must, therefore, be informed that neither of his propositions are admissible, especially the last, because, if the Honourable Court should undertake to defray the expense of the nuptials of the female children of one of the Jáḍejás, the rest of the fraternity would expect the same consideration, to which they would be equally entitled with the Rájá of Murví; the introduction of such a practice, independently of the great expense attending it, would also be liable to be abused.

"The Governor in Council is desirous, however, to be informed what would be the probable amount of the expense attending the marriage of a female of this class, in case the Honourable Court should view the subject in a different light, and should authorize the incurring it on the present, or on any future occasion.

"With respect to the retaining the establishment suggested by Lieutenant Ballantine, Captain Carnac is to be instructed to acquaint him that his proposition cannot be sanctioned, and to be called upon to report when the mehtás were employed by the native governments, as alluded to by Lieutenant Ballantine, as also the causes which led to the discontinuance of that establishment. Captain Carnac is at the same time to be required to exert his utmost vigilance in ascertaining how far the engagements entered into by the Jáḍejás with Lieutenant Colonel Walker, have been fulfilled; and on discovering any breach of such engagements he should rigorously enforce the penalties. Had the annual reports required by the instructions of Government of the 31st of March 1808 been regularly attended to, the chieftains would have observed a continued anxiety on the part of the British Government to enforce the engagements they had contracted; and the formation of those reports would also have led to a spirit of inquiry, and ensured in a certain degree the fulfilment of those engagements, inasmuch as it would have proved to the chieftains of Káṭhiáwáḍ the anxiety felt by the British Government on the subject. The Governor in Council relies on Captain Carnac's attention to the regular transmission of those returns in future; and if, as directed in the last paragraph of the instructions adverted to, no measures have been 'concerted with the Gaikáwáḍ government in respect to the best means for obtaining periodical notices of the operations, making it also a rule to submit (exclusive of such intermediate reports as may become necessary,) one general statement on the last day of each year, how far the amended system has been acted on, and observed; what deviations are known, or suspected to have been made from its rules; and what measures pursued for their enforcement; the whole to be accompanied with an estimate of the number of lives that may under the blessing of Divine Providence be thus ultimately saved to the community'. Captain Carnac will immediately enter upon a consideration of this extremely interesting subject with the Gáikawáḍ government, and report the result to the Governor in Council.

"If penalties to any extent should be recovered, it will then be matter for consideration how far the sum thus raised should be rendered applicable to the affording assistance to any of the Jáḍejás who may stand in need of such assistance, in the manner contemplated by Colonel Walker, in his Report of the 15th of March 1808, nor is the Governor in Council aware that any application of it would be more creditable to the national character.

"The Governor in Council entertains, therefore, every hope that by judicious management Captain MacMurdo may prevail on the chieftains of Kachh to abandon this abominable practice. No time could he more advantageous for his preferring his application, considering the pecuniary concessions which the British Government have made to the State of Kachh; and he is authorized to inform the Ráo that he could not make a more acceptable return than by following the praise-worthy example of the chieftains in Káṭhiáwaḍ, in engaging to promote the highly interesting object of abolishing the inhuman custom of female Infanticide."

This resolution was substantially communicated to Captain Carnac for his information and guidance. It is to be regretted that the Bombay Government, while it refused its assent to the specific measures which he had proposed towards the suppression of Infanticide, failed to suggest others for the accomplishment of that object. The injunction for him to make strict inquiry into the extent of the observance of their engagement by the Jáḍejás, the renewal of the demand for an annual report, and the request that he should further deliberate with the Gáikáwáḍ's government about the whole affair evinced the continued anxiety of government that the good cause which it had now had so long at heart should not be overlooked.

Captain Carnac, on receiving the reply from Government, felt constrained to offer to it an explanation and vindication of his own past procedure connected with the matters to which it adverted, and to make some fresh suggestions for the advance of the cause, which, to appearance, had for several years been well-nigh overlooked. His letter on these subjects addressed to Mr. Warden, the chief secretary, was dated the 16th September 1816. It is characterized both by spirit and ability. The following are its most important portions.

"The humanity of the British Government in endeavouring to suppress this horrible practice has been acknowledged by the whole country; and it has formed a constant part of my duty to enjoin the Gáikáwáḍ commander, and my assistant in Káṭhiáwáḍ, to be careful in observing those Jáḍejás who had bound themselves to renounce it. The accounts which I have been able to obtain are neither commensurate with my own expectations, nor with those of Government and the Honourable Court.

"In 1812, during my employment in the negotiations at Nawánagar, Vithal Ráo Diwánjí [the Gaikawáḍ's minister] in the hopes of satisfying my inquiries, established several mehtás in the principal Jáḍejá towns, with instructions to communicate the birth, preservation, or murder of female children, as soon as they received information of such occurrences. But the jealousy with which these men were regarded rendered their exertions nearly abortive; and while no Jáḍejá would himself communicate the condition of his wife, they found it in vain to ask for information from his neighbours. The duties of these mehtás were of that questionable nature that gives general dislike, and were likely to produce a feeling of opposition that would defeat all their inquiries. It was to the establishment of these men that Captain Ballantine alluded in his letter to me of the 8th of July last. They were withdrawn when the Peshwa resumed his rights in Gujarát, for the reasons stated in Captain Ballantine's letter. That gentleman probably supposes, that though such officers could gain little information, their presence operated as a check, and made the fear of discovery tend to the abolition of female Infanticide; and it seems reasonable to think that it should have this effect. No better plan having yet been devised, Captain Ballantine has only done his duty in recommending to the adoption of Government that which seemed to him the best fitted for the object in view.

"Considering the little apparent advantage that has been gained by the Diwánjí's mehtás being stationed where they were, I felt diffident in recommending to Government the adoption of a measure which showed so little prospect of success, or in submitting any new plan which must in a great measure be speculative, and probably when tried little successful. I am sorry also that it has hitherto been entirely out of my power to concert any practical plan with the administration at Baroda, by which I could promise myself the satisfaction of making an annual report on the success of Colonel Walker's measures. But at the same time, I hope the Right Honourable the Governor in Council will not consider my exertions in the cause of humanity to have been remiss, merely because the means hitherto used have been inadequate for arriving at a knowledge of the domestic transactions of upwards of 5,000 families, particularly interested in concealing their actions. I also beg leave to assure Government that the expense attendant on any feasible plan would not have deterred me from proposing it both to the British and Gáikawáḍ Government; sensible that the liberality of the former is equal to its humanity, and that I should have met no reluctance on the part of the latter to come forward in so charitable an affair.

"Influenced by these sentiments, and convinced that there exists at present no means of rendering Government any satisfactory report on the practice of Infanticide in Káṭhiáwáḍ, I submit with deference the following observations on a new method of obtaining information of the destruction of female infants, and shall be happy to gratify my own feelings by carrying that or any better plan which the wisdom of Government may devise, into effect.

"We may consider that every attempt to arrive by direct means at a knowledge of the practice of Infanticide has been, and will be, unsuccessful. Few men in any country will, without reward, accuse another of an act considered by the ruling power as a crime, but which is looked on by themselves and their companions without horror, or with approbation. If they did inform, it would be probably found that they were actuated by a spirit of revenge, and not of justice. This observation is very applicable to the natives of India generally, and particularly so to those among them who practise those cruel religious observances which demand the appearance of solemnity and mystery, and which impose on the ignorant an impressive notion of the sanctity of their institutions. Any native not inspired by a deep-rooted enmity would therefore most probably hesitate before he would accuse his neighbour of an action deemed criminal by the Government, but wearing an appearance of divine approbation, and said to be practised by the caste from remote antiquity. Though he can have no doubt, if he belonged to another caste, of the humanity of the Government which considered Infanticide a crime, yet, as Colonel Walker justly remarks, 'the Hindus, with a facility proportioned to their credulity, generally ascribe their peculiar institutions to a divine origin; and by connecting their observance with religious duties they have passed inviolate through many ages.' It would be difficult to make a Hindu conscious that in aiding the exertions of Government he was also not opposing the will of the gods. Even if there were no prejudices of this description, the trouble which it would be necessary to impose on an informer, in order to make him prove his assertions, would deter any but an enemy from stating what he knew.

"The Jáḍejás, though proud, are like, the other natives of India, very avaricious. The object which could not be gained by speaking to their feelings might be effected by working on their disposition. The reward of a hundred rupees to him who could satisfactorily establish in another the perpetration of Infanticide might bring to light numerous circumstances of which we now remain in ignorance. Nor would the expense of such remunerations fall on either the Native or British Government. By the bond to which the Jáḍejás have subscribed, they have rendered themselves liable to punishment at the will of the Sirkár, and it could not be considered a severe punishment to insist on the payment of a fine which would more than defray the charges attendant on receiving the information of their guilt. It may not be deemed irrelevant to furnish Government with what I conceive an adequate scale of rewards and punishments. An informer against the Jám should receive 1,000 rupees; against the inferior Rájás, 500; against their near relations, 250; and against a poor Jáḍejá, 100. The Jám, if proved guilty, should be fined 30,000 rupees; an inferior Rájá, 10,000; their near relations, 2,500; and a poor Jáḍejá, as much as he could pay without ruin.

"The difficulty of inducing any one to come forward against so powerful a man as the Jám renders it necessary that his reward should be liberal, which for the sake of example it is desirable that a person in his high station should be detected and severely punished. Whatever are the practices of the chiefs will also be those of the *bháïyád*. The pride of the lower Jáḍejás is to support the customs of their clan, and to follow the steps of their great relations in every act. We can never, therefore, expect the practice of Infanticide to be fairly laid aside till the principal Jáḍejás are either induced or forced to set the example; I have therefore stated the reward of the informer against the Jám, and the punishment of that chieftain at a high rate.

"The very alarm which the promulgation of the plan of rewarding informers would excite might greatly tend to occasion the preservation of many female infants. Aware that no feelings of kindness, of religion, or of general interest for the caste, could induce a poor Jáḍejá to resist the temptation of reward; every man would be afraid of his neighbour and his domestics; while there must be many, not of the Jáḍejá tride, who are informed of the state of their families, and who can therefore gratify their avarice with less dread of censure.

"The advantages of their plan, however, are opposed by disadvantages; and these would grow into an evil of some magnitude to the whole body of the Jáḍejás, unless provided against at the first outset. The hopes of reward might induce many to bring forward false accusations, and also such as might have an appearance of validity, without being grounded on fact. The informer should, therefore, be bound to give proof for the specific information which he brings, under pain of being severely punished if his information should turn out to be false. The only account which it seems probable an informer could bring, appears to be, that he knew of the pregnancy of a certain Rajputní, and that the event was never published to the community. Should the issue have been a female child, and it had died, it would require some discrimination on the part of the person investigating information to determine whether the child might not have been still-born, or died shortly after its birth. In either of the last-mentioned cases that informer should receive no more than a third of the reward. But if it should so appear that the Jáḍejás wife against whom the accusation is preferred, had not been pregnant, or had suffered an early abortion of her offspring, the accuser should be punished rigorously, or otherwise, according to the circumstances of the case.

"The evils of goindás (informers) in respect to the Jáḍejás cannot, I presume, be felt in any degree to the same extent as they are in Bengal. The information which they are required to yield admits of circumstantial proof, and is not like that concerning robberies and murders frequently dependent on presumptive proof; and it is consequently not likely to be given but when there exists, or have existed, some undeniable, and in some measure, public, grounds for its being true.

"I propose this plan with much deference to the wisdom of the Right Honourable the Governor in Council, sensible that it may appear better in theory than it may prove to be good in practice; but I am at the same time hopeful that it may be better than no plan at all, in rendering the exertions of my predecessor a permanent benefit to the country. I beg to assure the Right Honourable the Governor in Council that I require no stimulus to exert myself in this cause of humanity, since nothing would give me greater gratification than to have the self-satisfaction of reflecting that I had been instrumental in accomplishing so philanthropic an undertaking. But Government must be aware that my success is entirely dependent on subordinate agents, nearly as far removed from me, as I myself am, from the seat of Government; and that whatever interest I may take in the subject, my individual exertions can be of no further use than in stimulating them to a zealous attention. I have every reason to believe that neither Captain Ballantine nor the Diwánjí have been less active than the most humane man could wish, but the means in their power were not fitted to enable them to command success.

"The expense of marrying the daughters of the chiefs of Káṭhiáwáḍ would probably be as follows; the marriage of the Jám would amount to 30 or 35,000 rupees; that of the daughter of a minor Rájá, such as the Rájá of Murví, Gondal, and Rájkoṭ, to 15 or 16,000; that of the daughter of one of the near relations of the rájá would require from 5 to 7,000 rupees; and that of a poor Jáḍejás daughter from 1,000 to 1,500 rupees.

"It would evidently be enormously expensive for any Government to defray the charges of marrying even only one daughter to each family, and it might be impolitic to marry that of one person, and not of another. The Murví Rájá, however, might be made an exception, since it was he who first saved his daughter; and since it was by his means that Colonel Walker laid the first foundation of the superstructure he afterwards raised. I conceive the Gáikawáḍ Government would willingly share with the British Government the expense and the honour of presenting a dowry to the first female child saved from the barbarity of an unfeeling parent."

On the receipt of this communication, the Bombay Government "ordered, that the Resident at Baroda be informed, that the Right Honourable the Governor in Council objects to adopting a system of the nature he has suggested for ascertaining how far the chieftains of Káṭhiáwáḍ adhere to their engagements to abstain from female Infanticide, under a persuasion that it would be extremely offensive to the feelings of the Jáḍejás and must, until further orders, trust to the vigilance which he and his assistant can bestow on that object, on which however, an annual report, framed from the best data that can be procured will be expected. Neither can the Governor in Council approve of the plan of portioning the daughters of the Jáḍejás, the expense of which would be to an extent beyond the amount of the fines which can be expected to be recovered."

In a later communication it was added, "Although we do not feel ourselves at liberty to go to the extent of defraying the expenses of the nuptials of the two daughters preserved by the Rájá of Murví, as it might be drawn into an inconvenient precedent, we readily adopt your suggestion of testifying our sense of the Rájá's meritorious example by authorizing you to present him, in the name of the Court of Directors, with some suitable ornament for his dress, leaving the selection of it to your judgment." In acknowledging this order Captain Carnac said, "I beg leave to remark, in reply to the observation that the plan I proposed would be extremely offensive to the feelings of the Jáḍejás, that it seems very problematical if any plan that can be devised will not be the same; for since the abolition of Infanticide was a measure pressed on the Jáḍejás contrary to all their feelings and prejudices, I do not see that if they are unwilling to abide by their engagements we can prevent their continuance of the practice, except by a measure contrary to their wishes and feelings." The views of the Bombay Government were approved by the Court of Directors, who trusted that by exacting the legal penalties in all cases in which the Jáḍejás might be detected in violating their engagements, and publicly marking with special approbation every striking instance of honourable adherence to those engagements, the practice of female Infanticide might eventually be brought into general disuse and abhorrence.*

On the 20th June, 1817, Captain Ballantine handed up to Captain Carnac what he esteemed "a complete register of all the Jáḍejás known in Káṭhiáwáḍ." Making every allowance for errors, this was an important document. It was accompanied by a list of *sixty-three* Jáḍejá females, the total number known to have been saved during the first ten years of Colonel Walker's engagement, and by the remark, "I too much fear the object of our interference for the suppression of this singular custom has too generally failed for us to select any individual party for the just vengeance of Government and offended nature." It also hinted that other inducements than prohibitory engagements,—such as those which had been formerly suggested by himself and Captain Carnac,—were needful in the exigencies of

* Parliamentary Papers on Infanticide, 1789-1820, p. 107.

the afflictive case. Captain Ballantine's views, supported by Captain Carnac, were duly communicated to the Bombay Government and the Court of Directors. The ultimate notice taken of them we give in the language of the latter body, in a dispatch dated the 1st March, 1820.

"We have learned with great pain that your humane endeavours to accomplish the suppression of the barbarous and unnatural practice of female Infanticide in the Peninsula of Káṭhiáwáḍ have hitherto proved to a great degree unsuccessful, notwithstanding the engagements which were contracted by the Jáḍejá chiefs of that province in 1807 with Colonel Walker, to abstain from the commission of that offence.

"The register appended to the report of the assistant to the Resident at Baroda, under date the 20th June 1817, shows that the lives of only sixty-three female infants have been saved in consequence of your interposition in the course of ten years, a number extremely disproportionate to the number which must have been born within that period. Indeed the facts stated by Captain Ballantine,* that in the Táluká of Drápha, which contains 400 Jáḍejá families, there is not a single female child in existence, and that in no family has more than one female child been preserved, demonstrate the inveterate prevalence of this horrid custom.

"However mortifying may have been the result of your past endeavours, we are persuaded that you will not allow it to operate as a discouragement to further and persevering efforts in the same cause. We think you may do much by addressing yourselves to the interests of the Jáḍejás, and the renewal of the decennial engagements with the Káṭhiáwáḍ chieftains will have furnished you with an opportunity of calling upon them to enter into fresh engagements, under proper securities, to abandon the practice in question. We are not without hopes also that the additional influence which we

* Dispatch dated 1st April, 1818.

acquired in that part of Gujarát by the cession of the Peshwa's tribute,* may, if judicioulу exercised, be the means of enabling you to enforce a stricter adherence to their engagements on the part of the Jáḍejás.

"We entirely approve of the measure of distributing among those who observe their promises the fines which may be levied upon those who violate them."

The Hon. M. Elphinstone was at this time governor of Bombay; and nothing can more distinctly mark the great difficulties experienced in dealing with Infanticide in Káṭhiáwáḍ, than the fact that this talented and benevolent man, after visiting the province, felt himself unable to make any new suggestion calculated to hasten its suppression. "No effectual check can be imposed on this atrocious practice," he wrote, "as long as it is so completely congenial to the general feeling of the people, unless by employing hired agents, as proposed by Major Ballantine, whose duty it should be to detect offenders of this description; and such a measure would lead to so much intrusion into the most private and domestic proceedings of the superior castes (among whom alone Infanticide prevails), and would be open to so many abuses on the part of the informers, that I do not think the chance of success would compensate for the disaffection which it would create. It may also be doubted how far we have a right to interfere to such an extraordinary pitch with the private life of a people with whose civil government and internal police we do not pretend to have any concern. We must therefore be content to follow the footsteps of our predecessors (without attempting to go beyond them) in their most meritorious endeavours to discountenance this enormity; and we may safely flatter ourselves, that as the manners of the people become softened by a continuance of tranquillity and good order, they will gradually discontinue

* [On the conquest of the Peshwa in 1818, and the succession of the British to his sovereignty.]

a practice which is not more inconsistent with reason, than repugnant to natural instinct." The weight of Mr. Elphinstone's remarks must be felt by every considerate mind. Yet a vast deal more interference with the tributaries of Káṭhiáwáḍ than was contemplated at this time afterwards become absolutely necessary for the promotion of their own interests, as well as for the advancement of good government by the paramount power. *Salus populi est suprema lex.* It is in consequence of timely and appropriate interference, indeed, that to this day these tributaries have been preserved in the possession of their lands without the slightest encroachment. While Britain is supreme in India, it should be held responsible for the wellbeing of every native State within its borders.

CHAPTER V.

REMONSTRANCES OF COLONEL WALKER WITH THE COURT OF DIRECTORS OF THE EAST INDIA COMPANY ON THE EVASIONS OF THE JA'ḌEJA'S TO IMPLEMENT THEIR ENGAGEMENTS TO ABANDON INFANTICIDE, AND HIS FINAL COUNSELS ON THE SUBJECT TO BRITISH OFFICIALS.

Though the British functionaries in India were, at the time at which our narrative has now arrived, well-nigh baffled with Infanticide in Káṭhiáwáḍ, there was in Britain one individual who could offer the most valuable advice on the subject. That was Colonel Walker, who had done so much for its suppression during his own distinguished career in Gujarát. This benevolent officer, when residing in 1819, on his property of Bowland on the Gala-Water, asked and received from the East India Company copies of all the late Dispatches from Bombay on the subject, and prepared and submitted to the Court of Directors two communications respecting them, the ability, zeal, and earnestness of which can scarcely be sufficiently admired.

The first of them headed "Memorandum of Colonel Walker," was dated the 19th July of the year now mentioned, and was as follows :—

"In offering my opinion upon the means of suppressing female Infanticide in the West of India, I must first observe that this object should be accomplished without violating the feelings of the natives, and without having recourse to actual coercion. I must also beg to refer to my own proceedings which succeeded in obtaining the consent of the people to relinquish this barbarous and unnatural practice. It was accomplished, no doubt, with great difficulty, but it was so far a spontaneous act that it was solely effected by persuasion and reason. It is under this influence alone that the measure can ultimately be expected to prove successful; but from the peculiar habits of the people of this part of India the practice of destroying their children cannot be overcome by the mere dictates of natural affection. When this tie was once abandoned, it would be long before it could be again recovered; and it would be necessary that they should be continually watched, and urged to the performance of a duty which is seldom neglected even by the brutes. This is an unfavourable picture of human nature, but it is the unavoidable consequence of a long familiarity with depraved sentiments, and a perseverance in vicious habits. It was foreseen that the mere engagement which these people had contracted for discontinuing Infanticide, however solemn and authentic, would not be sufficient unless they were looked after with vigilance; unless they were frequently encouraged; and unless those instances in which they infringed their own voluntary engagement were detected and punished. The mode of punishment was provided by their agreement. I am persuaded that a system of this kind would have succeeded, and have preserved, in a great degree, the engagement inviolate for the abolition of Infanticide. Occasional infractions might have happened, and were to be expected; but the general principle would have been maintained, and in time the custom would have been forgotten, and have disappeared. It must have been, indeed, by the same process that it was established; for it was impossible that a practice so contrary to every feeling of nature could have been established at once, and without the utmost repugnance. Many persons must have persisted in saving their children, and thus disobeyed a horrid and inhuman institution, until they became reconciled to it by custom and usage.

"It was under the influence of a similar train of reasoning and reflection that I suggested to the Government, when I quitted India, to exact an annual report of the progress of Infanticide, and that it should be the object of continual care and solicitude. Before I retired from the service I had the satisfaction to see that the principles for its abolition had made no slight impression on the minds of the people, and in a short period they had saved a considerable number of infants. But from the report which has now been received from India, it would appear that the whole number saved in the course of ten years is little more than sixty, and perhaps not a third more than were presented by their parents to me in Káṭhiáwáḍ with feelings of affection and delight. From those feelings which were publicly displayed, and which had all the appearance of the most tender maternal effusion, I must own that I thought myself warranted in entertaining the most sanguine hopes that this blot on human nature would be utterly eradicated.

"In the present state of the subject, and with reference to the peculiar state of the society in which this crime prevails, I would take the liberty of suggesting some remedial measures, which may still avert the fate of those unhappy children.

"The first circumstance which requires attention is to see the people often, and by frequent intercourse to inspire them with sentiments more favourable to humanity. It is scarcely to be expected that the Jáḍejás will seek our society without greater encouragement than it is the habit of our countrymen, generally speaking, to afford to the natives of India; and we must therefore visit them in their villages. They must be sought out in their recesses, invited to attend the public kachérís, and the subject brought as often as possible under public discussion. This should not be done in a controversial manner, but with the complacency and benevolence of instruction, which seeks rather to convince than to confute an unreasonable opponent. In these situations opportunities would frequently arise of enforcing the heinous nature of the offence, of calmly discussing its tendency, of exposing its crime, and of contrasting the abominable practice with the universally contrary usage of the rest of mankind. By the effect of example, by the force of conversation, and by diffusing good and just notions of human nature, these men would be gradually alienated from their absurd and guilty conduct. It is not founded on religion; it is disavowed by the great body of the people, and prevails only among a single tribe.

"They would not withstand any systematic exertion which might be directed to its overthrow; and, in fact, did it not yield to an attempt which was made in a doubtful situation, amidst a multitude of other occupations, and which was not pursued for a long time? The same facilities, and greater, now exist to ensure success. The Gáikawaḍ authority may be disposed more readily to co-operate with us, while our own is better established, and while we possess an actual share in the Government of the country. The collector of the newly acquired revenue in Káṭhiáwáḍ would be a natural and an essential agent in this humane work. By means of the police, which is under his control, and by the frequent intercourse which his office obliges him to hold with the natives, he would have opportunities of communication superior perhaps to any other person. Let the collector,* the agent in Káṭhiáwáḍ, the agent in Kachh, and the Gáikáwáḍ authorities, heartily, and in concert, exert themselves, and they would be irresistible. It is with no improper or invidious motive that I have observed on the great superiority of these means over the new and imperfect influence which we had when the attempt

* [The office of Collector in Kaṭhiáwáḍ was united with that of Political Agent.]

was first made to suppress this odious crime. But I would not rest the success of this interesting measure alone on vigilance, and the active use of even all the agents in our power. I would employ other stimuli, and not neglect those that may be calculated to produce an effect on the grosser passions of those who persevere in the practice of Infanticide. I would not encourage the idea of an expensive agency, nor the direct and professed employment of spies, which are more likely to defeat than to promote the object; but there are surely means of ascertaining the result of a birth in a family, without either offending its delicacy, or requiring much expense. The fact of a pregnancy is always public, and the report of the neighbours would often be sufficient evidence. A few detections would arrest the practice. If the intercourse was as frequent as I have recommended, many things would be casually learnt, and little indeed could be concealed. In the course of this intercourse, many acts of friendship, of courtesy and attention, could be conferred on the Jáḍejás, which would be attended with little expense, but which they would highly value; they are both greedy and necessitous. The present of an inferior turban, of a dopaṭṭah, of a snuff-box, of a pair of spectacles, or of any other trifling article, would be prized by them as a mark of honour, and as a profitable acquisition. These little favours would be the means of bringing them together, of inducing them to come into our society, and finally of reconciling them to our views. It is by association and a constant attention that they are to be reclaimed.

"I cannot conclude these hasty remarks without observing that the character and reputation of our Government must suffer materially should those people be allowed to resume a practice which they had abandoned with all the formality of a regular and solemn compact. May it not be said that we were more indifferent in the cause of humanity than in exacting a rigid and scrupulous compliance with the terms of a treaty which involved a paltry revenue, or some insignificant district? We may by kindness and by patience bring them back to the path of their duty. The voice of nature, and the influence of the women, will unite in assisting us, and in this struggle against a deplorable practice we shall finally prevail, while our motives must be applauded, and cannot be mistaken. Were the power of Government never applied but in cases so obviously beneficial and disinterested the rudest minds would bless them; and the feelings of men, as well as their reason, would render them both agreeable and irresistible."

Colonel Walker's second communication, which was dated the 27th August, 1819, contained the expression of his more mature thoughts of the position at that time of the question of Infanticide, and the best means of contributing to its suppression. In point of vigour of language, and judiciousness of suggestion, it is even more remarkable than that now quoted.

"Since I had the honour of addressing you under the 19th ultimo," he writes to the Court, "I have been able to peruse with more leisure and attention the proceedings which have been held on Infanticide from the time that I left India. . . .

"After a careful perusal of the documents with which I have been favoured by the indulgence of the Honourable Court, I have found it impossible to suppress the conclusion, that the subject had either been forgotten for years together, or that some imperious and uncontrollable circumstances had rendered our interference utterly impracticable. From whatever resistless cause this has arisen, it is deeply to be lamented, and the consequences are far more formidable than even the immediate effects are in the loss of so many thousand lives; but the consequences are still more serious, as the enforcement of the engagement must now be infinitely more difficult by the long neglect and disuse of its provisions. There is no more effectual way of destroying the most sacred laws and obligations than by usage; while they acquire fresh strength and vigour by a regular appeal to their authority.

"At the time that I left India the subject was familiar to the Jáḍejás; there was an impression of interest on their minds; a return had appeared of parental affection; and above all there was the necessity of obeying a legal enactment possessing their own solemn sanction, and for the enforcement of which the British and Gáikawáḍ Governments were pledged.

"Instead of this picture, the Jáḍejás have now found out that the engagement, which was at first so reluctantly yielded, and strenuously urged, means almost nothing, since it may be eluded with impunity; may be violated without detection and without reproof. If they had imagined that there would be so little danger in its violation as they evidently, at present, believe to be the case, I should without any doubt have found much less difficulty in obtaining their consent to discontinue the custom of destroying their daughters. Could they have foreseen that the whole would afterwards have rested on their own freewill and choice, they would neither have been apprehensive of inconvenience nor of punishment, and would have saved themselves and me much trouble from a useless opposition. This reflection is not new, and I viewed the difficulty with which these people were first led to discontinue this extraordinary custom at the time that I was using every effort to overcome their prejudices, as no unequivocal proof of the stability of the arrangement. This is stated in my Report to the Bombay Government.

"The consequence, in short, at this moment operating in Káṭhiáwáḍ is the impression of weakness and vaccillancy on the part of the British Government, or that they are incapable of giving effect to their own measures.

"It may seem idle to trace out the nature and extent of the evil that remissness or accidents have produced. I should not indeed have made these observations were I not clearly of opinion, that in the application of any remedial measures it is most particularly necessary that we be distinctly aware of the nature and the extent of the mischief, otherwise it will never be counteracted. I am aware also that the truth cannot be stated in all its broadness and honesty to the Company's Government in India, as it might irritate instead of conciliate; yet it should be stated, though with as much delicacy as the nature of such truth will admit.

"I have now a more agreeable duty to perform in adverting to the interest which seems to be everywhere felt and expressed at present for the suppression of this crime. The communications of Captain Carnac and of Captain Ballantine breathe the spirit of feeling and humanity, which is natural to their character. They are men who love their country, their friends and mankind. They will, I am persuaded, pursue the subject with a renewed degree of earnestness and warmth, and by a judicious direction of their exertions finally accomplish the abolition of Infanticide. They will embrace every means and opportunity of maintaining unimpaired the honour of their country, by supporting its reputation for humanity and philanthropy. They are the best judges of local circumstances, and have the best means of taking advantage of them.

"I expect this from those gentlemen, and that they will unite a kind of enthusiasm in the cause.

"I cannot avoid taking this opportunity of expressing my own obligations and warmest thanks to Captain Carnac, for the spirit with which he repelled the insinuation contained in the resolution and minute of the 19th September 1817.* It is with the utmost unwillingness

* [The resolution and minute here referred to are as follows:—"The report of Captain Ballantine, whilst it affords satisfactory proof of sixty-three female children having been preserved by our interposition, exhibits a melancholy picture of the almost universal continuance of the horrid practice of female Infanticide to an extent little expected, after the reports of the success generally, but inaccurately, attributed, to Colonel Walker's influence and exertions."

that I have at all alluded to this subject, but I conceive that I could not pass it over in total silence, and must trust in the Honourable Court of Directors doing me that justice which I have on so many occasions gratefully felt and acknowledged at their hands. I may, however, be allowed to observe, that the attempt to throw reproach and censure on my influence and exertions is in point of fact, at least, inaccurate. The exertions and responsibility of an individual in the public service must necessarily terminate with his office; but I can affirm with truth that I have never been able to divest myself of care and solicitude for those interests which I left behind me in India; and especially for that measure by which I hoped to rescue a great number of helpless infants

Captain Carnac's notice of this minute was as follows:—"The Right Honorable the Governor in Council is aware that Lieutenant Colonel Walker, under the instructions of Government, had effected every measure which was calculated to ensure the suppression of Infanticide in Káṭhiáwáḍ. That officer had not only obtained the consent of the Jáḍejás to abandon a practice consistent with their dearest feelings and prejudices, but by his influence also contracted engagements adapted to that desirable object.

"If these engagements have not been fully enforced from their origin, and subsequent to the departure of Lieut. Colonel Walker to England, and that owing to such relaxation female Infanticide is not entirely extinguished in Káṭhiáwáḍ, I presume, with every deference, that whatever success has attended the endeavour to suppress the abominable practice is justly due to the influence and exertions of my predecessor.

"At the same time the disappointment which has been experienced can be traced exclusively to the want of a system by which a detection of the guilty could be ensured, and not to any indifference on the part of the local officers to the enforcement of the engagements contracted by the Jáḍejás. I have had the honour on several occasions of bringing the subject in the most urgent manner to the attention of Government, and in submitting recommendations on the ways and means for an effectual abolition of Infanticide, have implored Government to devise any plan which in its wisdom might be efficacious.

"While my suggestions have been deemed objectionable, no other plan has intermediately been prescribed, and doubtless the want of it is frequently affording the most melancholy evidence of an evasion of the excellent engagements contracted by the influence of Lieutenant Colonel Walker."]

from a premature death. I have endeavoured to second this wish, by every excitement which a frequent correspondence at so great a distance could effect, to impress on the minds of my European and native friends an attachment to those principles which had always regulated my own conduct, and particularly never to relax their efforts against those who violate the laws of nature and society. This was all that I could do, and was perhaps more than was to have been expected from an unemployed individual. The most arduous part of the enterprise was unquestionably the procuring of the engagements on the part of the Jáḍejá chiefs to abolish the practice of destroying their daughters; the solemn acknowledgment that it was contrary even to their own religion; and that such was their abhorrence and detestation of it that whoever should be proved guilty of the repetition of the crime should be branded with all the infamy, disgrace, and privation of privileges involved in the loss of caste.

"The recognition of these things as general principles, and principles of law, I hold to be the grand achievement in the removal of this scene of guilt, desolation and misery.

"If the practical benefit has not followed, it cannot, by any fair inference, be imputed to me; and this conclusion seems firmly founded in the fact, that in the course of a short period after the engagement was procured, as many lives were spared through its agency as for all the succeeding years.

"But, perhaps, the following quotation from the proceedings of the Bombay Government itself might be produced as a proof that the failure had no dependence on my influence and exertions.

"'Had the annual reports' (they observe, in their consultations of the 16th of August 1816) 'required by the instructions of Government of the 31st of March 1808, been regularly attended to, the chieftains would have observed a continued anxiety on the part of the British

Government to enforce the engagements they contracted, and the formation of those reports would also have led to a spirit of inquiry, and ensured, in a certain degree, the fulfilment of those engagements, inasmuch as it would have proved to the chieftains of Káṭhiáwáḍ the anxiety felt by the British Government on the subject'. In this passage they have themselves correctly traced, however late, one of the principal errors which has been committed, and which was in their own power at any time to have corrected.

"It may be said there was nothing to report; let this be admitted; report that fact, for it was a fact little expected, and the knowledge of it would have given an impulse to investigation and vigilance. It has at length produced this very effect; and however inefficient the means adopted might have proved, the appearance of activity and interest must have prevented many bad consequences.

"I shall now turn with pleasure to the circumstances which are still favourable to this cause of humanity, and which may encourage us to expect that this revolting practice will be overcome.

"The Court of Directors, the Government and its assistants in India, appear at present to take great interest in the success of the measure. This is one favourable class of circumstances.

"Again the prejudices of the Jáḍejás with which I had to grapple, if not entirely done away, are at least suppressed and disavowed. They appear so far to move within the range in which nature acts that they express no pride in the destruction of their offspring, and feel no shame in rearing them. It is evident that a very favourable change has taken place, since all the infants they have saved has been the consequence of their own choice; and as some of their daughters have been reared within very recent dates, the principle of natural affection is even at this moment producing its effect. This, therefore, is upon the whole a second class of favourable circumstances; but they can be favourable only to an enlightened and resolute mind; a mind that calculates coolly, that regards no obstacle as contemptible, and yet will not be appalled by the greatest.

"One of the principal objections to the remedial measures proposed to and rejected by the Bombay Government, without the substitution of others, is, that they uniformly consist of small details. They suggest to me the idea of a conqueror proposing to lay a vast region at his feet by merely disarming or taking captive a few of the videttes or outposts. It appears to me that there are two great principles, of which all the minor details must be merely ramifications. The first principle is the maintenance of the authority of Government in connection with the solemn engagements of the Jáḍejás; and the second is the adoption of that conduct towards the natives which I have endeavoured to illustrate in the letter which I had the honour to address you last month. I have taken the liberty of suggesting in that communication what I thought might be usefully enjoined; but much must be left to the discretion, temper, and good sense of the local authorities.

"There must be intercourse, reasoning, and such dignified and manifest benevolence, that the foul breath of malevolence shall never be able to sully it. In short reason, persuasion, and the aid of women, who more readily feel than men the cruelty of such a practice, would do much to put a stop to Infanticide; and in a few years it would be looked on in Káṭhiáwáḍ with as strong a feeling of horror as it is now in England.

"I shall take the liberty of offering some remarks on each of these points. In the first place the authority of Government must be maintained, and the engagement which has been mutually contracted, exactly fulfilled. We must show that we are serious, and that we are determined to be obeyed. This will be more difficult now than in 1808, but still it must be done.

"I would begin by sending to every Jáḍejá chief an

authenticated copy of his engagement, and apprize him in the most solemn and precise terms of the determination of the Company and the Gáikáwáḍ to exact the performance of an obligation which has prescribed to all parties sacred and imperative duties. These separate addresses to the chiefs would sooth their pride, and prevent them from taking offence; but that none may be able to plead ignorance of the intentions of Government, I would follow up the measure by a public Proclamation, and give it as wide a circulation as possible. This should be addressed to the bosom and understanding of every Jáḍejá. It should declare the feelings and the intention of Government upon the subject. It should strongly mark the abhorrence of the crime, and explain the nature of his own obligations in consequence of his engagement to renounce Infanticide. He should be told that the bear, the tiger, the wolf, the hyena, and whatever is fiercest in nature, preserve their offspring, and risk their own lives for their safety. He should be asked what was to be expected from a being in the shape of a man, but who is so far from having any thing of the nature of a man, that his bosom is unvisited with even that tenderness which moves and controls the most savage beasts of prey! That where the monstrous inhumanity of Infanticide exists it is impossible that any good can exist: That it involves a violation of good faith, as well as the recognized principles of religion, and that no trust can be reposed in the perpetrators of this horrid crime: That therefore Government are resolved to punish such outcasts of human nature by withholding from them every mark of confidence and regard, as well as by inflicting pains and penalties according to the nature of the case. That on the other hand, those who give evidence of a sincere and hearty return to nature and the principles of religion, shall be regarded with affection, and enjoy every mark of esteem, of favour, honour, and emolument, of which circumstances will admit.

"When these and other considerations have been promulgated, it would be necessary that they should be acted upon with firmness and vigilance; for *early* relaxation in particular would prove extremely injurious, not only to this cause, but to the respectability of Government in general.

"In the proclamation I have above suggested, and in all public declarations on the subject, it might be useful to point to the Táluká of Dráphá, of 400 families, who have never saved a female infant, and who are enduring the marks of Divine vengeance, in the extreme poverty and misery to which they are reduced. The Rájkumárs of Benares, also, who have proved faithful to their engagement, might be mentioned as an honourable instance, and in fine, they should be reminded of every obligation and example which can be supposed to bear on the question, and is likely to produce any influence upon their sentiments. The feelings and compassion of the chiefs should be roused by frequently expressing our indignation against the crime; and by correspondence and remonstrance to inspire a natural horror of it in every breast.

"In order to observe and to give due effect to these preliminary measures, the servants of Government, Natives or British, should have instructions to watch over the operation of the engagements in their several districts, and to report upon every occurrence of a birth among the Jáḍejás, or even the surmises of its consequences. As they are not very rigid in the seclusion of their women, and as all those who are in the lower stations of life, who form the great majority in every society, must necessarily be employed in occupations, which expose them to public view, a case of pregnancy can scarcely ever be concealed. There is no attempt made indeed to prevent it being known, and surely it would not require much discrimination of judgment, nor the exercise of a very officious or impertinent curiosity, to ascertain a circumstance which is so notorious. But there are other circumstances of less direct evidence, from which very fair and correct inferences may be drawn, and of which we may avail ourselves, in cases where stronger testimony may fail. It is well known that among Hindus of all descriptions the birth of a son is an object of congratulation and rejoicing. Whenever a birth in a Jáḍejá family was unattended by these cheerful and happy symptoms, where it was passed over in silence and without notice, we might with very considerable certainty conclude that the birth was a female. Upon this surmise or suspicion an inquiry might be made, and I do not imagine that there would either be any impropriety or indelicacy in questioning the family as to the result. In many cases I am disposed to think the Jáḍejás would not deny the fact, and any attempt to equivocate would form a strong proof of guilt. Cases of a suspicious nature must occasionally occur, and come under our observation; but the miserable children of poverty must not become the victims of vengeance, while the more aggravated guilt of those that range in the higher ranks of life are passed over in silence and with impunity. By taking advantage of every opportunity, by appearing active and inquisitive, and deeply interested in the event, we should convince these people that we are determined in future to prevent the perpetration of the act.

"At any rate every servant of Government should have injunctions to ascertain the consequence of a birth by all the means that may be in his power; nothing should be too trifling for his notice which may bear on the point; he should collect even the rumours of the country upon the subject, and report to his superior; he again to another, if such there happen to be, and so on till each case reach the assistant of the Resident, and then the Resident himself, who should lastly report to the Government at Bombay. I would beg to recommend that the report of the Resident should be made at least every three months for the first year or two, or till it appear that the measure is proceeding so securely that an annual report, which must never be dispensed with, shall be deemed sufficient. Quarterly reports for a time, indeed, would be highly beneficial, and if they were mere blanks, still I think they should be punctually made. They would prevent the subject from falling into neglect, and by maintaining a spirit of inquiry make it manifestly appear that we are in earnest. I would even suggest, if it could be attained, to engage the chiefs themselves to make returns of births, and not only of females, but of males, which would be a check upon the evidence in regard to the former. This would be gaining a step of decisive importance, not only to the cause, but might increase the small number of useful facts which we possess on the state of population in India. There is every reason for suspecting that the chiefs have been transgressors of their own engagements, but the form alone of making a quarterly return to Government would add to the general excitement, and would ultimately produce good. The great object is to apply as many principles as possible of common cohesion, and to put in motion the whole of the moral machinery which can be discovered for the abolition of this unnatural practice. I am at the same time perfectly aware that the nature of the subject must render it peculiarly difficult to obtain correct information, and accurate evidence, of a fact which is commonly perpetrated in secret. The means of concealing the sacrifice itself are extensive, but as they make no mystery of the pregnancy of their women, the result cannot be so easily disguised, and into this it is our business to inquire.

"If there is any reason to believe, or even suspect, that the birth has been a female, and that nothing has been offered to the view or notice of the public, such circumstances occurring must afford a proper subject for investigation. It is not to be expected that this investigation should always produce conviction; but the purposes of humanity would be fully answered by the inquiry, by showing the party that he was watched, by alarming him with the possibility of detection, and by a natural consequence to prevent the repetition of the crime.

"I should be disposed to consider a court, or Pancháít, as the most prudent and legitimate means for the examination of the question. It would be a tribunal congenial to the natives, and its decision would give them no offence. As the Court would be entirely composed of natives its proceedings would be regulated by their feelings, and the nature of the inquiry. Should, however, any objection be made to the Pancháít, or prevent it from assembling, I would have recourse to the trial by lots, or to any device, however defective or imperfect, which might show that we were attentive to the subject, and ever on the watch for its detection.

"It is evidently necessary that the whole system should be supported by rewards and punishments; but a considerable diversity of opinion may prevail as to their nature and mode of application. The crime may be rendered more frequent by the severity of the laws which are enacted to prevent it, while there may be as much danger of encouraging it by too great tenderness in punishing. The offence is of such an odious description that it cannot be considered as a fit object for the exercise of clemency. But at the same time it has been so long legalized by custom, and so common in its practice, that it may not be proper to inflict the last severity of the law on the first transgressors. Afterwards, however, and when the ordinance has been for some time generally observed, the criminal may be prosecuted as a common murderer.

"Cases of delinquency should in every event be always punished by fine, and branded with infamy. The chiefs should be particularly held to their engagement, and punished with a pecuniary penalty to the extent of their means and the degree of their offence. The poverty of many Jáḍejás, however, must render the mode of amercement with respect to them impracticable, and the punishment of those who violate the engagement under such circumstances must be limited to disgrace, or ejection from caste.

"To this may be superadded the displeasure of Government, the reproach and correction of society. I have said in a former communication that I would not have recourse to coercive means, and if possible I would still adhere to this rule; but the authority of Government must at all events be maintained, and this gross departure from duty punished. If all other means therefore should fail, I would not hesitate to apply those of coercion, taking care to show that it is a matter of necessity, and not choice.

"Rewards and punishments always suppose something done to merit the one, or incur the other; but it is generally a less difficult task to repay a good deed, than to discover the best means of punishing a crime so as to prevent its repetition.

"I have endeavoured, in my letter of the 19th of last month, and more particularly in its enclosure, to point out various marks of regard which might be shown, at little expense, to the observers of the engagements. They should have less the appearance of bribes than of marks of honour; but at the same time instances may occur in which it may be necessary to display the generosity and liberality of Government. This must be particularly necessary in cases of extreme poverty, and inability to rear the offspring which has been saved. This revolting practice may have begun among these people from want, fear of future evil, and a redundant population; it has been continued from prejudice and habit. Such cases of extreme poverty and distress have actually occurred. Several instances are stated by Captain Ballantine to have happened, and an affecting appeal appears to have been made by the parties for pecuniary relief, which will not escape the humane attention of the Honourable Court of Directors. I would suggest the adoption of a Regulation, which, while it might serve as some check on the perpetrators of Infanticide, would be an encouragement to those who follow a different conduct. The latter should receive as much praise and publicity as possible. In this point of view it might be found useful to publish in the cachérís and in places of public resort, after a report has been transmitted to Government, the names of those who have been faithful to nature and their engagement, and of those who have been proved to violate the dictates of both. While one class would thus be marked as unworthy of trust or confidence, the other would be placed within the view of distinction and preferment. Might it not be a beneficial excitement to confer an honorary medal on the Jáḍejás who save their daughters? The silver of a few rupees might answer the purpose; the medals would contain a suitable inscription; and the persons receiving them should be invested with them, by the highest local authority of the district, and in as public a manner as possible.

"From the increased share and influence which we now possess in the revenue and government of Káṭhiáwáḍ we have proportionally increased means of binding the principles and directing the sentiments of the natives. These are so obvious that it is almost unnecessary to point them out. Amongst the circumstances of which we have the command is the power of employing only in the transaction of public business meritorious natives, and of selecting, especially for places of honour and trust, those Jáḍejás who may have saved their children.

"The Company, in a great measure, possess all those means of preferment and of profitable appointment which formerly belonged solely to the native rulers. A plan founded on this principle, systematically and judiciously pursued, would have a far better chance of success than one which proceeded solely on compulsion. Avarice seems to be the most powerful obstacle at present against which we have to struggle or contend; and the most effectual and natural way of counteracting this passion would be to oppose its influence by a new source of advantages. The fines recovered from delinquents should constitute a fund sacred to the benefit of those who have saved their daughters, which should be distributed by the Resident according to the merits and wants of particular cases. The arrangement and distribution of the fund in this manner would be one means of satisfying the country that the humanity of the Company's government was quite disinterested. I shall only add, that every reasonable hope of abolishing Infanticide in Kachh is strongly connected with our giving effect to what is already become law in the neighbouring country of Gujarát.. The accomplishment of this most desirable object ought to be considered as a prudent and legitimate measure for the consolidation and stability of our Government or influence in that quarter of India.

"In concluding these remarks, and submitting them to the consideration of the Honourable Court of Directors, it may be necessary to apologize for their freedom. My only, but I hope satisfactory, excuse, is that peculiar interest which I feel in common with the Court on the subject of female Infanticide, and my great anxiety that those measures for its suppression, which have been honoured by their approbation, and cost me no small pains and solicitude to effect, may not in the end prove totally worthless and abortive.

"I have delivered my sentiments with candour, and with that plainness which truth seems to me to require; but with feelings of the most respectful regards for the prosperity and honour of the Company, with which the dearest interests of this country are closely connected.

"It is unnecessary for me to make any professions of attachment to a service from which I have enjoyed so many benefits, into which I entered at an early period of my life, and in which I have witnessed so many eventful scenes; none of them however of a more extraordinary nature than that which is the subject of this address.

"I shall be happy if the desultory thoughts which I have at different times thrown together upon this important subject shall be deemed worthy of the attention of the Honourable Court; and I shall conclude by earnestly wishing and praying for the final triumph of humanity over a barbarous and inhuman custom."

It does not appear that these valuable and spirited documents were, at the time they were written, communicated by the East India Company to its officials in India. On the members of the Court of Directors, they could scarcely fail to make a deep and salutary impression. They were certainly taken in good part by those to whom they were addressed, who a few years after their receipt evinced their gratitude to Colonel (then Major-General) Walker for his important services in India, by appointing him to the government of St. Helena. They formed part of a return to Parliament ordered to be printed 17th June, 1824; copies of which duly reached India, where they were not overlooked by parties more immediately concerned with the suppression of Infanticide. We find Major LeGrand Jacob, Acting Political Agent in Káṭhiáwáḍ in 1841, thus noticing them in a letter addressed to the Bombay Government:—"The philanthropists of Great Britain who have written on this subject, even including the venerable Colonel Walker himself, who addressed the Honourable Court with some severe strictures on the apathy of Indian functionaries as regards the crime, seem to me to have been carried away by their zeal in a noble cause to overlook the circumstances in which we are placed in this country, and to forget what was due to their exiled countrymen. A handful of Englishmen, scattered over a territory as large as Europe, can move but very slowly beyond the tide of public opinion. We experience the same difficulty in steering the course desiderated by a more enlightened and distant nation, as the æronaut has to encounter in directing his vessel, the want of an opposing force to the current we move in. In this particular province, nearly the size of Ceylon, and with a population of seventeen lakhs, the Political Agent can only devote great attention to the suppression of infanticide by sacrificing some other equally important duty; and it is surprising that a person of Colonel Walker's experience and sagacity should not, in his recriminatory letters on this subject to the Honourable the Court of Directors, written after his return to England, have made sufficient allowance for the fact, that a man cannot go beyond the limits God has been pleased to assign to mortal strength and intellect. The lapse of time that had occurred between these letters and Colonel Walker's departure from India, as also the altered nature of our position in this Peninsula, with an earnest zeal for one particular object, somewhat shutting others out of view, may be viewed in justification of the philanthropist's remarks."* In these pithy remarks there is much truth. They do not amount, however, to a vindication of the remissness of such of the officials in India as may be supposed to fall under the censure of Colonel Walker, so delicately and modestly expressed by him. We are bound to demand and enforce from our allies and tributaries the implementing of the righteous engagements which they have formed with our country. Our first duty in all the provinces under our supervision, after securing their general peace, is the prevention within their borders of the criminal destruction of human life. While we know the difficulties from time to time encountered in securing these and other philanthropic objects arising from the causes alluded to by Major Jacob—the paucity of European officers in the largest districts of India, their multifarious engagements, and the obstructions which native prejudice,

* Letter dated 23rd Oct. 1841.

custom, and apathy present to their labours, we know also that the zeal and devotedness and talent of our officials, as exemplified in measures and pursuits in which Major Jacob has borne an honourable part, as we shall afterwards see as our narrative proceeds, can with the blessing of God effect wonders.

CHAPTER VI.

ATTEMPTS TO PROCURE AN ENGAGEMENT FROM THE JÁḌEJÁ'S OF KACHH FOR THE ABANDONMENT OF INFANTICIDE—THEIR SUCCESS AND FIRST PARTIAL RESULTS—THE JÁḌEJÁ'S OF CHORWÁḌ AND CHÁ'RCHAT AGREE TO DISCONTINUE INFANTICIDE.

WE have already seen that Colonel Walker, when reporting the success of his endeavours in reference to the formation of an engagement on the part of the Jáḍejás of Káṭhiáwáḍ to abandon Infanticide, had but slender hopes that their brethren in Kachh, would soon follow their example.* It is to the credit, however, of the Bombay government and its officials, that they continued anxiously to urge the Jáḍejás of Kachh, to yield to the claims of humanity by abandoning this most cruel custom; and that, after much correspondence and intercommunication, the suppression of Infanticide among them was made a condition of the first regular treaty which was formed between that province and the British Government. Had the prince and nobles of Kachh been neglected in this important matter, not only would that province have greatly suffered in its moral interests, but the work of eradicating the horrid crime from Káṭhiáwáḍ would have been rendered still more difficult than it has ultimately proved to be.

The first party, after the departure to Europe of Colonel Walker, who sought to bring the people of Kachh to a right view of the atrocity of the crime of Infanticide was the zealous and persevering Jonathan Duncan, still the Governor of Bombay. He wrote a personal letter on the subject to Fatteh Muhammad, the minister of Ráo Ráydhan, which is not recorded, which called forth

* See above, p. 86.

the following strange reply, received on the 15th January, 1811. "With regard to what you have urged, founded not only upon the doctrines of Islamism and Christianity, but also upon the religious institutes of the Hindus against the custom of the destruction of females, as in practice among the Jáḍejá Thákurs (barons), I have read what you have stated on the subject of this horrid cruelty. Truly, the meditations of those whom God has exalted are derived from supernatural inspiration. The truth is, that among the Jáḍejás descended from the Jáḍá (Yádava?)* tribe the practice of female destruction has been handed down from generation to generation for the last five thousand years. It constitutes, in fact, nothing new. Some do not practise it, whilst others do, at the birth. Every person is vain of his own faith, as the Almighty has declared. Every tribe is gratified with its own tenets, and in the chapter of the *Bakarat* [Cow, of the Korán] is the following divine saying: 'When you shall have witnessed the good as well as the evil of any particular religion, there will be found to exist nothing disgusting therein:' † and hitherto no attempt has been made, since the world has been divided into four quarters, and subdivided into seven distinct religions, by any Persian or Arabian sovereign who has flourished on earth, to interdict the custom among the chieftains in question; and it cannot be unknown to you that this class of people are either connected by the ties of brotherhood or by relationship with his highness the Mahá Ráo, my master (may his shadow be extended!); and it must be accordingly inexpedient and improper in

* See p. 76.

[† No such passage as this occurs in the chapter of the Cow. It is there said, however, "Surely those who believe, and those who Judaize, and Christians, and Sabians, and whoever believeth in God and the last day, and doth that which is right, they shall have their reward with their Lord, there shall come no fear on them, neither shall they be grieved." This passage has given rise to much controversy, though the majority of the Musalmans hold that it was afterwards repealed. See Sale, *in loc.*]

me, who have been cherished by his Highness, to discuss this question with the Jáḍejá people: in concurring with the following divine command, 'It will not be competent to you to bring into the right path every person to whom you may be attached, though the Almighty be able to direct in the way of truth whomsoever he wishes.'* This point therefore excepted, I request you will unreservedly command my services in this quarter, on all suitable occasions; and I shall discharge the duties of a good-wisher in the accomplishment thereof; not doubting at the same time, that you will always consider me as one of those who desire you well, and afford me the pleasure of your correspondence, such as I shall esteem the height of human felicity."

Mr. Duncan, undiscouraged by this evasive, though polite, declinature, renewed his remonstrances with Fatteh Muhammad, in the following epistle dated the 25th March, 1811. It is obviously penned in the native style; and it is somewhat indicative of the "brahmanized mind," which Sir James Mackintosh, the Recorder of Bombay,—who in his philosophical and judicial dignity and decorum had but little sympathy with his frequent oriental accommodations,—was jocularly wont to attribute to Mr. Duncan.

"I have of late had the pleasure of receiving a letter from you, on the subject of the fortunate consequences that attended the deputation of the late most worthy character, Captain Greenwood, to Mandaví, and respecting your reluctance to interpose for the prevention of the nefarious observance of female Infanticide, as being a long-established custom that has prevailed among the Jáḍejás of your quarter, and of which although you cannot yourself but disapprove, you wish to decline interfering in for fear of giving offence to your superiors. You should, however, consider what a high religious merit you must acquire in the sight of the Almighty by proving the happy means of putting an end to so im-

[* This passage is conformable to the doctrines of Islam.]

moral and detested a practice, as must by all the world be acknowledged to be the one here alluded to, and which might gradually be repressed, and in time entirely rooted out, by pursuing the same conciliatory means for that purpose as were followed three years ago in Káṭhiáwáḍ, by the respectable Colonel Walker, who after some amicable discussion, obtained, under the instructions of this Government, written engagements and obligations from all the Jáḍejá chieftains in that region to abandon so abominable a custom, in like manner as I had previously done two-and-twenty years ago from the Rajput tribe of Rájkumárs in the Zillah of Juánpur, in the province of Benares; since which, the acts of these Rájkumárs have remained unsullied with such barbarous and unnatural deeds as the murder of their own offspring. I enclose a translation of the engagement which these Rájkumárs on that account entered into, under date the 17th of December 1789, and the respectable Captain Carnac, Resident at Baroda, will forward a transcript of the engagement to the same effect entered into with Colonel Walker by the Jáḍejás of Káṭhiáwáḍ, both which writings I recommend your confidentially imparting, together with copies of my former and present letters to you on this important subject, to some of the most discreet of the head men of that tribe in Kachh, and on whom I cannot doubt the perusal and consideration thereof will produce a salutary effect, and awake their feelings to a sense of the murderous habitudes to which they and their ancestors have been thus long inured; such as I cannot suppose they will desire to persevere in after knowing that it has been relinquished by so many of their brethren both in the west and in the east, when they can, I trust, no longer desire to continue the solitary instance of such atrocity; in which case the Almighty will no doubt forgive the past, as being founded in their ignorance, and in those prejudices of education which it is so difficult in all countries to get the better of; whereas if they wilfully persist thus to put their own infants systematically to death, in defiance of the salutary example set to them by their brethren, it is to be dreaded that the Divine vengeance may one day overtake them and their country, in like manner as the history of other nations contains marked manifestations of, such as I hope they will avert in time, and seasonably shield themselves from, by the renunciation thus solicitously desired of them; nor can you in particular perform a service so agreeable to me as by contributing, by all the weight of your own influence, to the attainment of an object so highly interesting to humanity, respecting which I shall therefore wait your further report, with an anxiety proportionate to the importance of the reformation thus in view."

This, it is believed, was the last communication on the subject of Infanticide written or prompted by Mr. Duncan. He died on the 11th August following, greatly lamented by the Bombay community, of which, for the long period of sixteen years, he had been the honoured and efficient head.*

* The following is the inscription on the handsome and tasteful monument to Mr. Duncan in the Bombay Cathedral.

IN MEMORY OF
THE HON'BLE JONATHAN DUNCAN
GOVERNOR OF BOMBAY, FROM 1795 TO 1811.
RECOMMENDED TO THAT HIGH OFFICE BY HIS TALENTS AND INTEGRITY,
IN THE DISCHARGE OF VARIOUS IMPORTANT DUTIES IN BENGAL AND BENARES,
HIS PURITY AND ZEAL FOR THE PUBLIC GOOD WERE EQUALLY CONSPICUOUS
DURING HIS LONG AND UPRIGHT ADMINISTRATION AT THIS PRESIDENCY.
WITH A GENEROUS DISREGARD OF PERSONAL INTEREST,
HIS PRIVATE LIFE WAS ADORNED
BY THE MOST MUNIFICENT ACTS OF CHARITY AND FRIENDSHIP,
TO ALL CLASSES OF THE COMMUNITY.
TO THE NATIVES IN PARTICULAR HE WAS A FRIEND AND PROTECTOR
TO WHOM THEY LOOKED WITH UNBOUNDED CONFIDENCE,
AND NEVER APPEALED IN VAIN.
HE WAS BORN AT WARDHOUSE IN THE COUNTY OF FORFAR IN SCOTLAND
ON THE 1ST MAY 1756,
CAME TO INDIA AT THE AGE OF 16; AND, AFTER 39 YEARS OF UNINTERRUPTED SERVICE,
DIED AT THIS PLACE ON 11TH AUGUST 1811.

INFANTICIDE
ABOLISHED
IN
BENARES AND KATTYWAR.

SEVERAL OF THE BRITISH INHABITANTS OF BOMBAY,
JUSTLY APPRECIATING HIS DISTINGUISHED MERITS
IN PUBLIC AND PRIVATE LIFE
HAVE RAISED THIS MONUMENT,
AS A TRIBUTE OF RESPECT AND ESTEEM.
M,D,CCCXVII.

With the immediate effect of Mr. Duncan's letter, we are unacquainted. It would appear, however, that as the position of Fatteh Muhammad as prime minister in Kachh became more insecure, and his dependence on the Bombay government, which espoused his claims particularly as against Jám Jasájí of Nawánagar, became more imperative, he and the Jáḍejás seem to have made some expression, or other, of deference to its repeated entreaties. The promises given, of whatever nature they might be, were long kept in a state of abeyance; and the Bombay Government, with the growing disturbances in Kachh before its view, possessed no power of enforcing them. It wrote thus to the Court of Directors on the 22nd August, 1815:—"The events which have recently occurred in the province of Kachh, and led to the termination of all intercourse with that government, have deprived us of the means of encouraging the native chiefs in an adherence to their laudable resolution to abandon the inhuman practice of female Infanticide.

"We have, however, called on the Resident at Baroda to ascertain and report whether the practice has been discontinued wholly or in part in Kachh, and whether it has entirely ceased within the province of Káṭhiáwáḍ."

Noticing this communication,—with the unfaltering loyalty to the cause of the abolition of Infanticide which, to their credit be it said, they have never failed to evince, notwithstanding their long hesitation about interference in Satí and other matters of humanity,—the Court of Directors replied: "We must again enjoin you, in the most serious and earnest manner, to be unremitting in your endeavours to accomplish this humane object in the countries wherever the British influence can be felt or exerted."

On the 16th of August following, we find the Bombay Government, then under Sir Evan Nepean, detailing its further proceedings, in a despatch to the Court at home.

"In our instructions to Captain Carnac on the occasion of renewing our negociations with the state of Kachh, your Honourable Court will observe we apprized that officer, that 'the suppression of female Infanticide was, as he was aware, an object, for the accomplishment of which the British Government was extremely solicitous; and that the late Fatteh Muhammad having pledged himself to promote the entire suppression of that horrid practice, we trusted that Lieutenant MacMurdo would feel no difficulty in obtaining an obligation from the Ráo [Bhármaljí] to use his influence in prohibiting so unnatural and so inhuman a practice.'

"Captain MacMurdo has not yet acted upon that part of his instructions, having, in a private letter to our chief secretary, dated the 22nd of January last, explained that 'he could not touch on Infanticide just now; it would have needlessly irritated and alarmed the Jáḍejás, and we shall have time to go to work slowly and methodically with greater prospect of success.'

"We have only within these few days received Captain Carnac's reply to our reference of the 22nd of July 1815, which has been noticed by your Honourable Court, a copy of which, and of our Chief Secretary's letter in answer thereto, we have the honour of forwarding for your information.

"The impaired power of the Ráo, and the internal revolutions in Kachh, Captain Carnac states, have been made a pretext for paying no attention to the execution of our wishes; and under these untoward circumstances we have not been enabled to carry our views for the abolition of female Infanticide in that province beyond measures of representation; and now that we have obtained a political establishment in Kachh, we fear it may require no slight degree of exertions before any sure progress be made in the success of our object. Captain MacMurdo's attention, however, has been directed to the impressive injunctions of your Honourable Court; and as we have directed periodical reports to be submitted to us of the success of our exertions, we entertain a hope that by the vigilant and persevering efforts which will be bestowed on this interesting subject, this humane object will be ultimately accomplished."

Writing to Captain MacMurdo on this occasion the Bombay government said, "As the practice is not in Káṭhiáwáḍ connected with any 'religious feelings,' the Governor in Council is desirous of being particularly informed if it be so within the province of Kachh, as, inferrible from an expression made use of in the 4th paragraph of Captain Carnac's letter, the custom in Káṭhiáwáḍ was followed through selfish and mercenary motives; and its abolition was represented by Colonel Walker as one of the most popular acts of the Company's Government in Gujarát, even with the Jáḍejás themselves; the Governor in Council entertains therefore every hope, that by judicious management you may prevail on the chieftains of Kachh to abandon this abominable practice. No time would be more advantageous for your preferring your application, considering the pecuniary concessions which the British Government has made to the State of Kachh;* and you are authorized to inform the Ráo that his highness could not make a more acceptable return than by following the praiseworthy example of the chieftains in Káṭhiáwáḍ, in engaging to promote the highly interesting object of abolishing the inhuman custom of female Infanticide." Captain MacMurdo was at this time appointed the government agent at Bhuj. The instructions delivered to him were approved by the Court of Directors.

[* "Of the twenty lakhs of rupees claimed in name of indemnification and expenses, the British government shortly afterwards remitted their own portion, amounting to above eight hundred thousand, together with the yearly tribute of two lakhs of Korís; a liberality which at first equally surprized and delighted the Ráo, who found no great difficulty in raising the remaining balance by fines on his refractory chieftains, and demands, under the title of voluntary contributions, from those who had long enjoyed the revenues of the country."—Burnes's Sketch of the History of Cutch, sect. iii.]

The affairs of Kachh during the next three years got more and more into confusion and disorder. Husein Miyáṇ and Ibráhím Miyáṇ, the Sons of Fatteh Muhammad and his successors in the administration of affairs, did not well consort together; and various factions were formed by them for no very commendable purposes. Mán Singh, or Bhármaljí, the son of Ráydhan by a slave-girl,—who had been seated on the cushion through the influence of Ibráhím Miyáṇ aided by a Muhammadan chief named Miyáṇ Sotah and with the connivance of the Jáḍejás in preference to Ládobá the lawful son of Bháíji Báwá the brother of Ráydhan and the lawful heir, —devoted himself to intemperance, debauchery, cruelty, plunder, and murder, in which he was but too much encouraged by the example of his ministers and companions. He was by no means well affected to the British authorities, however disinterested they were in the advice which they tendered to him for the regulation of his own behaviour and the conduct of public affairs. Encouraged by the sympathy of the Amirs of Sindh, and the vauntings against the British for their entrance into Kachh of the King of Kábul who had absolutely no rights in that province, he sought, but in vain, to eject the British from Tuná and Anjár in Kachh, which they held as a material guarantee for the pacification of the province and reimbursement for a portion of the expences which they had incurred while seeking to promote that object. Among other atrocities, he directed the assassination of his nephew Ládobá, even though, at this time, there was no wish either on the part of his bháíyád or the British Government to disposses him of the authority which he himself enjoyed. He alienated the Jáḍejáṣ from his person and darbár. When asked by the Bombay Government to treat with kindness the widow of Ládobá, and her expected offspring,—for she was pregnant when her husband was murdered,—he became infuriated, on account of their interference, and collected his soldiers with a view to proceed against Anjár. The most vigorous remonstrances of Captain MacMurdo were unavailing for his correction on this occasion, and though ultimately afraid to attack Anjár, which had been re-inforced by British troops, he moved against Aḍisír in the east of Kachh, for the express purpose of causing a breach of the peace.

In the course of these proceedings the treaty of 1816 was both suspended and violated. The Marquis of Hastings, the Governor General of India, on due information from the Bombay Government, declared Bhármaljí a public enemy, and gave instructions to proceed to the extremity of war against him. The sequel we cannot better notice than in the words of Dr. Burnes. "Orders were issued to accept the spontaneous and long proferred co-operation of the Jáḍejás for his dethronement, as well as to request that body of noblemen to elevate to the masnad whomsoever they considered the lawful heir to that dignity. To give full effort to these instructions, a British army was forthwith assembled, under the command of Sir William Grant Keir, at Anjár, where it was joined by (Vijírájjí) the two Prágjís, Alyájí, and Méramaṇjí, the five principal Jáḍejá chiefs in Kachh, who expressed their readiness and anxiety to co-operate in the measures to be adopted. The Ráo, who had during this interval entered into a compromise with the chief of Aḍisír, quickly returned to Bhuj, where he was seized with a violent illness. He was consequently unable himself to make any preparations, or give orders in person; but his partisans and favourites collected a considerable force, and on the approach of the British army to the capital, some skirmishing took place. Captain M'Murdo then intimated to Bhármaljí the intention of his government to organize anew the affairs of Kachh, in concert with the Jáḍejá Bháíyád; and called on him either to stand by the consequences of resistance, or to surrender himself, promising, in the event of his adopting the latter alternative, that he should meet with safety and consideration. This proposal was not attended to till the Hill-Fort of Bhujiá, which overlooks the city of Bhuj, was taken by escalade on the following day; upon which through the negotiation of the minister, Lakhmídás, Ráo Bhármaljí was brought to the tent of the resident, and placed under a guard of British troops. Every respect was paid to him, consistently with the safety of his person, and the kindest attention shown to his health, which, from constant intemperance, and his recent indisposition, was now so completely broken, that he was scarcely able to walk or articulate.

"A few days after his surrender, Ráo Bhármaljí was formally deposed, and placed in a palace built by Fatteh Muhammad, which was selected for his residence. The Jáḍejá chiefs were then left entirely to themselves to choose his successor; and it was generally expected that the election would have been in favour of the infant son of the murdered prince Ládobá; but strange as it may seem, the only son of Bhármaljí, a child of three years of age, received the unanimous votes of the Bháíyád, and was accordingly raised to the throne by the name of Ráo Désal.* The minister, Lakhmídás Mehtá, is understood to have secured, by his influence, this decision in favour of the offspring of his fallen master. Necessary as was his dethronement, several of the Jáḍejás, acting from the same impression, still wished, after that decided step, that the government should be carried on in his name; and when they found that the proposal was objected to, they evinced their respect for his failings and misfortunes, by entreating that kindness should be shown him in his confinement, and that the succession should remain in his family. The election of the Bháíyád proved in the end more fortunate than if it had fallen on the weakly child of Ládobá, (whom, however, they declared the next heir to Désaljí, in the event of his not living to have issue,) as he died a few weeks after, and the race of Bháíjí Báwa, the legitimate branch of the royal family of Kachh, became extinct.

* [The present Ráo of Kachh.]

"The next requisite step towards the settlement of affairs, was the appointment of a regency, to carry on the government during the minority of his Highness Ráo Désal; and the Jáḍejás were again requested to nominate a sufficient number of persons for the purpose. Their choice fell on Jáḍejás Virájí of Rohá, and Prithirájjí of Nángarchá, the two most powerful chiefs in Kachh, Udanjí, a Rájgur Bráhman, the minister Lakhmídás Walabjí, and Shét Ratansí Jéṭhá. The name of the British resident was also included; but as the object of the Governor-General was to render Kachh, as far as possible, an independent state, the arrangement was at first objected to; and it was only through the earnest solicitations of the Jáḍejá Bháíyád, combined with those of the existing members of the regency, that his lordship at length consented to the appointment of Captain MacMurdo as president of the latter body. Matters being now settled on a firm basis, the regency proceeded to correct the innumerable abuses in every department of the state, and to discharge the useless and expensive levies of troops which Bhármaljí had maintained. A British force was subsidized for the defence of the country and the support of the government; and the honour of guarding the Ráo's palace was given up entirely to the Jáḍejás, to the perfect exclusion of the low-born wretches whom the late Ráo had introduced to that responsible duty.

"In conformity with the spirit of the measures which have been detailed in these pages, and, as better calculated to maintain a firm and honourable alliance between the two states, a new treaty, containing, in addition to most of the articles of that of 1816, many others, adapted to the improved condition of affairs, was shortly after concluded between the governments. It will be seen on a reference to it, that the British government wished carefully to abstain from all interference in the Ráo's internal authority; whilst it agreed to guarantee his power and the 'integrity of his dominions' from all enemies, foreign and domestic. A boon of a similar description was extended to the Jáḍejá chiefs, who had established a claim on us by their conduct during the late revolution, and whose possessions were also secured to them on their consenting to preserve their female children. In return for these important concessions, the advantages derived by the British government are almost nominal; for, with the exception of an annual subsidy of two lakhs and eighty thousand rupees equal to the support of one-half of the force which has been generally required, we receive nothing from the Bhuj darbár, to which Anjár and its dependencies have since been restored. In enumerating the benefits of the alliance, we must not omit, however, the grand victory in favour of humanity in the abolition of Infanticide; a horrid practice, which it has been our object, ever since our connexion with Kachh and Káṭhiáwáḍ, to put a stop to, and which we have certainly succeeded in diminishing in these countries."*

The treaty now alluded to was concluded on the 13th October 1819. It was entitled "Treaty of Alliance between the Honourable the East India Company and His Highness Mahárájá Mirzá Ráo Shrí Désaljí, his heirs and successors, concluded by Captain MacMurdo, on the part of the Honourable Company; and by Jáḍejás Prithirájjí, Vijíraji, Merámanjí, Prágjí, Prágjí, Mokájí, Alyájí, Naughanjí, Bhánjí, and Jaymaljí, by virtue of full powers from their respective governments." The portions of it which referred to Infanticide were the following.

Article 10. "The Honourable Company engages to exercise no authority over the domestic concerns of the Ráo, or of those of any of the Jáḍejá chieftains of the country. That the Ráo, his heirs and successors, shall be absolute masters of their territory, and that the civil and criminal jurisdiction of the British Government shall not be introduced therein.

Article 17. "His Highness the Ráo, his heirs and

* Abridged from Dr. Burnes's Sketch of the History of Cutch, with the change of some of the names, pp. 215-221.

successors, at the particular instance of the Honourable Company, engage to abolish in their own family the practice of Infanticide; they also engage to join heartily with the Honourable Company in abolishing the custom generally throughout the Bháíyád of Kachh.

Article 18. "Previously to the execution of the deed of guarantee in favour of the Jádejá Bháíyád according to the tenor of the 16th Article, a written engagement shall be entered into by them to abstain from the practice of Infanticide; and specifying, that in case any of them do practice it, the guilty person shall submit to a punishment of any kind that may be determined by the Honourable Company's Government and the Kachh Darbár."*

The Court of Directors in reference to these articles,

* This written engagement was dated the 9th October 1820. It is thus with accompaniments recorded in the "Treaties, Agreements, and Engagements" accurately collated with the originals, published by Mr. R. H. Thomas of the Bombay Secretariate in 1851, from which (pp. 271-272) we have taken the preceding articles.

"We, the Jádejás Sugrámjí, Jiwanjí, and Sumrájí, of Patrí, do hereby engage for ourselves, our heirs and successors, to abstain from the practice of Female Infanticide, and in the event of our continuing this practice, do consent to submit to any punishment that the allied Governments may think proper to inflict upon us, as stipulated in the 18th Article of the Treaty of Alliance, dated the 13th October 1819, between the Honorable East India Company and Mahá Rájá Mírzá Ráo Shrí De'saljí.

Dated 9th October 1820.

(True translation, G. J. Wilson, 1st Assistant Resident.)

Memorandum. The above engagement was subscribed by the following Jádejá chiefs.

Jádejá Vijírájjí, and Bháíyád of Rohá.
Jádejá Káthíjí, and Bháíyád of Nalyu.
Jádejá Hothíjí, and Bháíyád of Darsarí.
Jádejá Káíojí, and Bháíyád of Wainotí.
Jádejá Bhimání, Mánsinghjí, and Bháíyád of Khe'doí.
Jádejá Prágjí, and Bháíyád of Mhawá.
Jádejá Chandojí, and Bháíyád of Nángarchá.
Jádejá Naughanjí, and Bháíyád of Kothárá.
Jádejá Meramanjí, and Bháíyád of Suthdí.
Jádejá Mokájí, and Bháíyád of Terá.
Jádejá Alyájí, and Bháíyád of Vínján.

which are both express and satisfactory, thus wrote on the 22nd November 1822.

"We shall be much gratified to hear that the stipulations contained in the 18th article relative to the abolition of the practice of Infanticide have been observed. We are not, however, very sanguine in our expectations on this head, unless these stipulations are enforced by interference on the part of the Resident, which would not be reconcileable with our engagement in the 10th article, 'to exercise no authority over the domestic concerns of the Ráo, or those of any of the Jáḍejá chieftains of the country.'"

The Court seems in this instance to have forgotten, that any subject whatever, specifically embraced in the treaty, ceased to be a mere domestic concern, and was brought within the category of political exigency.

It was to the disadvantage of the speedy implementing of these provisions that Capt. MacMurdo died shortly after they were agreed to.

When Mr. Charles Norris of the Civil Service was resident in Kachh in 1822, the town and district of Anjár, for some time occupied by the English, were restored to the authority of the Ráo, on the agreement by the regency to pay the annual sum of eighty thousand rupees as an equivalent; and the British subsidiary camp was removed from the hill-fort of Bhujiá, in the neighbourhood of the capital, to the ground which it now occupies in its vicinity. On the occasion of these transactions, however, no notice was taken of infanticide.

The first information of the effects of the Treaty with Kachh on the subject of Infanticide received by the Bombay Government was conveyed to it on the 23rd

"The Jáḍejás Sugrámjí, Jíwanjí, and Sumrájí of Patrí, having entered into a written engagement to abstain from the practice of Female Infanticide, as stipulated in the 18th Article of the Treaty of Alliance between the allied Governments, the Guarantee of the British Government is hereby given to the aforesaid Jáḍejás that they and their heirs and successors shall be in the full enjoyment of their possessions and rights, they on their part performing the services due from them to His Highness the Ráo's Government.— J. Williams, Resident."

March 1823 by Mr. T. G. Gardiner of the Civil Service, then the resident at the Darbár of Bhuj. Noticing a tour which he had made in the province, he thus writes:—

"I found, the chiefs and their bháíyád hospitable, manly, open and liberal in their opinions, willing to listen to advice, pleased with the smallest attention, fond of their children, (the majority having two, and often a greater number; I mention this circumstance, as I have seen it stated that the Jáḍejás are in the habit of poisoning their male, as well as destroying their female offspring, in order that their estate might descend entire,) kind and conciliatory to their servants and dependents.

"I took every opportunity of inquiring of my visitors, the number, age and sex of their children, and where I could get information of a female infant existing, belonging to any of the chiefs, I requested, when practicable, that it might be brought to me. I am not aware of the expectations the Government may have formed on this subject, but considering the short period that has elapsed since the guarantees were given and accepted, I am not disappointed in discovering the fact, of little short of 100 female infants being alive, belonging to the tribe in Kachh and Wágar;* the list is of importance, as it will form the basis for future inquiries, and is much more satisfactory than vague numbers, founded on uncertain data.

"Among the chiefs, I believe the feeling is pretty general, that it is become their duty as well as their interest to preserve their female children, for the penalty being undefined, any infringement of the agreement might be visited in the severest manner, by a pecuniary mulct; on the other hand, the inferior bháíyád having little to lose, are not under the same apprehension, and no doubt the practice is still continued to a lamentable extent among them."

* [Wágar is the eastern district of Kachh. The actual number of female Jáḍejá children alive, as certified by the list forwarded by Mr. Gardiner was 91.]

The proceedings of Mr. Gardiner, as thus reported by himself, were approved by the Bombay Government, which in noticing them to the Court of Directors at home, on the 27th November 1825, added this further intelligence.

"We have much pleasure here in referring to a subsequent letter from Mr. Gardiner, bringing to our notice the case of Jáḍejá Ráydhanjí, residing at the village of Dhamarká, who had some years since voluntarily preserved two of his female children, owing to the casual circumstance of meeting with Lieut. Col. Walker at Murví, when that officer was endeavouring to stop the practice in Jháláwáḍ. Disappointed in obtaining any satisfactory arrangement in regard to some girás dues of his family, which had been seized by the Government during the time of Fatteh Muhammad, this person and his family had been living at his village, on the produce of their own labour and exertions, but from a wish to preserve appearances, and to maintain his daughters suitably to their rank and birth, Ráydhanjí had incurred expenses, which obliged him at length to appear at Bhuj, and to apply to Mr. Gardiner's predecessor for relief, when a temporary allowance of grain was given to him.

"Having consumed this supply, and being reduced to great difficulties, for the support of his family, Ráydhanjí came a second time to Bhuj with his daughters, alighted at the gates of the palace, soliciting support.

"The Jáḍejá chiefs being at Bhuj, Mr. Gardiner regretted that such a display should have taken place, and that measures had not been sooner taken to prevent it, as it might have a bad effect on the minds of the Jáḍejás who would perhaps attribute his distress more to the circumstances of his helpless family, than to the unsatisfactory state in which the arrangement about his girás claim had been allowed to remain.

"To remove this feeling as soon as possible Mr. Gardiner directed the same allowance of food to be issued to him during his stay, as to the other Jáḍejás in the habit of visiting Bhuj, and on his returning to Dhamarká, took care that he should receive a further allowance of grain sufficient to provide for his family, until he should be able to settle his *grás* or *girás*, [mouthful], heritable rights in his fields.

"The age of the children were stated to be 13 and 10; and the object of Mr. Gardiner's addressing us, was, to recommend a donation being made to Ráydhanjí to enable him to effect the marriage of his daughters, which would have taken place at an earlier period; a recommendation, which we accordingly concurred in, and authorized Mr. Gardiner to present him with the sum of two thousand rupees for that purpose.

"The chief obstacle to the success of the measures for the suppression of the practice of Infanticide, is stated by Mr. Gardiner to be the great repugnance which the Jáḍejás feel at the idea of intermarrying, and that could we ever hope to overcome their scruples, the inducement to preserve their children would be greater; whilst, on the present system, they have in prospect not only the expenses of marrying their female children into the families of Soḍhás, Wághélás, Jaitwás, Jhálás, and other Rajput tribes, but also of purchasing wives for themselves from the same class of people.

"Since the preceding paragraphs were written, we have received a letter from the Resident in Kachh [then Major Henry Pottinger] which does not place the conduct of Ráydhanjí in the most favourable light, as far as relates to the eldest of the two daughters; for, instead of procuring a suitable match for the young lady, and expending the money granted by the British government, as was clearly intended, he actually sold her in marriage, for a further sum of five thousand korís, to a relation of the Ráo, who was nearly eighty years of age, stone-blind and bed-ridden. The other daughter is betrothed to Punjájí Chandají Wághélá of Paláswá in Wágar, and the sum of one thousand rupees, presented to her, is in deposit in the hands of the potadár, and care will be taken that it is appropriated to the purpose intended by Government."

So much for Jáḍejá cupidity and selfishness, which would, doubtless, get their just rebuke from Major Pottinger.

In connexion with these notices of the progress of measures in Kachh for the suppression of Infanticide, it may be here mentioned, that Lieut. Col. W. Miles, the Political Agent at Pálhanpur, the most northern district of Gujarát tributary to the Gáikawáḍ and the English Government, was about the time to which they refer instrumental in getting the Jáḍejás who had spread from Kachh to Chorwáḍ, an island in the eastern Raṇ, and to the *táluká* of Chárchat on the opposite continent, to sign agreements for its complete abandonment, which, it appeared, they had partially done from the time of the negociation by Capt. MacMurdo of the treaty with Kachh in 1819. His dispatch on this subject was transmitted on the 25th June 1827, by Mr. Willoughby, assistant-resident at Baroda, who remarked, that "the measures lately adopted by Colonel Miles, are very judicious and reflect the highest credit on his humane exertions," a sentiment in which the Government fully concurred. With the view of keeping the chiefs to their engagements, Colonel Miles had proposed that a register should be kept of the birth of all female children among the Jáḍejás; and of this Mr. Willoughby stated his opinion that it was "well calculated to check a practice so abominable and revolting" as that of Infanticide. The Governor-in-Council wished inquiry to be made by Col. Miles about the probable consequences of such an arrangement before it should be carried into effect. We go so far as to say, that a general registration of births and deaths is a great desideratum for all the tribes and tongues of India. The consequence of such a registration would be the prevention of an unspeakable amount of crime both against life and property. With ordinary caution and consideration, it is to a great extent practicable.

CHAPTER VII.

MEASURES PROPOSED BY MR. ELPHINSTONE FOR KA'ṬHIA'WA'Ḍ—NEGLECTED BY CAPT. BARNEWALL—CAPT. BARNEWALL'S RETURNS—FORMATION OF AN INFANTICIDE FUND—MR. BLANE'S AGENCY AND RETURNS.

INFANTICIDE in Káṭhiáwáḍ attracted but little attention in Bombay for several years after the reception of Captain Ballantine's communication of the 29th June 1817. On the 9th of January 1821, however, very important instructions on the subject were communicated by the Honorable Mountstuart Elphinstone to Captain Barnewall, the successor of Captain Ballantine in the political agency of that province. They called upon him personally to seek the detection of the Jáḍejás breaking their engagements to preserve their offspring; to discountenance the crime by showing favour to the chiefs in whose districts it might be diminishing, and refusing favours to those on whose estates it might be continued; and to dispose of the fines levied on the chiefs by giving grants from the fund formed from them to the parents preserving their children. They were quite in the spirit of Colonel Walker's letters to the Court of Directors, and of the following tenor:—

"The Honourable the Governor has learned, with great concern, the very limited success that has hitherto attended the exertions of the British Government to put a stop to the crime of infanticide.

"Though the Honourable the Governor does not think that it would be prudent to authorize the employment of regular informers for the purpose of detecting instances of this atrocity, he feels the greatest anxiety to employ every practicable means for its suppression; and considering that the practice is entirely unconnected with religion, and unsupported by the opinion of the bulk of the community, even in the countries where it exists, he cannot but entertain a hope that more effectual means of extirpating it may yet be devised.

"You are requested to state your sentiments on this head, and to offer any suggestions that appear to you calculated to obtain the end in view. It is to be hoped, that from the direct communication which now subsists between you and the inhabitants, you will be able, in the course of your circuits, to obtain information in some of the many instances of this crime, which must occur. It will then be in your power to visit the offence, not only on the person who has committed it, but on the head of the village, or on the chief who shall appear to have connived at it.

"Your influence might likewise be always employed in discountenancing this atrocity and in encouraging an opposite course. When remissions, are refused to a chief, it may be noticed as one reason for rejecting his request, that he has not been zealous in repressing infanticide. On the other hand, when an abatement is granted, it may perhaps be possible to reserve to Government the right to recover the amount after a certain period, unless the chief and his bháíyád can prove their attention to the rule in question, by the production of a certain number of female children of their caste. The proportion must of course be much smaller than a calculation of the births in so many families would authorize us to expect.

"With a view to encourage parents in sparing their female children, you are authorized to throw all fines levied on chiefs for other offences, as well as for infanticide (after indemnifying the sufferers by each,) into a fund to be distributed in proportion to children so preserved."

The measure recommended in the close of this communication was obviously one calculated greatly to subserve the cause of the suppression of Infanticide among a people so perverted in their feelings and customs, even from those of instinctive humanity, as the Jáḍejás. It was nearly altogether overlooked by the party most deeply concerned in its execution. Captain Barnewall, indeed, seems never to have communicated at all with Government on Infanticide till the 16th July 1824, when he forwarded to it a letter containing some hopeful notices of slow progress, of which the following are the most important portions.

"Sir:—I request you will submit, for the information of the Honourable the Governor in Council, the annexed statement, showing the number of Jáḍejá females at present in existence in this peninsula. The last statement was forwarded in Major Ballantine's reports of 29th June 1817, and appears to have stated sixty-three as the whole number that could then be discovered to have been preserved during ten years.

"The contrast, with the return now transmitted, is so far favourable, as to exhibit, that during seven years, more than double this number of Jáḍejá females have been preserved; the number at present being 200, while 66 have died. Among this number, some are stated to have been destroyed; but the impossibility of establishing the fact, under a declaration to the contrary on the part of the parents, has rendered it impracticable to enforce any penalty against the parties.

"A constant intercourse with the Jáḍejás during my annual circuit, has given me opportunities of impressing on their minds the interest taken by the British Government in the suppression of the barbarous and unnatural practice, and the guilt attached to the commission of it by the dictates of their own religion. I receive continued assurances that they will discountenance it; but from this disproportionate number of females still existing, it is evident, that although this horrible practice may be somewhat subdued, it is still far from being relinquished.

"The mind and opinion of the tribe do not appear to have undergone that change on the subject that will alone overcome the existence of a custom so unnatural. The effects of the penalties enjoined by the engagements entered into by the Jáḍejás would operate in deterring the commission of the crime, if the means of detection existed, or its discovery was not opposed by difficulties that defeat the utmost vigilance. Proving it is almost impracticable, unless some part of the domestic establishment of a Jáḍejá betray him, a circumstance that seldom can be expected, as domestic servants are generally the old adherents and dependents of his family.

"The present chieftain of Nawánagar had a daughter born some months since; and as the head of the Jáḍejá tribes, it was particularly desirable he should have set an example, by preserving it, and showing by his doing so, his anxiety to support the existing engagements. I had been particular in every interview I had with this young chief, in engaging his influence and support with his tribe in discountenancing the practice; he promised me to discourage it in every way in his power; but no sooner was a daughter born to him, about ten months ago, than he determined upon its destruction. This information was acquired from a person in close intercourse with attendants on his family, an inhabitant of his town, but who would only communicate the information under a promise of his not being made the instrument of proving the offence; the circumstance was universally believed by others who resided in the principality, and the tribe in general; and from all the information I could procure, I have scarcely a doubt of the fact, though the chief, when called upon, openly denies it, avowing the child died a natural death, and challenging proof being adduced, well aware that none but his own immediate domestics can establish the charge, and that they durst not give any evidence but such as would acquit him of the crime.

"The fines levied for the commission of the offence might be expended partly or wholly in rewards to those actively engaged in enabling the British Government to give greater effect to the suppression of the crime; this appears the only temptation likely to induce an informer to come forward, that it would be politic or desirable to authorize, or that seems calculated to afford any increased facility in establishing the guilt of those perpetrating it."

Captain Barnewall, it will be observed, makes no reference here to the instructions which he had already received on some of the matters on which he addresses Government, while he actually recommends an adoption of one of the very measures which had been enjoined upon him by higher authority, as if it had occurred to himself in the first instance. This fact was noticed by Mr. Elphinstone at the Government Political Consultations held in Bombay on the 30th March 1825;* and a refresher of his memory was consequently sent to him, which led him to make the following explanations, on the 7th June.

"I have suffered no opportunity also to pass, when meeting the Jáḍejás, without representing to them the enormity of the offence of Infanticide, and pointing out how contrary it is to the precepts of their religion, and the dictates of nature. My former Report shows, that

* "Having been led to refer to Capt. Barnewall's report, of July 16th, 1824, on female infanticide in Káṭhiáwáḍ, I observe, that although he gives a satisfactory account of the increased number of female children preserved, and proposes a plan for further checking the crime of infanticide, he does not state the measures he had adopted in consequence of the directions contained in the annexed paragraph of my instructions to him of the 9th January 1821.

"I beg to recommend that his attention be drawn to the subject, and that he be requested to state, whether any fines have as yet been applied in the manner directed in paragraph 6. If they have not, the amount of all sums received since the date of that letter, and not appropriated to purposes connected with the grievance which led to their imposition, should now be formed into a fund, and distributed in the manner prescribed."—M. ELPHINSTONE.

much success has resulted from the arrangements of Colonel Walker; as the crime is now discovered by all, and the feelings of nature and humanity have obtained an ascendancy, which, it is to be anticipated, may be progressive in the minds of the Jáḍejás, and gradually lead to the entire abolition of this detestable practice.

"No fine has become hitherto available, because all that have been levied have been appropriated as compensation for the loss of property, or in payment of expenses incident on enforcing their recovery.

"The first that is likely to become available to the fund, is now in a course of recovery from the Gondal Rájá, for a breach of his engagements, amounting to Rs. 15,000; the proportion of this fine appertaining to the Gáikawáḍ, is rupees 8,086. 2. 42; the remainder, or rupees 6,913. 1. 56, the Company's share, will be credited to the infanticide fund, and appropriated hereafter under the sanction of Government.

"The occasions on which these fines have been imposed in the last four years, are exhibited in the annexed statement; most of them refer to the Khúmáṇ insurrection,* and the amount of them has been credited,

* [The reference is here to inroads made about 1820 by the division of the Káṭhís called Khúmán into the territories of their neighbours for the purpose of rapine and plunder. Various proprietors in the peninsula, including the Thákur of Bháwánagar, the chief of the Gohíl Rajputs, were fined for connivance at these depredations.

The divisions of the pure Káṭhís are three in number, the *Wálá*, the *Khu'mán*, and the *Khâchar*. In the first of these there are twenty tribes; in the second, ten; and in the third seven. The following lists of these tribes the author of this narrative a few years ago extracted from a Wanshâwalí of the principal Cháran at the town of Bábriá, three stages from Rájkot on the road to Goghá, I. Wálá, De'ruyá, Waikhá, Lálú, Karpaḍá, Kadaḍaḍ, Víkmá, Kágaḍá, Bhojak, Chák, Wajsí, Gowályá, Rájdaḍyá, Gigá, Wajmal, Phád, Jangiyá, Boghará, Kasturyá, (Kuḍar). II. Khúmán, Chándu, Chándsur, Mánganí, Man, Motiyár, Jhamar, Jogyá, Lunsar, (Waland). III. Kháchar, Dánḍ, Jhobalíyá, Hipá, Cháondiyá, Somasaryá, (Khara). Except the divisional names few of these can be of Scythian origin. A good many of them were probably brought by the Kaṭhís from Sindh, in which and the neighbouring wilds they were settled before they came into the peninsula of in part liquidation of the military expense incurred on that occasion; the fine of 4,000 rupees refers to a sum exacted as compensation for property plundered from a village subject to the Amrélí [Gáikawáḍ's] authority,

Gujarát, which now receives from them its designation. See above p. 55. Jhobalíyá is evidently a Sindhian corruption of the Arabic Jebálíyah, mountaineer.

The author of this narrative has collected many legendary and historical notices of the Káṭhís from the mouths of their bards; but he has found nothing so satisfactory respecting their history as the following statement of Major Jacob. "The exact period of the Kaṭhís settling themselves in this Peninsula is unknown, but it is believed to be towards the close of the fourteenth century. They came immediately from the North-Eastern quarter of Kachh, and appear to have been a nomade tribe, wandering with their herds wherever they could find pasture, and plundering by profession. Their first establishment in fixed villages is said to have taken place between two and three centuries ago, but even so late as the commencement of this century we find Colonel Walker speaking of them as addicted to all their former habits —the Jaitpur and Jasdhan families excepted, whose example he says 'may afford a hope that the rest of the Káṭhís may also be reclaimed.' Those who set this good example were formerly styled 'reformed Kaṭhís'—a term already become obsolete, but the establishment of the British supremacy has alone put to a stop to their predatory excursions, and many Káṭhís are yet living who have stuck their spears into the gates of Ahmadábád during such occasions. The lightness of the tribute paid by these tribes in proportion to their revenues, as compared with other communities, is owing to the greater developement of their resources, which habits of order have created, since these proportions were fixed by the Maráthá Mulukgírí commanders, and confirmed by Colonel Walker, in A.D. 1808. The Káṭhís owe their possessions chiefly to the general anarchy produced by the decline of the Mahomedan power—the Jhálá, Jádejá, and other tribes, purchasing immunity from their plunder by the cession of villages: Jaitpur, Bhílká, Menḍhará, etc. were thus given up by the Nawáb of Junágaḍ, less than a century ago, with reserved rights therein. The Káṭhís are evidently a northern race: their stature, features,—above all their blue and grey colored eyes, by no means unfrequent—give much of probability to the idea that they are of Scythian descent, with which their habits in some degree correspond. The Sun is their chief diety; its symbol is drawn on every deed at the head of the list of living witnesses, with the words *Shrí Surajni Shákh*. Their mixture with other tribes has inoculated them with respect for the Brahmanical deities, but the Sun is paramount."—Trans. of B. Geog. Soc. vol. vii. p. 20.]

and paid over to his Highness the Gáikawáḍ's ryots, as indemnification for their losses."

To Captain Barnewall's letter was appended a statement of the probable expence of the marriage of the 189 daughters of the Jáḍejás then existing, dividing them into four classes, and calculating the number of marriages likely to take place each year from the apparent age of the parties concerned. The total sum required amounted to no less an amount than rupees 355,590, which if actually paid would have turned the heads of all the Bráhmans, Bháṭas, Chárans, and other religious mendicants of the province. The fines levied for 1821-1824, which seem to have been principally inflicted for connivance at the depradations of the Khúmán Káṭhís amounted only to Rs. 40,233. 1. 33¼; and they had all been credited to the military expences incurred in the suppression of those depradations.

Still the Bombay Government did not abandon the idea of forming what has since been called "The Infanticide Fund," or what might more appropriately have been denominated "The Infanticide Prevention Fund." It extended its "great approbation" to the proceedings of Captain Barnewall as detailed by him in his second letter now quoted; directed that all fines under Rs. 20,000, which might not be given up to the sufferers on whom they might be levied, should be allotted to the Infanticide fund; and requested Mr. John Pollard Willoughby, of the Civil Service, Assistant in charge of the Residency in Baroda, to endeavour to prevail on the Gáikawáḍ Government to co-operate in the measures proposed, by devoting its portion of fines raised in Káṭhiáwáḍ to a similar purpose.

Mr. Willoughby, though then but a young member of the service, discharged the delicate and important duty imposed upon him with great tact and promptitude; and on the 18th of August, he thus reported his complete success.

"In conformity with the instructions of the Honourable the Governor in Council, I embraced a favourable opportunity afforded me in a late interview with his Highness the Gáikawáḍ and his minister, to explain to them the nature and object of the measures proposed; and it is with the highest gratification I am enabled to report, that I experienced but little difficulty in prevailing upon them to co-operate in the manner requested, to put an end to so barbarous and unnatural a practice.

"Having obtained this verbal acquiescence, I considered it expedient that the same should be recorded. With this view, I sent a written proposal to the Baroda darbár, copy and translation of whose reply is herewith transmitted.

"On reference to this, government will be gratified to observe, that the Gáikawáḍ's assent to adopt the same measures with respect to his tributaries as those already adopted by the British government, is given in the most liberal terms. It is moreover made retrospective of the period when Captain Barnewall received charge of Káṭhiáwáḍ; no limit in the amount of fines to be appropriated for the suppression of infanticide is specified; but an account of the manner in which they may be appropriated is requested may be rendered annually.

"The political agent in Káṭhiáwáḍ will be duly apprized of the acquiescence of this government having been obtained to the recommendation of the Honourable Board to co-operate in this benevolent design."

The written memorandum from the Gáikawáḍ Government here referred to was translated by Dr. R. H. Kennedy, and forwarded to Bombay by Mr. Willoughby. It bore that, "The case under consideration, is one of charity, and will procure the blessing of heaven on both governments; therefore whatever sums have been realized as fines on offenders since Captain Barnewall was placed in charge of the districts, or any extra revenue beyond the tribute as fixed for perpetuity by Colonel Walker, may be appropriated as above specified, the disposal being year by year duly communicated to us, and the arrangement is highly satisfactory to this government." The faithful co-operation of the Baroda government with the British authorities for the suppression of Infanticide, from first to last, has been very remarkable. It is the most pleasing fact connected with Maráthí history with which we are acquainted.

"The Infanticide Fund," which has had an important influence in the suppression of Infanticide, was now established by authority. Its public arrangement was that of Mr. Elphinstone. It is possible that a hint may have been first dropped on the subject in Council from another quarter, for in a minute in the consultations of 7th September 1825, he puts this question, "Is not the plan at present proposed, precisely that recommended by Mr. Warden in 1819?" It was one of the many excellencies of Mr. Elphinstone's Government, that it seldom allowed a good hint or advice from any source in any matter of importance to pass unimproved.

The judicious use of the Infanticide Fund, as has now been hinted, and will afterwards appear, has been one of the best auxiliary means for the suppression of Infanticide. From certain points of view, there appear to be some disadvantages connected with its administration exclusively in favour of the Jáḍejás. "It appears to me," says Major LeGrand Jacob in his letter on Infanticide addressed to Government on the 23rd October 1841, "that to devote for the use of one small section of the community the taxes levied on the whole, is erroneous in principle, more especially when we consider that it is the attainment of a public opinion, hostile to infanticide, that must form the surest guarantee against its recurrence at some future period, and which, if it now existed, would obviate the necessity of rigour. I would further observe, that the money now spent, though good in showing the favour of the British Government towards the party preserving life, has the evil effect of feeding the pride that was the cause of its destruction. It was once observed to me by a shrewd Jhálá, that the marriage expenses of his daughters were just as heavy on him as on the Jáḍejá, and that had his forefathers been murderers, he might also enjoy the aid of Government; an observation which, though rarely made amongst an ignorant community, proves that the grant of marriage gifts to one particular class must be considered merely suited to a savage state, calling for change whenever the people should advance a few steps towards civilization, and it ought doubtless to be the duty of an enlightened Government to hasten this change." Fully admitting the principles involved in Major Jacob's statement, we do not exactly see the partiality which he conceives to exist in the administration of the Fund so much in favour of the Jáḍejás in particular, as has been the case since its first formation. Infanticide was the greatest moral pestilence in the whole peninsula of Káṭhiáwáḍ; and any measure tending to its annihilation was for the benefit of the entire community of that peninsula. No Jhálá Rajput had any right to open his mouth against its appropriation to the Jáḍejás; as his own tribe, furnishing wives to the Jáḍejás without stipulating for the preservation of their offspring, was a guilty party in all the infantile murder which they committed. The time, it is to be hoped, is not far distant,—and proposals of Major Jacob which we shall afterwards have occasion to notice are greatly adapted to hasten it,—when neither Jáḍejá nor Jhálá will accept a gift, however small, for the simple discharge of the universal duties of humanity to children, in preserving their lives and aiding them in forming their family establishments. A transition state of society often requires appliances quite unsuited to the circumstances of a settled community.

But to proceed. The first presents from the Infanticide Fund, which were proposed by Captain Barnewall, were confirmed by the Bombay Government on the 24th April, 1826. They were four in number, and amounted altogether to Rs. 5,640. On the 23rd September of the same year, the political agent in Káṭhiáwáḍ was requested, if possible, to adopt another measure, also of a most beneficial tendency in the suppression of Infanticide, that of making arrangements according to the example of Major Pottinger the Resident in Kachh, for procuring a list of every child, male or female, born in a Jáḍejá family then living. In gratitude for the promptitude of Dádájí the late Thákur of Rájkoṭ in signing the engagement of Colonel Walker, his successor and son Surájí had, on the recommendation of the acting political agent Major G. J. Wilson and his assistant Mr. Langford of the Civil Service, received the *bhandárí*, or guarantee to a creditor, of the British Government, to enable him to raise a loan of Rs. 12,000 to relieve him of debts incurred in the marriage of his sister, whose life had been spared in consequence of that engagement. That chieftain got an advance of a similar sum from the Infanticide Fund to enable him to celebrate his own marriage. These were the first of a series of most commendable acts of paternal kindness, which the Bombay Government has not since failed to show to its proud but poverty-striken tributaries, the Jáḍejás of Káṭhiáwáḍ. The measures now referred to, though still inadequate to the destruction of the gigantic evil of Jáḍejá Infanticide, were not without their salutary effects.

The actual progress of the cause of the abolition of Infanticide in Káṭhiáwáḍ for the next few years, and up to 1828, is intimated in the following extract of a letter of D. A. Blane, Esq. then the acting political agent in the province.

"An infanticide fund has been formed according to the instructions of Government, and presents have been distributed to some of them who have preserved their female children. It was intended that each individual known to have a daughter living should receive some mark of the approbation of Government, and they were accordingly invited to Rájkoṭ for that purpose, by the late acting political agent. A few only attended, but all those who came received presents according to their rank. An account of this fund is herewith enclosed.

"A census of the Jáḍejá females in the Nawánagar táluká, which was made last year, enumerated 171 individuals, which is an increase of 95 on the number shown in the statement which accompanied Major Barnewall's report. Referring, however, to the ages specified in the census, it appears that the increase now exhibited must be partly owing to omissions in the former inquiry; but if there be any inaccuracy on this head, there is not, I imagine, the slightest doubt that the total is correct, and that there are at least that number of Jáḍejá females now alive in the Nawánagar districts.

"An equally favourable result will, I doubt not, be exhibited when a census shall have been made of the other tálukás.

"Without therefore over-estimating the success which we have hitherto obtained, much has unquestionably been effected towards terminating this horrid and unnatural practice.

"The chief motive with the Jáḍejás to the commission of Infanticide, is the pride which leads them to consider the other tribes of Rajputs unworthy of receiving their daughters in marriage; and as no Rajput can marry a female of his own tribe, they prefer putting them to death to the prospect of the dishonour which is likely to result from their living in a single state.

"Lákhá Fattanee, the most powerful sovereign of their race, who ruled over Kachh and Sindh is said to have sent two Bráhmans to find an appropriate match for his daughters, but they returned without being able to discover any one of equal rank, and as he was unwilling to marry them to any inferior, the Bráhmans recommended that they should not be allowed to live. They were accordingly put to death; and the example being thus sanctioned, the Jáḍejás have since destroyed their female children immediately at their birth.*

* [This story is evidently the same as that which we have quoted from Colonel Walker; see above, p. 66. The name Lákhá "Fattanee" of Mr. Blane, in which a misprint occurs, should be Lákhá Phulání. He is the person mentioned in the following extract from Dr. Burnes, who, when speaking of the indefinite traditions of the Jáḍejás, says, "They trace their descent from Sacko Goraro (*Lákhá*, or *Lákho* according to the Kachhí termination) a prince who reigned in Sindh a thousand years ago, four of whose sons Moor, Oner, Phool, and Manyabhaee (*Moḍ*, *Unaḍ*, *Phul*, and *Manyábhái*) emigrated into Cutch, on account of some family dissensions. The two last had no issue. The posterity of Moḍ ended in the third generation at Sacko Phoolanee (*Lákhá Phulání*), whose name is still known throughout this province. From Oner (*Unaḍ*) descended the present Jám of Nawánagar, and the Rajpoot Jharejahs of Cutch."—Burnes' Visit to the Court of Sinde, etc. 2 edit. p. 232.

The traditions referred to, it will be seen, when compared with Tod's Travels, p. 469-476,—a passage singularly absurd and unworthy of its author in many respects,—are not to be depended upon. We have already stated the definite results of our own researches on the early history of the Jáḍejás (see above, p. 56-57); and we expect the Ráo of Kachh to combine in some form, having at least the air of possibility, their earlier traditions.

—— Since the preceding note was written, we have received from Capt. Raikes, assistant political agent in Kachh, some valuable notes on the Jáḍejás, prepared principally from information communicated to him by His Highness the Ráo, from which we make the following extract.

" Towards the end of the 8th century, the reigning prince at Táṭhá was Lákhá Gorárá; he had eight sons by two wives; the eldest by one wife (by name Gur Rání) being Umar, by the other of the Cháwaḍá tribe, Moḍ. On the death of the reigning (prince, Umar succeeded to the gadí by virtue of his primogeniture. Shortly afterwards Moḍ, (Umar's half-brother), and another brother by name Maní conceived designs against the life of Umar, with the view of possessing themselves of the government of the country. Subsequent, however, to the perpetration of their bloody purpose, they found it necessary to retire into exile; and having relations in the western part of Kachh they determined on trying their fortunes there. The Sammás of Sindh and Cháwaḍás of Kachh were intimately connected by marriage; and the fortune-seekers had therefore, in addition to a limited number of followers, many friends and relations in Kachh. They would appear to have made speedy use of both. Moḍ, almost immediately after arrival,

"The expense of marrying their daughters might operate with the poorer Jáḍejás, but the preservation of a female was equally unknown in the most wealthy families.

"Amongst the other Rajputs, equality of rank and

slew Cháwaḍá Wágham, his maternal uncle, and assumed the sovereignty of the affairs of, at any rate, the western portion of Kachh. He subsequently bequeathed his newly acquired possessions to his son. There is nothing, however, sufficiently authentic known of the events of those times, beyond the names of the ruling princes, and some few others of the more important events of the period.

"To admit of the state of the province being illustrated, it will therefore be sufficient to record the names of the rulers for generations until indeed the death of Purájí, when the absence of legitimate male issue caused a break in the direct succession. The deceased prince left two younger brothers, their names were Le'thá and Dethá; and there are some of their discendants living to the present day. As, however, they were deemed incapable by those in authority of steering the frail bark through the sea of turmoil and treachery then existing, the widow of the deceased Jám, (such being the title under which the princes of Kachh reigned) sent to Sindh for the Son of Jáḍá by name Lákhá. He was by caste a Sammá, as had been all the previous Jáms from the time of Moḍ. Henceforward, however, the descendants of Lákhá, are called Jáḍejás or discendants of Jáḍá; although the caste of the tribe is Sammá. With Lákhá, also, came a younger brother, or half-brother by name Lákháḍá. Lákhá is supposed to have come to Kachh about A. D. 843." The son of this Lákhá (Lákhá Phulání) was the Red Ráydhan, who was the Jám of Kachh at Vinján, (according to the authorities on which we rely in p. 64) in A. D. 1464, or Samvat 1521 of the MSS. of the Jaina priests in Bombay.

The discrepancy between the Ráo's chronology and our own, here brought to notice, is great indeed; but we are able to solve it. The eighth century of the Ráo is the eighth century of the Hijira of Muhammad; and the "about A. D. 843" should be "about A. H. 843," the equivalent of which, Samvat 1521, is given as the year of the ascent of the gádí by Ráydhan, the son of Lákhá Phulání, = A. D. 1464-5. See above, p. 56.

It is probable that the title of *Jám* was given to the earlier Jáḍejás of Kachh only retrospectively, as till the conquest of the Sammás in Sindh in 1521, the real titular Jám would be in that country. The Jáḍejás, in claiming their designation from *Jáḍá*,—which is probable enough,—seem to be opposing their tradition, referred to by Fatteh Muhammad (see above, p. 76), that their denomination is from the *Yádavas* of the Mahábhárata.]

wealth is the chief consideration in contracting marriages; and the Jáḍejá females who have been preserved since the engagements entered into with Col. Walker, have been given in marriage according to this rule.

"As the example of the principal tálukdárs in sanctioning this practice may be expected to have great influence in diminishing crime, it is highly gratifying to observe that in each of the large tálukás either the chief himself or one of his nearest Bháíyáds have joined in establishing it by the preservation and marriage of their daughters.

"The principal Jáḍejá tálukás are Nawánagar, Gondál, Rájkoṭ, Murví, and Dharol. In Nawánagar the Jám's own brother has a daughter who is betrothed to the son of the Ráná of Porbandar, the head of the Jaitwá Rajputs. In Gondal the present chief's late brother, who preceded him on the Gadí, had a daughter, who is married to the son of the Rájá of Drángaḍrá, the head of the Jhálá Rajputs. In Rájkoṭ the late chief, father of the present Thákur, had a daughter, who is also married to the son of the Rájá of Drángadrá. In Murví the present chief has a daughter, who is married to the son of the Rájá of Wánkanír, a Jhálá Rajput. In Dharol several distant relations of the chief have married daughters, but none of his own family have yet concurred in setting an example to his subjects.

"When the prejudice with regard to marriage shall have been fully overcome, it may, I think, be anticipated that the Jáḍejás will adopt the same views respecting the expense of the celebration, etc. as the other tribes of Rajputs, with whom they have now become more intimately connected. In the census above noticed, 68 out of 171 appear to be married; of the remainder the greater part are of tender years, but a few have exceeded the age beyond which they should not remain single; and in such instances, if poverty be the cause, assistance, judiciously afforded, might have a beneficial effect."

Some of the facts mentioned by Mr. Blane were of an

encouraging character; and on his recommendation and that of his assistants, special presents were given to, and received with much gratification by, the Thákur of Murví, in consideration of the countenance which he himself had personally given to the cause of Infanticide abolition, and of the fact that his father Jehájí had been the first Jáḍejá to preserve a daughter under the benevolent arrangements of the British Government. These presents produced a good effect throughout the province, and led the recipient to declare that he would be more attentive than ever to the *dharm-nù kám,* the duty of charity, which the Government was so anxious for him to discharge.

CHAPTER VIII.

MR. WILLOUGHBY'S REPORT ON INFANTICIDE IN KÁṬHIÁWÁḌ — HIS PLANS FOR ITS EXTINCTION HIGHLY APPROVED OF BY THE BOMBAY GOVERNMENT—CONSEQUENT PROCLAMATION ADDRESSED TO THE JÁḌEJÁ'S.

FOUR distinct eras are apparent in the history of the suppression of Jáḍejá Infanticide. In the first, during the time of Duncan and Walker, we have that of zealous and anxious negociation for the accomplishment of this benevolent object. In the second, that of their immediate successors, we have an almost complete inactivity, arising principally from a false confidence, cherished more by the government in Bombay than the officials in the provinces, that the Jáḍejás, however reluctantly, would themselves ultimately seek to implement their engagements and recognize the voice of nature and humanity. In the third, extending from the government of the Hon. Mountstuart Elphinstone to that of Lord Clare, we have that of an awakened interest for the prevention of the crime by the inquiries of the local officials, the discountenance of offenders, and the appropriation of fines for the encouragement of the Jáḍejás preserving their children. In the fourth, commencing with the appointment of Mr. John Pollard Willoughby of the Civil Service to the Political Agency in Káṭhiáwáḍ in 1831, and continuing to the present time, we have that of decided, judicious, practical, and successful effort for the completion of the great and difficult work*

An earnest of Mr. Willoughby's zeal and ability in the good cause had been obtained in the tact and promptitude which he had shown in effecting the arrangement with the Gáikáwáḍ's government relative to the Infanticide Fund which we have lately noticed; and the suitableness of the measures which he devised and executed for accomplishing the object which the Government had so long at heart more than exceeded the expectations which that earnest encouraged. He had not been long in office, when he "called upon the chiefs in whose territory the revolting crime of infanticide prevailed to send in registers of the number of the female children that were then living, in order to afford data for ascertaining how far the humane efforts of Government to abolish the inhuman practice have been attended with success"† These returns, he proposed to submit to Government, with a scale of distribution of the balance of the Infanticide Fund, then available, among the Jáḍejás who had preserved their children, and whose poverty or other circumstances might recommend them to the pecuniary aid of Government. Some time occurred between the demand for these reports and their reception; but they were no sooner in Mr. Willoughby's hands then he gave them his best and most anxious consideration, with a full personal review of all the efforts which had previously been made to suppress infanticide, with the causes of their failure. The result of their

* A somewhat similar recognition of these eras, is made by an able and eloquent writer in the Calcutta Review (vol. i. p. 415). "The ten years subsequent to the supposed final settlement of Col. Walker, may be regarded as the period of *delusive slumber*. The next eighteen or twenty years may be viewed as the period of *partial reviviscence* and *mingled despondency*. We now come to the third period, commencing about the year 1834, which may be reckoned that of *wide-spread energetic action*."

† Letter of Mr. Willoughby addressed to Mr. Williams, political commissioner in Gujarát, dated 24th April, 1833.

perusal and digestion, in the light of past experience, was the preparation of a communication to Government, the most valuable in point of practical wisdom and decision which the great problem of political humanity in the West of India had yet called forth, and which has really formed the basis of the measures which, there is reason to believe, have after so many years of anxious effort been ultimately crowned with absolute success.

The document now referred to is dated the 26th November, 1834. It is divided into three sections,—containing a detail of the measures previously adopted for the suppression of infanticide; an analysis and review of the census which Mr. Willoughby obtained; and the "observations and suggestions upon the proceedings which appeared to be called for and expedient with the view of ensuring a more rigid enforcement of Colonel Walker's arrangements for the suppression of the crime, and for evincing the deep and lively interest which the British Government must ever feel in securing that systematic infanticide, the grossest stain that ever disgraced humanity, shall be entirely suppressed." In justice to Mr. Willoughby and the cause which he had so warmly at heart, as well as to our own narrative, we shall insert its larger portion.* To parties practically engaged in the suppression of infanticide in other districts of India, it cannot fail to be specially valuable. To them the clearness and minuteness of its details must enhance its value.

Our first extracts refer to the *Census* which Mr. Willoughby transmitted to Government.

"I now proceed to the second head of my letter, or to analyze and remark upon the Census, herewith transmitted, of the number of Jáḍejá Females, who are either now alive, or who have died a natural death. These are drawn out in a new and I think improved form, a

* The first section of Mr. Willoughby's report is unnecessary for the reader of the preceding narrative.

separate return having been obtained from each Jáḍejá District. In order, moreover, to afford data, whereon to found a judgment how far the engagements are maintained by comparison of the number of Jáḍejás of both sexes, a return of Male Jáḍejás, of and under the age of twenty, has been included in a separate column. In the course of my investigation various improvements in this return have suggested themselves, and some measures appear called for to ensure as much as possible the accuracy of future returns; but these will be more appropriately noticed under the third head of my report. In regard to the accuracy of the present census, I am unable to assert that such has been completely attained.* I have reason to hope, however, that its general accuracy may be depended upon, though it is very likely errors may exist, and more especially in regard to the ages assigned, on which point the ideas of the natives of India are extremely loose and unsatisfactory. The returns were procured by circulars (in some cases several times repeated) issued to the chiefs themselves; but in several instances I subsequently tested their accuracy and fidelity by sending persons privately to ascertain from personal observation whether they truly represented the number of Males and Females of the Jáḍejá tribe now alive. And I am gratified to report that in no case was any discrepancy detected, except in regard to the age and names of some of the parties, and in one or two instances the number of males being under-rated. The returns are twenty-eight in number and the following is an abstract of the results they exhibit:—

* [It may be observed, once for all, that the first censuses of the Jáḍejás were not only imperfect but in some respects erroneous.]

Number.	Districts.	MALES of and under age 20.	FEMALES.					Excess of Males.	Excess of Females.	Remarks.
			Married.	*Bethrothed.*	*Unbetrothed.*	*Deceased.*	*Total.*			
1	Nawánagar	613	86	77	178	39	380	233	...	This return has been partially tested and found correct.
2	Dharol-Dhorájí. ...	208	11	...	73	9	93	115	...	This return has been tested and found generally correct: additions and alterations are inserted in a supplementary return.
3	Gondal	86	18	6	20	1	45	41	...	
4	Murví..................	61	3	3	1	7	14	47	...	An investigation was instituted by the agent, which proved this return to be correct.
5	Rájkoṭ	15	2	...	1	5	8	7	...	Do.
6	Drápha	67	1	...	9	4	14	53	...	
7	Vírpar Khadeḍrí...	52	2	4	4	...	10	42	...	Do.
8	Murílá-Dérí.........	63	...	1	13	3	17	46	...	
9	Sisang Chánḍalí. ..	37	3	...	10	2	15	22	...	
10	Satodar Wáwaḍí ...	38	6	5	13	8	32	6	...	Do.
11	Koṭra Níájí	24	...	1	1	...	2	22	...	A mehtá of the agent ascertained this return was correct
12	Khírsará	12	3	2	11	1	17	...	5	Do.
13	Rajpurá	30	...	...	2	3	5	25	...	Do.
14	Jhália	28	5	1	5	2	13	15	...	Do.
15	Mália	16	...	2	2	1	5	11	...	
16	Loḍaká	9	...	...	2	...	2	7	...	
17	Menganí.............	6	...	1	5	...	6	...	...	A mehtá was sent to this Táluká and ascertained the return was correct.
18	Pál	5	...	...	1	2	3	2	...	Do.
19	Bhaḍawá	18	...	1	1	1	3	15	...	Do.
20	Virawá	2	...	...	...	...	...	2	...	Do.
21	Kotharia	3	...	...	1	1	2	2	...	Do.
22	Sháhpur..............	3	...	...	...	...	...	3	...	
23	Waḍalí	8	...	...	1	...	1	7	...	
24	Kotaḍa-Sánganí ...	3	...	...	1	1	2	1	...	
25	Káksíálí..............	4	...	1	1	...	2	2	...	
26	Mhawá	2	...	...	1	...	1	1	...	Do.
27	Gauridhar	5	...	...	...	2	2	3	...	
28	Gatká	4	...	...	1	1	2	2	...	
		1422	140	105	358	93	696	731	5	

"The present Census therefore exhibits the undermentioned results:—

1. Number of Males of and under the age of twenty is.............................. 1,422
2. Number of Females of all ages known to have been preserved is 696

Excess of Males therefore is 731

"Of the Females 140 are married, 105 betrothed, and 93 are stated to have died a natural death. In regard to this return, however, it is requisite to observe that an omission has occurred in not ascertaining the number of male Jáḍejás who have died. An allowance on this account is therefore necessary, otherwise the inference drawn from the comparative returns of each sex will be more favourable than correct. To rectify this omission, it will be sufficient to presume that a proportionate number of casualities have taken place among the males, as in the other sex, and in this case the number of deaths which may probably have occurred among the male Jáḍejás born during the last twenty years, will be as follows:—

696—93=603: 93: : 1422 gives $219\frac{1}{4}$.

"The above results, while they afford a most cheering prospect of ultimate success, if proper care and precautions are taken to ensure that the Jáḍejás adhere to their engagements, still at the same time establish beyond doubt the melancholy fact that the dreadful crime of Infanticide has never been completely subdued. The number of females alive in 1824, according to Major Barnewall's return, was only 219. The number now alive is 603; but notwithstanding this great and gratifying increase during the last ten years, the continuance of the unnatural crime is established by the disparity which is still apparent between the number of males and females.

"I am, however, able to place the *progressive* increase of the number of females rescued from destruction in a more striking and satisfactory point of view, by the following further analysis of the census herewith transmitted, since it shows that there are

Males.	*Females.*	*Males.*	*Females.*
67 of the age of 20	13 of the age of 20	41 of the age of 9	30 of the age of 9
20 ......do. 19	4 ......do......... 19	96 ......do. 8	38 ......do. 8
26 ......do. 18	11 ......do......... 18	76 ......do. 7	43 ......do. 7
24 ......do. 17	9 ......do......... 17	93 ......do. 6	36 ......do. 6
41 ......do. 16	29 ......do......... 16	89 ......do. 5	53 ......do. 5
59 ......do. 15	27 ......do......... 15	118 ......do. 4	40 ......do. 4
42 ......do. 14	15 ......do......... 14	108 ......do. 3	35 ......do. 3
48 ......do. 13	21 ......do......... 13	103 ......do. 2	46 ......do. 2
83 ......do. 12	26 ......do......... 12	130 ......do. 1	44 ......do. 1
32 ......do. 11	13 ......do......... 11	19 age not specified.	7 age not specified.
125......do. 10	33 ......do. 10		

"The total number of females now alive is 603, whereas the number shewn in the above Total is only 571. The difference consists of Females above the age of twenty not included in the second analysis. It follows, therefore, that of the females now alive, 68 were born during the first five years comprehended in the Table, 102 during the second, 176 during the third, and 225 during the last five years of the period.

"It will be observed that the return shews that 93 deaths occurred among the number of Females preserved. An analysis of this column will also exhibit results far from unsatisfactory, and in many cases the diseases of which they died are specified and will be found to be of that description to which infancy is peculiarly liable, such as small pox, measles, convulsion, and fever.

Among the casualties		*occurred at the age of [years]*	
	1		25
do.	2	do.	24
do.	3	do.	20
do.	1	do.	17
do.	0	do.	16
do.	1	do.	15
do.	1	do.	14
do.	1	do.	12
do.	1	do.	11
do.	4	do.	10
do.	3	do.	9
do.	5	do.	7

Among the casualties		*occurred at the age of [years]*	
	1		6
do.	6	do.	5
do.	1	do.	4
do.	5	do.	3
do.	7	do.	2
do.	1	do. months	18
do.	3	do ,,	12
do.	1	do ,,	9
do.	1	do ,,	8
do.	8	do. and under	3
do.	1	still born.	
do.	35	age not specified.	

"The above Total, therefore, proves that Colonel Walker's settlements were at all events adhered to in 57 cases of the number of casualties; and the only doubt which exists applies to the remainders where the age at which the casualty occurred is not inserted, an omission which I hope may be attributed to the carelessness of some of the parties by whom the returns were furnished.

"There is still another point of view in which the present census is to be regarded with the highest satisfaction. The Government of 1817 justly remarked that the countenance of Infanticide in Káṭhiáwáḍ was placed beyond doubt by the simple fact that no instance had occurred of a Jáḍejá having saved more than one daughter: the present return shows:—

2	instances of a Jáḍejá's	having	4	daughters alive.
13	do. of Jáḍejá's	having	3	do.
80	do. of do.	having	2	do.

"The only other point to be noticed as matter for congratulation is that almost in every Jáḍejá Táluká either the chief himself or one or more of his relations have set the example of preserving their daughters; some of whom are alive and have intermarried into the families of the other Rajput tribes of this province. The moral effect likely to result from this happy circumstance can scarcely be estimated, and cannot fail to promote in the highest degree the success of our exertions towards the full and complete extinction of the crime.

"Taking in detail, the petty Táluká of Khírsará, situated only a few miles from Rájkoṭ, stands pre-eminent. Here the dreadful crime must have been completely subdued, there being actually an excess of females, over the males. In the petty Táluká of Menganí the number of each sex is exactly equal, and in that of Satodar Wáwaḍí there are 38 males and 32 females, of whom 24 are alive. These results were so gratifying that I sent persons into these districts, who ascertained that they were quite correct, except in the case of Satodar Wáwáḍí, where 6 males and 2 females had been born subsequent to the furnishing of the return. The requisite alteration has therefore been made in the original registers.

"In all the other Districts the number of males greatly preponderates over the number of females, and in those noted below, the excess is so great as of necessity to lead to the conclusion that the shocking practice still prevails in them to a considerable extent.

Drápha—*Males alive*	67	*Females alive*	10	*Excess of Males*	57
Murví ,,	61	do. ,,	7	do. ,,	54
Virpar-Kaḍeḍí ,,	53	do. ,,	10	do. ,,	42
Mulilá-Derí ,,	63	do. ,,	14	do. ,,	49
Sesáng-Chándalí ,,	37	do. ,,	13	do. ,,	24
Koṭaḍá-Niyájí ,,	24	do. ,,	2	do. ,,	22
Jhália ,,	28	do. ,,	11	do. ,,	17
Rájpurá ,,	30	do. ,,	2	do. ,,	28
Waḍálí ,,	8	do. ,,	1	do. ,,	7
Rájkoṭ ,,	15	do. ,,	3	do. ,,	12

"It is mortifying to observe that the Táluká of Murví, from its position in the above tables has not benefited by the example set by its chief twenty-five years ago, who was the first to renounce Infanticide. The return of the districts of Rájkoṭ, the head-quarters of this Agency, and therefore more immediately under the surveillance of the agent, is far from satisfactory. Whether this arises from accidental causes cannot be ascertained; but the fact that in fifteen years the number of females alive has only been increased by one is calculated to give rise to great suspicion that Colonel Walker's measures for the suppression of the crime have not been observed in this district. It is due, however, to the chief himself to state that he preserved two daughters, although both died between the age of 8 and 9 months. When one of his daughters, moreover, was dangerously ill with fever he evinced a desire to avoid the imputation of not having acted up to his engagement, by apprizing me of her illness, and requesting that the medical officer attached to the agency would attend her. When this application was made, the infant was past recovery, but notwithstanding this, I think that the chief's sending a message to me at all, shewed a disposition on his part to wish it to be understood that he was anxious to preserve his daughters."

Whatever may have been the accuracy of these returns, furnished, it will have been observed, in the first instance by the Jáḍejás themselves, it must be admitted that Mr. Willoughby here turns them to the best account.

Our next series of quotations from Mr. Willoughby's report embraces the *measures* which he proposed for the extinction of Infanticide in Káṭhiáwáḍ.

"I now come to the third and last head of my letter, or to suggest measures which seem to me calculated to secure for the future the entire extinction of Infanticide, and to impress upon the Jáḍejás in particular, and the community in general, the lively interest felt by the

British Government and its fixed determination to accomplish this humane object.

"In the first place, I would suggest that immediate measures be taken to obtain a full and complete Census of the Jáḍejá population of this province. The great importance of possessing information of this kind never appears to have attracted attention; but without it no data can exist for computing according to the generally received rules of population, the number of Jáḍejá females which are born, and thence deducing, with reference to the number actually preserved, how far existing engagements are observed by the tribe. I have myself much felt the want of this information, since the only estimate I can find on my records respecting the extent of Jáḍejá population is contained in the 108th paragraph of Colonel Walker's report of March 1808, where on the information of an intelligent native, it is computed that there are 5,390 families in Haláḍ and Machu-Kántá, divided into twenty-two separate branches; and Major Carnac in his letter of the 16th of September estimates the number of families at 5,000. If these computations in any way approximate the truth, it is quite obvious that the present census of females proves that the crime of Infanticide must still prevail to a large extent. I have also experienced considerable difficulty in estimating the number of victims annually sacrificed previous to Colonel Walker's arrangements, when the murderous custom was observed by the tribe generally. In the 109th paragraph of the report of March 1808, the annual Infanticides in Gujarát are estimated to have been 5,000, and those in Kachh at 30,000, but in the 13th paragraph they are according to another estimate stated to amount in the one case to between 1,000 and 1,100 and in the other to 2,000. Colonel Walker admits that those calculations were founded on hearsay evidence, but states it to be his opinion that whilst he deemed the first exaggerated, he considered the last underrated. For the credit of humanity, however, I am inclined to hope that even the lowest estimate was beyond the number of victims who annually perished; and in support of this belief I beg to refer to a letter to Col. Walker from Sundarjí, dated the 23rd of August 1805, in which the number of births among the Jáḍejás is stated to be between 5 and 600, annually. The writer does not even state whether the estimate includes both sexes; but from his reply Colonel Walker evidently understood that it only referred to females, and this was most probably intended.*

"I think, however, it will be satisfactory not only to Government but also to the Home Authorities, to set this question at rest, and therefore suggest that a general Census of the tribe be now made, which will also be attended with the beneficial effect of making every individual Jáḍejá acquainted with the feelings of the British Government on the subject of Infanticide. I do not anticipate that it will be necessary to incur any considerable expense in carrying this design into execution. All that I ask at present, is for permission to entertain a *Kárkun* (clerk) to be expressly employed on this duty; and an English writer will ultimately be required to render the Returns from the different districts into English. The Kárkun would be directed to visit every district, and annex to his letter the form of the return in which the census should be embodied, specifying the number of females in each district, and the names, ages, profession and occupation of each member of the Jáḍejá tribe, and dividing the married from the unmarried members. The chiefs of each district will be required to afford every aid in their power in framing these tables; and one great advantage which may very possibly ensue from a Kárkun being so employed, is perhaps the discovery of some case of Infanticide for in-

* [This estimate of Sundarjí Shivají to which Mr. Willoughby refers, if applied to the females of both Káṭhiáwáḍ and Kachh, was tolerably correct. See above, p. 72.]

vestigation; and it is scarcely necessary to observe that one instance of detection followed by severe punishment, would contribute more to the extinction of the crime than any other measure that can be resorted to.* The expense of this arrangement will be as follows, and the amount of it, if thought proper, might be defrayed from the Infanticide Fund.

One Kárkun Rs. 50, and 10 Rs. bháttá, when actually absent from Rájkoṭ.

One peon, Rs. 6.

Stationery, etc. 4.

Total Rupees 60 per mensem, or Rs. 730 per annum.

"In the second place, I would propose that every Jáḍejá chief should be required to furnish a half yearly Register of all marriages, betrothals, births, and deaths occurring among his tribe residing in his district, and that if he omits to do so, or furnishes a false return, that he should be severely fined. These registers should be considered due on the 1st of January, and the 1st of June in each year, though for some time to come complete regularity cannot be expected, and want of it should be treated with some degree of indulgence. The Kárkun employed in taking the general Census will be very useful in ensuring uniformity and regularity in framing those returns; but the great advantage of requiring them will be the constant reminiscence they will give to the Jáḍejás of their engagements, and of the resolution of the British Government to compel adherence to them.

"In the third place, the Political Agent in this province should be directed to consider it to be his imperative duty (and I am sure he will at the same time regard it as the most gratifying he could be called upon to perform) to furnish an annual Report on the last day of each year, on the subject of Infanticide, accompanying the same with a Register of all marriages, betrothals,

* [The correctness of this observation will soon be abundantly apparent.]

births and deaths, that have occurred among the tribe within the year of report. This is no new suggestion on my part, for in the correspondence on my records I find allusion made to instructions issued many years ago by the Honourable Court of Directors, that in addition to such intermediate Reports as might become necessary, one general statement should be submitted at the end of each year, shewing how far the amended system had been acted on and observed, what deviations are known or suspected to have been made from its rules, and what measure pursued for their enforcement, with an estimate of the number of lives saved. These orders from some cause appear to have been overlooked or lost sight of, but as was justly remarked by the Government of 1816, a report of the nature adverted to, would convince the Jáḍejá chiefs of the continued anxiety on the part of the British Government to enforce their engagements, and would lead to a spirit of enquiry conducive to the fulfilment of them. Under the arrangement, my next report on this subject should be considered due on the 1st of January 1836.

"In the fourth place, I beg to suggest the promulgation of a proclamation by Government throughout Káṭhiáwáḍ requiring the Jáḍejá Chiefs to enforce the observance of the infanticide engagements within their respective jurisdiction, announcing the determined resolution of Government to suppress the crime, and noticing, either in terms of approbation, or of condemnation, those chiefs who by the present census are proved to have either adhered to, or departed from their engagements. I take the liberty of submitting for approval a draft of the kind of Proclamation I think might with advantage be issued, to which I would annex a copy of the renewed engagements entered into in 1812 by the Jám of Nawánagar for the abolition of the crime of Infanticide. If this measure be approved of, I beg further to suggest that seven hundred copies of the proclamation should be lithographed in Gujarátí at the presidency and be forwarded to me for distribution throughout the province.

"There is only one part of the proclamation which seems to me to require particular notice, viz. the promise it contains that rewards shall be granted to persons who may afford information leading to the detection and conviction of any one who may commit Infanticide. I find that almost all my predecessors have suggested this measure, but that the suggestion has never been acted upon. Major Carnac, in particular, pressed it upon the attention of Government, and proposed the following scale of rewards to informers and of fines to be imposed in case of conviction.

	Rewards.			*Fines.*	
1st.	An informer against the Jám Rupees	1,000	1st.	The Jám ......if convicted Rs.	30,000
2nd.	An informer against an inferior Rájá	500	2d.	An inferior Rájá ...... „ ... „	10,000
3rd.	An informer against a near relation	250	3d.	Their near relations... „ ... „	2,500
4th.	An informer against a poor Jáḍejá	100	4th.	A poor Jáḍejá, „ as much as his means allowed without absolute ruin.	

"In my draft of a proclamation, I have adopted no scale, but merely intimate generally that informers will be recompensed in proportion to the rank of the person convicted, and with the view of deterring persons from bringing forward false accusations that such recompense will only be given in cases of conviction.

"I am strongly of opinion that in such a sacred cause as that of the extinction of infanticide every practicable measure should be adopted calculated to ensure success, and rewards to informers appears to be one of them. It is quite true that information so obtained would be liable to suspicion, because it would most probably originate either in enmity or avarice. This to me, however, is not a sufficient reason why testimony so encouraged should be wholly rejected, although it is obvious that great caution and discretion will be required in making use of it. Under the system recently introduced into this province for the trial of offenders, the chances of any evils resulting from the adoption of such a measure will be greatly diminished, for I would propose that all persons accused of the commission of Infanticide should be tried by the High Court of Criminal Justice for Káṭhiáwáḍ,* except perhaps where the rank of the offenders is such as to render it expedient that he should be dealt with according to the special instructions of Government. The Political Agent stationed in the province, will institute the preliminary inquiries, and commit for trial, and the ultimate publicity of the proceedings would under all circumstances, whether of acquittal, or conviction, produce a most salutary effect throughout the country. The community in general certainly regard infanticide as a crime of the deepest dye; but the experience of twenty-five years has amply proved that if not stimulated in some mode to exertion, no one is likely to incur the obloquy, reproach, and enmity usually encountered by informers and accusers. Unless, therefore, this feeling can be overcome we can never hope to see conviction follow one of a thousand instances of the perpetration of the crime. How is the fact to transpire except upon the information of some one present when the infant was born, or even of some one engaged in the nefarious proceedings. From the

* [This Court, from 1831 of the Political Commissioner for Gujárat, but since 1835 of the Political Agent for Káṭhiáwáḍ, was formed for the purpose of trying such criminal cases as the separate jurisdictions might find it difficult to treat. It is composed of the Political Agent, its president, the Jám of Nawánagar, the Nawáb of Junágaḍ, the Thákur of Bháwanagar, the Ráná of Porbandar, when they choose to attend it, (or their deputies) and such other Tálukdárs, or their agents, as may be specially summoned by the Political Agent to act as assessors, with a substantive voice both as jurors and judges, the Agent having the casting voice. Its sentences are reviewed by Government. It is the first step, we hope, to the amalgamation of the multifarious Káṭhiáwáḍ jurisdictions, which the chiefs should ere long allow to share the fate of the Scotch feudal jurisdictions. It is a remarkable fact that notwithstanding the profuse shedding of innocent blood in Káṭhiáwáḍ by infanticide, it has never yet been induced capitally to convict for murder, however atrocious!]

secrecy with which the crime is perpetrated, and the consequent difficulty of discovery, the penal part of Colonel Walker's settlement has remained entirely a dead letter, and will ever continue so, unless persons can be induced to denounce those who commit the crime. I, therefore, think Government should recognize the principle I am advocating, being of opinion that in the attainment of an object of such magnitude we should not be particular in our inquiries respecting the motives of the agent through whose information a case of Infanticide is clearly established against any one. On the receipt of the lithographed proclamation, a copy should be sent to each Tributary, with an admonitory letter, to aid either directly or indirectly in putting down a practice of such great enormity.

"There is also another part of the proclamation which requires briefly to be alluded to. In noticing those districts where from the great disproportion of the sexes it is manifest that the crime still prevails, I have intimated in general terms, that should this great disparity continue to be shewn in future returns, the British Government will feel bound to take into consideration whether any relations can be maintained with those who prove themselves so utterly regardless of the duties of mankind. I have endeavoured to word this part of the proclamation in such a manner as not to alarm the chiefs of Káṭhiáwáḍ generally respecting their estates, but at the same time to convey an intimation to the Jáḍejá chiefs that the compact between them and Government is composed of mutual obligations; and that if they do not perform their part of the same it is thereby rendered null and void. No one can be a stronger advocate than I am, that existing relations with the chiefs should be maintained, that we should be content with the tribute paid to former Governments, and allow them to enjoy their hereditary estates and privileges without molestation. Should however it be established by the certain though presumptive evidence to be obtained from returns of the nature now transmitted, that the crime of Infanticide still prevails in any particular district, I think, after the warning contained in the proposed Proclamation, the chief of that district should be severely fined, and that if this does not produce attention on his part to his engagement to suppress the crime, I think that an example should be made, and that he should be deprived of the sovereignty of his district. The case must be very glaring where I should propose such an extreme measure for adoption, and should only be resorted to when all other efforts directed to the accomplishment of the object in view, have been tried and failed.

"In the fifth place, I would propose that every Rajput in Káṭhiáwáḍ should, in a circular letter from the Agent, be himself enjoined, and be requested to enjoin, all Rajputs subject to his authority to make it a stipulation in every marriage contract of the daughters with a Jáḍejá that the issue of the union shall be preserved. In the 58th paragraph of his report of March 1808, Colonel Walker alludes to the apathy and indifference with which the abominable practice has always been regarded by the rest of the Rajput community, although, as that able and enlightened man remarked, the other Rajput tribes 'possessed a simple and effectual remedy by refusing to alliance their daughters to the Jáḍejás, unless on the condition of rearing their daughters.' They in fact countenanced it by such alliance by permitting their own offspring, and are stated to have viewed the practice with less abhorrence from the increasing facility it afforded of marrying their own daughters, that first of duties of the Hindu parent. My present suggestion is therefore founded on the above remark. I do not think the circular would be generally attended to; but if ten, nay even if one victim were saved, the object in view would not be entirely lost. At all events the issue of such a circular would afford another striking proof of the intense anxiety felt by Government completely to suppress Infanticide, and this alone in my opinion renders it expedient.

"In the sixth place, I beg to recommend that the following marks of approbation be extended to the chiefs and inferior members of the Jáḍejá tribe who have adhered to engagements to preserve their female issue, and that the expense incurred in making the same should be debited to the Infanticide Fund.

1st.	To the Chief of Khírsará, a remission from the amount of the annual tribute of 10 annas, or Rupees	1,000	0	0
2nd.	To ditto a present of cloths of the value of Rupees	100	0	0
3rd.	To the Chief of Ménganí, a remission from his annual tribute of 4 annas, or Rupees	921	0	0
4th.	To the Chiefs of Satodar Wáwaḍí do. do.	395	12	0
5th.	To the two Jáḍejás, who have preserved four daughters, a present to each of cloths, or in money of Rupees	300	0	0
6th.	To those who have preserved three daughters, a present of ditto, or in ditto of Rupees	150	0	0
7th.	To those who have preserved two daughters, a present varying according to the circumstances of each, from Rupees 25 to Rupees	50	0	0

"It is, I consider, a fortunate circumstance that the chiefs of Khírsará and Menganí petitioned for remission from their tribute for the past year on account of the failure of the monsoon, but which after enquiry into their resources I declined to grant. There will therefore be no mistaking the real cause why such an indulgence is now extended to them. I should not, however, conceive it desirable that the whole of the above remissions should be paid direct to the chiefs. They are undoubtedly entitled to the greater share, but the inferior Jáḍejás living under their authority who have preserved a daughter are entitled to a part. I shall, therefore, require from the chiefs a statement of the amount of Revenue paid last year to them by each of the inferior Jáḍejás, and pay to the latter a corresponding portion of the remissions, should Government be pleased to sanction them.

"In the original draft of this report, I had suggested that a present should be made to the Jám of Nawánagar on this occasion. The return from his districts shews 613 Males and 380 Females, which proves that Colonel Walker's arrangements have taken root in them to a very considerable and gratifying extent. On this account, and because I conceived it would be politic to conciliate this Chief as the acknowledged head of the Jáḍejá tribe in Káṭhiáwáḍ, and to induce him cheerfully to co-operate in carrying into effect the humane efforts of Government, I thought that such a distinctive mark of approbation might conduce to success. The Jám, however, has not himself preserved a daughter, and during Major Barnewall's agency he was strongly suspected (although he denied the charge) of having committed Infanticide. It has moreover been suggested to me by my Assistant Captain Lang (whose interest in the success of the measures for the suppression of the crime is as great as Government could desire), that such a present might induce the Jám and the other Jáḍejá Chiefs of rank to believe that the crime of Infanticide, as far as they were [in the past] concerned, would not be very narrowly enquired into, provided they could show that a considerable number of females are preserved within their respective districts. I think that considerable weight attaches to this remark, and shall merely at present suggest that when the Proclamation is transmitted to the Jám, the satisfaction of Government be conveyed to him at the progress made in his districts in suppressing Infanticide, accompanied by urgent exhortations that he will adopt the strictest measures to ensure its complete extinction.

"Such are the measures which after a long and deep meditation on the subject, I presume to propose for the consideration of Government; and I beg to state that they are considered by natives of the province competent to form a correct judgment, calculated to give increased efficiency to the measures adopted by Colonel Walker for the suppression of this terrible crime. It is scarcely necessary, I hope, to state that I feel, as every man, and more particularly every Christian should, most deeply interested in its complete abolition, or that I shall strenuously exert myself to ensure success to whatever subsidiary measure may be directed to compel obedience on the part of the Jáḍejás to their engagements. Both Captain Lang and myself embrace every opportunity of speaking upon the subject, with the detestation it merits, and of stimulating the tribe among which the custom prevailed to abandon it, and thereby restore themselves to that scale among human beings which they forfeited from its prevalence among them. By unceasing endeavours to expose the enormity of the offence, and to shew that it is at direct variance with the precepts inculcated by the religion of those who perpetrate it; by extending favor to those who renounce the practice; by promulgating the fixed resolution of Government to punish with the utmost severity those who still adhere to it; and from the success, partial as I fear it must be regarded, which has attended our efforts for its discontinuance, I am sanguine that through the divine blessing complete success may be ultimately obtained."

With regard to *Infanticide in Kachh*, Mr. Willoughby writes as follows.

"A report on the subject of Infanticide in Káṭhiáwáḍ would be incomplete without a brief allusion to the prevalence of the same crime in the adjacent province, Kachh. It must be quite obvious that if the crime is not suppressed in Kachh, the effect will be most inimical to its suppression in Káṭhiáwáḍ, since the members of the tribe residing in each province are intimately connected with each other. It was doubtless under this impression that Colonel Walker entered into a correspondence which does him the highest honor with Futteh Muhammad Jamádár, the regent of Kachh in 1807-8, with the view of enlisting him in the cause of humanity. I have of course no means of ascertaining how far the crime has been subdued in Kachh; but from our intimate connection and powerful influence with that Government since 1819, it is by no means improbable that greater progress has been made in that province than in this, and that if I were informed of the measures that may have been adopted there, some of them may be found to apply equally to the circumstances of Káṭhiáwáḍ. The care and pains also which are reported to have been bestowed upon the education of the young prince recently elevated to the supreme authority in Kachh, cannot fail to facilitate the object in view, for I am convinced that when the chiefs of the tribe can be prevailed upon practically to renounce the custom, but little difficulty will then be experienced in inducing the inferior Jáḍejás to follow the example."

In concluding his admirable paper, Mr. Willoughby gives the following information respecting the *Infanticide* Fund.

"In conclusion I annex to my report a statement of the Infanticide Fund on the 15th of September 1834.

The Balance due to Fund on the 26th April 1833, the date of the late account was Rupees				51,146	1	8
Intermediate receipts have been Rupees	31,781	3	6			
Do. Disbursements, do. do	1,000	0	0			
Surplus receipts are therefore, Rupees				30,781	3	6
Balance due to the Fund on the 15th September 1834, is Rupees				81,927	5	2

"In the 4th paragraph of my letter of the 24th April 1833, I expressed an intention to propose a scale of distribution of the Fund among those who had preserved their daughters, or whose poverty and other circumstances might render them deserving of favor or pecuniary aid from Government. The results of the present census, however, induce me to abandon this intention, because they lead me to anticipate many applications for assistance towards defraying the expense of marriages for which we should be prepared . It is a creditable feeling among the Jáḍejás and one which should be kept alive as much as possible, that it is not laudable to apply to Government for pecuniary assistance, and during 1833-34 only three applications were received. In two of these cases a donation of 400 Rupees was granted, and in the third, Rupees 200. I have no doubt that these grants will encourage other applicants to come forward, and as of the number of Female Jáḍejás now alive as many as 463 are unmarried, I do not think the Fund should be trenched upon at present, to a greater extent than is necessary to carry into effect the recommendations made in the 22nd paragraph of my report.

"To avoid delay, I have taken the liberty of forwarding this communication direct to Government, but as soon as copies can be prepared they will be forwarded for the information of the Political Commissioner for Gujarát.—Rájkoṭ, 24th September, 1834."

The plans propounded in this most important document, it will have been observed by the reader of the preceding pages, are not in every instance distinguished by novelty. Its interest consists in its embodying together all the devices of a valuable character which were the fruit of the judgment and experience of the benevolent men who had already turned their attention to the subject of which it so ably treats; in its placing these devices in a practical position; and in its showing how they might work in harmony for the accomplishment of the great end in view. Some of its suggestions, however, are of a novel character, as that respecting a full and complete census of the whole of the Jáḍejá population, which had not hitherto been considered either necessary or desirable, and that respecting the continued maintenance of a system of Jáḍejá registration. The measures which it proposed were partly of a coërcive, and partly of a hortative, character. Though in some points of view they might be liable to objection on general grounds in certain states of society, they were certainly all expedient and necessary in the case of the Jáḍejás and infanticide. Its only defect consists in its overlooking distinctive measures of enlightenment and education for the province in which the crime of of infanticide prevailed; but Mr. Willoughby, as we shall afterwards see, wished that such measures of moral influence and power should be adopted with reference to the general circumstances of the whole population of the province, and not merely of those of one particular tribe viewed in connexion with a special crime.

On the receipt of this communication in Bombay, it was immediately circulated in Council by Lord Clare, then the Governor, who personally felt much interest in its contents, and who immediately called a meeting of his colleagues for its special consideration. Mr. James Sutherland, the senior member of Council, recorded his opinion upon it to the effect, that "if any measures can obtain the object in view, I think they are now before the Board." Its suggestions were considered by Mr. Ironside, the other civil member of Council, "most valuable." After deliberate attention was given to its facts and reasonings, the decision of Government upon it was thus conveyed to Mr. Willoughby.

"His Lordship in Council directs me, in the first place, to return to you his warmest thanks for your interesting and able Report, which displays throughout an unremitting zeal in the cause of humanity, united with the soundest judgment and discretion in treating of the measures best calculated to effect the abolition of the barbarous practice in question.

"The forms of the returns which accompanied your letter are lucid and well devised, and the judicious measures taken by you to test their accuracy warrant a confidence in their general correctness; and the Right Honourable the Governor in Council is happy to express his entire concurrence in the conclusions at which you have arrived, after analyzing the returns in the able way you have done in paragraphs 8 to 11 of your Report, that 'improvement is progressive, and that a cheering prospect exists of ultimate success.'

"The measures suggested in the 13th to 16th paragraphs of your despatch are entirely approved by the Right Honourable the Governor in Council; and the expense of the establishment required for the preparation of the proposed census and returns, as stated in the

13th paragraph, is sanctioned by his Lordship in Council, and will be borne, as you recommend, by the Infanticide Fund.

"The proclamation by Government, which you propose to promulgate throughout the Peninsula, is approved by his Lordship in Council, with two exceptions: the degree of criminality attaching to infanticide compared with other crimes as taken from the Shástras, the Right Honourable the Governor in Council thinks may without disadvantage be omitted in a proclamation by the British Government; and his Lordship in Council prefers, upon the whole, that the denouncement of punishment, towards the conclusion of the proclamation, against those who continue to commit the crime, shall be general, rather than that it should be specified that the offender should be tried by the Káṭhiáwáḍ High Court of Judicature, or otherwise dealt with. Seven hundred lithographed copies of the proclamation, altered as above, in the Gujarátí language, will accordingly be prepared and furnished to you as soon as possible for promulgation. To each copy of the proclamation will also be appended a copy of the renewed engagement entered into in 1812 by the Jám of Nawánagar, the head of the Jáḍejá tribe in Káṭhiáwáḍ.

"The Right Honourable the Governor in Council prefers the general promise of reward to informers in cases of infanticide, on conviction, proportioned to the rank and power of the offender, as contained in the proposed proclamation, to the graduated scale proposed by Major Carnac.

"The following therefore is the system which is approved by the Right Honourable the Governor in Council, with regard to cases of infanticide. The Political Agent will institute a preliminary investigation, and if persuaded of the guilt of the party, will make a report to Government, and suggest in each case the course to be pursued with reference to the actual circumstances, the rank of the offender, and other considerations of importance, whether that the guilty party should be at once punished by a fine, or in any other way, or whether the case should be tried by the High Court of Criminal Judicature for Káṭhiáwáḍ.

"The tenor of the 20th paragraph of your Report, relative to the general notice which the proclamation intimates will be taken of chiefs within whose tálukás Infanticide is found to prevail, is concurred in by the Right Honorable the Governor in Council; and his Lordship in Council also entirely approves of the circular letter which, in the 21st paragraph, you propose to issue to Rajput chiefs in Káṭhiáwáḍ, calling upon each, when giving his daughter in marriage to a Jáḍejá, to make it a stipulation that the issue of the union shall be preserved, and to oblige every Rajput subject to him to do the same.

"His Lordship in Council has much satisfaction in sanctioning the rewards enumerated in the 22nd paragraph of your Report, to be borne by the Infanticide Fund, and approves also the communication which you propose to make to the Jám of Nawánagar, as stated in the 23rd paragraph.

"The Resident in Kachh will be directed to make known to you the steps taken for the abolition of infanticide in that province, and their result; and the Right Honorable the Governor in Council requests that you will, on all occasions, communicate freely on this interesting topic with that officer, to whom corresponding instructions will be issued.

"In conclusion, the Right Honorable the Governor in Council directs me to observe, that he views your exertions in this all-important cause with peculiar satisfaction, and exhorts you to a continuance of those efforts which have so justly entitled your proceedings now reviewed to the unqualified approbation and acknowledgements of Government. — I have, etc., CHARLES NORRIS, Chief Secretary."

Armed with this high approval and authority, which

was certainly extremely creditable to the government of Lord Clare, Mr. Willoughby set vigorously to work to carry into effect his own measures, as detailed and described by himself. Not one of them did he permit to remain in abeyance. He was ably and vigorously aided in their execution by Captain, now Lieutenant-Colonel, William Lang, then his own assistant in the political agency of Káṭhiáwáḍ, and who, as ultimately the chief British authority in that province, has next to himself been the most efficient instrument in the abolition of Infanticide within its borders.

The proclamation to the Jáḍejás, sanctioned by Government and issued by Mr. Willoughby, ran in these words.

"The British Government having recently had under consideration the prevalence of female Infanticide in Western India, is pleased to declare it to be its fixed determination to put an end to so revolting and barbarous a practice.

"From Returns lately received from the political agent stationed in Káṭhiáwáḍ, it appears that although a considerable degree of success has attended the measures adopted in that province for the suppression of Infanticide, the crime is proved to be still committed, by the great disproportion observable in the number of male and female Jáḍejás. This melancholy fact, therefore, pressing itself upon the attention of Government, the Right Honourable the Governor in Gouncil considers it requisite to call upon the chiefs of the Jáḍejá tribe to adhere to and maintain within their respective districts the engagement they voluntarily and unconditionally entered into with Government twenty-five years ago, through the medium of their friend and benefactor the late lamented Colonel Alexander Walker, to abandon the detestable and heinous custom of murdering their own offspring.

"His Lordship in Council further requires the active co-operation of the whole community of Káṭhiáwáḍ in giving increased efficiency to the measures adopted for the extinction of infanticide, the grossest stain that ever disgraced the human race; and hereby declares, that whosoever shall afford information sufficient to convict any Jáḍejá of so inhuman a proceeding, shall receive the protection of Government, and be rewarded in proportion to the rank and consequence of the party convicted. Humanity and a due regard to the precepts of their religion should induce the Hindu part of the community to aid, by every means in their power, the efforts of Government completely to suppress the crime.*

"With the view of enabling Government to ascertain how far the measures for the suppression of infanticide are adhered to, the political agent has been instructed to make a full and complete census of the Jáḍejá population of Káṭhiáwáḍ; and the chiefs of the tribe are hereby called upon to aid in the framing of this Return, which, when completed, will at once enable Government to detect where the crime is still committed. The political agent has also been directed to require from the chiefs half-yearly, and himself to furnish annually, a statement exhibiting the number of births, deaths, marriages, and betrothals occurring within their respective jurisdictions; and those who neglect to furnish this statement, or who may furnish an incorrect Return, will be severely punished.

"As a measure of prevention against Infanticide, Government considers it expedient to suggest to the whole of the other Rajput tribes of Káṭhiáwáḍ that they should refuse to give their own daughters in marriage to the Jáḍejás, except under a stipulation that the female issue of such marriage shall be cherished and preserved.

"The Returns recently received from Káṭhiáwáḍ show,

* [Here, in Mr. Willoughby's draft occurred the references to the Hindu Shástras which the Governor in Council had requested to be erased. See above, p. 194. They were contained in Colonel Walker's engagement, to which, *pro tanto*, we have already objected on that account. See p. 81.]

in the undermentioned districts, such a great disparity between the number of male and female Jáḍejás as can only be accounted for by the continued prevalence of the dreadful crime in those places.

No.		*Males alive.*	*Females alive.*	*Excess of Males.*
1	Drápha	67	10	57
2	Murví	61	7	54
3	Virpar	58	10	48
4	Mulila-Dérí	63	14	49
5	Sesáng Chándalí	37	13	24
6	Kotrá-Niyájí	24	2	22
7	Jhália	28	11	17
8	Rájpura	30	2	28
9	Waḍálí	8	1	7
10	Rajkoṭ	15	3	12

"The chiefs of these districts are hereby warned, that should similar results be shown from the periodical Returns hereafter to be furnished, they will be severely punished for not adhering to their engagements to renounce the crime. It will not be deemed sufficient by Government that they themselves shall adhere to their engagements to preserve their female children; but they are equally bound to secure that those engagements are observed by every member of their tribe subject to their authority. Should they neglect this warning, it will become requisite for the Governor to take into consideration whether any relations can be maintained with chiefs who act in such a manner as to prove themselves utterly disregardless of the precepts of religion and of the best feelings of mankind. In seeking to abolish infanticide the British Government is not actuated by any motive of ambition or self-interest, but simply by an anxious desire to erase the foulest stain that was ever attached to the name of man. The possessions of the chiefs of Káṭhiáwáḍ are guaranteed to them, and protection is extended to them on certain conditions; and it is the sincere wish of Government that they should continue to enjoy them, and all their privileges and immunities, free from molestation. The compact is however reciprocal and mutual, and the chiefs have stipulated that they will cease to disgrace humanity by destroying their own helpless offspring at the moment of its birth. Should they not adhere to this condition the compact is broken, the favour and protection of Government will be withdrawn, and the severest penalties be imposed until the inhuman custom is completely eradicated.

"It is more gratifying to Government to be able to notice some of the Jáḍejá chiefs in whose districts the crime has been wholly, or in a great measure suppressed. The Jám of Nawánagar is entitled to praise for the progress which has been made towards its complete extinction within his jurisdiction, which is to be attributed to the care taken by that chief in enforcing a due observance of the engagement he entered into for its suppression. The British Government confidently relies on his continued exertions and co-operation in ensuring success to the measures it has adopted for the abolition of a custom which, owing its origin to avarice and a mistaken pride, reflects most seriously on this character of the tribe of which the Jám of Nawánagar is in Káṭhiáwáḍ the acknowledged head.

"Among the other tálukás, Government is pleased to notice in terms of high approbation the following chiefs as having ensured to themselves the favour and protection of Government for having adhered to their engagements:

No.	*Districts.*	*Males of and under 20*	FEMALES.					*Excess of Males.*	*Excess of Females.*
			Married.	*Betrothed.*	*Unbetrothed.*	*Deceased.*	*Total.*		
1	Khírsará	12	3	2	11	1	17	...	5
2	Menganí	6	...	1	5	...	6	...	...
3	Satodar	38	6	5	13	8	32	6	...

And at the same time to hold up to the tribe in general, as an example for imitation, the undermentioned Jáḍejás, who have preserved four and three daughters each:

No.	Names.	Belonging to		Number of Daughters.
		District.	Village.	
1	Jáḍejá Khánjí	Nawánagar	Lálpur	Four.
2	" Báwají	"	Bálwá	Three.
3	" Ráébjí	"	Máchardá	"
4	" Dosájí	"	Pimpurdí	"
5	" Khántarjí	"	Pipaliá	"
6	" Dádájí	"	Sígach	"
7	" Bábájí	"	Dánthání	"
8	" Báwájí	"	Pásawá	"
9	" Mégrájjí	"	Amrá	"
10	" Harbamjí	"	Chíkárí	"
11	" Saghájí	Dharol	Rádhár	"
12	" Junájí	"	Líhálu	Four.
13	" Varaájí	Gondal-Dorájí	Janjmír	Three.
14	Kímaní Rupábhái	Virpar-Kaḍedí	Metia	"
15	Jáḍejá Lákhájí	Khírrá	Wárá	"

Government have also derived the greatest satisfaction from observing that the Returns show as many as 80 instances of Jáḍejás having preserved two daughters each. His Lordship in Council, with the view of testifying the sense he entertains of the meritorious conduct of the chiefs and inferior Jáḍejás above alluded to, has instructed the political agent at Rájkoṭ to grant remissions of tribute and honorary presents to them.

"The British Government is pleased further to declare, that although it will always be more satisfactory to Government, and more creditable to the Jáḍejás themselves to perform the first of parental duties without seeking pecuniary aid from Government in defraying the expenses of the marriage of their children; nevertheless that the local agent is authorized to receive and attend to applications when circumstances render such aid indispensable.

"In conclusion, the Right Honourable the Governor in Council is pleased to annex to this proclamation a copy of the engagement by which every Jáḍejá chief of Káṭhiáwáḍ bound himself, twenty-five years ago, to discontinue the dreadful custom of female infanticide; and at the same time to declare it to be the fixed resolution of the British Government to maintain the same, and that any person charged with having violated it, will either be placed on his trial for the heinous crime of 'child-murder,' before the High Court of Criminal Justice recently established in Káṭhiáwáḍ, or be dealt with in such other mode as may be deemed most expedient and conducive towards the complete suppression of the practice."

In point of propriety and plainness, this proclamation was all that could be desired.

CHAPTER IX.

CONVICTION AND PUNISHMENT OF JA'ḌEJA'S FOR INFANTICIDE BY MR. WILLOUGHBY AND CAPTAIN LANG—LETTERS TO CHIEFS DISSUASIVE FROM INFANTICIDE—SPECIMENS OF REPLIES—MR. WILLOUGHBY'S REMOVAL TO BOMBAY AND HIS SERVICES THERE.

On the distinct warning of the proclamation contained in the preceding chapter, Mr. Willoughby had soon occasion to act. In October 1834, information reached him, that Surájí, the thákur, or baron of Rájkoṭ, of whom better things had been expected and who had received much kindness from Government,* had been accessory to the murder of a daughter on the 6th November, 1833. That chieftain, after a searching private investigation of his case and a lengthened public trial by Mr. Willoughby and Captain Lang his first assistant, was duly convicted of the horrid crime, and fined to the amount of Rs. 12,000, a sum equal to about half the free annual income of his estates,† which were at-

* See above, p. 165.

† The baronial domains of Rájkoṭ consist of about 55 villages, of which 13 are alienated from revenue charge to the Thákur. The estimated population of them is 20,000, exclusive of the British camp. The annual income of the Thákur is about Rs. 60,000, of which Rs. 20,503 are paid in tribute to the British Government, which on the other hand pays Rs. 3,600 per annum for the site of its camp. The station was chosen from its central position; its proximity to the river A'jí, which passes the eastern wall of the native town; and the abundance of forage in its neighbourhood.

tached till it was paid; bound over to observe his engagements with the Government under proper securities; and compelled to dismiss his khárbhárís, or native ministers, who had failed to report the birth which had taken place, though formally called upon by Mr. Willoughby to supply such information. The sanction by Government of this punishment was conveyed in a letter dated the 2nd June 1835. His trial elicited some facts of curious but painful interest. At the time of the birth in his family, there were present the widow of Patél Mandan a friend of the mother, and two slave-girls, while several Bráhmans were in attendance outside to mark the *véla*, or precise time of birth, had it been that of a son. One of the Bráhmans, who was the first witness examined on the trial, on learning that a girl was born, went immediately home, "knowing that no present would be made for such an issue." Ratanbáí, the midwife called, was too late in her attendance. When she arrived, she found, as she testified, one of the slave-girls holding the child on the bed, "which was not as it ought to have been;" and observed it carried out gasping by another of the slave-girls, along with the afterbirth, from which it had not been separated while it was in the room. The mother cried, and, according to one witness, she said nothing, while according to another, she declared her "fate was hard." She was afraid to complain much, for she feared that if she did so, her husband would put her away, because, on a former occasion, "Surájí had abstained from all intercourse with his first wife for seven or eight months, for she had saved a daughter." The murder of the child was actually perpetrated by the afterbirth having been placed on its mouth, to prevent respiration. The father made no confession of his guilt to the political authorities. To understand the extent of the horrid wickedness and depravity of the Jáḍejás in Káṭhiawáḍ and Kachh, we have only to imagine five hundred cases of a like disgusting character occurring annually for many centuries in all their families without exception.

Mr. Willoughby thus conveyed to Government his opinion of the punishment, with which this convicted malefactor should be visited:

"He is of the age of twenty-two, and in rank takes precedence of all but three of the Jáḍejás of Káṭhiáwáḍ.* No circumstances exist which render him deserving of personal consideration. He has not even expressed contrition for the heinous crime he has committed. He is evidently alarmed for the consequences that may ensue, but he does not appear to feel ashamed of the unnatural deed he has perpetrated. The evidence against him is clear and conclusive, and Government possesses the undoubted right to inflict whatever punishment it deems most advisable. Although, however, I do not consider Surájí to possess any claim to consideration personally, on other grounds I am induced to recommend that in this, the first case of infanticide that has ever yet been clearly proved in Káṭhiáwáḍ, justice should be tempered with mercy; the motive for which is, that extreme severity would, in my opinion, be injurious to our future efforts to effect the complete extinction of the practice. It must be obvious that to secure this, we must enlist the feelings of the community on our side, so that they may be induced to view the custom with general execration, and to aid our endeavours to wipe away so foul a blot on humanity. We must (more especially in the first instances that are brought to light) avoid the danger of exciting sympathy in favour of delinquents, thereby deterring persons from informing against them, who might otherwise be disposed to do so. In short, unless we are able to carry public opinion with us, and inflict such penalties only as are likely to be recognized as just by the respectable portion of the community, our endeavours in the cause of humanity will be long retarded, or may altogether fail. I think also some regard is due to the feelings under which the Jáḍejá acted who gave information against Surájí; for I am quite satisfied

* [The Jám of Nawánagar and the chiefs of Murví and Gondal.]

he never would have come forward had he thought that the formal trial of his chief would have ensued, or that any other punishment would be inflicted beyond a fine, and exacting security against the recurrence of the offence.

"The following therefore is the course which I would respectfully recommend for the consideration of the Right Honourable the Governor in Council.

"1st. That a fine of 12,000 rupees be imposed upon Surájí, to be credited to the Infanticide Fund, and that his táluká continue under attachment until it is paid.

"2nd. That he be required to renew the engagement by which himself and family are already bound to renounce infanticide, and that he furnish the security of two or three of the principal Jáḍejá chiefs for the observance of the same.

"3rd. That an additional article be inserted in this contract, providing that on any expected birth in his family, the chief is to advise the political agent of the same, to enable him to take measures for ascertaining the result, and for securing the fulfilment of the engagement.

"4th. That he be required to dismiss from his service Jaṭhá Balwant and Dalpat, mehtás, declaring them incapable of being reëmployed by him, and requiring them to leave his territory ten days after the receipt of the order.

"5th. That he be informed that a repetition of the offence will subject him to a forfeiture of his estate, and to such other punishment as Government may see fit to award.

"I think that on these conditions the chief may be pardoned. The amount of the fine is suggested with reference to his resources and embarrassments. The 3rd and 4th conditions will I have no doubt be considered humiliating; but they are justified by the circumstances of the case. With regard to the mehtás, I beg to explain, that for many years past they have had the exclusive management of the Rajkoṭ táluká; they have greatly abused their trust, and enriched themselves at their master's expense. In 1825, the whole of the Rajkoṭ bháíyád petitioned against them, and Major Barnewall in consequence removed them from authority, and declined having any communication with them; they reinstated themselves in power during Mr. Blane's agency, but their dismission and expulsion is now expedient: 1st, for having failed to communicate the destruction of Suráji's daughter, although from their situation they could not have been ignorant of the event; 2nd, for having been instrumental in furnishing me with a false return of the Jáḍejá children of Rajkoṭ, and for having, when expressly questioned by me on the subject, declared this return to be correct. I greatly rely on the efficacy of this measure; the example will be salutary, and induce this class to give information against those who may violate the engagements in force, to discontinue the practice of Infanticide."

At the same time that Mr. Willoughby made these proposals, he had with much regret to communicate to Government information of the death of the Jáḍejá on whose statements, in the first instance, Surájí had been brought to trial. The death of that Jáḍejá had been thus intimated to him by Captain Lang in a letter dated the 6th December, 1834.

"It is with much regret that I report to you the death, on the 25th ultimo, of Moḍjí, the Jáḍejá Grásiá of Gauridhar; an event which, happening as it has done, so soon after the conviction of the Rajkoṭ chief of the inhuman crime of infanticide, which you are aware was effected chiefly by his means, is the more to be lamented; since, in addition to the almost irreparable loss the cause of humanity has sustained in the demise of a Jáḍejá Rajput, who had not only good sense enough to abjure the horrid practice of Infanticide because it was proscribed by the British Government, but, as I firmly believe, sufficient principle to detest the crime for itself, and to volunteer to come forward to denounce it when practised by other members of his tribe, his sudden death is not unlikely to be connected (in the minds of so prejudiced a race as the natives of this province are, especially in such matters) with his exertions in that cause, which ought, on the contrary, to render his name revered amongst them.

"To counteract as far as we can the evil effects which might arise from such ideas, and to evince to the community in general the high sense of his services and respect for his memory entertained by the British Government, I deem it my duty to recommend, in the strongest manner, that the sum of 1,000 rupees should be presented to the family to assist them in defraying the expenses of his déáḍá; and that a further present of a pair of bangles, or anything else which may be considered more eligible, be made to his eldest son. I address this letter to you in consequence of your having the Rájkoṭ infanticide case in hand, and my knowing that it was your intention to recommend the employment of the deceased on a small allowance of the Infanticide Fund.

"I beg to add that, at the urgent request of Míráji, the eldest son of Moḍjí, I have advanced the sum of 1,000 rupees, including the price of a small supply of opium from the warehouse, which, in the event of my present suggestion not being complied with, will be recovered by instalments from the revenues of Gauridhar." The recommendation here given in behalf of the family of Moḍjí was supported by Mr. Willoughby.

On Mr. Willoughby's report of the conviction of Suráji, the following minute was penned by Sir Robert Grant, on the 16th May, the considerate character of which is as conspicuous as the propriety of its language.

"Mr. Willoughby should be informed that Government highly approves the humanity and ability with which he has in this instance followed up his former very meritorious exertions for the suppression of the atrocious crime of Infanticide.

"He should also be requested to convey a similar assurance of the approbation of Government to Captain Lang, who has so effectively seconded his efforts.

"The evidence adduced before Mr. Willoughby and Captain Lang incontestably establishes the guilt of the chief of Rájkoṭ; and the barbarous insensibility which the chief has evinced on the occasion proves him to have little claim to forgiveness.

"At the same time, I entirely concur in the judicious and enlightened observations contained in the 20th paragraph of Mr. Willoughby's letter, with respect to the principles and considerations by which we ought to be guided in dealing with this inhuman offender.

"The measures recommended by Mr. Willoughby in his 21st paragraph should be entirely approved, as being sufficient, under the crisis, for the punishment of the crime committed, and as promising to be efficacious in preventing the perpetration of like enormities in future.

"I am unwilling to suggest any further precautions, as none that are necessary are likely to have escaped Mr. Willoughby's intelligence. At the same time, so much depends on the due fulfilment of the duty to be imposed on the chief by the third of Mr. Willoughby's suggestions, namely, that he is to advise the Political Agent of any expected birth in his family; and both the temptation to avoid and the facility of evading the performance of this duty seem so great, that I am induced to propose it for Mr. Willoughby's consideration whether it might not be well to give the chief to understand that no son hereafter born in his family, without previous annunciation of an expected birth to the Agent, would be regarded by the British Government as legitimate. This suggestion, however, need not be adopted if Mr. Willoughby deems it unnecessary.

"The death of Jáḍejá Moḍjí, to whom the detection of this case of Infanticide was principally owing, is an event greatly to be deplored. It must be consolatory, however, to the British Government to be able to mark their sense of his merit by bestowing on his family those tokens of approbation which Captain Lang so properly recommends.

"In observing, however, the remark of Captain Lang, that the sudden death of this meritorious person immediately after his successful exertions in the present case, is not unlikely to be regarded by the bigotedly prejudiced race to which he belonged, as a judicial infliction on him on account of those exertions, it is impossible wholly to suppress a suspicion, which would probably have occurred to Captain Lang had there been any ground for it. Captain Lang will, of course, have sufficiently informed himself of the particulars of the Jáḍejá's death to be satisfied that no reason exists for imputing it to unfair means.

"The present which Mr. Willoughby suggests, in the 24th paragraph of his letter to the Mehtá who assisted the prosecution of the inquiry, should be paid accordingly.

"The female witnesses, through whose evidence the chief's guilt was brought home to him, appear to be persons in his power; of course, it has not escaped Mr. Willoughby to use all proper means for their protection.

"The example which in this instance is to be made of the chief of Rájkoṭ will, I trust, produce a salutary effect, not merely on the surrounding chiefs, but on the Jáḍejá population of Rájkoṭ, among whom, the census reported by Mr. Willoughby, in his letter of 24th September 1834, proves that the crime of Infanticide was of frequent occurrence."

This minute, after being approved in Council, with the exception of the clause about the non-recognition of the legitimacy of a son whose birth might not be duly reported, was substantially communicated to Mr. Willoughby, on the 2nd June. The punishments which Mr. Willoughby had proposed were carried into effect;

and there cannot be a doubt that their infliction had a most salutary influence throughout the whole province of Káṭhiawáḍ. They showed to the Jáḍejás the determination of the British Government no longer to trifle with their violation of their engagements by the perpetration of crime.

Other convictions and punishments of a similar character followed them. On the 10th of September of the same year, information was given to Government of the conviction by Captain Lang of Jáḍejá Virájí of the village of Khírsará of the murder of his daughter; and he was sentenced to undergo imprisonment for one year, to pay a fine of Rs. 3,000, on pain of a further imprisonment for two years, and to furnish security that he would never again be guilty of infanticide. In consequence of his superior having attempted to screen him from justice, certain rewards which it had been intended to give to him for his general repression of the crime were withheld from him. To the investigation of this case, Mr. Willoughby and Major Lang, as in the former one, devoted much time and attention. It is rather a remarkable fact that, shortly after these punishments were inflicted, an old Jáḍejá of a poor family at Mhawá came forward from fear, and confessed that he had been instrumental in directing the death of a granddaughter, born to his own half-witted son. He was dealt with as much leniency as circumstances admitted, and sentenced to pay a fine of a hundred rupees, afterwards reduced to fifty, or in default of which to suffer imprisonment for three months.

The proclamation of Government against Infanticide was communicated by Mr. Willoughby to the chief Jáḍejás and Rajputs furnishing them with wives, and their principal agents, in a series of personal confidential communications and circular letters, about a hundred in number, and of a highly suitable and appropriate character. Of these, that addressed to the Jám of Nawánagar, and dated the 21st July 1835, may be taken as an example.

"After compliments. I have the pleasure to forward for your information two copies of a proclamation recently published by Government in this province upon the subject of female infanticide, to which I request your attentive consideration.

"I have been instructed on this occasion to convey to you the satisfaction derived by Government on observing the progress which has been made in the districts subject to your authority, in abolishing this inhuman custom, since the return lately furnished by you shows that 380 infants have been preserved.

"I confidently rely on receiving from you the most cordial co-operation in carrying into effect the measures in progress for ensuring the entire abolition of a practice so entirely at variance with the usage of mankind. I am happy to inform you that his Highness the Ráo of Kachh pledged himself to use his exertions to extirpate this heinous sin from his dominions; and I look to you as the chief of the Jáḍejás of Káṭhiáwáḍ to follow His Highness the Ráo's example, by affording me every assistance in accomplishing the same object in this province. By doing so you will greatly add to your reputation, and establish for yourself and family the strongest claims for a continuance of the friendship and protection of the British Government.

"I request you will do me the favour to give every publicity to the Government proclamation; and it would be highly conducive to the end in view were you on this occasion to summon to your presence your Bháíyád and the whole of the Jáḍejás subject to your authority, and inform them of your fixed resolve to punish with the utmost severity, and expel from the caste, any person who may still adhere to the barbarous custom of putting their female offspring to death, at the same time requiring them to renew existing engagements for its discontinuance.

"You will observe that Government has resolved to obtain a census of the Jáḍejá population of Káṭhiáwáḍ, and to require from the chiefs of the tribe half-yearly returns of all births, marriages, betrothals, and deaths occurring in the district. The object of these returns is to enable Government to ascertain from the results how far existing engagements are observed; and I request your assistance towards rendering the returns of your district as full and accurate as possible.

"The British Government has established a fund for the relief of Ját̤ejás in indigent circumstances and unable to defray the marriage expenses of their daughters. I shall on all occasions be most happy to pay every attention in my power to such representations as you may make on behalf of Ját̤ejás so circumstanced.

"It is impossible to convey to you an idea of the intense interest felt not only by the Government of India, but by the authorities in England, to effect the entire extinction of the unnatural crime of infanticide. Persons at a distance can scarcely credit the existence of such a custom among a high-minded race of men whose Shástras, or religion, denounce it as a crime of the deepest dye, and so great as not to admit of expiation. In suppressing it Government is alone influenced by motives of humanity and the purest philanthropy. It sincerely desires to effect the end in view by persuasion and by an appeal to the dictates of reason and religion; but should these means fail, the severest penalties will be inflicted upon those who still adhere to the detestable custom; and finally, it will become matter of serious consideration whether Government can with propriety keep any terms whatever with persons who, after having voluntarily renounced the practice, and repeated warnings and admonitions, may still prove themselves to be utterly regardless of one of the first and most important duties of mankind.

"Favour me with an early reply to this communication, and apprise me of such measures as you may adopt for giving effect to the wishes and orders of Government."

The answers received to the communications now referred to, and of which the preceding is a specimen, were in many instances of a very interesting character, showing the degree of attention, which, with their concomitant measures, they had awakened, and illustrating both the habits and feelings of the natives, and their professed appreciation of the motives and actings of the British Government. A few of them follow.

1. "All is well here. Write regarding your own welfare; your letter, dated A'ṣháḍh Wad 11th has been received. You have therein written regarding arrangements for the suppression of the custom of putting our daughters to death; all this is right. I shall assemble intelligent men together, and after due deliberation write you a reply." *From Jáḍejá Shrí Ranmaljí Jám of Nawánagar.*

2. "All is well here; write to us of your welfare. Your letter regarding the preservation of our daughters. and the proclamation on that subject has been received, Jáḍejá Déwají and all our Bháíyád are now at Rájkoṭ. I have written several times to my Wakíl (agent) to exact security from them, and to send the deeds to me. He has, however, not yet done so. My Bháíyád state that they are ready to execute the required writings as soon as Jáḍejá Déwají has done so. I will write to you hereafter on this subject. My father was an instrument originally in this business, and I myself act up to his example. I will not fail to pay due attention to the orders you have now issued." *From Jáḍejá Shrí Prithíráj́jí, Chief of Murví, and his son Kuérshrí Ráojí.*

3. "The British Government formerly adopted measures for the suppression of infanticide; but since receiving your letter of the 21st July, forwarding a proclamation on this subject, and observing that it is your fixed determination to abolish the custom, I have accordingly communicated the contents of your letter and proclamation to the whole of the Jáḍejás and the Bháíyád, and exacted security from them to abstain from the practice, and to the effect that if any of them should

disregard the present engagement he shall be expelled from the caste, and rendered liable to any punishment the British Government may think proper to inflict. I have spared no pains and trouble to inform them thoroughly of this. The measures adopted become the virtuous and humane character of the British Government, and are strictly in accordance with the precepts enjoined in the Hindu Shástras. He who now shall commit the dreadful crime will reap the fruits of his guilt; and he who, knowing that the crime has been committed by another, shall hesitate to reveal his knowledge thereof, must participate in the guilt and sin which are the consequences; who would participate in such sin? Let the Sirkár be convinced of this. Nothing will be left undone in this matter. But should, notwithstanding, any instance of the crime occur, the Sirkár is all-powerful to punish. Half yearly returns will be transmitted as directed. The new year will commence from the Dasará, (festival at the close of antumn) six months after which the first half-yearly return will be forwarded." *From Jáḍejá Chandarsinghjí, Chief of Gondal.*

4. "I have received your letter dated the 20th June. I am willing to pay the fine of Rs. 12,000 therein imposed upon me. I am, however, not in circumstances to pay the whole of this sum at once. I rely on your goodness to grant some indulgence in this respect; you have desired that whenever there might be the prospect of an increase to my family, I should inform you of the same. This I will carefully attend to. In regard to the security demanded from me that I shall hereafter abstain from the practice of infanticide, I beg to state that I abjure the custom for ever; and if ever I am found guilty of the crime, my possession will be at your disposal. Should you still insist upon exacting security, I am bound to afford it. I have, agreebly to your orders, caused the departure of Mehtás Jaṭhá Balwant and Dalpatrám Khushál from my territories. In reply to your orders that I must not injure Paṭél Lakhman's

mother, the midwife, and other persons who gave evidence, or their relations, etc., I beg to state that Lakhman Paṭél is like a son of the Darbár, and there is no one it regards so much as it does him.

"I this day, in the presence of four saukárs (merchants) and two other persons, called Lakhman Paṭél, and gave him promises of encouragement. I have received the proclamation on the subject of infanticide which you transmitted to me, and shall adopt arrangements for carrying the orders therein contained into effect. Whatever the English Government determines upon doing is designed for our good, and I am anxious to obey the wishes of the Sirkár. I beg you will be so good as to grant me some indulgence in paying the fine imposed on me; the way to be that which yourself may be pleased to determine. My estate is at the will of the Sirkár. This is my petition." *From Jáḍejá Surájí, Chief of Rájkot.*

5. "I continue to act agreeably to my engagements, and the wishes of Government. In this business, the object of Government is to uphold the Hindu religion.* The unfortunate above will not understand this, and wretchedness will be their portion. Three daughters have been lately born in my family, and have been preserved. I have drawn up a return of them in the form formerly furnished me by you, and have sent this return with the usual letter to you. I am obedient to your orders, and desire to act according to the wishes of Government. This, sir, is my representation." *From Jáḍejá Bhominégjí, Chief of Kotaḍá Sánganí.*

5. "I have received your letter with the proclamation, and have placed it on my head. I will obey the order of Government. *From Jádejá Jasájí, Chief of Lodíká.*

6. "Your letter, and the proclamation regarding the

* [This is one of many cautions to our countrymen in the matter of indiscreet references to Hinduism.]

preservation of our daughters, have been received. The Japtidár Kumásankar, assembled the whole of our Bháíyád together, and communicated the contents of your despatch to them. In obedience to the orders of Government we have never nor will henceforward put our daughters to death." *From Jádejá Khánjí, Patháji Kantharjí, Lákhájí Késarjí, Nánábhái A'lábhái, of Satodar Wáwadí.*

7. "I have received your letter with the proclamation. I have assembled my Bháíyád and formed engagements that they should not put their daughters to death. I am under the same obligation to preserve my daughters. Five months since my brother, Jádejá Haribhái, got a daughter, which he preserved. This I wrote for your information." *From Jádejá Dosájí, Chief of Pál.*

8. "I have thoroughly informed the chief Jádejá Chandarsinghjí of these matters, and the arrangements directed by you shall immediately be adopted, as you have already been informed in a letter from the chief himself. He who conceals his knowledge of a crime so heinous as that of Infanticide is guilty of a deadly sin, and concernment in the murder; who then would share the enormous guilt attached to such concealment? The labour which you have undertaken from motives of the purest philanthropy, and the orders you have issued, will be cordially aided and obeyed even at the peril of our lives." *From Bahájí Bachájí, Minister of the Chief of Gondal.*

9. "I have received your letter, forwarding a proclamation regarding the suppression of the wicked crime of Infanticide practised amongst the Jádejás. I have published the proclamation amongst the Grásiás and others residing in the villages included in my farm. With Colonel Walker originated the adoption of measures for the abolition of Infanticide, but it is you who have vigorously carried those measures into execution upon a systematic plan. The ears of the community

are at last opened, and they begin to see with their eyes. The inhuman custom continued, and your predecessors came and went, but no one has been so fortunate as to deserve that credit before God and eternal fame with posterity which you have obtained. I shall adopt the arrangements you have directed, and communicate with you on the subject from time to time. I rejoice in two things—the exercise of virtue, and the attainment of that celebrity which is the inevitable concomitant." *From Bâbá Wasaikar, Farmer of the Taluká of Dharol.**

10. "Your letter, dated the 7th August last, has arrived, and afforded me great pleasure. The proclamation regarding the daughters of Jáḍejás has also arrived, and I have conversed with the Ráná on the subject. The Jaitwá tribe is not numerous; there are only four Okalís, divisions. Orders have been issued to all of them to abstain from female Infanticide. The Ráná is very much pleased that the attention of Government is engaged on a subject of such immense interest, and so conformable to the religion of all nations. The Jaitwá tribe, however, was not included in Colonel Walker's arrangements for the suppression of Infanticide, because this (i. e. Porbandar) is a dharmaráj or place where religion is much respected, and the custom does not prevail; the four Okalís consist of only ten houses. I am much rejoiced that the precepts of religion are to be enforced, and I will co-operate." *From Mehtá Nathuram Manjalji of Porbandar."*†

11. "Your favour, together with the proclamation, has been received. The Jáḍejás, in putting their daughters to death, commit a great sin. The Shástras describe this sin as one of the greatest enormity. The custom of Infanticide is not sanctioned by any of the Puránas that I have ever heard of. A woman cannot be deprived of

* [This letter is from a native of Wasai (or Bassein) near Bombay.]

† [Of the practise of Infanticide by the Jaitwás of Porbandar, Colonel Walker was well aware. See above, p. 72.]

life, even if she is the most depraved and abandoned of her sex. The guilt, therefore, of putting an innocent infant to death is of the blackest dye. The British Government, in abolishing this inhuman practice from motives of religion and humanity, has gained for itself the highest reward of virtue. There are certain tribes of Rajputs who put their daughters to death. The causes which appear to me to have led to the practice are mentioned below. These causes, however, no longer exist, and it is unaccountable their still continuing to practice the crime.

"The causes I mentioned are as follows:—1. Up to the reign of Prithiráj Cholá, the bride was the property of the strongest who succeeded in taking possession of her person from the pavilion erected to celebrate her marriage. The contentions which ensued in consequence were of the bloodiest description. 2. The Súmrá tribe of Rajputs gave a daughter in marriage amongst the Sammá tribe of Rajputs. Some cause originating in this connexion led to a lasting rupture between the tribes. 3. The daughter of the Rájá of Tháthá was carried away by the Khalifah or Diwán of Baghdád.* 4. The Musalmáns during their reign

* [This was a considerable time before the Sammás of Sindh came into notice, the Khalif referred to being Walíd, who died A. H. 96 or A. D. 715. It was in connexion with the daughters of Dahír of De'wal or Tháthá, that Muhammad Kásim, his general, the conqueror of Sindh and the Panjáb, met his death. Respecting this affair the most satisfactory account is the following, from the pen of Sir Henry Elliot. "Our authorities differ respecting the mode of Muhammad Kasim's death; but it must be admitted that there is much more probability in the statement of the *Futúhu-l-buldán* than in that of the *Chach-Náma*, which is followed by all the later writers. The former states, that he was seized, fettered, imprisoned, and tortured to death by the Khalif's sanction; the latter, that the two daughters of Dahir, who had been sent to the capital for the Khalif's haram, complained that they had already been violated by their father's conqueror; upon which, the Khalif, in a fit of wrath, ordered that he should be sewn up in a raw cowhide, and so transmitted to Damascus. When his body was exhibited to the unfortunate girls, they declared that their assertion was untrue, and that they had uttered it merely to be avenged on the des-

forcibly possessed themselves of the daughters of the Rajputs, and great hatred and opposition between the castes ensued in consequence.

"To the above causes was owing the practice amongst the Jáḍejás of putting their daughters to death. The present times are, however, those of religion and virtue, and violence cannot be exercised by one individual against another. It is therefore unnecessary to continue the practice of infanticide. The greater portion of Jáḍejás do not adopt this dreadful crime; but those who do so will abstain, in obedience to the will of Government. As you have written to me to co-operate in the abolition of the custom, and as it is a work of piety, no endeavours will be spared on my part. Write in return, commanding me to do you service." *From Runchodjí Diwán of Junagaḍ.**

troyer of their family and country. The tale goes on to say, that the capricious tyrant, in an agony of remorse for his hasty conduct, ordered them to be immured alive. Others say, they were tied to horses' tails, and so dragged about the city. The whole story certainly savours more of romance than reality, but the reason which has been advanced against it—namely, that the sewing up in a hide was a Tátár mode of punishment, and not Arab—constitutes no valid objection; for, though it undoubtedly was practised by the Tátárs—as when the savage Halágú murdered the last Khalif of Baghdád—yet an earlier example might have been discovered in the Arab annals. Even before the time of the Sindh conquest, we find the adherents of the first Muáwiya enclosing the body of the Governor of Egypt in the carcass of an ass, and burning both to ashes. And as for the general tone of romance which runs through the version of Muhammad Kásim's death, we find a case somewhat parellel in contemporary history; for when Musá the conqueror of Spain, was treated with similar indignity by Sulaimán—the same relentless Khalif who persecuted the conqueror of Sindh—and was lingering in misery and exile at Mecca, the head of his son, who had been murdered at Cordova was thrown down at his father's feet, while the tyrant's messenger taunted him in the midst of his agony and despair."—Appendix to Arabs of Sindh, unpublished, pp. 31, 32.]

* [This Bráhman minister of the Muhammadan state of Junágáḍ was one of the best informed natives whom we have met in India. He had even a tolerable knowledge of Arabic, a language to which few of his caste ever pay any attention. He takes an intelligent view of some of the causes of infanticide.]

"I have derived much pleasure from the receipt of your letter. My people abuse the custom of the Jáḍejás, and it is becoming of the just government of the Sirkár, the protector of religion, to adopt the arrangements it has done; every one is pleased with this. Before we give our daughters in marriage to the Jáḍejás, we shall as directed, take the requisite writings from them to abstain from female infanticide. I write this for your information." *From Ráwat Jétarjí Motharjí, Shareholder of the village of Ratanpur Dâman.*"

There is an air of apparent simplicity and earnestness in these communications. The cause is easily discovered. The conviction of Suráji and the other Jáḍejás who had been found guilty of infanticide showed them that the British Government had really determined no longer to be trifled with. The respect and obedience which they express is certainly greatly in advance of the early days of British intercommunion with the natives of Káṭhiáwáḍ,

Mr. Willoughby, to whom they were addressed, was soon removed, in the exigencies of the public service, from Káṭhiáwáḍ to the seat of the presidency. On leaving Gujarát he gave over charge of the Political Agency at Rajkoṭ to Captain Lang, his first assistant, who was both theoretically and practically acquainted with all his plans and proceedings; and who ably and strenuously represented in the province all his views and feelings. In Bombay, he was not lost to the cause of the suppression of Infanticide. First, as Political Secretary to Government; then, as Chief Secretary; and lastly, as Member of Council, he continued for a period of twelve years its prime reviewer and director at the seat of authority, under all the governors from Sir Robert Grant to Lord Falkland, who, without exception, had the good sense to rely on his thorough consideration of every communication respecting it, and the judicious counsel which he had ever to offer. His services in Bombay for the suppression of Infanticide were scarcely less important, indeed, than those in Káṭhiáwáḍ, the scene of the crime.

It felt to the lot of Captain Lang in due time to remove the attachment from the estate of Surájí, the Thákur of Rájkoṭ, on his payment of the fine imposed upon him; to receive the securities for his observance of his renewed engagements to abstain from the practice of infanticide; to arrange the affairs of his State, which for a considerable time had been in a condition of pecuniary and fiscal disorder; to secure the banishment from it of the agents through whose unfaithfulness it had been involved in trouble; and to sanction the appointment of their successor. All these delicate duties, he discharged in a manner which called forth the expression of the highest approbation of Government.

CHAPTER X.

MR. JAMES ERSKINE'S REPORT ON INFANTICIDE IN KÁṬHIÁWÁḌ AND THE ESTIMATE FORMED OF IT BY THE BOMBAY GOVERNMENT.

MR. JAMES ERSKINE, of the Civil Service, succeeded Mr. Willoughby in the political agency in Káṭhiáwáḍ. He was a man of education and ability, but neither his mental nor economical habitude peculiarly fitted him for the important duties of the office to which he was thus called. The suppression of Infanticide, however, comparatively speaking, received much of his attention. He addressed a long communication to Government on the subject, by way of a report for 1835 and 1836, on the 30th June, 1837.

In the document now referred to, Mr. Erskine, in the first instance, adverts to the cases of the crime which had been brought to the cognizance of the agency since Mr. Willoughby's report of September 1834. After mentioning those of Suráji, Viráji, and Durgáji of Mhawá, to which we have already referred, he notices several which had been judicially investigated without the crime being proved. He then compares his own returns of the Jáḍejá population with those of Mr. Willoughby, showing, that overlooking a few errors and defects, the latter, notwithstanding that in the first instance they had been furnished by the Jáḍejás themselves, were not on the whole calculated to mislead Mr. Willoughby in his judgment of the state of the Jáḍejá population. He shows in particular that during the eighteen months subsequent to Mr. Willoughby's proclamation seventy-three females had been preserved, "upwards of forty of whom, would in the absence of Mr. Willoughby's exertions have met with inevitable destruction;" and that there was the appearance that the tálukás of Dráphá and Murví had wholly abandoned the crime of Infanticide.

After noticing Mr. Willoughby's report, and the decisions of Government to which it gave rise, Mr. Erskine proceeds to state his own views of the difficulties which still existed in the way of the final triumph of the cause of humanity,—which he represents as still very great,—and to point out what he conceived to be the defects of the coercive measures then in force. He complains of the sudden and unexpected strictness of the British Government in 1834 and 1835, after so many years of aparent apathy, though he ought to have been aware that after all the negociations, and entreaties, and warnings of the Government, this strictness could not on the part of the Jáḍejás be legitimately objected to; and he intimates that all over the province Suráji was considered a martyr, while a correct estimate of the feeling of the people on the subject, might have taught him, that however inadequate their views of the crime of Infanticide might be, they acquiesced in the justice of Suráji's punishment.* He considers the system of informers destructive to the social system and embarassing to Government, overlooking its necessity, and aggravating its evils. He declares the inability of Government to protect informers and witnesses from the vengeance of delinquents; while he ought merely to have recognized a simple difficulty in the matter, even

* The author of this narrative can give his own testimony on this subject. During several long journeys in Káṭhiáwáḍ from the year of Suráji's condemnation to the present time, he has observed enough to convince him that the sympathy of the *people*, however deficient in intensity, has all along been in favour of Government in the matter of Suráji's punishment.

though there was reason to fear that some of the witnesses in the cases which had passed before the review of Government, had not met with fair treatment. Rigorous investigations ordered by Government and consequent punishment on conviction, he holds, lead to stricter vigilance in the commission of the crime by those who practice it; and he intimates his own personal failure during his agency to convict any party, though he had brought several persons to trial, a fact which might have been accounted for by his neglect of private preliminary investigations. He holds that by ourselves punishing inferior Jáḍejás, we transfer the responsibility from chiefs to vassals, contrary to the principles of Colonel Walker's political settlement of the province, forgetting that the chiefs were bound to surrender their vassals to justice, that it is quite competent for Government to employ their authority in every instance that they may seem disposed to make a good use of that authority, and that in the matter of infanticide both chiefs and vassals were actually made amenable, by the precise terms of their engagement with Colonel Walker, to the British and Gáikawáḍ authorities, and though he himself in another portion of his letter says, "To try the people who commit the crime by their brothers and instigators needs only to be mentioned to demonstrate its inutility." He objects to the trial of criminals before the High Court of Justiciary in Káṭhiáwáḍ, on the ground that "to select Káṭhí and Musalmán assessors would have the effect of impressing the Rajputs with an idea of injustice," forgetting that such an objection as this is applicable to every class of people coming before that court as well as Jáḍejás. And he declares that he considers the punishments actually inflicted by Government as inexpedient, till a wholesome public opinion is prepared to sanction them.

Passing from the coercive measures of Government Mr. Erskine comments on those of a "sumptuary" character. The rewards given to Jáḍejás who had preserved their daughters, he thinks well bestowed. He questions, however, the propriety of the allotment of funds to aid in the marriage of the daughters of Jáḍejás. He justly complains of the extravagant expences of these Rajputs in the matter of marriage. He states that the kindness of Government in dealing with them had in certain instances been misapplied.

Mr. Erskine concludes his report by making certain suggestions to Government in aid of the cause which he had at heart. He acknowledges the help which he had received in maturing them from Captains Lang and Jacob his own assistants in Káṭhiáwáḍ; Captain Burnes, assistant political agent in Kachh; and Colonel Shirreff, the commandant at Rájkoṭ. And he recapitulates, principally from Colonel Walker's papers, the history of the Jáḍejás, with the view of showing the importance and applicability of his measures to their actual circumstances.*

* In this digression of Mr. Erskine, he notices the family prospects of the higher Jáḍejás with respect to the marriage of their daughters. The Ráos of Kachh had preserved none of their legitimate females till the present generation. Jám Tamáchí of Nawánagar saved a daughter sixty-three years ago, who was married to the Rájá of Jaudpur, when he was on a pilgrimage to Dwáraká. A sister of one of the Jáms before the invasion of Káṭhiáwáḍ had been married to the viceroy of Ahmadábád. These were the only instances of daughters being saved in the family of the Jáms till within three years of the date of Mr. Erskine's report, when the Jám, having been out on a visit to Mr. Willoughby on the confinement of his wife, found on his return home a female child a few hours old, whom he consequently spared, declaring that it was his *nasib* or fate. "The Jám," says Mr. Erskine in a memorandum annexed by him, "professes to give his daughters to the chief of the Drángadrá family, or his eldest son and heir, as head of the Jhálá tribe; to no others in Káṭhiáwáḍ; but he has never yet given one.' In Rajputáná, Jaipur, and Jaudpur only, but they will not take them. [?] But only one daughter of Jám Lákhájí's has been preserved for these ten generations, and she was given to Rámsinghjí of Jaudpur. Jám will take from Drángadrá, Bháwanagar, Sodha; from the head family of each only. The Drángadrá Rájá will give his daughter to Jám and Ráo of Kachh, Porbandar, and (the Bháíyád of Kachh). He will take from the head Jáḍejás such as the Bháíyád of the Jám, and

Mr. Erskine's suggestions were the following. 1. All the Rajput chiefs in Káṭhiáwáḍ should be required to "enter into an engagement that they will not give their daughters to any tribe who will not give their daughters in return." The effect of this arrangement, it was said, would be, that "the pride and the determined wickedness of the Jáḍejás will thereby be struck at and their proper position in society be defined without any violent measures." 2. The Jáḍejá chiefs, agreeably to a proposal of Captain Lang, should be required to limit the expences of the marriages of their daughters,* and they should be informed "that Government would

Wághe'lás, Chawaḍás, and Gohils. The Rájá of Bháwanagar will give to the Jám and to the chief family of the Jhálás. He will take from the Pramárs, petty Jhálás, Wághe'lás, and Jaitwás; will give to Jáḍejás and Jhálás, and will take from petty Jhálás and Jáḍejás. Jáḍejás and Soḍhas will also give their illegitimate daughters to Musalmáns. Instances have happened of this . . . . . Wághe'lás will take from Jhálás, Pramárs, Rahtoḍs, and will give to Jhálás, Jáḍejás, and Gohils. Pramárs will give to every sect of Rajputs, and will take from Jáḍejás, Gohils, and Jhálás."

* The following is an important extract of a letter on this subject addressed by Capt. Lang to Mr. Erskine, dated 14th April, 1837. "I take the opportunity of informing you, that when lately absent from Rájkoṭ, I remarked with sincere pleasure in many, indeed almost all the Jáḍejás I met with, considerable anxiety as to how they were to dispose of their daughters in marriage, and was requested by several to make some arrangements for them on this subject. This feeling, I never observed before, and it shows most clearly a determination, for the present at all events, to renounce the inhuman practice of infanticide. Every possible attention ought of course to be paid to their wishes, which are simply that they should be able to bestow their daughters on their equals in rank, and not be obliged to incur a larger sum on account of the marriage expenses of these than is incurred by other Rajputs whose daughters they receive in marriage. As the Jáḍejás formerly preserved very few females, there was no difficulty in getting them married into Jhálá families, even superior to their own in rank; but when the number of female Jáḍejás increases, the other Rajput tribes, and particularly the Jhálás, to whom the Jáḍejás prefer giving their daughters, will no doubt be ambitious of forming much higher connexions than they are satisfied with or even think of at present, the more especially as the Jáḍejá tribe is very much more numerous in Káṭhiáwáḍ than the Jhálá. It is therefore, I think, highly

assist the indigent to the same extent as any other caste." 3. A penalty for the practice of infanticide should be specified, to consist in loss of *girás*, or heritable territorial rights, and degradation. 4. The principle of the responsibility of chiefs for the conduct of their vassals should be observed. 5. "The minute scrutiny of the census to be the test, and all chiefs to grant their efficient aid to the census."* 6. An amnesty should be granted to offenders for a limited period. "In the Government letter of the 9th July, 1836, 5th paragraph, the views of Government are more vehemently expressed as to the rigour to be pursued in cases of suspected infanticide; 'Captain Lang's remark of the necessity of a clear and rigorous examination of every case to which the smallest suspicion attaches, is, in the opinion of the Right Honorable the Governor in Council, perfectly just.' I therefore beg to submit to the wisdom of the Honorable Board the proposition that the period of two years or such other time as Government shall decide shall be granted to the Jáḍejás and others in the habit of committing the crime during which time no investigation

desirable that all the most respectable Jhálá chiefs and Grásiás should be invited to attend at Rájkoṭ, the former deputing others to act for them, if they prefer it, in order to discuss the subject with a few of the most respectable Jáḍejás in presence of the political agent. No measures, except of persuasion, could of course be used, but it might be pointed out to the Jhálás how much the success of the case depends upon them, and that Government would expect from them every reasonable assistance in furthering it. I am strongly of opinion, that much good would result from this in enabling the Jáḍejás to dispense with the heavy expense which now attends the marriages of their daughters; but even if nothing else were gained, it would serve to evince the deep interest which we take in everything connected with the abolition of infanticide, and our willingness to assist in every way in our power in promoting the great object in view. Should the experiment succeed with the Jhálá Rajputs, it could afterwards be extended to the other tribes, to whom the poorer among the Jáḍejás now give their daughters occasionally, and all eventually must do when the happy period arrives when infanticide, that foul blot on human nature, shall no longer exist in Káṭhiáwáḍ."

* Mr. Erskine in another portion of his letter says, "It may appear

shall be made either with regard to former or late cases, and that the result of the Census at the termination of that period shall be the test." 7. The assistance of the Ráo of Kachh should be secured, and an assembly of Jáḍejá chiefs should be held at Bhuj to concert measures for regulating their marriage practices so as to make them tend to the suppression of infanticide. 8. Education should be vigorously promoted in the province of Káṭhiáwáḍ."

Into the reasons of the last mentioned recommendation, Mr. Erskine enters at length, and with propriety and tact.

"I now come to the last proposition which my judgment dictates to me to be submitted to the Right Honourable the Governor in Council, to the end of the abolition of the iniquity, and I confess my implicit conviction that it is not only the best, but the only means by which Government has it in its power effectually and finally to eradicate the atrocious crime now under consideration: I mean education, mental improvement, and moral amelioration of the mass of the people. '*Virtutis indagatrix expultrixque vitiorum*,' and without which all our best efforts must be abortive among such a population. Drowned in ignorance, superstition, and vice,

inconsistent with the view of the question I have expressed throughout this report regarding the evils of domestic inquisition for me to recommend the continuance of the census which must involve inquisition to a certain extent. I should greatly rejoice were there any plan which seemed at all feasible by which the step might be avoided. But after the repeated breach of faith on the part of the Jáḍejás it is evident that it would be trifling with the subject to rely on their promises, and no means exist but the census of ascertaining the fact of having kept their engagements or not. Besides, conciliatory conduct on the part of the censors, one of whom Government has already sanctioned is to be a respectable woman, and care in paying every attention to the feelings of the people which the nature of the case will admit will soften as much as we have it in our power the evil which it is indespensably necessary to incur." All this is as reasonable as it is inconsistent with Mr. Erskine's general scrupulosity as to the invasion of Jáḍejá privacy, the privacy of atrocious murderers.

what engine can be used to reclaim them? As to the Jáḍejás themselves, any reasonable man would at once declare that no law could control their iniquity. The voice of conscience, the representative of God in the hearts of men, is entirely hushed in the breasts of those relentless wretches. To awaken within them this divine monitor, to what earthly power can we appeal? It is true that no one becomes infamous at once, but it is equally so that no one sunk in the deepest abyss of iniquity can ever suddenly become virtuous. It has been well remarked, that, 'when we look into the history of the world, two things are seen upon every page, man's ignorance and man's wickedness. History presents another truth: the most ignorant individuals, as well as nations, have been the most vicious and degraded. (The Jáḍejás themselves are a forcible example of this truth.) The present condition of the world reveals slavery and misery where the people are ignorant, and liberty and happiness where there is mental and moral light; where the mind is not improved by virtue and knowledge, it will be governed and debased by the passions and appetites, and employed in planning and executing that which destroys happiness and present improvement. How far human suffering may be attributed to ignorance, or how many of the evils which have and do still exist among the inhabitants of the earth originated from ignorance, would be difficult to ascertain, but we know enough to be assured that the amount of suffering from ignorance is unmeasurable, and the evils unmeasurable.' Ignorance has not only multiplied evils by misapplying what is good, but has given an imaginary existence to many of the most fearful nature which have long distressed and enslaved the human race. Ignorance and error have always led to the commission of the most atrocious deeds of wickedness, and to the habitual adherence to crime."

"I have already exerted myself towards this object by disseminating copies of two small works in Gujarátí which I originally procured from my friend Mr. Wilkinson.* I have distributed copies to every Jáḍejá, and many other Rajput chiefs, many of whom eagerly accepted them. I have with the assistance of the two pandits whom I brought with me from Bombay, translated several different works into Gujarátí for distribution among the chiefs and such as will value them. A short history of the state of England, moral tales, grammars, spelling-books, &c. are already completed, and ready to be transmitted to Bombay to be lithographed. If Government will in their wisdom grant an amnesty towards this blind and misguided race, I will occupy my time in travelling over the province, addressing myself

* [These were translations from the Hindí and Bríj Bháshá into Gujarátí of two tracts, composed almost entirely on the principles of Hinduism, under the auspices of Mr. Lancelot Wilkinson of the Bombay Civil Service, a most zealous agent in the cause of the suppression of Infanticide among the Rajputs of Central India. Of one of them the following notice is by Mr. Wathen, Chief-Secretary to the Bombay Government and an eminent orientalist.

"This work is the production of a Bráhman named Omkár Bhaṭṭa. It commences with praise of Vishnu in the shape of Gowardhan, and mention of the blessings to be acquired by offering up prayers to that deity.

"He then proceeds to satirize the Rajputs of Málwá, and describes them as a dirty and vicious tribe, who have lost all their original virtues from following impure practices. He them proceeds to point out the great sin incurred by killing a human being, and states that it is not to be expiated by any subsequent penance or pilgrimages. The poet points out that it is not allowed or enjoined by any of the holy books, but on the contrary that they command life to be invariably cherished. He abuses them for their avarice, in killing their daughters to save the expence of giving a dowry. He recommends them by every argument and quotation he can, to put a stop to the unnatural practice of killing female children; and promises eternal rewards and lasting blessings to those who will introduce a reform among their tribes by conforming to the real maxims and rules of religion." Of this work, somewhat modified, 700 copies were printed by the Government and sent for distribution to Káṭhiáwáḍ. It was an unsuitable document for the patronage of a Christian Government. We must not preach superstition or practise imposture, either directly or indirectly, even to promote the cause of humanity.]

to the chiefs themselves personally, calling upon any latent good feelings which may still lie, though dormant, in their breasts, exhorting them to adherence to their engagements and the practice of virtue. By such means, even with the limited acquaintance I possess of the manners and customs of the natives of the Peninsula, I feel confident of gaining a large number of converts to the cause of virtue, even if I should not succeed in entirely abolishing the atrocity. In the letter dated 27th April 1836, from the Honourable the Court of Directors, it is clearly stated that 'Mr. Willoughby's report on the effect of our measures for the suppression of infanticide in Káṭhiáwáḍ is highly creditable to him, and is on the whole satisfactory. For though it shows that the practice still prevails very extensively, it shows also that a great and progressive decrease has been produced by the efforts of the British Government.' It is impossible not to concur in the observations of Mr. Willoughby when he says, that 'to effect the complete extinction of the practice, we must enlist the feeling of the community on our side.'*

"This is the direct and most true policy, 'truth prevails by delay and exposure;' and by a steady adherence to such principles the truth must eventually conquer. The principles upon which I propose to act are all in perfect accordance with the above expressed opinion." "Again let us consider the immense advantages we shall acquire by having effected this desirable reformation by gentle means instead of violent. When its final abolition shall have been effected the people will look back with astonishment at the wickedness of their fathers, and learn to bless the British Government, who had conducted them by sure and firm steps to a state of virtue and happiness."

The education of the Jáḍejás and other tribes in Káṭhiáwáḍ is undoubtedly a necessity, to complete their

* [The necessity of this has been universally admitted.]

aversion to infanticide and other atrocious crimes. The kind of education, required by them, on which Mr. Erskine says but little, is undoubtedly that of Milton as defined to Master Hartlib, "the end" of which "is to repair the ruins of our first parents by regaining to know God aright, and out of that knowledge to love him, to imitate him, to be like him, as we may the nearest by possessing our souls of true virtue, which being united to the heavenly grace of faith, makes up the highest perfection." Though an ordinary economical education cannot fail to be highly useful to the Jáḍejás, it is only that of a right religious character which can be blessed to the renovation of their hearts and the radical change of their course of life.

Mr. Erskine, in the conclusion of his letter proposed that an amendment of Mr. Willoughby's proclamation should be re-issued to the Jáḍejás, and that a meeting of Jáḍejás should be called by him for conference on the subject of infanticide. And he refers to enclosures showing the state of the Infanticide Fund, which had a balance in its favour of Rs. 1,115,525. 6. 2.; and of agreements, entered into by certain chiefs of Málwá for the abolition of Infanticide on the solicitation of Mr. Lancelot Wilkinson, whose zeal in the cause was worthy of all praise.*

* These resolutions, adopted by ten Rájás and Rajput chiefs were the following. 1. "The chief cause which has led Rajputs to destroy their daughters is that several families of Rajputs will receive in marriage the daughters of Rajputs of several other tribes, but they refuse to give to them their own daughters in return. They thus are reduced to difficulty in getting what they deem a suitable match for their daughters. Under this fancied difficulty, they destroyed their daughters on their birth. On this account it has now been resolved, that every Rájá and chief shall issue in his own limits an injunction, that no Rajput shall give his daughter in marriage to another who is not ready to give him his daughter in marriage in those families who will give their daughters. 2. It has been already resolved that any Rajput who shall destroy his daughter shall be deprived of his patrimonial rights and excommunicated, and these penalties doubtlessly will be enforced upon such an offender, but he also, who after preserving his daughter shall take any money from his son-in-law, shall be excommunicated; if he

On the arrival of Mr. Erskine's letter in Bombay, it was handed by Sir Robert Grant,—then personally busy with the case of the ambitious but contemptible projects of the Rájá of Sátárá for the ejection of the British from India,—to Mr. Secretary Willoughby, who went over it with the greatest attention and urbanity, notwithstanding the crudeness and rashness of many of its speculations and statements, making it the subject of an elaborate memorandum. The noble-minded Sir Robert Grant was not spared to take this valuable document into consideration; but it met with ample justice from Mr. James Farish, his temporary successor in the Government, and his associates in the Council, Mr. (now Sir George) Anderson, and Mr. J. A. Dunlop. The principal minutes upon it of these excellent gentlemen were the following.

"Mr. Erskine's Infanticide Report for 1835 and 1836 has been so fully analyzed by Mr. Willoughby, in his valuable memorandum on this important and interesting subject, that it will be unnecessary for me to enter at all into detail.

is poor and destitute of means, let his family and friends give him assistance to enable him to marry his daughter suitably to his name; if destitute of powerful friends, let the Rájá and chief in whose territory he resides give him assistance and provide for the marriage of his daughter. 3. Bháṭs and Cháraṇs have claims from of old against Rajputs on the occasion of their marriage. We hereby fix a maximum of what is to be paid to them according to the rank and circumstances of Rajputs; viz.

By Rájás to each Bháṭ and Cháran................	Rs.	1	0	0
By Thákurs of villages to ditto	„	0	8	0
By Rajputs holding rent-free lands to ditto........	„	0	4	0
By poor Rajputs in service as sepoys to ditto	„	0	2	0

No more than the fees as above fixed are to be given by any Rajputs on occasion of marriages. This is to be the custom; if any Rajput from a desire to procure a good name, wish to give more, let him do so on any other day. Against his so doing there is no prohibition." As framed by the Rájás themselves such economical arrangements as these are unobjectionable; but they are not in themselves matters for direct British interference.

"Both these gentlemen have brought to this subject the warmest zeal to accomplish the most benevolent object, and have been actuated in the measures they have adopted by the most earnest desire to suppress and put an end to the revolting and wicked practice of female infanticide, by every effort which has suggested itself for their judgment as best adapted to that end, though they differ in some respects. Mr. Willoughby's matured judgment, and knowledge of the people, lead me to acquiesce in his proposed amendments of the suggestions of Mr. Erskine.

"The success which has attended Mr. Willoughby's efforts is very strikingly shown by the number of female children preserved of those born in the last year of his agency, and the one following it, although as embracing only 12 instead of 18 months, and omitting the táluká of Nawánagar, they exhibit a result very much short of what might have been given.

"Whatever recommendation or otherwise the preliminary inquiry into charges may have in ordinary questions of a local nature, in those connected with infanticide I think them of very great importance, particularly as tending to prevent groundless or malicious charges being brought before the public, and the character of the accused unnecessarily injured. The suggestion of the Political Secretary should be adopted.

"The persecution which it appears the chief of Rájkoṭ has exercised towards the connexions of the party who informed against him should be inquired into, and redressed as pointed out in paragraph 21.

"It is to be regretted that Mr. Erskine had not more carefully looked into the proceedings of his predecessor, nor possessed the documents which should now be sent him as suggested in paragraph 48 of the memorandum, when he would have been satisfied that measures of a conciliatory character formed as much a part of his principle of proceeding as of his own; and in the conspicuous and acknowledged success which has attended those principles of proceeding, he would have found a more solid ground of commendation than any which he has adduced as the basis for condemning them.

"In Mr. Willoughby's remark upon the eight propositions of Mr. Erskine for effecting the great benevolent object in view in paragraphs 32 to 41 of the memorandum, I entirely concur. I am quite at a loss to conceive how in his sixth proposition he could have proposed the degree of impunity for the crime of which they have had such full knowledge, and of the penalties attaching to it through Mr. Willoughby's proclamation. On the eighth proposition, I think the Honourable Court should be strongly recommended to authorize an expenditure sufficient to ensure efficient measures for the diffusion of education in Káṭhiáwáḍ.

"The proclamation proposed should be amended by embodying much of that of 1834, so that it shall appear distinctly as a continuation of the former proclamations. I object to the circular because of the inconsistency that would be involved in our issuing a document speaking of the Shástras as containing a declaration of the true law of God. By avoiding such questionable, or rather erroneous statement, and simplifying and shortening the circular somewhat as proposed in 44, it would be much improved. The meeting of the chiefs, if it can be effected in the spirit anticipated by Mr. Erskine, will, I trust, be attended with the benefits he anticipates.

"In conclusion, I have to observe that the few remarks I have offered on the interesting reports before the Board, and the Political Secretary's valuable memorandum on it, touch but on few of the points which deserved notice. I felt, however, that I could not improve upon the several recommendations which Mr. Willoughby has offered, and I would therefore suggest that he be requested to frame, in the spirit of his 46th paragraph, a reply to Mr. Erskine, embracing them.

The whole subject will also be reported to the Honourable Court.—James Farish.

"I quite agree in the general propositions for the suppression of Infanticide, but entertain doubts of the advantages to be expected from general convocations of ignorant, prejudiced men, who are confessedly incompetent to enter into or comprehend our views, but who seem to me quite as likely to confirm and embitter each others prejudices, as to be converted to our way of thinking, while it may tend to give combined habits of action not desirable to encourage.—J. A. Dunlop.

"I entiely concur in the view Mr. Willoughby has taken of Mr. Erskine's report, and in the measures he suggests when he differs from Mr. Erskine.

"The mode Mr. Willoughby points out in his 7th paragraph for inquiring into these cases, I consider eminently wise, and it should be alone followed.

"Mr. Erskine's proposition that no proceedings should be held on these cases for two years, I should strongly object to, as unnecessary for information to put the Jáḍejás on their guard; for information of our abhorrence of the practice they already possess, as also of the penalties to which the practice renders them liable. It would tend to throw a doubt upon our former proceedings; to those proceedings, in some measure, the colour of injustice in our not having given such law of warning before, and lead to some doubt if up to this point we had really been in earnest.

"I do not see either any necessity for the proposed proclamation; it proclaims what is sufficiently known, and I do not suppose any one really suspects that any good would come of it.

"I admit that education and knowledge will ultimately change the feelings and habits of a whole people; but this is a work of time; and it is not to knowledge so gained that we must look for the cessation of this great crime, but to the measures of Government, used with prudence and conciliation. Our progress since Mr. Willoughby's administration has been great, and entitles him to the highest praise. Many have written much, but in his measures we find a practical result, and till we find a better and more practical result promised, and believe it will occur from other measures, I think those he adopted, and has now so satisfactorily explained, ought to be persisted in.—G. W. ANDERSON. J. A. DUNLOP.

The reply sent by Government to Mr. Erskine was the following. We insert it nearly in full as a complete explanation and vindication of the measures originally adopted on the suggestion and recommendation of Mr. Willoughby, and which when carried into effect, have really accomplished that suppression of the great crime of Infanticide which Government had so long and so much at heart.

Bombay Castle, 16*th February* 1839.

"SIR,—I am directed by the Right Honourable the Governor in Council to acknowledge the receipt of your report on Female Infanticide in Káṭhiáwáḍ, for the years 1835 and 1836, dated 30th June 1837, with its several enclosures; and in reply to communicate to you the following observations and instructions on the subject.

"In the 4th paragraph of your report, the different cases of infanticide which were investigated during the two years above mentioned are reviewed. These amount to 13 in number, five of which occurred in 1835, and eight in 1836. During the first year (1835) conviction followed in four cases, and even in the fifth case no reasonable doubt could be entertained of the guilt of the accused, although the evidence was deemed insufficient for a judicial conviction. In 1836, however, although in several cases strong presumptions of guilt existed, there was not a single instance of conviction. The Governor in Council considers the difference in the results to be as remarkable as it is unfortunate. It may doubtless, in part, be fairly attributed to increased vigilance and to the adoption of precautionary measures on the part of those by whom this revolting crime is committed, to conceal it, in consequence of the convictions of 1835. Government cannot, however, resist the impression that there must have been some defect or mismanagement in conducting the investigations of 1836. It appears to the Governor in Council obvious that these inquiries cannot be conducted on ordinary principles with any prospect of a successful termination. The mode adopted by your predecessor, whenever a case of infanticide came to his knowledge; was, in the first instance to hold a preliminary inquiry in private, previous to the accused party being placed publicly on his trial, in order to satisfy himself that reasonable grounds existed for the charge, and that it was sustained by sufficient evidence. I am desired to draw your attention to this point, in answer to some of the objections urged by you to the system you found in force, on your assuming charge of the administration of affairs in Káṭhiáwáḍ. One great advantage attending this mode of procedure is, that false accusations are thereby checked *in limine*, and the Governor in Council entertains no doubt that from the course adopted by your predecessor, had that officer continued in Káṭhiáwáḍ, several of the cases publicly investigated in 1836 would never have proceeded beyond the preliminary investigation above adverted to. 'The Governor in Council considers it to be the duty of the Political Agent to investigate every charge of infanticide which may come to his knowledge, without reference to the quarter from which it may proceed; but that, in the first instance, his inquiries should be private, and that when in this manner he has satisfied himself that fair grounds exist for putting the accused on his trial, he should do so, but not before. In every case, however, whether of abandoning or persevering in the inquiry, a full report of the proceedings held should be submitted to Government.'

"In the 7th paragraph of your report, the Jáḍejá population is contrasted from the date of your predecessor's proclamation, or the end of the year 1834, up to the middle of 1836. The following table shows the proportion of males and females, of and under the age of 20, in each táluká, except Nawánagar, from which district no census had, at the date of your report, been obtained.

Táluká.	*Males.*	*Females.*	*Táluká.*	*Males.*	*Females.*
1. Rájkot	22	11	15. Waḍalí	9	1
2. Shahpúr	12	...	16. Gatká	5	2
3. Mhawá	3	1	17. Páḷ	8	2
4. Kotará-Sángani	14	5	18. Virawá	2	...
5. Dharol	206	88	19. Bhádawá	6	2
6. Satodar Wáwaḍí	79	27	20. Koṭháriá	4	1
7. Drápha	95	20	21. Koṭhaḍá Niájí	31	5
8. Rájpurá	38	3	22. Shisang Chándalí	51	15
9. Jhália	26	9	23. Máliá	32	15
10. Mulilá-Derí	38	12	24. Khirsará	33	16
11. Gondal	325	97	25. Kákaiálá	5	2
12. Gauridhar	9	1	26. Murví	279	51
13. Lodiká	16	2	27. Virpar Khaḍeḍrí	59	18
14. Menganí	13	7			
			Total	1,422	413

"Altogether, however, there 424 Jáḍejá females living; of whom 4 are widows, 70 married, 92 betrothed, and 258 unbetrothed; and since your predecessor's returns 9 casualties have occurred.

"The Governor in Council considers the following remarks contained in the seventh paragraph of your report on the results exhibited in the above table, as particularly deserving of attention. 'It appears, therefore, that there are 123 male Jáḍejás of the age of one year and under now alive, and 73 females; this must be admitted to be highly satisfactory to the cause of humanity, as proving that in consequence of the measures put in force, 73 female infants have been preserved during the 18 months immediately subsequent to the proclamation, upwards of 40 of whom would in the absence of Mr. Willoughby's exertions have met with inevitable destruction. The year before the census has a show of 102 males, and only 20 females, evidencing that nearly 80 infants must have been put to death. But to pursue the scrutiny further, and from more narrow inspection of it, a more satisfactory result even than the above with respect to the prospect of the final extinction of the crime becomes apparent, namely, that there is every hope that the two tálukás of Murví and Dráphá have effected an abolition of the atrocious practice in their respective limits. There may have been isolated instances of the commission of the crime in the Murví táluká, but the indigent, and it is to be hoped penitent Grásiás of Dráphá, have at length vindicated their humanity from the blood stigma. The Drápha táluká shows an equality of the sexes during the year subsequent to the publication of the proclamation, the numbers being 10 to 11, although up to the proclamation the disparity was 84 to 10. In the Murví táluká during that year, the numbers are 20 and 13, whereas in that district there were only 38 females in all saved up to the end of 1834. In Gondal and the smaller tálukás the returns still continue unfavourable, and evidence that the crime of infanticide is still perpetrated." These results are deemed by the Honourable the Governor in Council to be exceedingly satisfactory, and must be hailed with delight by every friend of humanity. Still they do not exhibit to the full extent, the great measure of success which has attended the measures of the British Government for the extirpation of this dreadful crime. The 73 female infants preserved, are stated to be of the age of one year and under, whereas the point of comparison embraces a period of 18 months; consequently for the return to be correct, it should include all females of and under the age of 18 months, instead of one year and under. In addition to this, the táluká of Nawánagar is excluded from the calculation, and in this district the Jáḍejás are believed to be nearly as numerous as the Jáḍejás of all the other tálukás combined. On this point, I am desired to refer you to the table contained in the fifth paragraph of your predecessor's report on infanticide, dated the 24th September 1834.

"In the 10th paragraph of your report, a review is taken of the coercive measures adopted at the suggestion of the late Political Agent, for the suppression of infanticide, and in the 11th paragraph of those designated by you 'sumptuary measures.' In the latter case, the term appears to the Governor in Council incorrect. The measures called 'sumptuary' are, in fact, measures of conciliation adopted towards such of the Jáḍejás as preserve their daughters, contradistinguished from those of a penal nature directed against those who destroy them.

"After the results alluded to in the 10th and 11th paragraphs of this letter, the Governor in Council was totally unprepared for the remarks, 'that the measures hitherto adopted have been in some respects defective, and insufficient towards the final extinction of the practice, and are not likely if pursued to be productive of effectual success, [unless] under certain modifications which I shall take the liberty to suggest'; that they have been 'too partial, and superficial and not of that comprehensive and radical nature which is requisite in overturning a long established custom among a depraved and barbarous race'; and that attention has hitherto been directed 'towards the preservation of individual female children,' which 'may not only not be a step towards the final eradication of the crime, but may positively operate as a barrier without collateral and subsidiary measures.' It must be remembered that the measures of Government for the suppression of infanticide to which your remarks apply, are only of very recent date, and consequently, it can hardly yet be judged what is likely to be their result; but certainly the number of females preserved during the short period which has intervened since their adoption, afford no ground for despair, but, on the contrary, exhibit a wide field of promise and hope of final success.

"Although the Governor in Council is far from supposing that all has yet been done to effect the object in view, that is within the power of Government to effect, or that many measures may not be yet devised as auxiliary to those already in force for the suppression of infanticide, still he is of opinion that the annual census, if rigidly enforced, and followed up by those measures which may be necessary, according to the results which it may exhibit, is of that comprehensive and radical nature desired by you.

"You notice what you regard as the defects of the present system. The first of these is the sudden and unexpected strictness of the British Government in 1834 and 1835, after so many years of apparent apathy, and this is preliminary to condemning the severity of the punishments awarded on the cases of conviction which occurred during the late Political Agent's administration. The first question for consideration is, were the punishments awarded too severe? In support of your opinion that they were, allusion is made by you to some conversations, not with disinterested parties, but with some Jádejá chiefs, with whom the crime of infanticide is familiar and habitual. The case of the chief of Rájkoṭ is particularly dwelt upon by you. This chief was fined 12,000 rupees, was required to renew his engagements against infanticide, to report all births in his family, and was warned that a repetition of the offence would involve forfeiture of his estate. In a second case, imprisonment for one year, and a fine of 3,000 rupees, commutable to imprisonment for the further period of two years, was imposed. In the third case a fine of 100 rupees was imposed. These sentences were approved by Government and by the Honourable the Court of Directors."

"With reference to the objection made by you to the system of making use of informers in the detection of cases of Infanticide, the Governor in Council is not aware of any mode by which the crime can be detected, except through such agency. Such instruments should of course be used with great caution, but their agency is inevitable, unless Government are resolved to abandon all further endeavours to convict the guilty. On this subject, I am desired to refer you to the 18th and 19th paragraphs of your predecessor's report on Infanticide, dated the 24th September 1834, and to observe that much of the evil attending the system, as noticed by you, may be obviated by adopting the mode of procedure laid down in the 6th and 7th paragraphs of this communication. In the 15th paragraph of your report it is observed, 'the investigations which I perused on my arrival in Káṭhiáwáḍ, I confess filled me with surprise, and very nearly with horror, and I consider it impossible but that their effect was to alienate the people from Government.' The Governor in Council cannot concur in this remark, and he considers it inconsistent with the admission made in your 4th paragraph, namely, that the Rájkoṭ case 'was conducted with as much delicacy as the nature of the case admitted.' In the opinion of Government, if anything is more calculated than another to conciliate the people, it is measures of humanity and philanthropy similar to those adopted by the late Political Agent, which can never be regarded by the community as emanating from any sordid or interested motive. Another ground of objection urged by you to the use of informers, is the inability of Government to protect them from the resentment of those against whom they may appear, which likewise applies to witnesses. This the Governor in Council freely admits is a serious evil, but one which he conceives may be for the most part guarded against, if proper precautions are adopted, and any attempt to injure either informers or witnesses severely punished. In support of this argument you observe that three out of the five witnesses in the Rájkoṭ case have died, and that the general impression in the country is, that they were murdered; one of these individuals, the chief of Gauridhar, died, I am desired to observe, before your predecessor left Káṭhiáwáḍ, and a rigid scrutiny having been entered into respecting the causes of his death, nothing was elicited to show that his death had been occasioned by unfair means, except the suspicion excited by his having died suddenly. Regarding the other two witnesses, no information is before Government beyond the fact now reported by you of their being dead. As the Governor in Council presumes that an inquiry was instituted by you on the occasion of their death, you are requested to forward to Government your proceedings on that inquiry, in order that it may be ascertained on what grounds it is supposed they were murdered. It is further observed by you in the same paragraph, 'Jadarám, the informer in this case, has been ejected from his house in Rájkoṭ, by the chief, and the wife of one of the agency establishment treated in the same way for assisting in the conviction.' The Governor in Council is at a loss to conceive how the chief could have been permitted to act thus, or the cause of your not having interfered to prevent such conduct, and Government direct that even at this late period measures may be adopted for affording redress to the injured parties.

The Governor in Council is unable to agree with your reasoning on the Gaṇod case, which appears to be based on the supposition that 'the whole voice of the community is opposed to the law,' or that against Infanticide. Government are convinced that the feeling of all classes of the community, except those who commit the crime, is exactly the reverse. Besides this, on the principles laid down for your guidance in this communication for conducting these investigations, the Gaṇod case would not have proceeded beyond the preliminary inquiry, which could not have failed to detect the false accuser and his motives. Were Government to respect what is termed by you the '*lares* and *penates*' of the Rajput community, all the efforts which have hitherto been made to eradicate the crime of female Infanticide must be relinquished and we must sink into our former apathy and supineness as to whether Colonel Walker's engagements are adhered to or not.

"It is justly observed by you that the cases of conviction which occurred in 1835, have rendered future detection more difficult, by having placed the Jáḍejás on their guard, but this, as before observed, is unavoidable; but Government consider that even throwing difficulties in the way of child-murder is something gained towards the completion of our ardent wishes. This, however, is not the only result of those convictions, for to no other cause can be attributed the gratifying fact, that in the short space of twelve months, 73 infants were preserved, independently of those saved in Nawánagar, the census of which may probably add 50 more to the number, a fact which of itself establishes that the measures, so strongly objected to by you, are not quite so inapplicable and unsuited to the attainment of the desired object as supposed by you.

"The Governor in Council is fully satisfied that your predecessor never could have contemplated transferring the responsibility of the crime of infanticide from the chief to the vassal, in cases where the former can fairly be held answerable. No chief, however, is held responsible for any offence the perpetrators of which are discovered. If a robbery occurs within his limits he is bound by the custom of the country to produce the robber, or to make good the loss. This principle should be maintained in cases of infanticide, as advocated in the report of your predecessor of September 1834, wherein it is proposed by him that fines in the first instance, and ultimate deprivation of sovereignty in cases of manifest delinquency, should be resorted to whenever the annual census shows that the practice prevails in any particular táluká. Towards the close of the 20th paragraph of that report, it is observed, 'Should, however, it be established by the certain though presumptive evidence to be obtained from returns of the nature now submitted, that the crime of infanticide still prevails in any particular district, which I think after a warning contained in the proclamation now proposed the chief of that district should be severely fined, and that if this does not produce attention on his part to his engagement to suppress the crime, I think that an example should be made, and that he should be deprived of the sovereignty of his district. The case, however, must be very glaring where I should propose such an extreme measure for adoption.'

"The Governor in Council considers that you labour under an equally erroneous impression, in supposing that it was ever under the contemplation of your predecessor to suggest, that those accused of infanticide should be tried 'by their brothers and instigators.' Had the proposition of the gentleman, that cases of this nature should, in some instances, be publicly investigated before the Political Agent's Court of Criminal Justice in Káṭhiáwáḍ, been approved by Government, it would have been the duty of the political agent, as in all ordinary offences, to have associated with himself assessors free from bias, or from the claims of relationship or friendship.'

"You advance objections to what is designated by you the 'sumptuary measures' for the suppression of Infanticide, a term which, cannot be considered to convey a correct idea of the nature of those measures. It is admitted by you that the rewards bestowed on those who preserved their daughters were well bestowed, but you observe that 'as those who now save their daughters will not evidently be entitled to any reward for the future, after such repeated and obstinate evil conduct, this plan will cease to be an engine for putting a stop to the practice.' The Governor in Council cannot perceive why such should be the consequence. On the contrary, Government would advocate a continuance of the system, at all events for some time to come. Hereafter, the innate love of offspring may be trusted as sufficient for our purpose, but for the present it is conceived that an annual distribution of presents, on the plan adopted by your predecessor, will produce a beneficial result.

You next object to the system now in force, of the Government contributing towards the expence incurred by Jáḍejás in marrying their daughters. The

Governor in Council conceives that such contributions should be made with caution, and should be preceded by a strict inquiry into the circumstances of the applying party. The Infanticide Fund was expressly created by Mr. Elphinstone's Government for this object, and the present amount of its accumulated fund (108,930 rupees) shows that it is not likely soon to become exhausted. An unfavourable opinion however is expressed by you of almost every measure which has heretofore been adopted, to win the Jáḍejás into acquiescence with the humane views of the British Government. The distribution of presents made by Mr. Langford, in 1829, among the Dharol Jáḍejás, is condemned by you, because you consider the correctness of the returns obtained by that gentleman 'extremely doubtful.' You likewise view in an unfavourable light the honorary presents bestowed by Government in 1829, on the son of Jehájí, the chief of Murví, who was the first to set the example of renouncing the practice of infanticide, and you express an opinion that the praise conveyed to the Jám of Nawánagar, at the recommendation of the late political agent, was a measure of evil tendency. All the above measures, however, are regarded by the Governor in Council as wise and judicious. With regard to your observation, that 'no previous steps were taken to ascertain whether the Jám was entitled or not to such eulogy, I am desired to refer to the 23rd paragraph of the late political agent's report, dated the 24th September 1834, wherein it is stated that the return from Nawánagar exhibited 613 males and 380 females, 'which proved that Colonel Walker's arrangement had taken root to a very considerable and gratifying extent.' It was then mentioned by your predecessor, that he at first intended to propose that an honorary present should be conferred on the Jám, to conciliate him as the acknowledged head of the Jáḍejá tribe in Káṭhiáwáḍ, but assigning reasons why he had abandoned this idea. That officer contented himself with suggesting, that in forwarding the proclamation to this chief, he should be informed 'of the satisfaction of Government at the progress made in his districts in suppressing infanticide, and urgently exhorted to adopt the strictest measures to ensure its final extinction.'

"I now proceed, under the instructions of the Honourable the Governor in Council, to remark on the measures proposed by you for the suppression of female Infanticide.

"With reference to the remarks contained in the 17th paragraph of your report, the Governor in Council regrets to find that Captain Lang's opinion on your proposals was not obtained previous to their being submitted to Government, more especially as it is admitted by you that 'on some points a difference of opinion exists between you and that officer.' Captain Lang's long residence in Káṭhiáwáḍ, his intimate acquaintance with every Jáḍejá chief in the province, his extensive local knowledge, and above all, his zealous and successful exertions personally to extirpate the crime render the opinion of this able officer of more than ordinary value, and you are therefore requested to obtain his sentiments on this subject, and submit the same to Government.

"The first measure proposed by you is, that all the Rajput chiefs in Káṭhiáwáḍ shall be required 'to enter into an engagement that they will not give their daughters to any tribe who will not give them their daughters in return,' and you are of opinion that the chiefs will be induced to enter into an engagement of this kind. Government are not quite so sanguine on this point, and imagine that even if such a measure were agreed to, it would not be generally adhered to. Still, however, there appears no objection to an attempt being made to obtain the voluntary assent of the chiefs to the arrangement, which, if successful, would undoubtedly aid the objects in view.

"Your second proposition is, that the Jáḍejá chiefs shall be required to enter into a stipulation, that the expenses of the marriage of the daughters of their bháíyád shall not exceed a certain amount, to be fixed at a general meeting of the caste, and be informed that Government will assist the indigent to the same extent as any other caste, but not to a greater. The Governor in Council is aware of no objection to the first part of this proposition, but in regard to the latter, it does not appear that Government have ever contributed to the marriage expenses of any other caste but the Jáḍejá. This should continue after due inquiry into the circumstances of the party requiring relief.

"With regard to your third proposition, that specific penalties should be proclaimed for the commission of Infanticide, after a certain time, to be fixed by Government, the Governor in Council is more disposed to allow each case to be dealt with, as at present, according to its merits, but cannot agree with your opinion that it is advisable to fix a period prospectively from which to punish the crime.

"On reference to the 24th paragraph of this letter, you will perceive that the fourth measure proposed by you, namely, that the chiefs be held responsible for the conduct of their bháíyád and vassals, is not a new suggestion, and the Governor in Council directs that this responsibility be enforced to the extent therein mentioned.

"The fifth proposition, or that the annual census should be the test, and that the chiefs should be enjoined to aid in framing this census, requires no remark, since these propositions were sanctioned by Government in 1835.

"Your sixth proposition is, that 'the period of two years, or such other time as Government shall decide, shall be granted to the Jáḍejás and others in the habit of committing the crime, during which time no investigation shall be made either with regard to the former or late cases, and that the result of the census at the termination of that period be the test.' The Governor in Council is quite at a loss to conceive the grounds of this proposal. If acceded to, entire impunity for the commission of the crime would be the result, and it is to be feared that many would avail themselves of the license.

"It was the intention of your predecessor, had he remained in Káṭhiáwáḍ to have proposed the policy of complying with the prayer of a petition presented to him by the Jáḍejás for an amnesty for past offence. This, however, in the opinion of the Governor in Council, would not on any account be extended beyond the period when every Jáḍejá must have become aware of the determination of Government to do all in their power to suppress the crime. The proclamation of your predecessor was the vehicle through which this information was conveyed, and Government are pleased to authorize an amnesty being granted up to the end of 1835.

"The Governor in Council does not perceive any present necessity for appointing a second censor, (as recommended at the close of your sixth proposition), more especially when the difficulty which has been experienced in finding persons fit for this duty is taken into consideration.

"Adverting to your seventh proposition, namely, that Government should endeavour to obtain the aid of the Ráo of Kachh for the suppression of Infanticide, I am directed to state, that in the opinion of the Honourable the Governor in Council, nothing would so much facilitate the suppression of this crime as obtaining the cordial co-operation of his Highness and the British authorities stationed in Kachh. The sentiments of the Ráo, as alluded to when discussing this proposition, prove that his Highness is favourably disposed towards the suppression of this crime, and the force of his example will doubtless have a most beneficial effect in inducing his Highness's tribe to abandon the inhuman practice. Extract of this part of your report has been sent to the acting assistant resident in charge, Kachh, with instructions to concert measures with his Highness for the abolition of Infanticide, which all the chiefs under his Highness's control have long since renounced, and it has been suggested to him that the first measure to be adopted should be to take a census of the Jáḍejá population of Kachh, a measure which has proved so beneficial in Káṭhiáwáḍ, the census being annually renewed.

"With reference to your suggestion that a general convocation of the chiefs of the Rajput race should be held at Bhuj in the presence of the Resident in Kachh and yourself, I am desired to state that the Governor in Council does not deem it expedient at the present time that such a measure should be adopted.

"With regard to your eighth and last proposition, namely, that the British Government should endeavour to effect the object in view by the education, mental improvement, and moral amelioration of the mass of the people, I am desired to observe, that your suggestions on this head have been already considered, and for the most part approved of by this Government. As an auxiliary measure, the diffusion of education is deserving of great attention, but measures of a more active character ought not to be relaxed, since years must elapsed before it can be expected that any material effect will be produced by the diffusion of education. The Governor in Council is willing to admit that education and knowledge will ultimately change the feelings and habits of a whole people; this, however must necessarily be a work of time, and it is not to knowledge so gained that the British Government must look to the cessation of the crime of infanticide, but to measures of vigour, tempered with prudence and conciliation.

"With reference to the 20th paragraph of your report, the Governor in Council is of opinion that it will be expedient to republish the proclamation issued in 1834, such modification being introduced as the altered state of circumstances and the census may render necessary, the same being submitted before promulgation for the approval of Government. The proclamation proposed in your report, if issued, would merely proclaim what is already sufficiently known, and would not, in the opinion of Government, be attended with any beneficial result. The Governor in Council would moreover decidedly object to any announcement in the name of the British Government, speaking of the Shástras as containing a declaration of the true law of God.

"The progress made in this great cause since your predecessor's administration, has, in the opinion of Government, been great, and entitles that gentleman to the highest commendation. In his measures a practical result has been experienced, and until Government find a better and more extensive practical result promised and likely to occur from the adoption of other measures, the Governor in Council is unwilling to depart from those which have proved so advantageous.

"Adverting to the circular letter proposed by you to be addressed to the chiefs of Káṭhiáwáḍ, I am desired to state that the Governor in Council does not consider it expedient at the present moment that the same should be issued.

"Government are anxiously awaiting the receipt of your reports promised in the 23rd and 25th paragraphs of your letter now under acknowledgment, and I am desired to remind you that your annual Infanticide report for 1837 was due on the 1st January 1838.

"Although the Governor in Council, as already explained, differs with you in many points connected with this subject, still he considers the zeal and diligence exhibited by you in your present report to be highly creditable to you.

"Appreciating, however, as Government do your exertions in this cause, still they do not think that you have properly understood the real character of some of the measures which were adopted at the recommendation of your predecessor. A conclusion might be drawn from your report that that gentleman had aimed to effect his object by penal measures only, a conclusion which the Governor in Council considers highly erroneous. In support of this conviction, and in proof that measures of a conciliatory character formed as much a part of his principle of proceeding as of your own, I am desired to refer you to the following communications from your predecessor to the chiefs and other influential persons in Káṭhiáwáḍ, on the subject of his proclamation, and the census of the Jáḍejá population, copies of which are herewith forwarded.

"A selection from the replies returned to the above letters is likewise forwarded for your information, and for the purpose of being placed on the records of your office."*

It was well, perhaps, that such a letter as Mr. Erskine's should have been submitted to Government. In lack of such a document, we should probably have wanted the preceding clear defence of Mr. Willoughby's admirable measures, and the suitable suggestions which were made for carrying them into practical effect.

Mr. Erskine's subsequent communications with Government on Infanticide in Káṭhiáwáḍ were of a limited character. They reported the suspension,—which afterwards issued in the dismission,—of the native employed in making the annual census of the Jáḍejás, for accepting a bribe for concealing the death of a Jáḍejá female which had occurred in suspicious circumstances; and the difficulties experienced in getting his place suitably filled up, as Government preferred the employment of a pure native in that duty to that of an Indo-Portuguese brought to notice by Mr. Erskine. They mentioned the completion of the Jáḍejá census of the Nawánagar táluká, which on the whole exhibited gratifying results. They brought to notice the arbitrary remission of part of the term of imprisonment of Jáḍejá Virájí,† an act which justly met with the disapprobation of Government, though it was ultimately confirmed.

Mr. D. A. Blane, whom we have already had occasion to notice as a zealous agent in Infanticide suppression,

* See above, pp. 213-220. † See above, pp. 210.

was the successor of Mr. Erskine in the political agency in Káṭhiáwáḍ. On the 17th November, 1840, he acknowledged a call from Government for an Infanticide Report, and expressed his regret that he had found that the statements of births, marriages, and deaths had fallen into arrears. He was not able personally to supply the documents which were wanted, as he was soon transferred to the secretariate in Bombay. Captain LeGrand Jacob, the first assistant at Rájkoṭ,—Captain Lang having been appointed to the political agency of the Máhíkántá in the north of the continental Gujarát, where he soon effected great good both with prince and people,—took charge of his duties on his departure from Káṭhiáwáḍ; and they could not have fallen into better hands, as far as ability, integrity, foresight, knowledge of native customs and character, and calm and successful perseverance in the discharge of duty in spite of an acute and sensitive discernment of difficulties, were concerned.

CHAPTER XI.

CAPTAIN LE GRAND JACOB'S EFFORTS FOR THE IMPROVEMENT OF THE KA'ṬHIA'WA'Ḍ CENSUS—HIS REPORT ON INFANTICIDE, AND SUGGESTION OF INSTRUCTIONAL MEASURES—FOUNDATION OF CHRISTIAN MISSION IN KA'ṬHIA'WA'Ḍ—VIEWS OF THE GOVERNMENT OF CAPTAIN JACOB'S REPORT—ADDITIONAL NOTICES OF MEASURES ADOPTED.

On the 9th of September, 1840, Captain Jacob called upon the rájá of Murví to supplement the Jáḍejá census of his táluká by including that of the Jáḍejá females of A'dhoí, a district belonging to that chief in the province of Wágar on the northern side of the gulf of Kachh, over which he claimed jurisdiction; and some delay occurring in the implementing of his request, he ordered the mehtás of A'dhoí directly to supply what was wanting. On the 22nd March, 1842, he addressed the following judicious letter to the Bombay Government, the occasion of which appears from its contents.

"I have the honour to acknowledge your letter, No. 608, dated 4th instant, with inclosures, calling on me for an opinion as to the practicability of introducing into this peninsula some system for placing limits to the fees exacted at marriage festivals by Chárans, Bháṭs, and other members of the eleemosynary community, similar to that adopted by Bijí Singh of Jaudpur.

"In reply, I beg to state that I do not consider such an arrangement either practicable or expedient. In the first place, because of the number of independent chiefs, whose relative rank it would be difficult to fix; and if an assembly of delegates could be got together for the purpose, their mutual jealousies and pride would bar the attainment of the ends in view. To speak of the Járejás alone, whom Government, I conclude, have chiefly in view, the Murví chief being descended from an elder branch of the Kachh dynasty, considers himself at least equal in rank to the Jám of Nagar, who has five times his means, and far above the Gondal family, which state is twice as wealthy as his. Were it a question only of a single principality, as in Kachh, where the subordinate Bháíyáds have fixed rank in relation to the head of their tribe, the object might, perhaps, be attained by simple publication of a recommendatory letter from the chief to his mendicant tribes not to ask for more than such stipulated amount as he might fix, with due reference to the feelings of the community generally; and doubtless the establishment of any such system by the Ráo would have great effect in leading the chief of the Járejá tribe in this province to follow the example. In the second place, I doubt the expediency of introducing any such rule under British sanction. The custom of importuning for presents is injurious both to giver and receiver, by encouraging pride and mendicity. The influence of Bháṭs and Chárans in this peninsula has been considerably diminished since the period of our connexion with it; witness the entire change of the mode of obtaining security, whether for payment of tribute or for other transactions. As the nature of our system of Government becomes more and more understood and the people more enlightened, so will begging cease to thrive as a profession. We might slightly diminish present mischief by fixing a standard, but the doing so would only give perpetuity to an evil that the hand of time is gently eradicating." These views of Captain Jacob were approved by the Bombay Government. The fixture by authority of the British administration of gifts to Bráhmans, Bháṭs, and Chárans whatever reduction of expence to the chiefs might in the first instance be accomplished by it, would evidently give a sanction to the system of superstitious mendicancy, alike opposed to Christian principle and political expediency.

Previous to the date of the communication now noticed,—on the 23rd October 1841,—Captain Jacob had furnished to Government a full infanticide census for 1840, including that of the Jaitwás of Bardá and the suspected tribes in A'dhoí in Wágar, with an able general review of the late progress of the cause of humanity, a document, however, which was not finally disposed of by Government till August 1842.

Captain Jacob in the commencement of his communication explains the circumstances in which no regular report on Infanticide had been forwarded to Bombay for four years. "Shortly after the despatch of Mr. Erskine's Report in 1837, the fact of the infanticide censor, Munshí Ghulám Muhammad, having accepted a bribe to quash an accusation of child-slaughter transpired." "The removal of this person, otherwise so well suited for the situation, was a check that this particnlar department of the agency has scarcely recovered from, in consequence of his successor Jayasukrám, entertained 1st April 1839, having proved quite unequal to the office, and having been finally removed from it by Mr. Blane so recently as 1st April last, when Náká Wajerám, an intelligent Bráhman of the Nágar caste, was appointed in his stead. In the interval between the suspension of the munshí and the appointment of his successor, Mr. Gonsalves, a clerk in the office, was employed in taking the Nawánagar census, which will be found included in the accompanying tables."

Captain Jacob then proceeds to comment on the census which he forwarded to Government, noticing as he proceeds some important acts, arrangements, and proposals.

"For the above reason, the census now submitted must be received with some extra caution, the new censor not having had time to visit all the parganás; but I have checked the returns of both, by those obtained from the chiefs for the first half of the present year, as well as by the aid of attachment mehtás, where they were sufficiently trustworthy to be made use of. The only táluká in which there appears discrepancy is Gondal, the census of which was taken by the present censor, and unfortunately the detailed lists, whence the last census was framed, are not forthcoming in this office, so that I have no means of testing the present one by comparison of names."

"The results of the present census, as exhibited in the analysis appended, are extremely gratifying, with exception of the Sháhpur táluká, and A'dhoí purganá of Murví. In the former, not a single female has escaped the ruthless effect of Jáḍejá pride; in the latter, the census of which is now exhibited for the first time, and has been obtained with considerable difficulty, the proportion of males to females is nearly 17 to 1. Some excuse may be offered for this district, which had hitherto escaped the vigilance of the British Government, and separated as it is from Káṭhiáwáḍ, remained in comparative ignorance of the strenuous attempt to suppress infanticide that had here been made; but I can offer none for Sháhpur, the chief of which, by his breach of faith and criminal negligence, has justly laid himself open to the displeasure of a paternal Government.

"Jáḍejá Kaláji of Sháhpur is about 30 years of age, and by no means deficient in intellect; he must have been fully sensible that Government would hold the Jáḍejás to their engagements, since he had already been called to account on this matter, in the case of his brother Jáḍejá Bháwájí." "The revenues that he derives annually from his táluká, which now consists of four villages, of which one belongs to his Bháíyád, are estimated at 2,000 rupees, subject to a yearly tribute of 501 rupees to the British Government, and 157½ rupees to the Nawáb of Junágaḍ (*Zortalabi*) leaving him a clear rental of about 1,400 rupees. I beg, therefore, to recommend, that a fine of rupees 1,000 be imposed upon him, with a warning that, unless future returns give a result more favourable to humanity he should be deprived of all control over his táluká, and that he be required to furnish unexceptionable security against continuance of the crime; and in default of such payment and security, after the elapse of two months, that he be placed in confinement until those terms are complied with.

"Regarding A'dhoí [in Wágar], a more lenient course may be pursued, but the Murví chief might be warned of the danger he was incurring by thus permitting his Bháíyád, the other side of the water, to break at once the laws of nature and humanity, and the engagements he has entered into, on behalf of all subject to his authority.

"It is a much more pleasing task to revert to the state of all the other Jáḍejá tálukás of Káṭhiáwáḍ; and it must be highly gratifying to those benevolent men who have laboured for the suppression of Infanticide in this province to see the progressive return to the order of nature, in the relative proportion of sexes, that must be attributed to their labour alone. The total male population is shown to be 5,760, females 1,370; the proportion, therefore, of all ages is a fraction more than four to one, but the number of both sexes under 20 years of age, is, males 2,923, females 1,209, showing a proportion of two and a quarter to one, which favourable diminution chiefly arises from the preservation of female life during the last few years, which gives the general result as follows:

Proportion of males to females, under		10 years	1¾	to 1
Ditto	ditto	9 years	1¾	to 1
Ditto	ditto	8 years	1¾	to 1
Ditto	ditto	7 years	1½	to 1
Ditto	ditto	6 years	1¼	to 1
Ditto	ditto	5 years	1	to 1
Ditto	ditto	4 years	1	to 1
Ditto	ditto	3 years	1	to 1
Ditto	ditto	2 years	1	to 1
Ditto	ditto	1 year	1	to 1¼

"The correctness of these returns is further tested by the proportion of deaths occurring in 1840, which is shown as three to one.

"The total number of cases that have come under inquiry since the transmission of Mr. Erskine's Report, 30th June 1837, is seven, of which one only was proved, namely, that of Wakhatsingh of Nawágáum, a village under Máliá, connected with which the former censor, Ghulám Muhammad, lost his place for accepting a bribe, as before stated. The murder of Wakhatsingh's infant, it will be perceived, occurred before the publication of the Government proclamation, when you [Mr. Willoughby, secretary to Government] were political agent of this province in 1835, and cannot therefore be taken as any breach thereof, however much it may be of the laws of humanity; and yet Wakhatsingh had reared three daughters, and his accuser, Satájí, the Máliá chief, out of four had not preserved one."

"The census of the Jaitwá population now for the first time given, has been furnished, after some demur by theRáná's Government [at Porbandar], and has not yet been further tested. It approaches nearly to the proportions shown for the Jáḍejá population." "It was first brought to notice by Colonel Walker, that this tribe was equally addicted to the crime as the Jáḍejás themselves;* and it is curious to remark the coincidence between the proportions of sexes preserved in both tribes, though the vigilance of Government being bent on the Jáḍejás alone, has acted indirectly, and therefore with less force, on the Jaitwás."

"The crime of Infanticide is, I fear, by no means confined to either the Jáḍejá or Jaitwá population. I have heard assertions of its being extensively practised in Jaitwáḍ, and amongst the Muhammadan tribe of Sétás, but with the all but impossibility that exists of carrying through the common duties of the agency, I

* See above, p. 72.

have been unable to spare sufficient time for inquiry into the subject. The full extent to which infanticide is practised in the peninsula will be known only when Government is able to spare the services of an officer for this especial inquiry. I have the honour to annex translates of agreements entered into by the Mánká and Korangá tribes of Wágar,* who are accused of this crime, which I owe to the Government kárkun, Ishwardás, stationed at A'dhoí, and through whom the Jáḍejá census of that district has been obtained. These tribes are stated to be neither Muhammadans nor Hindus, but a mixture of the two, approaching in caste to the Wágars of Okhámandal. Writings have also been taken from the A'dhoí Jáḍejás, who had not before brought themselves under similar engagements, translations of which are given.

"The imperfection of our instruments must ever throw some degree of doubt on returns of population, that can be obtained only through their labour; but a further cause of hesitation in receiving the census as entirely to be depended on, exists in the difficulty that has been found in getting the Jáḍejás, of respectable rank, to show their females to a male censor. This repugnance was yielded to, in consequence of the Jám's earnest remonstrances, and as sanctioned by Government letter 9th October 1838. Mr. Gonsalves was accompanied by his wife throughout his tour in the Nagar states. The like treatment has been claimed by others, and a considerable portion of the females entered in the returns from which my tables are framed have no other guarantee for their existence than the word of their male relations. Their prejudices in this matter are so deep-rooted, and supported by public feeling and sympathies, that I conceive we should err in attempting to force them. Besides, it will never do to treat the Já-

* [These tribes, we believe, are converts to Muhammadism, from the Kulís, or aborigines, of the district.]

ḍejás of one táluká better than those of another. I therefore beg respectfully to recommend the extension of the principle already sanctioned for the Nagar Rajputs to the rest of the community; the wife or other nearest female relative of the censor might be granted a sum equivalent to half of what he draws, during the time actually employed in taking the census; every endeavour by persuasion should be made to overcome the prejudices of the inspected: but where decided repugnance may be evinced, it should be the duty of the censor to acquaint himself with all particulars through his wife, he being held equally responsible for the correctness of the statement as if taken by himself. I consider this addition necessary for the proper carrying out of the plan for suppression of Infanticide, so ably matured by yourself when political agent. Bribes may sometimes lead astray, but the husband cannot well help knowing the real facts of the case, and he will have a double motive for not suppressing them. At present, facility is, to a certain extent, offered for fictitious report, to skreen from guilt."

Major Jacob in the conclusion of his report frankly expresses his convictions as to the state of feeling respecting infanticide prevailing among the Jáḍejás and their neighbours of other tribes, and as to the expediency and necessity of adopting instructional measures for its improvement.

"I would now beg to point out wherein I differ from previous writers on the subject of Infanticide. The state of public opinion in this country has been supposed more strongly set against the crime than I believe to be the case. Complimentary letters or remarks, in reply to strongly expressed opinions by persons in power, are no criterion of real feelings, which must be judged of by acts. I can trace eye-service to Government, but no real service to humanity, in the profession of such of the community as pretend to take any interest in the matter. Of all the population, the most tender of life are the Shráwaks or Jainas, the monied classes, who possess great influence throughout the peninsula. They have in several places forced the Rajput, and other chiefs, to enter into agreements not to permit the slaughter of sheep, etc.; but though child-murder within the same district was notorious, as far as my knowledge extends, they have not so much as attempted to stipulate for the preservation of human beings.* Again, all the Rajputs who rear their daughters feel a direct interest in the continuance of the crime by others. They might at once prevent it, by stipulating before marriage that their daughters' children should be preserved, yet though pressed to take this step, I am not aware (my remarks are limited to this province) of an instance in which it has been done. If, therefore, as has been stated, the community in general consider the crime as one of the deepest dye, they would appear to make very little use of their opinions. The fact, I fear to be, that the population is in a state of semibarbarism, with whom philanthropy, apart from superstitious motive, is an unknown principle. They are, of course, the creatures of circumstances; and I say this, simply to denote that there is no public feeling to assist the penal machinery established by us for the suppression of the particular crime under review."†

"The general result of the measures hitherto pursued, supposing the returns to be correct, are doubtless most satisfactory as far as regards the end for which they were established, namely, the saving of life; but they are not free from evil in other respects, to diminish which is decidedly politic if the object could be attained by milder means. The distress caused to families by the feeling, that whenever accidental death may have

* [This statement is quite in accordance with what we have ourselves noticed in Káṭhiáwáḍ. See above, p. 71.]

† [This paragraph is followed by a passage which we have introduced at p. 132, above.]

occurred they are laid open to be victims of any one who owes them a grudge, and the entire tearing down of the Rajput curtain which inquiry inflicts, give rise to heart-burnings and animosities, even when the result is a conviction of innocence of the accused, and is particularly to be lamented; for it is sometimes impossible to arrive at a satisfactory decision without such process. The whole system in force is, moreover, one of perpetual and harsh inquisition into the domestic affairs of a proud tribe, carrying alarm into every family: if a wife be pregnant, if a child is born, if a daughter be sick, a messenger must be despatched to give notice to some superior power, who, if feud exists—and where does it not amongst a people like this?—may make each occasion a handle for oppression or annoyance. If an infant perchance die, the family are kept in a state of apprehension for an indefinite time as they can never be certain when an enemy may, or may not, prefer an accusation against them; and it is needless for me to mention, that in a state of society like this, subornation of evidence is a matter of daily occurrence.*

"Neither can the system be relied on, except during the pressure of a vigilant supervision, that is becoming more and more difficult from the increase of the business of the agency. If the heart remain unchanged, there must be danger of relapse when that pressure becomes relaxed; for we have no warrant for supposing the voice of nature to be alone sufficient to prevent falling back into a custom that was not sufficient to prevent its adoption; but I cannot bring myself to regard the present anti-infanticide measures as other than temporary, to be removed on the entrance of the Jáḍejás into the order of nature. I deduce from these reflections the corollary that, first, there is some risk of the coercive machinery breaking down, from want of

* [The inconveniences here alluded to are undeniable; but they form a strong motive to the Jáḍejás to abandon the crime which has given rise to the measures in which they have originated.]

power to guide it; but supposing the vigilance of the Government agents to continue, until the end be attained of the coercive process, there is, secondly, danger of relapse on its withdrawal. To keep it working after the end has been gained, would be as unjust as perpetual suspension of the Habeas Corpus Act, after the riots, for which it might have been suspended, had passed away. And, thirdly, that the saving of a number of human beings, leaving them to be brought up in ignorance and vice, the animal part saved, the moral powers totally neglected, is a questionable boon to the parties themselves, whatever it may be as to its humanizing effects on society in general.

"It is evident from the above observations, that I feel strongly impressed with the necessity of a line of policy that shall strike at the heart, and consequently at the root of the disease, and afford a permanent remedy; and I beg therefore to urge the propriety of attempting it without further delay. It is true that no immediate result can be expected from education; but the slow growth of its blessings is an argument for no time being lost in the attempt to impart them. We may save life by the census, but how can we protect it from misery and neglect afterwards? Whilst approving, therefore, of the present coercive system, I conceive that it should be looked on merely as a temporary expedient, and that it ought to be accompanied by healing and generous measures, namely, an attempt to create a higher tone of moral feeling throughout the community generally.

"The Infanticide Fund this day shows a balance of rupees 1,16,786 in hand; and I conceive that a large portion of this sum cannot be more judiciously expended than in the cause of education.*

"This letter has brought to light the existence of several tribes, by whom infanticide is supposed to be practised; and how know we, among the myriads of

* [This is followed by the general observations on the fund which we have quoted at pp. 163-4.]

the Peninsula, how many secret crimes of the deepest dye are perpetrated? It is evident that a state of society, where a race of wholesale murderers are looked upon with as much respect as others, must be vicious at the core. Such being the case, it occurs to me as fitting and proper that general should be superadded to partial measures; that the amelioration of the whole state of society be attempted; and that our spare funds, raised from the community generally, should no longer be exclusively devoted to the use of a particular class. With this view, I would give every encouragement to the cause of education, and to every means that may enlighten the intellect and improve the heart; accordingly I beg to recommend as follows:

"That a sum of rupees 4,000 be set apart from the Infanticide Fund for the erection of a school-house. On this subject I will here observe, that I have received four replies only to the circular letters addressed by me to all the principal men in the country [on the encouragement which might be expected from them of education], as brought to the notice of Government in my letter No. 183, of the 21st June last, and approved of in Mr. Chief Secretary Reid's reply No. 2,096, of the 27th of the following month. One only of these gave any definite answer. This was a letter from Ranmalsinghjí, the Kuwár [son, heir-apparent] of Drángadrá,* written by himself in Hindustání,† informing me that he highly approved of the proposed measure, and would subscribe 20 rupees a year towards its execution. Had the sum been somewhat larger, I should have solicited the favour of Government towards a chief who had shown himself so superior to his countrymen.

"That a sum of at least rupees 300 a month should be

* [The chief state of the Jhálá Rajputs.]

† [The Drángadrá family have considerable oriental linguistic attainments, knowing Gujarátí, Hindustání, Persian, and a little Sanskrit.]

set apart for the salaries of schoolmasters and current expenses of the establishment.

"That 1,000 rupees a year be devoted to the encouragement of annual essays in the vernacular language, on the subject of infanticide, part as prizes, and the rest for expenses of printing numerous copies of the best essay for distribution throughout the community. This measure would enlist the feelings of the rising generation against the crime, the scholars of the Rájkoṭ college might catch the spirit of emulation; and it is not unreasonable to hope, that before many years, a popular feeling would be created adverse to infanticide, that might enable Government to dispense with at least the harsh portions of the present coercive system, as the scaffolding is removed on completion of the building. In speaking as I do of the severity of the present system, I beg again to disclaim the slightest intention to disparage it. On the contrary, I conceive that humanity owes a deep debt of gratitude to the exertions of those gentlemen who have planned and matured the system. It has acted, and still acts, as a tempest that purifies the atmosphere; but which, nevertheless, no one wishes to see of long continuance. The atrocious nature of the crime, and the impossibility of eradicating it by any ordinary process has sufficiently, and by the result most satisfactorily, proved the necessity of the rigorous measures that have been established. My views are simply that other measures should be superadded, that might the more speedily enable us to dispense with what is now a necessary evil; and that the restrictions on the use of the Infanticide Fund should be abolished.

"The only objection that the above appropriation of the Mausulí* and Fine Funds, as far as I am aware, is susceptible of, is the engagement entered into with his Highness the Gáikawáḍ on the subject; but I cannot

* [Fines levied by the quartering of horsemen and foot-messengers on the chiefs.]

conceive, after that prince had once consented to surrender the funds, that it would signify to him whether they were bestowed in communicating knowledge, or in permitting the Jáḍejás and their friends to enjoy greater pomp at their festivals; on the contrary, his Highness might naturally be supposed willing to agree to anything that would so cheaply add to his fame, and no great difficulty could, I should think, occur in overcoming any scruples that might be found to exist; at any rate, the British Government is master of its own funds, and these could be applied to mental and moral purposes, whilst those under the gift of his Highness could be spent, as at present, in providing for the body."

It may be here mentioned, that a few months before Captain Jacob's reasonable and practicable proposals about the adoption of educational measures for Káṭhiáwáḍ were submitted to Government, incipient arrangements for the instruction and enlightenment of the province by the most efficient source of moral regeneration, the foundation of a Christian mission, were carried into effect. During a long tour through Káṭhiáwáḍ in 1835,—in the larger portion of which he enjoyed the valued fellowship and assistance of the Rev. William Fyvie late of Surat,—the writer of this historical narrative became practically acquainted with its claims on the Christian philanthropy of Europe and its promise in an evangelistic point of view; and having been afterwards asked to recommend a sphere of foreign missionary labour to the Irish Presbyterian Church, he briefly stated its peculiarities to that zealous and efficient member of the Christian Body, the evangelistic doings of which in the province of Ulster are so well known and appreciated. Káṭhiáwáḍ was consequently chosen as a field of foreign missionary exertions; and the Rev. James Glasgow, and the Rev. Alexander Kerr, with their esteemed partners, came to India with a view to their commencement. The Bombay Government readily gave them permission to settle in the province; and on their arrival at Rájkoṭ in June 1841, along with the writer of this notice who sought briefly to introduce them to their work, they received a most cordial and generous welcome from Major Jacob, Colonel W. D. Robertson commanding the station, and other friends there residing, and from several of the chiefs of the peninsula, including Surájí of Rájkoṭ, so unfavourably noticed in the history of infanticide, who was among them the first of these chiefs to hear from our lips the doctrines of salvation. We had not been long at the place, however, when we were all seized with violent fever, which in the case of Mr. Kerr proved fatal, while in another it had nearly the same termination. Mr. Glasgow remained at his post, after his sore bereavement and heavy affliction; and next year he was joined by his brother the Rev. Adam Glasgow, and the Rev. Robert Montgomery. The mission was further strengthened in the beginning of 1843 by the accession of the Rev. James McKee and the Rev. J. H. Speers, and in 1846 by that of the Rev. James Wallace. The Gujarátí, and, in some instances, other Indian languages, were speedily acquired by the missionaries. Stations were formed at Rájkoṭ, Porbandar, and Goghá, while Junágaḍ was temporarily occupied. Much information by conversation and preaching was communicated to all classes of the natives, both at their residences and during itineracies. An English and two Vernacular schools were founded at Rájkoṭ; and vernacular elementary schools at the other stations. Tracts and books were prepared and printed,—principally at Surat, at which one of the missionaries ultimately settled in consequence of difficulties of accommodation and action at Porbandar,—and extensively circulated. A few natives, from both Hindus and Muhammadans, were not wanting as seals of the Christian ministry. The Jáḍejás, with many of whom the missionaries have maintained intercourse, have shared in their efforts, and have undoubtedly participated in the salutary moral influences which they have begun to diffuse around them. They will doubtless prove, with the blessing of God, powerful auxiliaries to the cause of anti-infanticide and humanity in general throughout the province.

The reply of Government to Captain Jacob's communication was principally founded on a minute of Mr. Willoughby, but it was conveyed to him in a letter from Mr. L. R. Reid, Chief Secretary to Government, dated the 12th August 1842, of which the following are the most important portions.

"The Governor in Council considers the explanation afforded by you, of the circumstance of no report having been submitted to Government on this subject between June 1837 and October 1841, to be far from satisfactory."*

"The facts stated regarding the táluká of Sháhpur, strongly illustrate the evils arising from the orders of Government requiring the periodical reports on infanticide not having been attended to. Government is now apprised that during the four years now reported on, 'not a single female has escaped the ruthless effect of Jáḍejá pride.' Had this melancholy fact been earlier reported, preventive measures might have long since been adopted. Kalájí, the chief of Sháhpur, cannot plead ignorance in extenuation of his culpable apathy, or what may be more justly termed his connivance, at the perpetration of infanticide in the villages. This chief is represented to be a man of intelligence, and in 1836 was fined 50 rupees as a mark of the displeasure of Government for having been privy to the concealment of the birth of his niece, who, there were strong grounds for believing, was put to death shortly after birth. After the severe examples which have been made in Káṭhiáwáḍ, the fine of 1,000 rupees suggested by you to be imposed on Kalájí seems scarcely an adequate punishment, but as Government deems it safe to err on the side of leniency, even at this late period, in

* [For this delay Major Jacob, who was not in charge of the political agency during the larger portion of the interval, was in no degree responsible.]

enforcing the engagements against infanticide, the Honourable the Governor in Council is pleased to sanction the proposed fine; and you are requested, in requiring this chief to renew his engagements, strictly to warn and assure him that his continuance in withholding his cordial co-operation with the British Government for the suppression of this crime, will inevitably lead to the sequestration of his táluká."

"Adverting to the 8th paragraph of your report, I am desired to inform you, that as the district of A'dhoí has now, for the first time, been brought within the census, Government is disposed to make some allowance for the non-observance of his engagement by the chief who owns that district; but it is desirable that he should be warned, in the name of Government, and in writing, that this will be the last time he will receive such indulgence. I am, on this occasion, desired to refer you to the instructions of Government, contained in Mr. Secretary Willoughby's letter, dated the 29th June, No. 1841, directing you to extend to A'dhoí, the measures which have, for some years past, been in force in Káṭhiáwáḍ, for the prevention of infanticide.

"It is in the highest degree satisfactory to Government to observe, from the statements submitted with your present report, that notwithstanding the unfavourable result of the census of the district of A'dhoí and the Sháhpur táluká, still the excess of male over female registered births in the province of Káṭhiáwáḍ, within the 30 Jáḍejás táluká mentioned by you, was in 1837-38 only 27; in 1838-39, 29; and in 1839-40, 27; while in 1840-41, the census exhibits an excess of 32 females over the males.

"With reference to the 10th and 11th paragraphs of your report, the Governor in Council regrets much to perceive that out of seven cases of alleged infanticide investigated by the Political Agent, between May 1838 and September 1840, conviction should have followed in one instance only, although the presumption of guilt was more or less strong in four of the other cases, two only being proved false accusations."

"The fact stated in the 12th paragraph of your report, that although the Jaitwá tribe was not included in the arrangements adopted against the Jáḍajás, still that their adoption has indirectly tended to the preservation of females among the Jaitwás, is considered by Government to be very satisfactory, and the Governor in Council will look forward with great interest for your promised report in regard to this tribe.

"With reference to the 13th paragraph, I am desired to request that you will embrace the first opportunity of instituting inquiries, with the view of ascertaining whether, as is alleged, the crime of infanticide prevails among other tribes in Káṭhiáwáḍ besides those of the Jáḍejá and Jaitwá, and to inform you that it is satisfactory to Government to observe that you have succeeded in obtaining from the Mánká and Koranjá tribes of Wágar, and from the Jáḍejás of Adhoí agreements to renounce this practice.

"The Honourable the Governor in Council is pleased to sanction the arrangement proposed in the 14th paragraph of your report, that the wife or nearest female relative of the person employed to take the Jáḍejá census, be associated with him in the performance of this duty, as it will doutless constitute another check against false returns; you are accordingly authorized to grant to such female, during the time actually employed in taking the census, a monthly allowance equal to half of the salary drawn by the censor, to be debited to the Infanticide Fund, great care being taken to secure that the proposed limitation is duly observed.

"While the Honourable the Governor in Council admits that there is some force in the general observations offered by you in the concluding paragraphs of your report, he is not aware that it has ever been contended that public opinion in Káṭhiáwáḍ was so strong against the crime of Infanticide, as to induce the other classes, spontaneously to come forward and actively co-operate with the British Government, in its suppression. All that has been urged is this, that the voice of nature being with us, the measures adopted would at all events not be misunderstood, even if they are not viewed with decided approbation. In respect to the inquisitorial nature of the measures adopted by Government, it is, in the opinion of the Governor in Council, an unavoidable and necessary evil, since by no other means can the suppression of Infanticide be accomplished,* and Government must rely on the judgment and descretion of its agents to prevent the innocent suffering from false accusations. These have, on a few occasions, undoubtedly been preferred, but they have been heretofore invariably detected, and none but the really guilty have suffered punishment. It will afford the British Government the highest gratification to see that happy day when it can with safety relax the penal measures now in operation against Infanticide, but, as observed by you, the present system can only be relied upon 'during the pressure of vigilant supervision,' and even though other duties are neglected, the agent must never

* [On this matter the minute of the Mr. G. W. (now Sir George) Anderson is well worthy of notice. "Captain Jacob points strongly the injury done to the wounded feelings of Jáḍejá pride, by the inquisitorial character of the inquiries the very nature of the crime compels Government to sanction. But Captain Jacob sees, as well as any one else, that without these very inquiries the end in view would be as far from us as ever; and therefore we have the choice of having inquiry so made, or quietly allowing this infant-murder to stalk abroad as rife as ever. As to education, if we are to wait for its effects, to trust to its influence, we must look forward perhaps to not less than a century. No, we must sincerely persist in our present efforts in our present system to stop this course of murder; and once effectually checked, we may hope that the feeling and prejudice causing it may be overcome, and then the inclination cease. To accomplish that change of prejudice and inclination must be our continued effort; and it is evident our present system has already effected much of this. I would strictly continue it, yet certainly add to it as much of education as circumstances will admit."]

relax from that supervision. The complete suppression of this crime must be a work of time; but looking back to the past, and seeing how much has been effected within a few short years, Government is encouraged strongly to hope that a steady and continued perseverance in the measures now in operation will ultimately be crowned with full and entire success. On a reference to Mr. Willoughby's first report on this subject, dated the 24th September 1834, it appears that the number of Jáḍejá females then ascertained to have been preserved in Káṭhiáwáḍ of all ages amounted to 696, and your present report exhibits a total of 1,370, being an increase of 674 in less than seven years, which result exceeds the most sanguine expectations of Government.

"With reference to the propositions contained in the 21st and 22nd paragraphs of your report for the diffusion of education in the province of Káṭhiáwáḍ, I am directed to inform you that the Honourable the Governor in Council does not deem it expedient to mix up the question of education with that of infanticide; for Government has already once determined that the Infanticide Fund shall not be trenched upon for purposes of education; and that before departing from this resolution, the consent of his Highness the Gáikawáḍ is necessary. The Governor in Council is, however, of opinion that you should still endeavour to ascertain to what extent the chiefs and monied-men in Káṭhiáwáḍ are disposed to aid in the introduction of a general system of education in that province, and to report the result to Government.

"I am at the same time instructed to signify to you, that if it is deemed desirable, the Governor in Council has no objection to a prize being offered for an essay against the practice of infanticide, to be afterwards printed and circulated in Káṭhiáwáḍ; but that the offer should be made to the scholars of the Native Education Society in Bombay, as an object of emulation amongst them, and the amount thereof charged to the educational funds. Government will, however, await your opinion on the subject.

"With the view of proving that the British Government is resolved to persevere in its efforts to suppress the inhuman practice of infanticide, and in order that the subject may be kept alive in the minds of the people of Káṭhiáwáḍ, the Honourable the Governor in Council considers it advisable and expedient that you should embody the results of the present census in a proclamation, noticing in terms of commendation those chiefs who by these results are proved to have adhered to their engagements and the reverse of those who have not done so. This proclamation should be circulated throughout the province of Káṭhiáwáḍ. I am on this occasion desired to draw your attention to Mr. Chief Secretary Norris's letter, dated the 22nd November (No. 1,824 of 1834); and to request that you will be pleased to report whether the instructions of Government therein conveyed have been acted upon, and particularly whether the measure sanctioned in the 8th paragraph, of endeavouring to induce the heads of those tribes who give daughters in marriage to the Jáḍejás, to stipulate at the time of betrothment for the preservation of female issue by such marriages, has been carried into effect, and if so, with what success.

"With reference to the 22nd paragraph of Mr. Willoughby's Report on Infanticide on the subject of granting remission from, and delays in payment of tribute, and honorary presents either in clothes or money to such of the chiefs of Káṭhiáwáḍ as may distinguish themselves by a conspicuous adherence to their engagements to renounce the custom of infanticide, I am directed to state that the Governor in Council is desirous of being informed whether the present census does not enable you to point out any chiefs or inferior members of the tribe who have rendered themselves deserving of the indulgences and rewards proposed by Mr. Willoughby.

"In conclusion, I am desired to inform you that the

Honourable the Governor in Council considers you fully entitled to the high approbation of Government for the zealous attention you have bestowed on the interesting question of the final and complete extinction of infanticide in Káṭhiáwáḍ.

"A copy of your present report and of this reply will be forwarded for the information of the political agent in Kachh."

The letter addressed to Captain Jacob, from which we have made these quotations, was acknowledged by him in a communication dated the 28th November 1842, which contained various articles of valuable intelligence, and directed attention to several interesting enclosures.

Respecting Jáḍejá Kalájí of Sháhpur Captain Jacob thus wrote: "Certain favorable features in his case, that have come to notice since I framed my last report, induce me to plead in mitigation, if not remission, of his punishment. A small table appended will show that only eight persons are married within his Táluká, who have eleven sons and two daughters born since my last census. Although no daughter was alive at that time, yet four had been born, and the sickness previous to the decease of three of these reported; and persons it appears had been deputed by the political agent to inspect and report thereon—consequently except in the suspicious case in Bháwájí's family for which Kalájí was fined, it seems by no means impossible that the disproportion between males and females may be accounted for by natural causes. In addition to these ircumstances, the greater part of the Rájkoṭ Bháíyád waited on me in a body to intercede for Kalájí with Government, promising to hold themselves responsible that no deviation from the pledge to preserve life should hereafter occur in the Sháhpur family. I do myself the honor to annex translation of their petition; and it appears to me that it would further the cause of humanity if Government would be pleased to extend an act of grace to the petitioning chiefs in behalf of their kinsman. The leniency could not be mistaken, since the security it holds out for the future is greater than what would result from disregarding the guarantee as well as the feelings of so many respectable Grásiás; and it may be deemed wise to reserve punishment for cases where the possibility of innocence cannot be held forth to enlist the feelings of the people against the measures of Government."

Into these views the Government entered very readily; and Mr. A. Malet of the Civil Service, who was appointed Political Agent in Káṭhiáwád, in succession to Mr. Blane, was in due time instructed to carry them into effect.

Captain Jacob also reported the readiness of the Murví chief to follow out the views of Government in reference to A'dhoí, and to use his influence for the prevention of Infanticide among the few Súmrás resident on his estate.* In reference to the Súmrás he gave a similar assurance in behalf of the chief of Dharol. This information was satisfactory to Government, which gave directions that these chiefs should be kept to their promises.

In regard to the female department of the censorship, Captain Jacob thus wrote: "I regret to say that I have as yet been unable to make arrangements for securing the aid of a female censor." "The prejudices of the Nágar [Bráhman] to which the present censor belongs lead him to demur acceptance of the Government offer. The chief difficulty is the alarm of being called on personally to give evidence before any functionary of Government in cases of real or supposed infanticide. The Nágar caste is particularly tenacious of the privacy of their women; but this difficulty may I hope be got over, as any examination might, I think, be conducted through the husband, or at any rate on the understanding that the pardah should be respected. Should his

* The Sumrás, like the Jáḍejás, are portions of a tribe from Sindh. See above, p. 56.

Honor-in-Council view this point in a different light, it will, I fear, become necessary to change the present censor, who is otherwise very well qualified for his office." The reply to this part of Captain Jacob's communication was the following. "It is on all occasions the desire of Government to abstain from making any innovations on the prejudices of caste when the public interests or those of the community will not thereby be endangered, but that as by the adoption of the plan proposed by Captain Jacob, a great risk would be incurred of collusion or concealment another censor must be appointed, unless the individual now entrusted with that duty will agree to some female being associated with him who is not incumbered with prejudices of the nature mentioned by Capt. Jacob, since it will be highly important that the political agent should have the free and unrestricted power of questioning the female employed upon this delicate duty, and that in cases of supposed infanticide in which her evidence may be required by the political agent she should give it without fear or demur of any kind."

Referring to education as a "special antidote to the moral disease under review," Captain Jacob expressed his belief that unless the Government took the lead in the matter nothing could be expected from the chiefs, adding that the Infanticide Funds were ample for the object, and repeating his sentiment that being raised from the whole community they could not be better employed than in promoting the benefit of the whole community. With reference to this matter, Captain Jacob was again requested to inform Government whether he had "endeavoured to ascertain the extent to which the chiefs and monied-men in Káṭhiáwáḍ could be prevailed upon to aid in the introduction of a general system of education in that province."

In regard to a prize essay on Infanticide, Capt. Jacob recommended that the sum offered should be liberal, say a thousand rupees; that public competition should be invited; and that the Board of Education should decide on the merits of the competitors. The sums eventually offered by Government were six hundred rupees for the best, and four hundred for the second best essay, if worthy of reward, the adjudicators appointed being Mr. Townsend of the Civil Service, the Rev. Mr. Pigott, Secretary to the Education Society, and Dr. C. Morehead, Secretary to the Board of Education. The first prize was gained by Mr. Bháu Dájí, an alumnus of the Elphinstone Institution. No essay was given in worthy of a second prize.

Respecting the injunction of the Rajputs furnishing wives to Jáḍejás to stipulate for the preservation of their female offspring, Captain Jacob reported that he had complied with the instructions of Government but had not yet learned the result, adding that he was not sanguine of success, owing to native apathy and dislike to interference with family concerns, and to the supposed unwillingness of the Rajputs to deprive their daughters of a chance of a Jáḍejá alliance unless in the case of a unanimous concurrence. The political agent was requested by Government, awaiting the result of Captain Jacob's injunctions to the Rajputs, to prosecute the object aimed at.

In reply to the question relative to rewards from the Infanticide Fund, Captain Jacob stated that, while from his not having sufficient confidence in the accuracy of the census formerly forwarded by him he was not disposed to recommend the bestowal at that time of any honorary rewards on the Jáḍejás, he thought that small presents might be given to each of seven Jáḍejás reported as having four or five female children, if personal observation confirmed the census. This proposal received the approbation of Government.

The most interesting portion of Capt. Jacob's letter was the following. "I beg to transmit an application from the Jám of Nawánagar asking the assistance of Government for twenty-one members of his bháíyád to facilitate the marriage of twenty-two daughters, which I beg to recommend for favorable consideration. The Jám has all along regarded the anti-infanticide measures of Government with extreme jealousy; and it is a great point gained that he should by the step which he has now taken for the first time have thus tendered them a species of voluntary acknowledgment. The amount asked for is higher than the sums usually granted by Government on similar occasions; and an average of two hundred rupees for each daughter, making a total of Rupees 4,400, might be considered sufficient." The Government sanctioned the payment of five thousand rupees to the parties indicated by the Jám.

In conclusion, Capt. Jacob annexed an abstract of the census completed up to the end of 1841, making a few corrections in the previous lists. This list gave the total of Jáḍejá males in Káṭhiáwáḍ on the 31st December 1841 as 6,106, and of females as 1,662. The number of male Jaitwás was at the same time 125 and of females 48. Major Jacob expressed the hope that the annual report demanded by Government could now be regularly furnished.

CHAPTER XII.

COLONEL POTTINGER'S MEASURES FOR THE SUPPRESSION OF INFANTICIDE IN KACHH—VISIT TO KACHH OF SIR JOHN MALCOLM—EDUCATION OF THE RÁO DÉSALJÍ AND HIS EARLY DESIRES FOR THE ABOLITION OF INFANTICIDE AND OTHER CRIMES—REPORTS AND EXERTIONS OF COLONEL MELVILLE AND MR. MALET—THE VIGOROUS EFFORTS OF THE RÁO.

We have already incidentally referred to Major [now Sir,] Henry Pottinger as the successor of Mr. Gardiner in the residency at Bhuj, the capital of Kachh. He was early distinguished as a courageous and successful eastern traveller; and he was generally and deservedly esteemed an officer of ability and determination, as he has since sufficiently proved himself in the high appointments which he has held connected with both the Imperial and East India Company's Services. He entered on his office in Kachh in 1825. At this time, the Ráo Désaljí, the prince of the province elected by the Jáḍejás in the remarkable circumstances already mentioned by us, was only about eight years of age. Major Pottinger, according to arrangements also already referred to, was a member and president of the regency by which the affairs of the state were managed during his minority. The circumstance tended to the increase of British influence in the state, as well as facilitated the transaction of business.

Major Pottinger's early efforts in behalf of the abolition of infanticide, and of the difficulties encountered by him, have been thus summarily exhibited by himself, in a letter addressed by him to Mr. C. E. Trevelyan, deputy secretary to the Government of India, and dated the 31st August 1835.

"The suppression of Infanticide appears to me by far the most difficult subject that we have ever had to deal with in India; *Satis*, or the immolation of children on the Ganges, were nothing when compared to it. They simply required the fiat of the Government to put a stop to them in our own territories, but to even check infanticide we have to oppose not only sentiments which are strong enough to suppress the common feelings of human nature, and I may even say of the most savage wild animals, but to interfere in the most secret and sacred affairs amongst the higher classes of natives, of women; for no one who has been a short time in India, and has used his powers of observation, can have helped perceiving how scrupulously every man pretending to respectability refrains from any allusion to his females old or young.

"When I first came to Kachh, ten years ago, I set out with all the zeal of a new comer to root out the practice, but I soon discovered my mistake. The Mehtás, sent at my request, by the regency, were either cajoled by false returns, or expelled from towns and villages, not only by the classes charged with the crime but by the other inhabitants whom long habit had taught to view the business with indifference if not absolute approbation.* I next got the darbár to summon all the

* [On the 27th September 1826, Major Pottinger forwarded to the Bombay Government "a list of all the female Jáḍejá children that were living on the 1st of the present [native] year." It comprehended only 143 names. "I have made an arrangement," he wrote on this occasion, "in concert with the other members of the regency for the birth of every child, (whether male or female,) that occurs in a Jáḍejá's family being reported to the Darbár; and as all deaths are to be testified at the same time in the same manner, I hope these precautions will effectually put a stop to any instances of infanticide that may still be occasionally practised." This measure was approved by the Governor in Council, who considered it extremely desirable that a similar check should, if practicable, be introduced into Káṭhiáwáḍ as the Political agent there was immediately informed.]

Jáḍejás to Bhuj, and partly by threat and partly by persuasion, arranged with them to furnish quarterly statements of the births within their respective estates. This plan I saw from the outset was defective, but it was the best I could hit upon at the moment. It proved however an utter failure; within six months most of the Jáḍejás declared their inability to act up to their agreement, even as far as regarded their nearest relations.

"Several fathers, for instance, assured me that they dare not establish such a scrutiny regarding their grown up sons, and the few censuses that were furnished, I found to have been drawn up by guess work, from what may be termed the tittle-tattle of the village. My next idea was, that, as all the Jáḍejás profess to be blood relations of the Ráo of Kachh, they might be requested to announce to him as the head of the tribe, as well as Government, the fact of their wives being enceinte, and eventually the result. The scheme appeared feasible to the ministers, but when we proposed it to the Jáḍejá members of the regency they received it with feelings of equal disgust and horror. Two modes further suggested themselves of carrying our object. The one to use direct authority and force, but that would no doubt be at variance with the spirit if not the letter of the treaty. The other to grant a portion to every Jáḍejá girl on her marriage. This latter method, proposed to the Bombay Government by my predecessor, (Mr. Gardiner,) had been explicitly negatived, and that negative had been confirmed by the Honourable Court of Directors; under these circumstances I was obliged to remain quiet. Sir John Malcolm came to Bhuj in March 1830. He made a speech to the assembled Jáḍejás on the enormity of the crime, and told them the English nation would force the East India Company to dissolve all connexion with a people who persisted in it. The Jáḍejás of course individually denied the charge, but they afterwards inquired from me how the Governor could talk so to them at a moment when we were courting the friendship of Sindh, in which child-murder is carried to a much greater extent than even in Kachh, for it is a well known fact that all the illegitimate offspring born to men of any rank in that country are indiscriminately put to death without reference to sex.* Subsequent to Sir John's visit, an impostor of the name of Vijaya Bhaṭṭ went to Bombay, presented a petition to Government setting forth my supineness, and offering if furnished with some peons to do all that was required.† This petition was referred to me to report on, which I did as it merited, and matters lay in abeyance till the young Ráo was installed in July, 1834, when he adopted the most decided steps to enforce that article of the treaty which provides for the suppression of infanticide. He took a paper from the whole of his brethren reiterating that stipulation, and agreeing to abide the full consequences if they broke it. I officially promised the Ráo our support in all his measures, and we have been watching ever since for an occasion to make a signal example, but the difficulty of tracing and bringing home such an allegation will be understood from this letter, and it would be ruin to attempt to do so on uncertain grounds and fail. I do however think that our best, perhaps only chance of success rests with the Ráo, who is most sincere in his detestation of the crime, and his wish to stop it.

"I quite concur with Mr. Wilkinson‡ that infant-

* [The murder of illegitimate children is dreadfully prevalent, there is reason to fear, through all the native states of India. A few years ago a representation was made on the custom to the Bombay Government by an humble Dheḍ of Káṭhiáwáḍ.]

† [The party here referred to is an old Jaina priest, nearly deaf, named Gurjí Khántí Vijaya. Though he made a wrong movement in this case, and his proposed appliances were most inadequate, his zeal for the abolition of infanticide was creditable to him as a native.]

‡ [Mr. Lancelot Wilkinson of the Bombay Civil Service, who was at this time zealously labouring for the abolition of Infanticide in the minor Rajput states of Central India under the political superintendence of the Government of India.]

icide is carried to an extent of which we have hardly yet a complete notion in India. The Ráo told me very bluntly, that he had just found out that a tribe of Musalmans called "Sammas,"* who came originally from Sindh, and now inhabit the islands in the Raṇ, paying an ill-defined obedience to Kachh, put all their daughters to death merely to save the expense and trouble of rearing them. He has taken a bond from all the heads of the tribe to abandon the horrid custom, but, as he justly remarked, he has hardly the means of enforcing it.

"I had no intention when I took up my pen of saying so much, but have been insensibly drawn on to tell you all I know of Infanticide in Kachh. Of its origin, I can only repeat the general tradition of its being a scheme hit on by one of the Jáḍejás to prevent their daughters, who cannot marry in their own tribe, from disgracing their families by prostitution. The Jáḍejás of Kachh have, perhaps, adopted all the vices, whilst they have few or none of the saving qualities of Musalmans. No people appear to have so thorough a contempt for women, and yet, strange to say, we often see the dowagers of households taking the lead in both public and private matters amongst them. Their tenets are, however, that women are innately vicious, and it must be confessed that they have good cause to draw this conclusion in Kachh, in which I strongly suspect there is hardly one chaste female. We can understand the men amongst the Jáḍejás getting reconciled to infanticide, from hearing it spoken of from their very births, as a necessary and laudable proceeding, but several instances have been told to me where young mothers, just before married from other tribes, and even brought from distant countries, have strenuously urged the destruction of their own infants, even in opposition to the father's disposition to save them. This is a state of things for which I confess I cannot offer any explan-

* [Of the same stock originally as the Jáḍejás.]

ation, and which would astonish us in a tigress or a she-wolf."

To this important communication, we would take the liberty of adding a few supplementary and illustrative remarks.

1. Colonel Pottinger's zeal for the abolition of infanticide in Kachh, we are persuaded, effected everything which could be done for the suppression of that atrocity, in the absence of absolutely coercive measures. To these, in the first instance at least, that distinguished official entertained great repugnance, founded on what he conceived to be the restrictions of the treaty and the political exigencies of the case. He was doubtless perfectly conscientious in his judgment of that agreement and these exigencies. In our humble interpretation of the objects of the treaty, however, we consider that it allows a sufficiently broad margin for such coercive measures as were adopted in Káṭhiáwáḍ in 1834, and as have been ultimately resorted to by the Ráo Desaljí himself, acting on his own authority and with the advice of the British Government. The power now legitimately exercised by the Ráo could formerly have been exercised by the regency, though it must be admitted not with that degree of personal influence which the Ráo individually possesses. In the matter of infanticide, moreover, all the Jáḍejás who enjoyed the British guarantee were responsible by treaty to the British Government. Had Colonel Pottinger persevered in his original admirable plans for the registration of Jáḍejá births, and measures even still more inquisitorial, no blame could have been legitimately attached to him by any of the nobles or ignobles of that unnatural fraternity.

2. Sir John Malcolm was accustomed to make most enthusiastic references to his address to the Jáḍejás on the subject of infanticide on his visit to Bhuj in 1830. It is thus noticed in a despatch of the Bombay Government to the Court of Directors, dated, the 10th August

1831. "Our president took this opportunity to express his sentiments most fully on the subject of infanticide. The Jáḍejás knew, he said, the solicitude of the British Government for the abolition of that most barbarous crime, which so far from being countenanced or sanctioned by the usage of Hindus, was held in utter execration by all of that race except the few tribes of Rajputs by whom it was introduced and continued to be practised from motives of family pride. The Jáḍejás of Kachh, he said, had long been reproached with this horrid and inhuman usage, the abolition of which had never ceased to be ardently desired by the British, one of whose principal motives in contracting and maintaining the connexion with Kachh was its hope of accomplishing this highly valued object. He feared, he said, that little respect had been paid on this head by the Jáḍejás to the 17th article of the treaty of 1819, and he was well aware that men did not readily abandon the customs of their ancestors, but he felt it his duty to declare to them that by continuing the practice of Infanticide they incurred the risk of losing the protection of the British Government."

3. Colonel Pottinger founds his principal expectation of the abolition of Infanticide in Kachh on the personal and official influence of the Ráo Désaljí; and his efforts and arrangements for the instruction and training of that young prince were of the most judicious and meritorious character. Had he been his own son, he could not have been more attentive than he was to his intellectual and social interests. After securing for him instruction in the Indian languages, he placed him, for the acquisition of English and general culture, under the care of the Rev. James Gray,—formerly of the High School of Edinburgh, but then the chaplain of the station, specially selected for it by Sir John Malcolm,—a gentleman of unbounded benevolence of character, distinguished literary taste, poetical distinction, and exemplary Christian zeal. Mr. Gray was enthusiastically

fond both of his charge and its special duties, to which he devoted as much attention as the usages and interruptions of a Rajput palace permitted. The progress of his pupil was in every respect as satisfactory as could have been expected; and he displayed the most amiable and hopeful traits of character and ardent attachment to his tutor, to whose respected memory, on his lamented death in September 1830, he erected a handsome monument in the camp burying-ground at Bhuj.* Sir John Malcolm regretted much that he did not know a chaplain at this time on the Bombay establishment fitted, by his knowledge of the Indian languages and customs and desire of native improvement, to take Mr. Gray's place; and failing to get one of the Scotch missionaries, with whom he entered into communication on the subject, to leave his peculiar evangelistic work to undertake that duty,—the great importance of which he readily admitted, — and to enter the educational

* A very interesting biographical notice of Mr. Gray, by his son-in-law the late Robert Cotton Money, Esq., C. S., for some time Assistant Resident at Bhuj under Colonel Pottinger, is printed in the Oriental Christian Spectator for May 1831. Respecting his connexion with the Ráo it is there thus written. "Soon after Mr. Gray's arrival in Kachh [in 1826], several respectable natives, driven perhaps by curiosity alone, continually visited him; and, as some have told me, they thought a *padre* must know more than any other man. On observing the freedom from prejudice which the inhabitants of this singular little country have, he considered it no unlikely thing to gain at last admittance to the young Ráo as his preceptor. He was fortunate in possessing the friendly opinion of Colonel Pottinger on this point, whose influence as Regent during the boy's minority was meritoriously employed in cultivating the future King's mind, and moulding it to a form more suited to rule with European prudence and decision than oriental pomp and criminal partiality. By the Resident's permission, and the approbation of the other members of the regency, and to the great delight of his after favourite pupil, he commenced his labours as his tutor. He used to attend at the palace four times in the week. The liberality of Government placed in his hands the means of familiarizing the minds of the natives with the elements of Astronomy. Nothing used to delight him more than these trips, from which he returned with deeper feelings of affection for the young Ráo."

service of Government with liberal offers of preferment in that department, he left the tutorship vacant for a short time. On the recommendation of Colonel Pottinger, Captain John Crofton of H. M.'s 6th Regiment, a gentleman who had received a university education at Trinity College, Dublin, ultimately succeeded Mr. Gray, in 1832, and faithfully and effectively continued the work of instruction which had been so hopefully begun. The periodical reports of the progress of the prince by that officer to Colonel Pottinger were very encouraging, while at the same time they were judicious and discriminative.

On the 8th of July, 1834, the Ráo entered on his duties and privileges as ruler of Kachh, the regency having been terminated a year sooner than had at first been intended, on account of the progress of his Highness in education and training.

On the succeeding day, His Highness addressed the following letter, written in his own hand, to Lord Clare, the Governor of Bombay.

"I have had the pleasure to receive your Lordship's letter of congratulation.—By the favour of the British Government, I have been early placed on the throne of my fathers.

"I feel all the sentiments in the letter of your Lordship: they are good and kind. I hope by doing justice and showing mercy, to make my ignorant people know that I am not a tyrant, but a king, and father over them.

"Since 1819, Kachh has much improved. It is owing to the good and strong rule of my friend and benefactor Colonel Pottinger. Then there was war, now there is peace. He has made good arrangements. I have thanked the President in the public Darbár, and often in private, for all his kindness. Now, my Lord, I much like the approbation of the British Government myself, and, therefore, I hope your Lordship will thank Colonel Pottinger for all the good he has done to me, and to my subjects as President of the regency for many years. I have sent out a Proclamation against the murder of Female Infants; and this bad custom shall end.

"I hope to do many other good and proper things with the aid of my friend Colonel Pottinger. He knows all my plans, and he will write to your Lordship whatever I do.

"I desire very much the constant friendship of the British Government. I request of your Lordship to accept my friendship and gratitude, and to overlook my writing and style, which are not yet fit for the eyes of your Lordship.—I have, etc." Rá'o De'salji'.*

An extract of a letter of Lieutenant Crofton, dated Mándaví, September 30th, 1834, and addressed to Colonel Pottinger, will enable the reader to form a correct judgment of the Ráo's attainments and culture.

"I have felt considerable regret at the exaggerated estimate of the attainments of His Highness, formed by partial judges, which has gone forth to the public through the newspapers of the Presidency, but which I trust, for the sake of the Ráo, and what he most respects—truth—may meet with as little credence from Government, as the numerous libels of late uttered against yourself. The statement, made in my report of April last, is that which I consider to be rigidly correct: and no augmentation to the literary attainments of His Highness has been since made; for, you are fully aware that all the studies under me have been suspended since June last, and that, during the last four months, the time and attention of the Ráo have been devoted to patient and toilsome investigations into state papers, claims, and privileges, and in carrying into execution numerous salutary reforms, in effecting which your exertions were so long thwarted by ignorance, obstinacy, interest, and intrigue.

"That the knowledge of English acquired by his Highness is meagre must be admitted, and that a long-

* Oriental Christian Spectator, 1834.

er time and different circumstances would be required for obtaining a sounder and more extensive acquaintance with a language, difficult even to the cleverest foreigner in Europe. Still, though not an English scholar, His Highness very nearly approaches to an English thinker, and in manner and in feeling more resembles the English gentleman, than the Indian rájá. Perhaps there is not another instance in Indian history of a prince, like Ráo Désaljí, having made such a rapid progress in letters, or having attained, at so early an age, to such a strength and vigor of intellect. The clearness of apprehension, and the patience of investigation, which he has evinced since he came to the throne, and the justice and mercy of all his acts, alike prove him to be wise above his years, as to have benefited by the knowledge of European laws and ethics.

"The happiest results may be anticipated from a rule so auspiciously commenced, and must indeed follow from the firmness and mildness which His Highness has displayed, particularly in some late trying circumstances at Mandaví while removed from the benefit of your counsel, in which he has proved himself capable, by thinking maturely and then acting promptly, and fearlessly putting down the factions of all classes—even those formerly protected by reverence for caste. I naturally must feel anxious, while desirous of not exaggerating the acquirements in English of His Highness, that the Government should be fully acquainted with the sound common sense, keensightedness, patience in inquiry, judgment, justice, mercy, and temper, with which the Ráo transacts the affairs of his country, and how closely he scrutinizes every act of Government, to compare it with the principles on which he has read and been told that it proceeds. In his private and domestic character, he is a rare instance of all that is amiable and virtuous; and is as free from prejudice and bigotry as any Hindu can be, without relinquishing that faith of which he must be, as Rájá, the nominal professor; if not the real believer.* I can appeal to your own intimate knowledge of this young prince's character for all that I have said in his praise: and it must be obvious that by treating him more like a petty European Sovereign than as an Indian Rájá, in our communications with him, we must increase in him the high opinion he already entertains for all that is English.

"I need not observe to you, that the Ráo of Kachh will be the first to hail the adoption of English as the medium of political correspondence, for, as he lately remarked in your presence 'the language of Persia is not the language of truth but of compliment, and the worst of all original tongues for business.'

"In parting from His Highness, I have presented him a letter of friendly advice, and urged him by public and by private motives to pursue the course of good rule, which he has so well and so ably commenced, recommending him in all his difficulties and doubts to seek the guidance of the British president, and to remember that so long as he should merit the alliance of the British, the same power, which had defended and secured his claim to the throne, would never cease to support him in all his just measures and rights, against the evil and rebellious of his subjects.

"In conclusion, I beg leave most respectfully to express the deep sense of gratitude which I feel, for the steady support you gave me through a delicate and difficult duty,—and for the approbation of my humble efforts to effect, under your instructions, the objects of Government."

The Court of Directors, as well as the Government of Bombay, were much gratified by the accounts given by Colonel Pottinger and Mr. Crofton of the personal character of the Ráo, of the reforms contemplated by him

* ["Few or no kings have lost their thrones on becoming Christians." —Editor of the Oriental Christian Spectator. And surely, if even the supreme Government of India be Christian, the subordinate Governments of the country can be Christian also.]

in his public and private establishments, of his mode of conducting the affairs of his state, and especially of his determination to enforce the article of the treaty which forbids female Infanticide. Of this fact His Highness was duly informed.

We may be excused for introducing into this place, as directly bearing on the matters now referred to, an extract from a journal, addressed to a friend, of the first missionary tour in Kachh, performed by us a few months after the Ráo came into the possession of the full powers of his sovereignty.

"*February 23rd.* Colonel Pottinger kindly introduced Mr. Fyvie and me to the Ráo Désaljí. He received us at the palace with much cordiality, and proved very affable.

"The report of the attainments of His Highness, presented by Mr. Crofton to Colonel Pottinger on the resignment of his charge on the day that the Ráo ascended the masnad, and which is printed in the Oriental Christian Spectator for January last, appears to me to be remarkably candid and correct.

"His Highness's acquaintance with the English language is considerable. Of its vocables he has a creditable store, and a tolerably ready, though not a very correct, use. While of the English literature and science, properly so called, he has little knowledge, he has a general acquaintance with English life, and manners and customs. As an oriental linguist, he is deserving of much praise. With the Kachhí, Gujarátí, Hindustání, and Persian, he is familiar; and he is able to speak and read them with fluency. He is distinguished for his good sense; and manifests a vast deal more of correct and amiable feeling than I have seen among any of the grandees in India. There are few, indeed, of the natives of Bombay, whom I should prefer before him in this respect. There is a modesty on the one hand, and a self-respect on the other, which I have seldom seen united in a native of Asia. He is represented by those who know him as free from the prominent vices for which many of his predecessors were so lamentably distinguished, and which led to the misery of their subjects and their own ruin. He is much respected and beloved by his people, as well he may; and, under God, he may prove to them the source of the greatest blessings. He has commenced his reign, by declaring his determination to suppress infanticide; to prevent an increase of the Pawaiyás, (Eunuchs and Sodomites,) who have formerly not only been tolerated in the country, but received from it state endowments, and been recognized as entitled to receive *per annum* a loaf of bread and four pice from every inhabitant of the land; and to discourage other evil practices.* In reference to infanticide, he has brought all the Jádejás under new and strict engagements; and an offender he has signally punished. We took an opportunity of commending him for what he has done in this matter, and encouraged him to persevere. He expressed himself in a satisfactory manner on the subject; and clearly showed that the common feelings of humanity have full play in his breast. I cannot say so much for any other Jádejá whom we have seen, either in Káthiáwád or Kachh.

"The Ráo is certainly superior in some respects to the superstitions of the country. His suspicions of the vanity of idolatry, however, are not sufficiently strong to lead him directly to discourage its practice. He lives

* "To watch the progress of crime is most awful. In all Jádejá towns there is a large population of those degraded wretches the Pawaiyás, inmates of brothels for the most abominable wickedness. Mandaví, Nawánagar, Gondal and Rájkot are the chief seats of these debased specimens of humanity. In Mandaví there are 40 houses of Pawaiyás; in Bhuj from 15 to 20; in Nawánagar, 40. There are none in the Jhálá villages, and in Junágád only one or two. In Rájkot, Dharol, Murví, Gondal, and Dhorají, several. The Jádejás are, with few exceptions, in every way a disgrace to the name of man."—Report on Infanticide of James Erskine, Esq., 30th June, 1837. A few of these unhappy beings, who in the first instance are brought to vice and wretchedness by their parents, are seen even in the British territories.

in an atmosphere of contagion; and he has not escaped infection. He observes heathen rites; and he lately yielded to the solicitations of his mother, and repaired a temple which had been long neglected. The horrid practice of Satí, he has not yet opposed. A poor deluded woman of the town burnt herself with the body of her husband, about two months ago.

"His Highness seemed aware that Christians profess to worship only the great Creator, and that the English have no images in their temples. We regretted to find, however, that of the *principles* of Christianity he has no knowledge. His curiosity on the subject, it was not difficult to awaken. He readily received the books and tracts, which we gave to him, questioned us as to their contents, and promised to read them. I have little doubt that he will act according to his declaration. He observed that he is convinced that the English could not have attained to their present greatness without a good religion. The books with which I presented him, were Mr. Gray's translation of the Gospel in Kachhí,* and my

* "The Gospel is not only the first book printed, but the first book written in Kachhí. It was viewed as a great curiosity. The Ráo mentioned that while the language in which it is written is generally understood, and spoken by the lower orders of the people, it is never used even for a single note, and, of course, never taught in schools. He added, that Gujaratí and Hindustání are spoken by great numbers of the people, understood by all, except those in the north, who follow a pastoral life and have no villages, taught in schools, and used, more particularly the former, in all correspondence. The Resident, and the Ministers, expressed their assent to what he said on this subject. As all this authority possesses the greatest weight; as the testimony which we have received from natives, and our own observation agree with it; and as books in Kachhí can be read only by those who read either Gujarátí or Hindustání, it seems to follow as a consequence, that we ought to conclude that there is no occasion for multiplying them at present. Were missionaries settled in the country, they would of course seek the education of the lowest orders, and promote their instruction through the language most familiar to them. Mr. Gray, in making his version of the Gospels, (for I have now learned from his munshí that he translated the whole of them,) contemplated of course the use of them in connexion with Kachhí schools, which if God had spared him, his

two Exposures of Hinduism, and Refutation of Muhammadism. The Ráo read the introduction to the Refutation of Muhammadism in Hindustání, and observed that the discovery of truth must be the result of discussion. He seemed to derive much pleasure from the anticipation that the pamphlet would prove a curious treat to the darbár munshi. Mr. Fyvie presented His Highness with a copy of two of the Gospels, and Acts, a Summary of the Holy Scriptures, Forms of Public Worship, and a variety of small tracts in Gujarátí. He read a portion of some of the tracts, and conversed a little about them. He told us that Mr. Crofton had informed him that the Bible had been translated into many languages; and we took occasion to state the motives of the Christian public in giving it a universal circulation, and noticed the contrast between their conduct and that of the Bráhmans, who prohibit their followers, not of the sacred order, from perusing the Védas, and that of the Musulmans, who propagated their faith at the point of the sword. We promised to send him, through Col. Pottinger, complete copies of the Scriptures in English and Gujarátí. He said that he would receive them with much pleasure.

"His Highness seemed to be quite familiar with the statistics of his country. Colonel Pottinger mentioned to us, that he is an excellent man of business, and interested even in the *minutiæ* of his affairs. He spoke of both his instructors with much interest. He has erect-

benevolence would have prompted him to establish. If the present peaceful state of the country continue, the Kachhí language [as spoken in this country] will probably perish in the course of half a century. None will regret its decease, for no treasures of knowledge will perish with it. All the friends of the religious improvement of the people will hail their universal accessibility through the medium of Gujaráti and Hindustání, in which the Scriptures, and a variety of Christian publications, already exist. I have made these observations with the view of discharging a duty which I owe to the Bombay Bible Society, in whose behalf I edited the Kachhí Gospel, to which reference has been made, and the other philanthropic institutions whose sphere of labour is the West of India."

ed a monument to the memory of Mr. Gray; and he often peruses, he observed, a valedictory letter of advice addressed to him by Mr. Crofton. We recommended him to observe its counsels, and remarked that his own welfare and the weal of his people, must ever much depend on the attention which he pays to its precepts, and other moral instructions which he has received. *Yathá rájá tathâ prajá:* as is the king, so are the people. Mr. Money's death he noticed with much regret. In Colonel Pottinger, he seem to have much confidence, and to him he evidently bears both great affection and respect. The English, in general, he considers as his true friends. They are so in every sense of the term. To them, under God, is he indebted not only for his education, but even for his throne and the peace of his country, which a few years ago was the scene of rapine, plunder, and bloodshed. May he speedily learn from them the way of eternal life, and receive, through faith in the Son of God, the salvation of his immortal soul, and enter into that kingdom which passeth not away!

"When we were about to leave the room in which His Highness received us, he begged of us to wait to see a gigantic Zangibarian slave whom he had lately obtained in a present. We sat till the African Hercules came to make his salám, and in the interval conversed with the king on the subject of slavery. We were delighted to hear him announce, that he not only treated his slaves with kindness, but that he had given them to wit, on the occasion of the desertion of two of them, that they might all take their departure whenever they might feel inclined.*

* "The Ráo, on our rising to return home, after a long interview, proposed to show us all the curiosities of his palace and palace-yard. He personally pointed out to us every object of insterest. What struck us most was the darbár room of the Ráo Lákhá. It is constructed with a taste highly creditable to the workmen of Bhuj; and it contains many ornaments brought from Holland by a Kachhí who visited that

"I do not recollect any thing else worthy of particular notice in connexion with our gratifying visit to the Ráo. I have always viewed him with the greatest interest, especially since Sir John Malcolm made to me the proposals with which you are acquainted. We sent a few pamphlets in Gujaratí to his father, Bhármaljí, who has been at liberty for several years, and who is now conducting himself with general propriety.*

"Many natives called upon us in the afternoon. From the darbár munshi, who was formerly with Mr. Gray, I received a satisfactory account of the manner in which the Kachhí version of the Gospels was executed."

Little, or nothing, after this, was heard of the progress of anti-infanticide measures in Kachh for two or three years; though it was generally believed that the Ráo was continuing to make his influence bear on the abolition of the inhuman custom which was so destructive of the character of his tribe. In 1838, Colonel Pottinger had his political charge extended to Sindh, where, as resident at the Court of the Amirs at Haidarábád, his services, prior to the commencement of the unfortunate expedition to Afghanistán, and especially in connexion

country upwards of a century ago. The Ráo has an excellent collection of horses; and he evidently takes great delight in inspecting them. Those of the breed peculiar to the country, are very superior as Indian steeds. We saw, for the first time, specimens of the lions found in Káṭhiáwáḍ and Parkar, &c. They are as large and fierce-looking as any which I have seen elsewhere. We also observed some specimens of a small and curious deer found in Sindh."

* Bhármaljí owed his liberty to Sir John Malcolm, who in his minute on Kachh thus writes of him:—"The ex-ráo, I had been assured was penitent for his former crimes, and sincerely attached to his son, and was believed to have abandoned all hopes of restoration to the rank he had by his conduct forfeited.... And as I found the young prince, the minister, and all the Jáḍejá chiefs anxious on the ground of honourable feeling for the removal of the appearance of confinement (for it was nothing more), I had no hesitation in complying with their request."

with the treaty for the navigation of the Indus which was negociated by him, were of the most important character. On the 21st February 1839, the following letter was addressed by the Bombay Government to the acting assistant resident in charge (afterwards resident) in Kachh, Captain P. M. Melville, a distinguished staff-officer of the Bombay Army.

"SIR,—I am directed by the Honourable the Governor in Council to transmit to you an extract from paragraph 18th from the report of the Political Agent in Káṭhiáwáḍ, on female infanticide for the years 1835 and 1836, and with reference to the previously expressed abhorrence of the Ráo of Kachh of the crime of infanticide, and the measures he has already adopted for its suppression, to request that you will be pleased to embrace the earliest opportunity to concert measures with His Highness for the complete extinction of this revolting crime as far as his influence and authority may extend.

"I am on this occasion desired to state, that Government look forward to the most beneficial results from His Highness exerting his influence in inducing his tribe to abandon this inhuman practice.

"The first measure which suggests itself to Government to be adopted for the effectual suppression of this crime, is to cause a census to be taken of the Jáḍejá population of Kachh, a measure which has proved highly beneficial in Káṭhiawáḍ.

"The Governor in Council is of opinion that the form of the census should be the same as that observed in Káthiáwáḍ, and that the same should be renewed annually.

"A form of the Káṭhiáwáḍ census is inclosed for your guidance.—J. P. WILLOUGHBY, Secretary to Government."

To this communication was added a form of the census prepared by Mr. Willoughby for Kaṭhiawáḍ in 1834, and since used so beneficially in that province. It may be here introduced.

FORM OF REGISTER for taking a Census of the Jádejá tribe of Rajputs in the province of Káṭhiáwáḍ.

Where Residing.			Jádejá Families.																									
				Jádejás.							Children.																	
											Male.					Female.												
											Living.		Dead since last year.			Dead since last year.			Living.									
																			Widow.		Married.			Betrothed.			Unbetrothed	
District.	Táluká.	Village.	Number of Families.	Widower.	Married.	Unmarried.	Age.	Shákhá, or branch of the Tribe.	Profession.	Occupation.	Name.	Age.	Name.	Age.	Cause of Death.	Name.	Age.	Cause of Death.	Name.	Age.	Name.	Age.	To whom Married.	Name.	Age.	To whom Betrothed.	Name.	Age.

The birth of a daughter to the Ráo, on the 17th February 1839, gave His Highness an opportunity of showing a good example to his fraternity of the conservation of female life. This rarity of a spared Jáḍejá princess, however, died in infancy.

In a despatch dated the 5th May 1839, Captain Melville reported to the Bombay Government his proceedings consequent on the instructions just now quoted. To the proposition made by him respecting a Census, His Highness in the first instance demurred, as he considerd it to be repugnant to the feelings and privacy of Rajput life. He suggested, however, that a meeting should be convened of the Jáḍejá chiefs for the purpose of devising measures for the suppression of the barbarous practice. To this proposal Captain Melville cordially acceded. A meeting was accordingly convened, and the result, which was very discouraging, was thus described by him in a letter of the 5th May 1839 :—"The chiefs assembled in considerable numbers, and at the Ráo's particular request I attended their meeting in the palace at Bhuj. I addressed them in strong language, assuring them of the universal horror with which the crime that unfortunately distinguishes the Jáḍejás is viewed, and urging them by every motive I could suggest, to unite in an earnest effort to remove the stigma which rests upon their name. A long conversation enabled me to ascertain and to estimate with sufficient precision the sentiments and feelings of the assembly. The continued perpetration of the iniquity was not denied ; it was lamented indeed but extenuated and almost defended ; and I withdrew after an interview of several hours, with the conviction forced upon my mind, that of all the Jáḍejás assembled not one man, His Highness the Ráó excepted, entertained a sincere wish to put an end to the foul practice of Infanticide, or if left to himself would stir a finger for the purpose." The discussion on the subject continued for many days. A plan for establishing a fund to aid the poorer Jáḍejás in effecting the marriages of their daughters was proposed ; but though it was warmly supported by the Ráo it did not meet with general concurrence. Captain Melville was ultimately informed, "That the assembled Jáḍejás are ready and agree to furnish a census of their population, if required; but they would be better pleased [O trustworthy men!] if the Bristish Government would continue to repose in their prince, the Ráo, and in themselves the same confidence as heretofore; and they, on their part, promise to exercise a stricter watch in their several districts, and duly to report every case of infanticide which might come to their knowledge." Captain Melville advised the Ráo to take advantage of the consent thus yielded and to institute the census. He clearly saw the necessity of immediate action, for he found that infanticide was still most lamentably practised to an incredible extent throughout the country. "The Jáḍejá population," he wrote, "may number about 12,000 adult males [this was an over-estimate, as we shall afterwards see], and it is the opinion of well-informed persons that it would be difficult to produce 500 females, born in Kachh of Jáḍejá blood. Nor is the crime, I fear, confined to the Jáḍejás properly so-called. Many branches have from time to time been detached from the genuine stock; some by degradation and intermixture with foreign classes, and some by conversion to the Muhammadan religion. These separate tribes pass under the general denomination of the *ḍhang* [the dissolute]; their number may be about 5,000 men, and in all the practice of infanticide, to a greater or less extent, has been continued through every change of name and habit, and exists at the present hour."

Captain Melville was of opinion that the suppression of infanticide was easier of accomplishment in Káṭhiáwáḍ than in Kachh; but this the Bombay Government admitted only so far as opportunities of forming suitable connexions for females are more frequent there than in Kachh, where comparatively few Rajputs, except the Jáḍejás, are to be found. To counterbalance this advantage, it was justly added, Kachh had a prince willing by example and authority to co-operate with the

British Government in the suppression of the crime. The power of the chief of the Jáḍejás in Kachh, justice requires us further to add, is but limited, for previous to the benevolent interference of Britain in behalf of that province the Ráo there was rather among the chief Jáḍejás the first among equals than a general sovereign. It is well that Britain has been all along trying to give unity to the Kachh administration, without subverting the privileges of the nobles in that country, whose jurisdictions, however, it might be well still further to limit by some established system of representation at the darbár.

Captain Melville was requested by Government to assure the Ráo that every support would be afforded him in carrying into effect the measures necessary to enforce the fulfilment of the Jáḍejá engagements to suppress infanticide. In his despatch of the 23rd May 1839, he reported that the Ráo had commenced his arrangements for the census, but that a party, of considerable rank and and influence, had urgently requested that this measure should be postponed till they had arranged with the tribe—first to diminish by common consent the customary and well-nigh compulsory expences of Jáḍejá marriages; and secondly to establish a fund to aid in the marriage of their poorer daughters. The Government assented, from an impression of the expediency of carrying the Jáḍejás with it in ulterior movements, while hope was entertained that they were acting bonâ fide. Captain Melville, on the 18th of June, reported the detection by the Ráo of a case of infanticide committed by order of a Jáḍejá grandfather. The criminal in this case was fined proportionably to his means, on the advice of the Bombay Government.

In March 1840, Colonel Pottinger, who had returned from Sindh, took his final leave of the Kachh darbár, before proceeding to England. "I visited his Highness," he writes to the Bombay Government on the 24th of that month," at a public darbár held for the express purpose of giving me my final audience, and at which there was a very large assemblage of Jáḍejás and other persons of weight in the country. After I had conversed some time on various topics, I told his Highness that there was one subject on which I looked back with the deepest regret, on quitting Kachh, which was, the small progress that had been made during my long residence at the Bhuj darbár towards the abolition of infanticide. I took a review of all the measures that had been proposed and adopted during the last fifteen years, and concluded a lengthened discourse by distinctly stating to all who heard me that the day could not be far distant when the British Government would insist on the rigid fulfilment of that humane stipulation of the treaty which abolished child-murder. I said that the Jáḍejás could not doubt our ample power and means to enforce that engagement; that we had been anxious to leave it to them to devise the best manner of proceeding, but that they must not mistake the forbearance and patience which had been evinced for indifference, or suppose that we intended to abandon the great object in view. His Highness the Ráo entered most warmly into my feelings. He interpreted my observations in detail in the colloquial dialect, in order that they might be clearly comprehended, and declared that he fully participated in every syllable I had expressed, and assured me that no exertion should be wanting on his part to bring about a final and complete abolition of the degrading and wicked practice, for which his brethren were unhappily so notorious. He thanked me must gratefully for the advice I had so opportunely given the Jáḍejás, ere it was too late to repair their evil course by voluntary amendment, and emphatically called on all those of the tribe who were present, not only to reflect themselves on the warning they had received from me at the moment of my final departure, but to communicate what had passed to their families and relations, with the object of removing the foul stain, which (added His Highness) Colonel Pottinger has justly told you is so inhuman and sinful, that Kachh, notwithstanding its now happy freedom from most crimes common to mankind in general, is looked upon throughout all the world as a country distinguished for one atrocity, which throws every good quality it may otherwise possess into the shade.'

"The Jáḍejás who were at the darbár admitted, through their spokesman Jaymaljí of Térá, and Mairâmanjí of Mhawá, the undeniable truths that his Highness and I had told them, reiterated their oft repeated promises of setting about some effectual plan for a reformation, and begged me to be assured that my parting injunctions should neither be forgotten nor neglected."

Those who know the man and the subject can easily understand what Colonel Pottinger's discourse must have been, both in manner and matter. It produced the most beneficial effects. Within a few days after the Colonel's departure from Kachh, the Ráo intimated to Captain Melville his ardent desire to frame some effectual plan for the suppression of infanticide, which could be reported to him before he finally left the shores of India. He proposed the establishment of a darbár mehtá, with assistants in every district, to procure a census; but to this Captain Melville demurred on the score of expence, the lack of trustworthy agents, and the prejudices of the Jáḍejás. His Highness then caused a deed to be drawn up, which was executed by the Jáḍejás, containing four articles, in which they strictly bound themselves to render an exact annual census of their own population in their respective districts; to give information of every case of infanticide within fifteen days of its occurrence, or failing to do this to pay such a pecuniary penalty as might be exacted, and to furnish a report, supported by the testimony of four witnesses, of every premature or still birth; to allow all fines inflicted in violation of the preceding engagement to form a fund auxiliary to the marriage of poor Jáḍejás; and to receive the assistance of the darbár in sending one or two of its own mehtás round the country to direct and assist the chiefs in framing the census. Captain Melville proposed that in addition to the mehtás of the Ráo, one should be employed on the part of the British Government in testing the census made by the chiefs, which on the proposal of Sir James Carnac, was sanctioned in the modified form of devolving this duty on a clerk already employed in the residency with a small increase of salary. He failed to induce the Ráo, in imitation of the Gáikawáḍ and Satárá Governments, to put an end by proclamation to Satí,—the kindred crime of Infanticide, though sanctioned as a rite by Hinduism,—two cases of which had just occurred. He received the highest commendation of Government for his "zeal, judgement, and humanity" in his discussions on infanticide with the Ráo and other Jáḍejás.

The census prepared by the Jáḍejás was forwarded to Government,—along with an able and interesting, but painful, report,—by Capt. Melville, on the 8th December, 1840. From Captain Melville's communication we make the following extracts.

"The census has been rendered by the chiefs, in fulfilment of the first article of the agreement into which they entered with the Darbár. But the real agents by whom the enumeration has been made, are two meḥtás, deputed by the Ráo under the fourth article of the agreement, who have visited every town and village in succession, and drawn up the register of each according to a prescribed form. These mehtás are Musalmans of good repute, and of sufficient respectability. I have no reason whatever to doubt their honesty, but they are not men of such intelligence and high character as I should wish to see employed on so important a duty. When the census is to be renewed in the following year, I purpose proposing to his Highness to change the agents, in order to guard against collusion and deception; and as a further check, I intend to depute the mehtá now employed on the part of the British Government in Wágar, to points selected at random, and where his presence cannot be expected.

"On an examination of the Table, it appears that a population of 5,247 souls is composed of 4,912 males and 335 females. It must not, however, be understood that this is the real proportion between the male and female part of the entire Jáḍejá population; it is merely the proportion between males and females born of Jáḍejá parents, and now living. The wives of the Jáḍejás and the mothers of the children are not included, because they are all foreigners belonging to other tribes, and therefore have no part in the present calculation.

"Of the females enumerated, 77, it will be seen, are married, and these reside, for the most part, without the province; 42 are betrothed, but have not yet left their native homes; and 216 are in a state of celibacy. There is one, and only one, widow among the whole number, and but three orphans.

"It will be seen that there are now living 149 male and [only] 45 female children under one year of age; and 592 male and 89 female children between one year and five. Again, between the age of 5 and 15 there are 1,291 males and 103 females; between the age of 15 and 25, 963 males and 86 females. It may be calculated, therefore, that the number of female children preserved, during each of these periods of time respectively, has borne the following proportion to that of the male children, viz.

During the last year	1	to	3·3	decimals.
During the five last years	1	to	5·5	„
During the 10 years preceding	1	to	12·5	„
During the 10 years again preceding.	1	to	11·2	„

"By adding the several columns together it will be found that the survivors of all born during the last 25 years, 15 years, five years, and one year respectively, answer to the following numbers, viz.

25 years......	2,995	males,	323	females; or, 9·2 to 1
15 „	2,032	„	237	„ or, 8·5 to 1
5 „	741	„	134	„ or, 5·5 to 1
1 „	149	„	45	„ or, 3·3 to 1

"This decrease in the relative numerical superiority of the males may be also shown in another manner. I assume the mortality, from natural causes, of the two sexes to be equal; and on this assumption it follows that the proportion which one sex bears to the other, among the survivors of any specified date, must accurately represent the proportion which existed among those living at that date. There are now extant, of all that were living—

25 years ago........	1,917 males,	and	12 females.
15 "	2,880 "	and	98 "
5 "	4,171 "	and	201 "
1 year ago	4,763 "	and	290 "

"It results that the males and females then living bore to each other the following relation, viz:—

25 years ago	as 159·7 to 1
15 "	as 29·3 to 1
5 "	as 20·7 to 1
1 "	as 16·4 to 1

"And at this moment the proportion estimated is 14·6 to 1.

"The conclusion which may, I think, be drawn from the above calculations is, that the practice of infanticide has decreased since the period of our connexion with the Kachh state, and that it is still diminishing in a very sensible degree. This degree will, I hope, be greatly accelerated by the progress of the measures now in operation for the extinction of the crime. The census will be renewed next year; and an addition will be made to the register, showing the births, deaths, and marriages of the preceding 12 months. Under the second article of their agreement, the chiefs report to the Darbár all cases of premature or still births or deaths under suspicious circumstances, of the newly-born children. For neglect of his duty on this point, the Ráo fined the chief of Motálá 200 rupees. The only other fine which has been inflicted, since the commencement of the census, is that imposed upon Dhaljí, of Patrí, after an imprisonment in the Hill Fort of more than 12 months. The sum, therefore, of 1,200 koris is all that has as yet been appropriated towards a fund for the assistance of the poorer Jáḍejás, in defraying the marriage expenses of their daughters.

"In the 13th paragraph of my report of the 6th May 1839, I have stated that infanticide is less prevalent in the district of Wágar than in that of the Abráshiá, and I have assigned, as a reason for this, that in Wágar there are families of Wághelás with whom the Jáḍejás can intermarry, whereas on the Abráshiá the Jáḍejás are alone. The truth of the fact is proved by the present census, as we find the enumeration of the tribe in Wágar gives 888 males and 94 females, being a proportion of 9·4 to 1; while that of the Abráshiá by itself gives 1,724 males and 95 females, being a proportion of 18·1 to 1.

"In the 7th paragraph of the same Report, I have estimated the number of the Jáḍejás at 12,000. In this estimate I included both the pure and impure Jáḍejás; but experience has shown me that it is far too high, if taken as the number of the adult males, though it may not be very far from the truth, if considered to comprehend all the males of every age. The present census comprises only the Jáḍejá Bháíyád, the royal brotherhood or clan. The branches which it includes are the Khengár (to which the Ráo himself belongs), the Sáéb, the Ráéb, the Deda, the Bhimaní, the Amar, and the Hálá. It would be very satisfactory could we believe that infanticide was confined to the Bháíyád; but unfortunately it is but too certain that the baneful example has spread among other and more numerous tribes. It is calculated that the various families which have from time to time been separated from the stock of the pure Jáḍejás, and which are now acknowledged only as spurious and degraded offsets, amount at least to 7,000 males: to these must be added 3,000 for the Muhammadan tribes, which have been similarly parted; and amid all this population the crime of female infanticide is systematically and ruthlessly practised.

"What steps can be taken to check and extinguish this horrid vice, and so large a number of people, is a question of the gravest moment. The Bháíyád is but a third part of the number; the larger portion is not comprehended in the British Guarantee, and cannot be brought under the operation of our existing treaties with the Kachh state. To the Ráo alone, therefore, we must look for the application of any coercive measures; and His Highness is startled at the idea of criminal proceedings against so powerful a body of his subjects. Nor, indeed, do I know that such stringent measures are immediately desirable. I would rather seek to persuade the Ráo to call upon the leading men of each tribe (where such can be found) to enter into compacts, binding themselves and all their followers and relations to abandon the dreadful habit, and thus to obtain upon them such a hold as may justify the infliction of summary punishment hereafter. This is the best plan which I can at present devise; but my information is not yet sufficiently extended, or my views matured, to enable me to speak with confidence on this momentous branch of the subject, and I therefore beg to be permitted to reserve it for a future report."*

* On the subject of Satí, the kindred crime of Infanticide, Captain Melville added :—"I have taken frequent occasion to discuss with the Ráo the subject of Satí, and to urge him to denounce the cruel rite; but His Highness will not allow himself to be prevailed on to exert his power to this end. In reply to all my arguments, he refers me to the Jáḍejás, and reminds me of what, in the abstract, I cannot deny, that as the head of the state he is bound to consult them on every great question, and to abide by their advice. In conformity with this rule, His Highness has addressed to his Bháíyád circular letters demanding their opinions regarding Satí, and has assembled them in my presence, that I might hear them speak for themselves. Without a single exception, the Jáḍejás support and defend the rite of Satí, while their prince remains professedly neutral. I have endeavoured all along to prevail on the Ráo to act for himself, well knowing that a body of ignorant men like the Jáḍejás can never be induced to abandon any part of their an-

On the 11th of January 1841, Captain Melville thus intimated the issue of an important proclamation by the Ráo; calculated to hasten the issue of the complete suppression of infanticide in Kachh.

"I have the satisfaction of reporting for the information of the Honorable the Governor in Council, that His Highness the Ráo has issued a proclamation, addressed to the "*Sammátarí-no Patar,*" (a designation which includes every tribe and family tracing their descent in any way from the Sammás, and thereby claiming affinity with the Jáḍejás,) warning them that as the evil practice of infanticide which has hitherto prevailed among the Jáḍejás has been at length put down, it will not be permitted to continue among the other tribes which have followed the bad example, but that every case which may come to the knowledge of the Darbár will be very severely punished. And in order to facilitate the detection of the offence, the proclamation further declares that an informer shall receive as a reward one-fourth part of any fine which may be inflicted on conviction of an offender; but that a false accuser, or an accuser who fails to fully substantiate his charge, will meet with immediate and condign punishment."

Captain Melville annexed a list of the tribes to which this proclamation specially applied, which included all of them in which the practice of infanticide was known

cestral superstition, unless urged by some more powerful motive than the simple dictate of virtue or humanity. I believe that they would bow, and willingly bow, to the mandate which forbids Satí; and that if the Ráo would exercise the moral courage required on his part to issue the injunction, the rite would be at once and without a murmur abandoned. For the future I shall oppose, unless otherwise instructed by the Honourable Board, the proposition of the question in any form to the Jáḍejás in a body, and trust to time to bring about a change in the Ráo's feelings, which may render His Highness as sincerely desirous of employing all the power and influence of his station to abolish Satí, as he most truly and evidently is to put an end to Infanticide."

to exist.* These tribes are scattered throughout the country; and the authorities could hear of no men among them likely to prove useful instruments for working upon the masses.

The Government, in acknowledging the receipt of Colonel Melville's communications, expressed the high sense entertained by it of the "zeal, wisdom, and discretion which had distinguished his efforts for the suppression of infanticide in Kachh"; its entire satisfaction with the proclamation issued by the Ráo; its regret that His Highness had not yet been prevailed on to abolish Satí in his own dominions by his own authority, as had been done by his Highness the Gáikawáḍ and the Rájás of Sátárá and Kolápur and the chiefs of the Rewa-Kánṭhá and other districts; and its hope that Mr. Malet of the C. S., Colonel Melville's efficient successor in the residency at Bhuj, would use his best endeavours to get trustworthy persons employed in the Jáḍejá censorship, which should also, through the Political Agent in Káṭhiáwáḍ, be extended to A'dhoí.†

In September 1851, Mr. Malet reported to Government a case of Infanticide by a female of the Hothí tribe, said to have committed the evil deed, or to have allowed the child to perish from hunger, when she was

* "List of Tribes passing under the common designation of 'Sammátarí,' or descendants of the Sammás, (but not Jáḍejás of the Bháíyád) among which the practice of Female Infanticide is known to prevail.

Tribes which have become Musalman. Ker, Sammá, Nutiyár, Abadá, Gajan, Sár, Mandará. These are supposed to number about 3,000 males.

Tribes which are still Hindus. Kandardé, Pasayiyá, Abadá, Bhojdé, Kara Ráo. These have branched from the De'da. Gaján, Ráo, Dal, Mor, Dádar, Dunyá, Hápá, Bare'ch, Butá, Ustíyá, Nangíyá, Je'sar. These have branched from the Gajan. Kámya, Hothí, Thárá, Mokalsí, Othá, Waransí, Choghe'r, Bhámaní, Virával, Kandághará. These Hindu tribes are supposed to number about 7,000 males."

† It was in consequence of this request that Major Jacob procured the census of A'dhoí referred to at p. 255.

in a fit and her husband was absent. For concealing the crime the husband, named Udhájí, was fined by the Ráo a hundred koris, in default of which he was to suffer imprisonment for one year, a punishment certainly too lenient. The criminal stated in mitigation of his offence, however, that the head of his tribe had never consented to put a stop to the crime of infanticide. This brought to the recollection of the Ráo that the persons charged with the proclamation forbidding infanticide had been informed by the Hothís of Bandará and Tumáḍí, that they did not intend to abide by the Ráo's orders on this point. They were accordingly called to Bhuj for conference, when they requested some days to consult the goddess *Mátá*, under whose protection they had been ostensibly located in their lands and villages for several generations. This "divinity," they afterwards reported, gave them no orders on the subject; and they declined to make engagements without her injunctions.* The

* The following epistle of the Hothís is both painful and curious. "The worshippers of Mátá Kunarjí and Dansinghjí write to his Highness the Ráo De'saljí.—You have sent here Thákur Rághují; he has told us not to destroy our female children, and called us and the Tumaḍiwálá to Bhuj, after which we came here and took the orders of Mátájí; but this is not the order of Mátájí, so we cannot keep our children alive without the order of Mátá. Formerly the Sáhib and Lakmidás Mehtá called us, and said, that our girás would not be unjustly taken by the Darbár, to which purport they would give us a writing, and that we should agree not to put to death our female children; but at that time we neither gave a writing nor received one; but now His Highness says that we are to preserve our female children. On this we requested the orders of Mátájí, but Mátájí gave us no order, therefore we cannot preserve our children. Those who formerly among us preserved their children, and those who married them have perished, and have left no posterity. How, therefore, can we preserve them? We are the faithful servants of the Ráo, and from the power of Mátájí and the Ráo our characters in former time were preserved (when they did not consent to stop child-murder); why should it not be so now, when it is in your power? This place was privileged by your ancestors fourteen generations ago, since which time it has always remained an asylum; therefore do you give an answer to the Sáhib on this subject, for we cannot consent to this." A sufficiently plain avowal of systematic murder!

Ráo's own superstitious feelings made him hesitate for some time about the course he should pursue with them; but he was willing to follow the advice of the British Government. The representatives of that Government at Bombay,—on the suggestion of suitable compulsory measures by Mr. Malet,*—were of opinion, that "the heads of the Jáḍejá tribes having declared the crime punishable if committed by any of his subjects, the Hothís came under the same obligation as others, and if detached in the perpetration of the crime, should be made liable to the same punishments."

The result of the proceedings in Kachh in the Hothí case was thus notified by Mr. Malet.

"After acquainting his Highness with the sentiments of Government, I had a long conference with him on the methods to be pursued towards the Hothís, both as affecting them and with reference to the Jáḍejá bháíyád, and those other tribes who are by the Ráo's proclamation amenable to punishment for infanticide. His Highness consulted his minister and several of his bháíyád, and the result of the conference was, that to recede from the demand originally made on the Hothí chiefs for their agreement to abstain from infanticide and for a census, would weaken the arrangements now in force, and greatly dissatisfy the Jáḍejá bháíyád.

"I need but mention two principal reasons for these conclusions, with which I beg most respectfully to state my concurrence: firstly, the especial sanctity of Mátá Bandará and Mátá Tumaḍí, the abodes of the principal chiefs, would effectually prevent the discovery of infanticide unless the census were duly taken, and even

* 1. "To send *mausu'ls* [horsemen or foot-messengers billetted till the demands which they enforce are complied with] at a daily increasing rate, until the chiefs consent to sign the agreement. 2. To sequestrate the *girás* of those refusing to sign the agreement within a stipulated time. 3. To remove from the country all those who persist in committing a sin, which the *Darbár* and the British Government have determined, as far as their means can ensure to put a stop to."

if discovery could be made, would render His Highness ever dependent on our aid for its punishment: secondly, the Jáḍejás would be dissatisfied at finding that a tribe, which, although many of its members are of pure blood, is inferior to their own, could refuse, with at least present impunity, to concur in what they had agreed to, they would repent their own conduct and ever endeavour to evade their engagement.

"For these reasons His Highness the Ráo determined again to endeavour to procure the assent of the Hothí chiefs to the abolition of infanticide and to a census. To strengthen his persuasions, I informed the Hothís that I was ready to enforce their obedience to the Ráo's orders to discontinue infanticide, and that the two Governments would severely punish the crime, forcibly pointing out to them the evil consequences of their contumacy. I considered it better for various reasons, with which it is unnecessary to trouble Government, not to proceed to Bandará or Tumaḍí in person.

"Notwithstanding the Ráo's endeavours and the persuasion of the respectable persons he sent to the Hothís, they were inflexible, and His Highness was compelled to request my aid. I therefore addressed letters to the chiefs of the two villages, in which, after stating the reasons for my interference, I informed them that it was His Highness's firm determination not to allow persons guilty of infanticide, and disobedient to his orders, to reside in his dominions, and that they were allowed fifteen days for preparation to leave the province. I sent these letters by 20 Mausúl Swárs [horsemen], 10 to each village, thinking it better to avoid by such parties the possibility of the chiefs involving themselves further by resistance, and to show the other tribes the consequences of disobedience to their own Government. I am happy to say that the objects were effected, the Bandará chief repairing to Bhuj the next day and the Tumaḍí chief the day after. There appeared at Tumaḍí, at first, a disposition to resist, but it soon evaporated.

"I enclose a translation of the acknowledgement by the Hothís of their improper conduct, which I considered it right, as a memento, to affix to their agreement to abstain from infanticide in future. With this exception, it is the same as that given by the Jáḍejás, and transmitted to Government by Lieutenant-Colonel Melville, in his letter of the 11th April 1840.*

The proceedings of Mr. Malet and the Ráo in this case met with the entire approbation of the Government, at the head of which, at this time, was the Hon. G. W. Anderson. They were of a very décided character.

The infanticide report of Kachh for the year 1841 was presented to the Bombay Government by Mr. Malet on the 1st July 1842. It brought to notice his zealous endeavours for the accuracy and improvement of the census, and contained the following statement, which called forth the commendations of Government both to himself and the Ráo.

"I am happy to observe the more just proportion of females to males under one year old in this census. Last year it was 1 to 3·31; this year it is 1 to 1·22; and although infanticide must be still inferred, I think it as satisfactory as could be expected. The Sáéb, Amar, and Ajání tribes have actually more female than male children of that age.

* "I, Hothí Kuwarjí of Baḍá Bandará write, that there was a treaty made between the English and Kachh Governments in the year Samwat 1875, A.D. 1819, in the 17th article of which all the Jáḍejá Bháíyád agreed not to destroy their female children; in that agreement the whole of the tribes concurred. Therefore the Darbár many times has reiterated its orders, but we, from our foolishness, did not agree to this; but now Munshí Gul Muhammad came to our village to make the census, and we would not, according the custom of the country, allow him to take it. This was on our part a great fault, therefore the Sirkár sent on us 10 Mausúl Swárs, and we went and prayed for pardon of our offence from the two Sirkárs, and agreed, according to the agreement of all the Jáḍejás, to keep our children alive according to the four paragraphs written underneath, etc.

"Here follow the four paragraphs contained in Enclosure 2, to Colonel Melville's letter of the 11th April 1840."—9th January, 1842.

"On the whole Jáḍejá population, the proportion of females to males has risen from 1 to 14·6 last year to 1 to 10·5 this year. The married and betrothed females, deducting of course those under one year old in both years, were, last year, 1 to 1·268; this year 1 to 1·127, a slight but satisfactory increase."

Of the Ráo's earnestness and determination in the suppression of infanticide, and of the efficient assistance received by him from the Residency and the Bombay Government, there could be no doubt.

CHAPTER XIII.

MR. MALET'S REPORTS ON INFANTICIDE IN KA'ṬHIA'WA'Ḍ AND THE NOTICE TAKEN OF THEM BY GOVERNMENT—NATIVE ESSAYS ON INFANTICIDE.

The first of the regular annual reports on Infanticide in Káṭhiáwáḍ was forwarded to the Bombay Government on the 27th September 1843 by Mr. Arthur Malet, transferred from Kachh to the political agency in the more southern province. The Jáḍejá returns showed an increase of 137 males and 195 females, the totals being 6,243 and 1,857. Those of the Jaitwás gave a total of 153 males and 25 females. Those of the Súmrá showed that the practice of infanticide among this Muhammadan tribe,—portions of which were found in the Nawánagar, Dharol, and Murví districts,—had not been general, though extensive, the total at the end of 1842 being 351 males and 141 females. The A'dhoí Mánká-Korangá returns exhibited totals of 69 males and 25 females. Donations, as usual, had been granted from the Infanticide Fund in aid of the marriage expences of poor Jáḍejás females. Only one case of suspicion of infanticide had arisen in the course of the year; but it had originated in an erroneous report of the sex of an infant.

The conclusion of Mr. Malet's report was as follows:

"The censor employed up to the end of 1832, though a trustworthy man, could not be prevailed on to permit his wife or any near female relation to take a part in his duty. I have this year therefore been obliged to remove him; and he is replaced by a kárkun hitherto employed in the judicial department, named Rámchandra Krishnají, not so intelligent a person, but considered trustworthy. I regret, however, that I have not yet found any respectable person so free from prejudice as required by Government in the sixth paragraph of that letter. The wife of the present mehtá is to be examined in her own house; and this examination, if necessary, can be conducted by the Political Agent or an assistant. More than this I see no probability of attaining at present.

"I carefully explained to Jáḍejá Kalájí of Sháhpur the consequence of any future deviation from his duty, and wrote the same to the chiefs who interceded for him.

"The A'dhoí census will in future fall under the Political Agent in Káṭhiáwád.*

"With reference to the seventh paragraph, I have taken every opportunity personally to inculcate on the chiefs the necessity for their contributing towards the spread of education in Káṭhiáwáḍ, and I addressed letters also to them, but I much regret to say without success. I shall not, however, lose sight of this most desirable object, concerning which I hope at some future period to address you more at large. As connected with this subject I may mention, that the missionaries from the North of Ireland of the Presbyterian persuasion are endeavouring to found schools in this province. The stations they wish, I believe, more particularly to occupy are Rájkoṭ and Porbandar. Surájí, I am told, promised them ground to build on, and the Ráná has, I

* [The district of A'dhoí in Wágar in the eastern portion of Kachh, as has been already incidentally noticed, belongs to the Thákur of Murví, the descendant of Aliájí the eldest son of Hamír (see p. 50) murdered by Jám Ráwal, who claimed the sovereignty over it in opposition to the Ráo of Kachh, the descendant of Khengár, the second son of Hamír; but the point at issue having been most fully and ably investigated by the authority of the Bombay Government, under the special commission of Mr. J. G. Lumsden, of the C. S., the claim of the Rájá of Murví to the sovereignty of the larger portion of A'dhoí was satisfactorily established.]

hear, been repairing a house for them, but objects to allow them to become the proprietors of ground."

"Captain Jacob's injunctions noticed in the 8th paragraph have only in two instances as yet been replied to, the Thákur of Walá professed his readiness to act as the others, but could not separately make any promise; the Rájá of Drángadrá intimated that he would on an expected occasion of a marriage obtain the opinions of such as might be present, but his death prevented this. I shall, however, endeavour on all occasions to inculcate the necessity of such a stipulation, and can I at any time get the consent of any influential chief I think it not unlikely that others may follow.

"The distribution of the Rs. 5,000 to Jáḍejás of the Nawánagar táluká will appear in the Report for this year.

"The 11th paragraph of Mr. Willoughby's letter requires the future transmission of the infanticide reports on the 1st January each year. I regret to state that this cannot take place: the reports from the chiefs are not due until that date, and until their receipt the mehtá cannot proceed on his circuit. Were the report considered due in June each year it might be forwarded with punctuality."

The Government, under Sir George Arthur, expressed its satisfaction with Mr. Malet's report; and recommended him to implement all the measures to which he had directed attention. It fixed the 1st of April, afterwards extended to the 1st of June, for the transmission of the annual report.

Mr. Malet's Infanticide Report for 1843, was forwarded to Bombay on the 30th August, 1844. It embraced the returns of the Jáḍejá, Jaitwá, and Sumrá population, but not those of the Mánká-Korangá, as the district of Adhoí belonging to Murví had again been lately placed under other superintendence. It was viewed by Government as of a satisfactory character. The year 1843 was the first in which the infanticide censor had, during his tour of inspection and inquiry, been accompanied by his wife. Mr. Malet's instructions to these parties were most strict, that every Jáḍeja female should be seen by one or other of them. To the younger children the censor himself found easy access. Those of more mature age were visited by his wife. No suspicion had arisen, in consequence of their investigations, of any case of actual infanticide.

Mr. Malet stated that he continued to lose no opportunity of inculcating upon the chiefs the necessity of making arrangements for the advancement of education in the province, but that he saw little probability of being able to awaken their interest in that most important object. He also mentioned that he did not lose sight of the instructions of Government relative to stipulations in Jáḍejá marriage settlements for the preservation of the female issue. He encouraged a few poor Jáḍejas, to apply for assistance in the marriage of their daughters.

The Returns for 1844 were forwarded to Government by Mr. Malet on the 10th August 1845.

"There is nothing in these statements," he observed on that occasion, "that calls for particular notice. There appears to be a steady progression; and as the censor and his female relation see every one of the females, and their names are regularly entered and compared with former statements, I hope there is no ground for suspicion. No suspicion of infanticide has occurred this year.* Of the unmarried females noticed in the 10th paragraph of my letter No. 102 August 30th 1844, one has been married. No application has been made this year for assistance, the disbursements on that account being for former demands. There is, I think, a dislike to apply for aid, except in cases of necessity. There is no progress towards Education on the part of the Chiefs, and I do not at present see any probability of it."

* Gondal was not visited this year for want of time. It was carefully examined last year, and no ground for suspicion exists.

In reply to this letter, the following important communication, founded on a minute of Mr. Willoughby, was addressed by Government to Mr. Malet, on the 19th January 1846.

"I am directed by the Honourable the Governor in Council to acknowledge the receipt of your letter, dated the 10th August last, No. 130, submitting your annual report, for the year 1844, on Female Infanticide in the Province of Káṭhiáwáḍ; and forwarding five statements containing the information specified in the margin.*

"The first and second statements submitted by you shew the following results:—

Caste.	*No. of Male Population.*			*No. of Female Population.*		
	In 1842.	In 1843.	In 1844.	In 1842.	In 1843.	In 1844.
Jádejá	6,129	6,176	6,430	1,841	1,959	2,175
Jaitwá	153	153	154	52	53	57
Sumrá	351	364	372	141	i57	164

"Hence it appears that in each instance the increase in the number of females, especially, among the Jáḍejás, has during the years 1842, 1843 and 1844, been in a greater proportion than the males. This result is very satisfactory, more particularly since from the 2nd paragraph of your letter, it appears that every one of the females entered in the census passes under the personal observation of the censors.

"In statement No. 3, the proportion of males to females, from ten years of age to one year and under, amongst the Jáḍejá, Jaitwá and Sumrá populations in Káṭhiáwáḍ is shewn to be as follows:—

* 1. A Census of the Jáḍejá, Jaitwá and Sumrá populations of the province of Káṭhiáwáḍ for the year of report. 2. A comparative Table of do. for the years 1841-42, 1842-43, and 1843-44. 3. Tables of the proportions of the Male to the Female sex from ten years of age to one year and under, amongst the Jáḍejá, Jaitwá, and Sumrá populations of this province. 4. Tables shewing the different ages of the Jáḍejá, Jaitwá and Sumrá populations. 5. Statement of the receipts and disbursements of the Infanticide Fund during the year 1844.

Caste.	Under 10 years.		Under 9 years.		Under 8 years.		Under 7 years.		Under 6 years.		Under 5 years.		Under 4 years.		Under 3 years.		Under 2 years.		Under 1 year.	
	Males.	Females.	Males.	Females.	Males.	Females.	Males.	Females.	Males.	Females.	Males.	Females.	Males.	Females.	Males.	Females.	Males.	Females.	Males.	Females.
Jádejá	1,711	1,207	1,532	1,179	1,313	1,188	1,167	1,029	1,035	887	903	877	891	755	703	620	400	451	274	232
Jaitwá	25	...	22	...	25	25	15	25	18	16	10	15	5	...	12	14	3	6	2	2
Sumrá	102	67	107	82	99	58	90	70	77	60	69	50	53	41	39	37	29	22	9	6

"The following further table shews the result of the census of the Jáḍejá population in Káṭhiáwáḍ, as obtained in 1834, 1837, 1841, and 1844.

	Under 10 years.		Under 9 years.		Under 8 years.		Under 7 years.		Under 6 years.		Under 5 years.		Under 4 years.		Under 3 years.		Under 2 years.		Under 1 year.	
	Males.	Females.	Males.	Females.	Males.	Females.	Males.	Females.	Males.	Females.	Males.	Females.	Males.	Females.	Males.	Females.	Males.	Females.	Males.	Females.
Mr. Willoughby's census in 1834	125	33	41	30	96	34	76	43	93	36	89	53	118	40	108	35	103	46	130	44
Mr. Erskine's do. in 1837	108	22	35	12	97	28	85	32	105	25	93	12	95	25	125	16	102	32	123	60
Captain Jacob's do. in 1841	232	73	150	54	225	65	201	58	176	56	165	70	143	116	140	111	122	95	46	128
Mr. Malet's do. in 1844	1,711	1,207	1,532	1,179	1,313	1,188	1,167	1,029	1,035	887	903	877	891	755	703	620	400	451	274	232

"The Governor in Council desires me to draw your particular attention to the extraordinary disproportion between the male and female Jáḍejá births during the last ten years which your census for the year 1844 exhibits, when compared with the three censuses of your predecessors, for the years 1834, 1837, and 1841.

"The result of your census leads to the very improbable inference, if the numbers of males and females shewn under each age be correct, that the numbers of male and female births amongst the Jáḍejás in Káṭhiáwáḍ have for the last ten years been annually decreasing from natural causes in the ratio of from ten to twenty per cent. For instance, according to your census, the numbers of males of ten years of age in 1844, was 1,711, while those of one year and under were only 274, being in the ratio of 6¼ to 1 in favor of the former, and this too notwithstanding the generally admitted fact, that of all children born alive at least one third die before attaining the tenth year.

"The disproportion between the number of females of the age of one and ten years, is nearly similar to that existing amongst the males of the same ages, namely 1,207 of ten years and 232 of one year and under, being in the ratio of about 5⅕ to one.

"You are requested most carefully to inquire into this point, and submit any explanation you may be able in regard to this great and extraordinary disproportion, which the Governor in Council can at present only account for by the supposition that the above results have been obtained from incorrect data.

"From statement No. 4, accompanying your report, it appears that the greatest age amongst male Jáḍejás is 86, and of female 53 years. Amongst the male Jaitwás it is 79, and of female 35 years; and amongst the Sumrá males it is 72, and of females 37 years.

"From statement No. 5, the total disbursements paid from the Infanticide Fund during the year 1844, including marriage donations, and the maintenance of the Infanticide Establishment, amounted to Company's

Rupees 2,047-12-4; or Rupees 1,609-4-11 less than the expenditure of the preceding year. The Balance in favor of the Fund on the 31st December 1844, amounts to Company's Rupees 1,21,809-13-3, or Rupees 798-3-4 more than on the 31st December 1843.

"The information contained in the 2nd and 3rd paragraphs of your letter is very satisfactory.

"The Governor in Council was prepared by your previous reports for the announcement contained in the last paragraph of your letter. He requests, however, that you will not relax in your efforts to induce the principal chiefs to contribute towards the diffusion of Education in Káṭhiáwáḍ, for unless they can be persuaded to do this, under the condition prescribed by the Honorable the Court of Directors, Government will be unable to aid in the accomplishment of this very desirable object.

"The Governor in Council considers it very creditable to the Jáḍejás that no application has been made by them during the year 1844 for aid from the Infanticide Fund. Although, however, applications for assistance ought not to be encouraged, reasonable support should be extended in cases of destitution and distress."

A more satisfactory proof than this of the attention and vigilance of the Bombay Government, even in matters of minute detail connected with the infanticide returns, cannot easily be conceived.

Mr. Malet gave a prompt reply to the letter of Government, pointing out the sources of most of the errors which had occurred in his office, from a misplacement of figures in some of the columns of the census tables. The amended returns submitted by him, it was remarked by Government, however, were still defective, as apparent from the improbable fluctuation, shown by them of the male and female children of different ages. For instance, in two of the tálukás there were more male and female Jáḍejá children between the ages of seven and eight than between those of six and seven; and in one of them, more male children between five and six than between four and five years, and nearly double the number between the age of two and three than between that of one and two years of age, while experience proves that the opposite would be the more probable and correct result. But we need not dwell on these incidental mistakes, more especially as the Jáḍejá and other statistics will afterwards pass before our notice in a more perfect form. Mistakes in a census conducted by natives unacquainted with the principles of statistical registration were in the first instance almost unavoidable.

At the close of 1844, the name of the successful candidate for the first prize for an Essay on Infanticide was announced. It was that of Mr. Bháu Dájí, then an assistant teacher in the Elphinstone Institution, and now a graduate of the Grant Medical College, and a successful medical practitioner in Bombay. It was one of four Essays which had been sent in to the adjudicators,* of which none were considered worthy of the other prize. After the suggestion of a few judicious amendments in it by Mr. Willoughby, under the authority of Government, 600 copies of it in English, and 1,500 in Gujarátí, were printed and lithographed. The Gujarátí copies were intended principally for circulation in Káṭhiáwáḍ and Kachh.

The Hindu authorities quoted in this Essay as seemingly hostile to infanticide, we have already introduced into these pages.† After pointing out the general sinfulness of infanticide,‡ it thus warmly expostulates with the cruel and unnatural Jáḍejás, its principal perpetrators in India.

"Many of the Jáḍejás say, [that infanticide origina-

* E. H. Townsend, Esq., and the secretaries of the Board of Education and the Bombay Education Society.

† See above, pp. 29-31.

‡ "The protection of our offspring is the most sacred of all our obligations. It is also a powerful law of our nature. Its influence throughout all ages and on all nations, stamps it with an authority which cannot be slighted with impunity. The meanest insect is subject to it in common with man, and it is therefore no prejudice of education, no

ted] from the Rájá Jáḍá, who sent his Rájgur to find a suitable match for his daughter, but not finding one, he requested the Rájá to kill his daughter, which atrocious deed was done. From that time the Jáḍejás say, they continued to murder their daughters to uphold the

ordinance of wilful tyrants, but the wise and absolute enactment of the author of our being. This law, which discloses to us, at once, the will of the Creator and the duty of the creature, is violated by the commission of infanticide.

"It is treason against the Divine authority. The prerogative of God to appoint the time of his creatures is subverted.

"The infinite wisdom and paternal goodness of God are arraigned and condemned. The moral government of the Deity is disregarded and insulted; whatever is decent is outraged, whatever can be binding is broken.

"It is a treason against the social compact. Society has claims upon the infant from which it cannot be fairly absolved, except by the dispensation of him who, having formed the bonds at the beginning, has alone a right to loose them at his pleasure. The person who commits infanticide extinguishes not only the affection due to the infant, but the duties he owes to his country and mankind at large.

"It is treason against the revealed will of God. His express command is to commit no murder; and the person, who murders and allows to be murdered his own child is no less guilty than he who assassinates his neighbour, for it is God's property not his own. Parents have no more right to kill their children, than children have to kill their parents.

"Infanticide shows as little feeling as courage, and he is indeed a coward who murders, or allows to be murdered, an innocent being unable to offer resistance.

"Infanticide is a dastardly, barbarous, and selfish act.

"A child is the very image of innocence, helplessness, and amiability. —Can there be greater barbarity than in destroying these pictures of ourselves? In the midst of war and of its licenses, not to spare those tender beings is regarded as a deep crime, even in an enraged and cruel conqueror. What then must be the heart of the parents who crush the innocents whom even a brutal enemy forbears to injure? Can imagination itself conceive ought more harrowing to the feelings?

"Infanticide, being the most revolting of murders, is punished among all civilized nations, with death. The law of England, which will be enforced wherever its sway is acknowledged, punishes it also with death. In any civilized country the author of such a crime, especially when he is the father of the child, would be looked upon as a monster and his name held in detestation and infamy, and he would in England be torn to pieces by the people. Has God then made good and evil, guilt and innocence different in different countries? Or is not crime the same in all, and to be shunned, as injurious to man, and hateful to God?"

honour of their chief and clan. This resembles a child's tale; if, however, the Rájá did murder his daughter only for the reason assigned, both he and his Rájgur deserve to be classed among the most infamous of the human race, as the parent has no right to kill his offspring. It is an act stigmatized, both by divine and human law, as a foul crime. It is very clear that Jáḍá, who according to your legend, killed his daughter first, and with whom the practice originated, acted against the severest denunciations of religion and against custom; for, at that time daughters were preserved and not killed. Your ancestors were bold enough to commit a bad deed. Should you therefore desist from doing what is just, and what is your duty, and what is expected from the meanest creature? Beware, then, of this insidious enemy, *custom*. Were all sects of Rajputs to follow your example, in murdering their daughters, where, may I ask, would you find wives?

"Some unthinking persons are ready to say, 'If we relinquish the custom, others will continue it. Where then is the good of our doing so?' But what course of wickedness will not such reasoning justify? The robber, the assassin, may use the same plea, and say, 'What is the use of our ceasing to rob and murder? Others will still continue to do both.' Would you think them justified in the argument? Remember that society is composed of individuals, and that a custom cannot be abolished unless some of the community first break through it.

"I have been told that some of the Jáḍejás consider it no sin to kill a child before its cries are heard. This is worse than delusion. Is the enormity of the crime diminished, or annihilated by the difference of a few moments? The destruction by a mother of even an unborn infant is considered highly criminal by the Shástras.

"Little credit is due to those who follow in a beaten path, whilst on the contrary the world, in all ages, has looked with admiration upon those who have been daring enough to break through custom that they have known to be wrong. You say, 'To whom shall we affiance our daughters? none but princes are worthy of them. As we are not able to marry them to princes without crippling our means, we kill them. Pay the marriage portions of our daughters, and they shall live.' This excuse is furnished by the richer portion, and those who are possesed of some authority. The poorer classes of the Jáḍejás give a base, and more contemptible excuse. They say, 'We will not be called the brothers-in-law or fathers-in-law of any one. Why should we demean ourselves by giving our daughters in marriage to others'? Let me ask you, do you demean yourselves by taking women in marriage from those tribes which you consider inferior to your own? If you do not, why should not the brothers and relations of your wives be fit persons to marry the daughters to whom their own female kindred have given birth? Do what you please, the fathers and brothers of your wives are still the grandfathers and uncles of your sons. Is it then degrading to give your daughters in marriage to a person of that caste from which you take your wives?' . . . . It must be a strange kind of Kshatriism indeed, not that of the ancients, which requires the killing of daughters to maintain it. If the honour of a tribe is to be upheld by blood, then may butchers call themselves the bravest of men. Had these mighty kings sought for their equals as husbands to their daughters, where could they have found them? Are you then possessed of more pride than even such great men as these? Whence do you derive that pride? You are not even in rank the highest of your own tribe. The Sesoḍiás, the Raṭhors, the Pramárs, are higher than you. But you say, you are warriors. That such is a legitimate source of pride, I do not deny. There was a time when your forefathers followed no other occupation than that of war. These might have indulged in the pride to be derived from it. But are not the Musalmans, the Maráthás, and the English warriors? They who have conquered you one after another? Have they not more real cause for pride, than you? Is it degrading to honor another man? But, even if you were so proud as to suppose that you do not honor your son-in-law, or your brother-in-law, for their own sake, but for the sake of your daughters or sisters. All the gifts you bestow are for their benefit, for their happiness. Tell me what is degrading in this? It exists only in your distorted imaginations.

"Some of you inconsiderately say, 'If we rear our daughters, they may perhaps be guilty of light conduct and bring disgrace on the family.' If it be proper to kill daughters, because you fear that if they live, they will eventually be lowered, or perhaps be guilty of immoral conduct, upon the same principle you might destroy your sons and wives, for they too possibly may be guilty of that which may lower them or even entail disgrace on their family. But how do you know, I ask each of you, that the infant which you murder will not become as fair and beautiful as Padminí, and that Ráj-put princes of the noblest blood will not come to seek her hand? Do you see them with your own eyes? Do you apply to them the touchstone of opportunity? Nothing can surpass that folly, which, to gratify vanity and to gain popular applause, violates the laws of God and man. It is like preferring common glass to diamond. Among you, originally, one man spent a vast sum of money in the marriage of his daughter. Bráhmans, Bairágís, and Bháṭs lavished praises on him. The common herd of mankind heard of it with admiration; persons possessed of little knowledge and foresight tried to rival him in pomp and ceremony. It followed that the custom became general. It came to be considered dishonourable to perform marriage ceremonies at little expense. Thus the birth of a daughter came to be looked upon as a curse, in consequence of the expense which her marriage entailed. To avoid this inconvenience the Jáḍejás have doomed their daughters to death. Thus folly and vanity have led to crime; vanity in the rich, to throw away thousands upon mere ceremony; and folly in the poor, to imitate them. And now, every daughter you murder, you look upon as so much money saved; and the sons, that are born to you, you preserve as a source of gain. Thus to you the birth and rearing of children is a matter of rupees, annas, and pies. Parental feeling is distorted in your breast.

"An intelligent Jáḍejá Rajput wrote to the benevolent Colonel Walker in the following words:—'In Kaṭhiáwáḍ and Kachh-Haláḍ, the Rebaḍís or goatherds allow their male kids to die when there are many of them brought forth, and Chárans follow the same practice with their male buffaloes, both being unproductive;' and thus his meaning appears to be, that your motives for committing infanticide are of no higher value than those of the goatherd and the Cháran for killing their goats and other animals. Ignorant and avaricious men among you may say, 'We are obliged to spend some thousands of rupees for the marriage of a daughter; this sum would have remained to us, and we should have been rich to-day;' others may say 'Look at that thákur; his *sansár* is broken up; his estate is frittered away; had he but killed his daughters he would still have been rich.' It is true that an expenditure of money is incurred by the marriage, but it is really not attributable to the rearing of daughters. It is, to the nonsensical custom of spending large sums of money at the time of their marriages. And why do you spend them? The folly of wasting your money is not only ridiculous, but it is monstrous, when it leads you to murder your children by way of preventive."* In this reasoning, there is undoubtedly much tact and propriety.

One of the Essays sent up to Government in competition was in the Sanskrit language, and entirely written on Hindu principles. It was written by Raghunáth

* The Gujarátí version of this tract is good, though it contains a few anglicisms, originating doubtless in the comparative neglect of vernacular literature by even the best of the native students of English. In this respect, however, it is less faulty than many productions which we see now issuing from the press.

Párwatí Sháștrí. Though it was unsuitable for publication, it contains a few curious passages worthy of notice.*

* The author thus attacks Infanticide from the approved *examples* of the Shástras.

"In the *Bhágawat*, [Purána, Skanda x. 6.] for instance, it is related that there was a very cruel king, named Kansa, and, it having been prophesied that Kṛishṇa, a son, of his sister [Devakí], would kill him, Kansa on hearing of his birth ordered that all the infants who had been born in his country at the same time should be slain. Pútaná [a Rákshasí, or female incarnate demon], therefore, and others, on becoming acquainted with this order, killed very many infants. Then Pútaná having imbued her nipples with poison went to the house of Nanda [the foster-father of Kṛishṇa] with the intention of killing Kṛishṇa, and thus addressed his mother [foster-mother] Yashodá—'Having heard of the birth of your beautiful son I have come to see him; it is therefore proper that you should shew him to me.' On hearing this, Yashodá, not being aware of the deceit, placed Kṛishṇa in the lap of Pútaná, and proceeded to occupy herself in her domestic affairs. Pútaná then gave her poisoned breast to Kṛishṇa, but he, knowing the treachery sucked so powerfully, while Pútaná called out Quit, quit, that her breath was exhausted and she expired. Thus as the divine Kṛishṇa killed Pútaná, so will God kill those who murder their infant daughters.

"It is related in the *Bála Kaṇḍa* of the *Rámáyaṇa* that the Ṛishí Vishwámitra requested Dasharatha [the father of Ráma] to allow Ráma to accompany him in order to protect a sacrifice that he intended to perform against the Rákshasís [female devils], and that Dasharatha complied with his request. The Ṛishi then departed with Ráma and his younger brother, and having arrived at a forest deserted by men, beasts, and birds. Ráma inquired how this forest had become thus deserted. Vishwámitra replied that it had been occasioned by a female Rákshas, named Táḍaká, who devoured men, beasts, and birds, and that from fear of her all had fled from the forest, and that it was for the purpose of killing her that he had brought him (Ráma) there. Ráma, recollecting that his father had enjoined him to obey all the commands of Vishwámitra, then slew Táḍaká. But, afterwards on reflecting that he had, by the command of the Ṛishi, killed a female, he became grieved and thus addressed his brother Lakshmaṇa "Why am I grieved that I have slain this female Rákshas in obedience to the command of the Ṛishi who is fully conversant with the Ve'das and Shástras? Yet I fear that the kettle-drums of my fame will not be sounded by the exulting people for this deed, that on account of it my glory will not become resplendent in the world, and that the Guru of my race Vasishṭa will be ashamed of it."

These stories, well-known to the natives, are sufficiently incongruous and grotesque to fall within the sphere of Hindu belief.

CHAPTER XIV.

REPORTS OF COLONEL LANG ON INFANTICIDE IN KA'ṬHIA'-WA'Ḍ—SCHEME FOR EDUCATIONAL MEASURES—EXTINCTION OF RAJPUT INFANTICIDE AS A CUSTOM IN KA'ṬHIA'WA'Ḍ—CONGRATULATION OF MR. WILLOUGHBY—LATEST NOTICES OF ANTI-INFANTICIDE MEASURES IN KA'ṬHIA'WA'Ḍ.

In 1846, Major (now Lieut.-Colonel) William Lang was nominated to the political agency of Káṭhiáwáḍ, in which, before his assignation to the adjoining province of the Máhikánṭhá, he had long acted as an assistant. A better appointment to the office could not have been made by Government. This zealous and able functionary was thoroughly acquainted with every district and chief of the peninsula, with the habits and usages of the people, and with the duties of the agency in all their details; and at the same time greatly and universally beloved for kindness, simplicity, and uprightness of character, indefatigable attention to business, and soundness, solidity, and impartiality of judgement. The measures for the abolition of infanticide suggested by Mr. Willoughby had his fullest approval; and his influence had hitherto been exerted in carrying them fully, faithfully, and energetically into execution. High expectations were formed of his exertions in the cause; and they have been in no degree disappointed. It has been his honour to report the cheering fact that infanticide no longer exists among the Rajputs in Káṭhiáwáḍ as a custom, whatever it may do in exceptional cases as a crime.

Colonel Lang's first report on infanticide was that for 1845. It was forwarded to the Bombay Government on the 25th August 1846. Noticing the Returns of the Jáḍejá, Jaitwá, and Sumrá tribes, which it embraced, it thus proceeds:—

"The increase in the number of the female children in all these tribes, which has been going on since the introduction of the present system for the suppression of infanticide in 1835, continues to be shown in the returns now submitted. In the case of the Jaitwá and Sumrá population, the increase is equal in both sexes; but the Jáḍejá census is not so favorable, as it shows an addition of only 165 female children to 202 males. I fear, however, that there are still a great many inaccuracies in these returns. The proportion of births of both sexes to the number of married Jáḍejás appears generally to be exceedingly small, and in Vírpur-Kharéḍí and several of the smaller Tálukás, there is not a single birth of either a male or female child during the year under review. The number of grown up Jáḍejás in Vírpur-Kharéḍí, it will be observed, is sixty-five; and I have ascertained from the censor that forty-four of these are married. It is exceedingly improbable, therefore, that a year should have passed without a single child having been born to any of these; and in this Táluká I find that last year's return was equally blank, which makes it amount almost to a certainty that there must be some concealment of the births that actually take placc. I have therefore sent for the chiefs of all the tálukás in which no births of either sex are registered during last year, and shall endeavour to ascertain the true state of the case. I have also directed the native agent to ascertain, as some guide to the censor for the future, the proportion of births to married men amongst one or two other castes where he has the means of doing so; and have instructed the censor to be very particular for the future in noticing all these points when making his tour of the different tálukás, and when his suspicions are excited by any disproportions either in this respect, or with regard to the numbers of children of different sexes and ages, never to rest content till he has made the fullest inquiries on the spot, and adopted every other means in his power to satisfy himself that there is nothing wrong."

Notwithstanding the imperfections of the census now referred to,—for which the remedies suggested by Colonel Lang were entirely suitable,—neither he nor the native censor had any suspicion of the actual commission of infanticide during the year under review by any particular Rajput in the province.

In reference to the Essay on Infanticide of Mr. Bháu Dájí, which had not yet reached Káṭhiáwáḍ, Col. Lang expressed his belief that the circulation of it, if it were adapted to the circumstances of the people in plainness and simplicity of style, might be highly useful. At the same time, he suggested the propriety of "two prizes being again offered, for general competition throughout the presidency, for the best essays against female Infanticide, to be composed in the Gujarátí language and in a style sufficiently simple to be comprehended by the Rajputs themselves." These prizes he thought, also, should be continued from time to time, as the productions which they would encourage might be generally useful in Gujarát as school books.

Colonel Lang's report contained additional information and proposals of an important character. It mentioned that he had been anxiously seeking, though hitherto without success, to get the Rajputs furnishing daughters in marriage to the Jáḍejás to have stipulations made, as long ago proposed, for the preservation of their female issue. It recommended the renewal of presents to such Jáḍejás as had preserved four daughters and upwards. It thus, also, in an encouraging manner, noticed the subject of education for the province of Káṭhiáwáḍ.

"I am happy to be able on this occasion to report that the continued endeavours of my predecessor [Mr. Malet] to enlist the chiefs of the province in the cause of education were crowned before his departure [to Bombay as chief-secretary] with as complete success as could well be desired, in as far at least as relates to their subscribing for the establishment of a superior school at Rájkoṭ, with the view of introducing a better system of education throughout the province generally. As is known to Government, many letters had been written to the different chiefs both by Mr. Malet and his predecessors, but with little if any effect. On visiting Nawánagar, however, in November last, Mr. Malet spoke to His Highness the Jám on the subject, and persuaded him to consent to an annual subscription at the rate of one per cent on his tribute. He then addressed letters to the other principal chiefs, informing them of the good example which had been set by the Jám, and calling upon them to follow it. This was immediately done by His Highness the Nawáb of Junágaḍ, who, in consideration of his rank and the smaller amount of tribute paid by him, agreed to subscribe at the rate of two per cent. The Rájá of Drángadrá likewise speedily responded to the call; and circulars were afterwards written by Mr. Malet to all the remaining chiefs and tálukdárs in the province. The whole of those who have yet sent replies have agreed to the plan of giving one per cent on their tribute except the Thákur of Bhawanagar, who wrote in reply that he had formerly proposed to give one rupee for each day of the year, but his kárbhárí had not forwarded his letter, and that he would now reserve the point for discussion with Mr. Malet when he met him, as he had a number of grievances connected with the introduction of certain new regulations into his capital to complain of. I received this letter shortly after Mr. Malet's departure, and wrote in reply urging him to follow the example which had been set by so many of the other chiefs, and I had hoped, ere this, to have received the Thákur's reply, agreeing to do so, which I have no doubt will eventually be sent.* In the mean time, however, I beg to submit a statement shewing the names of the several chiefs and Tálukdárs from whom replies have been received up to the present time and specifying the amount of tribute paid by each, and their respective subscriptions for the general improvement of education in Káṭhiáwáḍ calculated upon it.†

"Iṭ will be observed, from this statement, that the sum already subscribed is Rs. 4,398-13-1 (Rs. 4,510-6-0 subsequent correction) ‡ per annum; and if all the other chiefs and tálukdárs agree to the same arrangement, which there is every prospect of their doing, the amount realized during the year from this source will be between nine and ten thousand Company's rupees. Mr. Malet did not address the Amrélí and Okhámandal Kamávisdárs [collectors],§ considering that Government would doubtless prefer applying to His Highness the Gáikawáḍ through the Resident at Baroda. It is not, I hope, too much to expect that His Highness will readily follow the example of His Highness the Nawáb of Junágaḍ, in the higher rate than the other tributaries which

* [The Bhawanagar state afterwards agreed to subscribe a thousand rupees per annum to education.]

† [The principal annual subscriptions in this list are those of the Jám of Nawánagar (Jáḍejá), Rs. 1,110-0-5; the Rájá of Drángadrá (Jhálá), Rs. 406-11-4; the Nawáb of Junágaḍ (Musalman), Rs. 1,253-4-11; the Thákur of Rájkoṭ (Jáḍejá), Rs. 189-14-0; the Ráná of Porbandar (Jaitwá), Rs. 279-12-0; the Wálá Víkamsí of Jaitpur (Káṭhí), Rs. 502-9-11.]

‡ [To this was afterwards added Rs. 2,212-13-9, making a total of Rs. 6,723-4-3.]

§ [The Amrélí and Okhámandal districts belong to the Gáikawáḍ, the latter district having been presented to him by the British Government for a slight consideration, that it might avoid entanglement with the celebrated shrine of Dwáraká situated within its boundaries. The Gáikawáḍ ultimately refused to contribute to educational purposes for these districts.]

he has agreed to pay on his tribute, and grant two per cent, from the whole of his receipts from Káṭhiáwáḍ, for the improvement of the system of education throughout the province; in which case, our Government would be graciously pleased to do the same (and it is surely not too much to ask for such a grand object). It would at once swell the funds available for this purpose to upwards of thirty thousand rupees a year.

"With so gratifying a prospect before us, as far as the funds required are concerned, it is desirable that no time should be lost in commencing the erection of a capacious and handsome school house at Rájkoṭ; and on this point, therefore, I shall feel obliged by your obtaining for me the instructions of the Hon'ble Board, as to the amount which it is considered proper to expend upon the building, and the plan of the college or school in Bombay, or elsewhere, best adapted to the purpose, on which it would be advisable to erect it. I hope, likewise, that early instructions will be issued to the proper authorities at the presidency for the selec tion f the fittest man that can be found for the situation of head Gujaráti master, and of fully qualified men for those of Gujaráti teachers in different departments. With such ample funds, the establishment of a good English School, under a thoroughly qualified European Master, may probably be eventually contemplated by Government; but I am myself humbly of opinion, that our first efforts should be confined to the introduction of the best possible system of vernacular education throughout the province; and with this object, although I would of course have the head school at Rájkoṭ, I humbly conceive it would be necessary to establish branch schools, all of them under teachers educated in Bombay, at the most centrical places in different parts of the province; to afford to all desirous of securing for their children a thoroughly good vernacular education the opportunity of sending them to one of these schools, from which they could afterwards be sent to the Head School at

Rájkoṭ if desirous of prosecuting their studies in the higher and more difficult branches, instruction in which would necessarily be confined in a great measure to the Rájkoṭ School. All these branch schools would of course be under the entire control of the Head-Master at Rájkoṭ, and it would form an important part of his duty to visit them as frequently as possible, and to select from each the most able youths for further instruction at Rájkoṭ, provided their parents were willing to send them there, for the greater encouragement to which, it may hereafter be advisable to allot a limited number of scholarships to the Rájkoṭ school. As regards an English school in the present low state of education in Kaṭhiáwáḍ, I doubt not many might be induced to attend it for a time; but few, I fear, would be likely to remain long enough to obtain more than a smattering of English, whereas the same period spent in attendance at a throughly efficient vernacular school, would suffice for the attainment of a tolerable education in their own language, and impart to those, who had the time and inclination to prosecute their studies further, a taste for cultivating the higher branches of knowledge, so far as they could be taught from Gujarátí works. I am aware that the great want of these forms at present a serious objection to confining our efforts to vernacular education alone; but this seems only to make it the more incumbent upon us to adopt some more efficacious measures to obtain a supply of the necessary works on different subjects in the vernacular languages of the country, since the education of the great mass of the people, in any language but their own, seems to my humble judgement, altogether impossible." "I offer these observations, however, with much diffidence, as it seemed necessary without delay to allude to the several points connected with the introduction of a new system of education into Káṭhiáwáḍ which are deserving of the maturest consideration of Government. The two School-Masters who have now been at Rájkoṭ for so many years, although educated in Bombay, appear scarcely to have produced the slightest impression; so that if the vernacular system is to be adopted for the present at least, it must be evident that every thing will depend on the Head-Schoolmaster who may be selected being a very superior man in every respect, and no expense therefore should be spared in securing the services of the best man available for the duty in Bombay as well as those of the best qualified subordinate Teachers in the different branches of education."

The Government in acknowledging, through Mr. Malet, the receipt of Colonel Lang's communication, expressed its belief that it was probable that the concealment of births in certain of the tálukás was of design; intimated that as the Essay on Infanticide was in a condensed form in the course of being printed, it would await the result before determining about additional prizes; sanctioned the rewards proposed to be given to certain of the Jáḍejás for the preservation of four or more daughters; declared its satisfaction with the liberality of the chiefs in the matter of education, while at the same time it expected that additional funds would be forthcoming from their associates; and requested that, in future, communications on the subject of education should be kept distinct from that of infanticide. At a later period, the Government set apart a lákh of rupees from the Infanticide Fund as its own contribution and that of the Gáikawáḍ to the cause of education in the province. This sum bears interest from the 5th June 1847, which added to the voluntary contributions of the native chiefs,—the scheme of a continued per-centage on their tribute having been abandoned,—forms, as a beginning, a respectable appropriation, of about eleven or twelve thousand rupees annually, to the great cause of public enlightenment in one of the most benighted, though remarkably interesting, provinces of India. A high central Vernacular and elementary English school, with suitable buildings and a suitable native superintendent, has been founded at Rájkoṭ, and branch schools at some of the capitals of the principal native chiefs, to a few of whom, now minors, tutors have also been appointed. The final arrangements for them have been made by the Government Board of Education in Bombay, in concert with Colonel Lang and one of his assistants, Major Aston, formerly a zealous secretary of the Native Education Society. Their moral influence will greatly depend on the system of instruction to be ultimately adopted.

The reports of Colonel Lang for the years 1846, 1847, and 1848, which were all duly forwarded to Government, show a constant anxiety on his part for perfecting the Returns, which he was enabled in a large degree to effect by the employment of an additional censor, and the comparison together of the proportions of population in different tribes.* No suspicions of any cases of actual infanticide occurred during these years.† The infanticide fund was employed as usual in paying the expences of the censorship, and aiding poor Jáḍejás in the marriage of their daughters. Colonel Lang's proceedings were viewed as highly satisfactory in every respect by Government. Copies of the Essay against Infanticide were forwarded to him for distribution in Káṭhiáwáḍ; and he was informed that a notification was about to be issued offering additional prizes for Essays on the same subject.‡

Colonel Lang's report for 1849 was presented to Government on the 31st December, 1850. It intimated his continued anxiety and endeavour to get important

* The ordinary expence of the censorship in its improved form is, we believe, Rs. 116 a month.

† One chief had been accused, however, of neglecting to report the birth of two daughters.

‡ The second prize,—an essay worthy of the first not having been found,—was gained by Kuwarjí Rustamjí, whose production, in the form of a simple dialogue, was published both in English and Gujarátí. The competition, owing to the little information possessed by native youth respecting Infanticide in Western India was but limited. The adjudicators were the Rev. G. Pigott, C. J. Erskine, Esq. C. S., and H. J. Carter, Esq. Secretary to the Board of Education.

economical arrangements made between the Jáḍejás and other Rajput tribes calculated to facilitate their intermarriage and to diminish the expence of their nuptial celebrations.

"When I lately met His Highness the Jám at Balambá, I found him still fully alive to the necessity of making some arrangement for decreasing the heavy expense attending the marriage of the daughters of Rajputs in general and Jáḍejas in particular. Mr. Ogilvy [Resident in Kachh] had kindly got His Highness the Ráo to send over three agents on His Highness's part to discuss the subject, several communications since I last met the Jám having passed between him and the Ráo regarding it. I had also influential Rajputs with me belonging to Jháláwáḍ and other parts of the province, all most willing, as far as I could ascertain, to enter into any arrangements which their superior chiefs might consider practicable. I found the Kachh agents, however, still in favor of alliances with the Rajput families in Rajputáná; and they seemed to think that by giving daughters not only to the chiefs themselves but also to other members of their families, and even to their superior subordinate chiefs, there would be an ample opening made to dispose of all the daughters of our superior Jáḍejá chiefs, and that in cases where alliances were formed with others than the chiefs themselves of Rajputáná, the honor and dignity of the Jáḍejá chiefs would be sufficiently upheld by getting all other suitors for their daughter's hands to come to their capitals to be married. I remember, however, that this very practice of getting the bridegroom to come to their houses to be married, was one of the principal sources of expense complained of by the 'Idar Patáwats* and other Rajputs in that part of the country, who look upon it as derogatory to send their daughters to be married as is universally done in this province; and I pointed this out to

* [The landholders of 'Idar in the Mahikánṭhá province, north of the Mahí river in the continental Gujarát.]"

the Jám and the Kachh Agents, and urged the necessity of making some arrangement, the benefit of which would not be confined to the principal chiefs, but extend to all the inferior classes of Rajputs subject to them, whether belonging to the Jáḍeja or any of the other tribes.

"After sundry consultations the Jám came one morning with the Kachh Agents, and told me that they were fully satisfied that the only measure they could adopt likely to be generally beneficial was to introduce the custom of giving their daughters in marriage in the most respectable families from which they now received their wives. But if they confined themselves in disposing of their daughters to this part of the country, it would be necessary that the other chiefs to whom they would in that case be obliged to give them, should join them in a general arrangement for the disposal of their daughters also, in the families of inferior chiefs to those with whom they had heretofore been in the habit of forming marriage alliances. The Jám therefore proposed that I should speak to the Rájá of Drángadrá* and the Ráná of Porbandar† and others on the subject; and both he and the Kachh Agents stated that if all would agree to enter into this arrangement they were fully prepared to do so, ánd that the opportunity of the Jám's daughter's marriage a few months hence, when influential agents from all the other Rajput talukás would be present at Nawánagar, might be taken for concluding it. I have since spoken to the Rájá of Drangadrá and the Thákur of Murví on the subject, and both appear to be most willing to agree to whatever the Kachh and Nawánagar authorities may require to get this arrangement effected; and I have also ascertained from the Rájá, who is the principal chief to whom both the Ráo and the Jám would in this case have to look for alliances for their daughters, that he would

* [The head of the Jhálá Rajputs.]

† [The head of the Jaitwá Rajputs.]

not object to concede the point, if required, of having to proceed to Bhuj or Nawánagar on all occasions of marriage with the daughters of their chiefs, which would of course be a highly honorable alliance for his family."*

Arrangements such as those here contemplated, if actually made, would be of great importance in the disposal of Jáḍejá females, the difficulty of their marriages according to the views of their tribe having been long, as the reader must have observed, the principal temptation to the unnatural crime of infanticide. The proposal to effect them received the approbation of Government.

Colonel Lang, in noticing the Returns which he forwarded to Government on this occasion, made the cheering intimation, that "the proportion of female children to males in all the tribes [Jáḍejá, Jaitwá and Sumrá] is now so nearly equal, and the progressive increase of the female population so regular, that if the returns can be depended upon in other respects, there would appear to be every ground for believing that the practice of infanticide must have become almost entirely extinct in this province." Never was a triumph of Christian philanthropy of such magnitude as this intimated in greater simplicity of spirit and language.

The actual state of the case, as set forth by the Returns forwarded by Colonel Lang, is thus recorded in the following letter addressed to him by the Government of Lord Falkland, through Mr. Secretary Goldsmid, on the 22nd April 1851.

"It appears from the information furnished by you that the population of Female to Male children, ascer-

* Colonel Lang added :—"I hope I have also persuaded the Jám to allow me to present an elephant on the part of Government to his daughter on the occasion of her approaching marriage [with the Mahárájá of Jaudpur], instead of postponing for a time the collection of the Tribute, as the former would mark much more strongly to the chiefs of Rajputáná, the interest taken by the British Government in the young lady's welfare, and might therefore be more advantageous to her. As directed, however, I have left it entirely optional with the Jám, to receive either of these indulgences he may prefer."

tained to have been born during the year of report is as under.

	Males.	*Females.*	*Excess.*
Jáḍejá	288	278	10 Males.
Sumrá	16	18	2 Females.
Jaitwá	4	5	1 Female.

While a comparison of the present census with those of preceding years exhibits the following results :—

	1844.		1845.		1846.		1847.		1848.		1849.	
	No. of Male population.	*No. of Female population.*	*No. of Male population.*	*No. of Female population.*	*No. of Male population.*	*No. of Female population.*	*No. of Male population.*	*No. of Female population.*	*No. of Male population.*	*No. of Female population.*	*No. of Male population.*	*No. of Female population*
Jáḍejá	6,430	2,175	6,617	2,334	6,600	2,423	6,846	2,779	7,256	3,030	7,353	3,237
Sumrá	372	164	378	271	382	199	411	248	466	308	462	308
Jaitwá	154	57	157	60	169	75	237	116	256	132	251	141

While the proportionate percentage deduced from the above table is :—

Years.	*Jáḍejás.*	*Sumrás.*	*Jaitwás.*	*Years.*	*Jáḍejás.*	*Sumrás.*	*Jaitwás.*
1844	33 4-5	44 1-10	37	1847	40 2-3	60 1-4	44
1845	35 3-10	45 1-5	38 1-5	1848	42 4-7	60 4-10	51 1-6
1846	36 4-5	52 1-10	44 3-8	1849	44	66 3-4	56 1-5

"The foregoing results, I am desired to remark, are most satisfactory, and show the efficacy and suitableness of the measures adopted by Government in 1834, at the recommendation of the Hon'ble Mr. Willoughby then in charge of the Káṭhiáwáḍ Agency, for the suppression of the crime of Infanticide; and appear to justify the observation at the close of your 6th paragraph, that if the returns can be depended on, (and there seems to be no reason to doubt their general accuracy) there are grounds for the gratifying belief that the practice of Infanticide must have become almost entirely extinct in Káṭhiáwáḍ.

"Well and ably have you, in the opinion of Government, continued and carried out by means of conciliation and persuasion the good and humane work in which Mr. Willoughby so indefatigably toiled for the extirpation of the crime of Infanticide from Káṭhiáwáḍ; and the vigorous measures which that gentleman originated for effecting that object have by the judicious proceedings of yourself and of those who succeeded him in the province been brought to a most successful and gratifying termination."

At the time that the Report now commented upon by Government was received in Bombay, Mr. Willoughby, after a lengthened and distinguished service in India, was on the eve of his departure for Europe. It was a matter of high gratification for him, and thanksgiving to God, to observe the success which had attended the measures for the suppression of the dreadful crime of female infanticide which he had been instrumental either in arranging or devising. That success, he justly remarked in his minute on the occasion, "had been far greater and much more rapid than the most sanguine [acquainted with the real difficulties of the case] could have anticipated." He justly attached great importance in securing the desired issue to the vigorous manner in which the cases of proved infanticide had been treated by him before he left the province of Káṭhiáwáḍ. "I recollect," he added, "that by some, whose opinions I valued, I was thought to have invaded too strictly the sanctity of Rajput domestic privacy,* and that the measures I had recourse to were too harsh and likely to outrage the feelings of the whole Rajput community. But I argued that those philanthropic men Governor Duncan and Colonel Walker never intended that the engagements which they induced the Jáḍejás to enter into should be waste paper; and although I was aware that I was touching on delicate ground, I felt assured that I should find a powerful ally in those feelings of parental affection, which

* [So it was denominated, while, as all our readers must have seen, it was a privacy which had not a particle of sanctity connected with it.]

exist in the human breast in every stage and degree of civilization. The result has certainly proved that I was not mistaken. The few examples made in the first instance sufficed, and on Major Lang the more grateful task has devolved of completing the good work, by measures of conciliation and persuasion; and I need not add how highly I approve of the manner in which this most able, humane, and intelligent officer has performed his part." We have seen in the letter already quoted the estimate formed by Lord Falkland and his other colleague, Mr. Blane, of the labours of Mr. Willoughby, and of Colonel Lang and his other successors, in this great service of philanthropy. The sympathy of the Bombay community was entirely in accordance with their judgement of Mr. Willoughby's merits in the case, though,—as it often happens with regard to the laudable exertions of the officials of the Indian Government,—it was but partially informed of the value, amount, and result of his endeavours. A public testimonial to Mr. Willoughby, recognizing not merely what he had done in the case of infanticide, but his general countenance and support of the cause of philanthropy and enlightenment in India, was determined on; and many unsolicited subscriptions to that memorial were immediately forthcoming from Europeans and natives, both at the seat of the presidency and its outstations and the native states which had benefited by his wise and merciful arrangements.* Her Majesty's Government, too, may be supposed to have marked its sense of obligation to Mr. Willoughby, by nominating him, without his appearing as a can-

* At a meeting of Mr. Willoughby's friends held on the 21st April, 1851, the following, amongst other resolutions, were passed.

1. "That the friends of Mr. Willoughby, on the occasion of his departure from India, after an extended and uninterrupted employment of thirty-two years in the most important departments of the Civil Service, are desirous of expressing the regard and esteem which they entertain for him in his personal character; the high opinion which they have formed of him, as a most able and devoted servant of the Government; and their gratitude for his philanthropic labours in the abolition of Infanticide in the province of Kâṭhiâwâḍ, and the public

didate for the office, one of the Directors of the East India Company under the new act which has come into operation in 1854. It is the ordinance of God, however, that independently of the acknowledgements of man, genuine benevolence should never fail to receive its own reward.

The Reports on Infanticide in Káṭhiáwáḍ forwarded by the Bombay Government since Mr. Willoughby's departure to Europe have fully confirmed the belief of the actual suppression of the dreadful crime among the Rajputs of that province. The census of the Jáḍejás for 1850, submitted by Colonel Lang on the 26th December 1851, shows a total of 292 male and 267 female children born and preserved during the year under review; that of the Sumrás, of 24 males and 18 females; and that of the Jaitwás of 10 males, and 4 females.* The Jáḍejá census for 1851 gives a total of 222 males and 216 females born during that year; the Sumrá, of 15 males; and the Jaitwá, of 8 males and 2 females. The Jáḍejá census for 1852, forwarded in the temporary absence to sea of Col. Lang by Captain J. T. Barr, his first assistant in charge, on the 14th April 1854, gives 214 male and 180 female

spirit which he has uniformly evinced in the support of the Philanthropic, Educational, and Literary Institutions of Bombay; and resolve to open a Subscription for the commemoration of his name in this Presidency, in connexion with the cause of Native enlightenment and improvement.

2. "That a Subscription be opened, of which a portion shall be appropriated to the establishment of a Fund for the improvement of Vernacular Literature, and a portion for the Education of Native Females. The Fund to bear the name of Mr. Willoughby: Subscribers being at liberty to appropriate their contributions to either or both of these objects."

The third resolution had reference to the presentation to Mr. Willoughby of a piece of plate with a suitable inscription.

* The Court of Directors, on noticing the disproportion between the males and females of the Jaitwás here mentioned, remarked that it was "very desirable to ascertain the cause of the difference." The attention of the Ráná of Porbandar and the Jám of Nawánagar was called to the circumstance, but they gave no explanation of the fact, which, though worthy of remark, was probably entirely incidental.

births; that of the Sumrás 4 male and 8 female births; and that of the Jaitwás 3 male and 9 female births. Variations in the proportions of the sexes intimated in these returns can easily be accounted for without the supposition of any case of actual infanticide. No suspicions against any of the Rajput tribes now mentioned were entertained, except in a single instance, in which they were proved to be unfounded. On the 12th of July 1854, however, a female of the Mhawar clan of the Miáná tribe, near Máliá on the gulf of Kachh, was convicted before the Political Agent's Court of Criminal Justice in Káṭhiáwáḍ of Infanticide—of having occasioned the death of her newly-born twin infants by designedly withholding from them the requisite nourishment, and sentenced to a year's imprisonment for the crime, a punishment quite inadequate to the offence, even in the view of certain extenuating circumstances.* The most painful fact brought to light in this case, of which information was first given by an attachment mehtá, was the existence of the practice of infanticide by the wild herdsmen of her clan, hitherto overlooked in attempts to suppress the crime, as proved by the number of males in it being 94, while that of the females was only 24. Anti-infanticide engagements have since been exacted from the Mhawars; and they have been brought under the censorship which has been so successfully applied in the case of the Jáḍejás.

* The Miánás, so denominated from Mián, or Míyán, one of their leaders, are land-pirates from Sindh who settled in this district and on the opposite coast about a hundred and forty years ago. They used to set out on their predatory excursions on foot. The native assessors of Capt. Barr, who presided in the Court of criminal justice on the trial of the woman above referred to, begged for a remission or mitigation of the punishment, on the ground of her being an instrument in the hands of her husband, and her occupation to some extent with an elder daughter lying sick of small pox when the starvation of the infants occurred; but Lord Elphinstone and his colleagues properly declined to comply with their prayer for the condonation of "murder." The woman had intimated her intention to the midwife to destroy her children; so there could be no doubt of her guilt.

The historical incidents in the pursuit of anti-infanticide measures in Káṭhiáwáḍ during the last three years, though few, have been of some importance. The Jám of Nawánagar succeeded in negotiating a marriage for his daughter with the Mahárájá of Jaudpur, though he did not live to see the completion of the nuptials. The young bride on the happy occasion, on the suggestion of Colonel Lang, received from the British Government out of the Infanticide Fund, a present of an elephant and other articles amounting in value to five thousand rupees. Colonel Lang had resolved to endeavour, on the assembly of Rajputs at the festivities, to get them to consent to reduce the ruinous expenditure incurred on such occasions, but he was prevented from accomplishing his wishes. Writing to Government on the 18th December, 1852, he says, "I take this opportunity of acknowledging the receipt of Mr. Secretary Lumsden's letter of the 13th July last, and the copy of the report sent with it of the measures adopted for the prevention of female Infanticide in the Mainpurí District. I had hoped at the marriage of the late Jám's daughter to have got some arrangement made for diminishing the expenses now attending Rajput marriages in this province, by inducing the most influential Grásiás to enter into an agreement to marry their daughters into the same families, or families of the same rank, from which they get their wives, but the unfortunate death of the Jám just before the marriage took place prevented anything being done, and when I lately visited his son and successor I found that although professing, and I believe sincerely, his willingness to enter into any arrangement which may be proposed by His Highness the Ráo of Kachh regarding Rajput marriages for the future, he is unwilling to do anything himself in the matter independent of His Highness the Ráo. Major Jacob kindly came over to Nawánagar for a few days when I was there, and as he made himself acquainted with the feelings both of the Ráo and the Jám on the subject, I think some good might be done by getting a deputation of influential Rajputs from the different tribes in Káṭhiáwáḍ, commissioned by the principal chiefs, sent over to Bhuj to discuss the matter with His Highness the Ráo, and endeavour to get some arrangement effected regarding their future marriages through Major Jacob. I have heard from that officer that His Highness greatly approves of the Mainpurí measures as far as he understands them, and there can of course be no question of the great advantage of any measures which will enable the Rajputs here and in Kachh to reduce the expenditure now incurred at their daughters' marriages, without subjecting themselves to any invidious comparisons or remarks from their fellow Grásiás.* I shall therefore

* [The Mainpurí arrangements here referred to were effected by the influence of Mr. Charles Raikes, the magistrate of that district under the Agra Government, and Mr. W. H. Tyler the officiating commissioner of the Agra Division, in 1848. The Chohán, Ráṭhor, and other Rajputs of Mainpurí, Agra, E'tawá, Farakhábád, among whom female infanticide had prevailed to a great extent, agreed to diminish the expences of marriages and to regulate these expences according to the four following grades.

"1st *grade.* For Rájás or Talukdárs. The dower to be demanded in behalf of a son from the parents or guardians of a marriageable daughter shall not exceed Rs. 500. One third of this sum to be paid at the period of *lagan;* one third at the door of the girl's father when the marriage procession arrives; and the remainder in the shape of pin-money *(kanyádán,)* etc.

"2nd *grade.* For Zámíndárs, Rs. 250. One third, etc. as above.

"3rd *grade.* For others in easy circumstances, Rs. 100. One third, etc. as above.

"4th *grade.* For all other decent people, one rupee."

It was resolved, too, that by these chiefs no *demand* should be made in excess of the sums now specified, while a father might give more if he chose; that "the insolence of Bráhmans, Bháṭs, and Barbers, and others who abuse decent people for not spending large sums at marriage ceremonies," should be represented to the magistrate for redress; and that only a moderate number of persons should be invited to marriages.

While there was scarcely a daughter found in the houses of the Chohán Thákurs in 1842, there were 1,482 girls living, of six years and under, in October 1851.

The direct anti-infanticide measures pursued in the Mainpurí districts were the following:—

"In Chohán and Phátak villages the watchmen are ordered to give ascertain from Major Jacob whether His Highness the Ráo would be willing to receive a deputation of the description I have proposed, and if so and Government approves of the measure, I have no doubt that I could get one sent by the principal chiefs of this province at anytime that would be most convenient to His Highness the Ráo."

This subject of reducing the expenses of Jáḍejá marriages is still under the earnest consideration of the Rájkoṭ agency, though, to use the words of Captain Barr, "owing to the departure of that experienced officer (Colonel Lang) from Káṭhiáwáḍ and Colonel Jacob from Kachh, little progress has yet been made in effecting the object in view."

From the resolution of Lord Elphinstone's Government dated 11th May 1854 on the Infanticide Report of Káṭhiáwáḍ for 1852, we make the following important extract. "The number of male and female children of these three castes ascertained to have been born during the year 1852 was :—

	Males.	*Females.*	*Excess of*	
			Males.	*Females.*
Jáḍejá	214	180	34	...
Sumrá	4	8	...	4
Jaitwá	3	9	...	6

"The total ascertained population of the three Classes in 1852, contrasted with the years 1842 and 1847

information of the birth of a female child forthwith at the police station. A barkandáz goes to the house and sees the child. The Thánádár informs the magistrate, on which an order is passed that after one month the health of the new-born child should be reported. The watchmen are further bound to give information if any illness attack the child, when a superior police officer (either thanádár, moharí, or jamádár, at once goes to the village, sees the child, and sends the report to the magistrate."—Report on Measures adopted in the District of Mynpoory, for the prevention of Female Infanticide. Agra, 1852. Later proceedings in these Districts have been very satisfactory.]

and the annual average of the five years ending in 1846 and 1851 respectively show the following results.

	Males.					*Females.*				
	1842.	*Average of 5 years ending 1846.*	1847.	*Average of 5 years ending 1851.*	1852.	1842.	*Average of 5 years ending 1846.*	1847.	*Average of 5 years ending 1851.*	1852.
Jáḍejá.........	6,129	6,390	6,844	7,338	7,813	4,841	2,147	2,779	3,225	3,686
Sumrá.........	351	349	411	467	498	141	166	248	307	346
Jaitwá.........	153	157	237	245	244	58	59	116	128	139

"The proportion-percentage which the female bore during the years 1842 and 1852 to the male population of these castes was as follows:—

		Jáḍejás.	*Sumrás.*	*Jaitwás.*
In the year	1842	30	40 1-6	34
Average of the 5 years ending	1846	33 2-3	48 1-8	37 9-15
In the year	1847	40 2-3	60 1-4	44
Average of the 5 years ending	1851	43 11-12	65 1-3	58 1-4
In the year	1852	47 1-6	69 2-5	57

"*Resolved* that these results, as shewing a steadily progressive diminution of the disproportion in the aggregate number of the two sexes, and the fact that no grounds exist for supposing that during the year of report any case of Infanticide occurred in the province of Káṭhiáwáḍ are highly gratifying.*

"That the First Assistant Political Agent in charge be so informed, and that with reference to paragraph 7th of his letter, the Acting Political Agent be requested to persevere in endeavouring to secure a reduction in the Jáḍejá marriage expenses."

This resolution was duly communicated to Captain Barr by Mr. H. L. Anderson, Secretary to Government in the political department.

With such competent and experienced political functionaries as hold office in Káṭhiáwáḍ and Kachh, and

* [It must be remembered that the *wives* of the Jáḍejás, belonging as they do to other Rajput tribes, are not included in the census; and that their absence aggravates the apparent disproportion of males and females.]

are expected soon to resume their duties in these provinces, and such vigilant superintendence as they will enjoy under Lord Elphinstone, who so ably directed in the first instance the successful measures for the suppression of the *Maryá* and other human sacrifices among the Khonds of the mountains of Orisá,* and his colleagues, the efforts of one of whom in the cause of anti-infanticide in Kachh as we shall immediately see were highly commendable and important, we cannot doubt that, with the blessing of God, the cause of the preservation of Rajput infants is safe in their hands.

* An interesting "History of the Rise and Progress of the Operations for the Suppression of Human Sacrifice and Female Infanticide in the Hill Tracts of Orissa" has just been published in the Selections from the Records of the Government of India (Home Department) No. V. This fasciculus contains the more important passages of Lord Elphinstone's able minutes on the best means of abolishing these horrid customs. The grand total of *Mariás* saved from sacrifice up to the 13th April 1853 was 1,260, and of *Poshiás,* 813. The existence of the rite of human sacrifice among the Khonds was first brought to light by Mr. Russell of the Madras Civil Service, in a report dated the 12th August 1836.

CHAPTER XV.

REPORT ON INFANTICIDE IN KACHH BY MR. LUMSDEN — HIS REMARKS ON THE STATISTICS OF THE POPULATION OF THE JADEJAS AND OF THE DIFFICULTIES OF THE MARRIAGE OF THEIR DAUGHTERS— REPORTS OF COLONEL ROBERTS AND THE REVIEW MADE OF THEM BY GOVERNMENT—REPORT OF MR. OGILVIE — REPORTS OF CAPTAIN RAIKES — REMARKS BY MAJOR JACOB ON CERTAIN PROPOSALS — LATEST SUMMARY OF ANTI-INFANTICIDE PROCEEDINGS IN KACHH BY THE BOMBAY GOVERNMENT.

The report on Infanticide in Kachh for the year 1842 was presented to the Bombay Government, on the 11th August 1843, by Mr. J. G. Lumsden, of the Civil Service, appointed political agent in that province in succession to Mr. Malet removed to Káṭhiáwáḍ. It is a document of great ability and importance, its author having become well acquainted with the history and economical position of the Jáḍejás during a service of several years in which, as special commissioner at Adhoí in Wágar, he laboured with singular application and success to unravel the mysteries of the complicated claims of the Bhuj and Murví families for the sovereignty of that district and the ownership of some of its bandars, or ports. The greater portion of it we transfer to our pages.

Mr. Lumsden handles the Jáḍejá *statistics*, as bearing on the progress of the cause of anti-infanticide, in a masterly manner.

After noticing the returns forwarded by Colonel Melvill,—according to which the proportion of males to females among the Jáḍejás had fallen from 146 to 1 to 105 to 1,*—he thus proceeds :—"The returns for the present year are for 104 villages and show a population of pure Jáḍejá blood of 6,909, which is not quite an excess of 200 individuals over the last, and therefore they afford the means of a pretty accurate comparison. It is gratifying to observe that in these returns the general average has fallen from 105 to 88 to 1.

"The proportion of males and females living under 1 year, is equally high with that of last year, or 1 to 1·2 which it is to be observed is very little in excess of the natural proportion of male to female births in many other countries, while in the column from above 1 year to 5 years the proportion of females has actually risen from 1 to 5·4 to 1 to 2·5 males. There is also a slight diminution in the proportion of deaths under 1 year, a column to which suspicion of unfair practises is most likely to attach, though in the present year none such have come to light nor has a single case of infanticide been detected.

"To pursue this interesting investigation, and to establish the proof of a progressive improvement, I have constructed a table based on the calculations made by Colonel Melvill and forwarded by him with his report on infanticide, No. 118, dated 8th December 1840." "Two facts [connected with it] alone require to be noticed. The first, that the successive returns during 3 years for periods of 25 years ago seem to establish that our remonstrances and exertions at that early period of our connection with Kachh were not altogether unattended with success. The other fact will require comment hereafter. It is the only subject of regret connected with the present report. The disproportion between

* Mr. Lumsden, *en passant*, corrects an error of Colonel Melvill's classification of certain tribes. The Ajáṇís mentioned by the Colonel as a separate tribe are merely a branch of the Khengáráṇí.

Jáḍejá females disposed of either by betrothal or marriage and those unprovided for, which was in 1840 only 1 to 1·437, of the latter and in 1841 only 1 to 1·127, has in the present year increased to 1 to 2·01, though in all three cases the female children under 1 year have been excluded from the calculation.

"I have stated that the census of the Jáḍejá population for the year 1841 was taken from 103 villages, and that another village which had been omitted by mistake has been included in the returns for the past year.. The parties who took the census in 1841 were two Muhammadan officers of the darbár. The returns, now under consideration, were drawn up by two Hindu mehtás, Madhavají mehtá and Desái Karamchand; and we have therefore a favorable opportunity of judging of their correctness by comparison. In 1841, there were born 177 daughters, while of girls above 1 year to 5, there were living 127. This gives an aggregate of 304 female children who should be accounted for in the columns for 1842 headed from above 1 year to 5, and upwards. In 1842, we find under the former column 2·75, and adding 10 (the number of deaths during the past year of that age) we have 285, leaving a balance of 19 girls unaccounted for, who may be supposed to have in the interval exceeded the age of 5, or their ages to have been wrongly reported. In 1841, there were living from above 5 to 15 years, 119 Jáḍejá girls. In 1842, we find by the column from above 5 to 15 years, that there were living no less than 147 girls to which should be added 3 who died during the past year. If we here suppose the 19 missing in the former column to have passed into this, we have still an excess of 12 girls above the number to be accounted for. But this excess might be occasioned either by a mistake among a class of people as careless as the Jaḍejás in reporting to successive and different mehtás the age of their daughters or by the additional village in the present table, or it might be due to omissions in the former census. If, then, we pursue the inquiry we find that in 1841, there were living of the third class, or girls from 15 to 25 years of age, 130. In 1842, we find in the corresponding columns 136. Here again we have an excess of 9 girls above the former census. Since we have also in this instance to add 3, who died during the preceding year, of Jáḍejá females who had passed their 25th year, there were registered in 1841 only 26 and in 1842 we have 29. None died of this class in the course of the year. The aggregate excess of the three last columns in the census for 1842, is therefore 12+9+3, or 24, to which, if we add the number of births during the past year 114, and deduct the aggregate of the deaths above 1 year or 10 + 3 + 3= 16, we have a total of 122, which if added to the number of the living in the former year, should exactly correspond with the number returned *as alive* in the present; and this is found to be the case, since 579 + 122 are 701.

"The agreement may also be shewn in a general way. There were alive in 1841, when the census was taken, 579 women; from which, if we deduct the deaths during the past year above 1 year or 16, we have 563 to be accounted for. Add 114, the number living under 1 year, and we have 677, which deducted from 701 leaves the same excess of 24. In seeking to account for this excess, we find that 9 females are living in the village of Waḍawá not included in the last year's returns, and that 15 girls of different ages must consequently have been omitted in the census for 1841.

"The exact agreement of the two tables is a subject of agreeable surprise, when it is borne in mind that His Highness employs but two mehtás in taking the census from which the tables have been constructed, and that as a greater guard against collusion the same mehtás did not prosecute these inquiries in the years 1841 and 42."

Of the *marriage arrangements* of the Jáḍejás of Kachh, on which so much must depend in connexion with the preservation of their female offspring, Mr. Lumsden thus ably treats.

"I have now to revert to the great and increased disproportion which the Jáḍejá females, disposed of by marriage and betrothal, bear to those who are unprovided for in the census of the past year. This is a subject of serious concern, since it is evident that if the Jáḍejás are unable to procure matches for their daughters, this alone will create a strong tendency to revive the inhuman practice which we are struggling to abolish.

"Female celibacy is viewed as a reproach and disgrace by all of Hindu extraction, and in the East (as Sir A. Burnes observes in a statistical account of Wagár and with reference to the preservation of Jáḍejá females) is but too frequently synonimous with prostitution. As the excellence of the present preventive system must tend evidently to aggravate this evil each succeeding year, it becomes a matter of the deepest moment to consider in time how it may be counteracted and to endeavour to devise a remedy.

"I confess my inability to suggest one at the present time; and it will be as well to recapitulate the difficulties with which the subject is surrounded in this country. The geographical peculiarities of Kachh separate its inhabitants in a great degree from intercourse with the surrounding countries and from any admixture of foreigners with its people. The greater portion of the Rajput population is of the Jáḍejá tribe. But no Hindu can marry a descendant of his own *gotra* or male stem. A Jáḍejá cannot therefore marry a Jáḍejí and the few remaining Rajput houses in Kachh are not sufficient to supply husbands for a tenth part of the Jáḍejá girls who will be marriageable in a few years. Their parents must consequently seek for matches beyond the province. 'It is not to be expected,' as Colonel Melvill justly remarks, "that the inhabitants of distant countries who can find wives much nearer home, should make long journies and incur heavy expences merely for the honor of a Jáḍejá alliance."

"There is a large class of the poorer Jáḍejás who gain their subsistence as cultivators of the soil. The subdivision of property, improvident habits, and the increasing population which is caused by a long period of tranquillity, are adding daily to their numbers. Is it to be supposed that men so situated can depute a person to seek beyond the province for an alliance for their daughters, or that they can generally relinquish their sole means of subsistence, and migrate with their families for a similar purpose. What then must be the result? It may be startling, but as it appears inevitable, it would be worse than folly to remain blind to the fact. If a remedy be not devised, and if aid be not in some shape afforded to this helpless class in the disposal of their daughters, we must expect to behold the introduction among them of an utter profligacy of manners, promiscuous intercourse and concubinage.

"There is indeed another refuge from such scandal and dishonor. It is to revert to the horrible practice from the opprobrium of which we seem at length to have rescued this country. With the intention of ultimately relieving the threatened evil, His Highness has of late years adopted a measure which has an immediate tendency to increase it. He is ambitious that his tribe should ally itself in marriage with the numerous and high caste Rajput families of Jaudpur and Márwáḍ. To this end he has broken off the custom of intermarrying with Muhammadans, which was formerly very prevalent among the Jáḍejás, stimulated, as he asserts, by the consideration that there are comparatively few great Muhammadan families, and therefore few advantages to be expected from their alliance. But he has not as yet prevailed upon the Jáḍejás to reform another custom to which in the eyes of a strict Hindu is a violation of the most important obligation in his creed and which constitutes its principal feature. From the

Ráo downwards, the Jáḍejás have employed from time immemorial Muhammadan cooks, and thus disqualify themselves for forming the connections about which he is so solicitous. It is His Highness's intention, I believe, to bring about an innovation. But though such an act would secure the applause of all Hindus he has not had the boldness to attempt it. The Jáḍejá chiefs are extremely jealous of their ancient usages, and many of them acknowledge in a measure the efficacy of the Muhammadan creed. Thus the whole of the Sáhebáni Jáḍejás are actually *muríds* (or nominal disciples) of the *pír* (saint) of Loháriá in Sindh. At present, therefore, this measure of the Ráo, like all half-measures, is a failure. While it deprives his tribe of a facility for the disposal of their daughters which they formerly possessed, it has not obtained for them the wider opening to which he aspires.

"It will not, I hope, be supposed that these remarks convey an approval of His Highness's intended reform, which I believe to have its origin more in the wounded vanity of the Hindu than in the far-seeing policy of the sovereign. I look upon it solely in its relation to the subject under discussion; its probable effect in providing fit and sufficient matches for the Jáḍejá girls, and in preserving the respectability of that aristocracy. Both of these ends are evidently in a measure *duties*. In this light to consider and even to respect prejudices, however childish, as they affect our efforts to uproot an odious custom (without merely exchanging one evil for another) cannot be viewed as contemptible. Setting Kachh aside, examples are not wanting, unfortunately, in any age or country to convince us that the impulse of a false creed, or that mere prescription originating in the most miserable vanity, are either of them sufficient to make monstrous acts assume the garb of duties and the most senseless practices to be regarded as sacred obligations.

"Since, then, the success of the Ráo's matrimonial

negociations in Márwáḍ seem to depend upon the light in which the Jáḍejás are regarded in those countries as pure Hindus, I would rather urge upon His Highness the completion of his scheme."

"The following palliatives for the evil of celibacy have been proposed on former occasions. A general marriage fund among the Jáḍejás was recommended by Colonel Melvill, who hoped to have interested Government in supporting it. This measure, which would have been highly politic and advantageous to the Jáḍejás, was lost by the passive opposition of that body. It was probably regarded as a precedent for taxation, of which they have been ever jealous. The fine fund, which was to have added to the resources of the former one, has up to this hour provided only 1,525 korís.

"An additional reason which might be supposed to act as a check upon marriage, by deterring the Rajputs of the neighbouring countries from contracting alliances with Kachh, was the amount of the customary expenses always heavy among Rajputs, but nowhere more so than among the Jáḍejás, and falling principally upon the father of the bridegroom. The abolition of several of the most vexatious was contemplated by Colonel Melvill, to whose influence I attribute the fact that their amount, of late years, has been much diminished. Still these fees remain, which may be justly characterized as the tribute of an ostentatious vanity on the one side, and as greedy and bare-faced plunder on the other. In appendix C, I have detailed them for the information of the Honourable the Governor in Council and my efforts will not be wanting to induce the Bháíyad either to suppress them entirely or to limit their amount for the benefit of the poorer classes.*

* *Extra Marriage expenses among the Jáḍejás of Kachh common to all Rajputs but peculiarly heavy in Kachh.* 1. *Pálu.* A present to the father of the girl by the father of the bridegroom according to the rank of the party, generally from 1,000 to 10,000 korís. His Highness the Ráo when he married a daughter of Drángadrá paid to the chief of

"Such is the state of matters at the present time. While dwelling upon the threatened danger, I may add that some prospect of amelioration presents itself from our recent conquest of Sindh and the increased intercourse which it is likely to lead to with this country. The whole of the Nagar-Párkar, the Thar, and the extensive and desert tracts towards Amírkoṭ and Jaudpur, are inhabited by the numerous tribe of Soḍhás, a race who abhor infanticide and from time immemorial have been allied with the Jaḍejás, whom they hold in high esteem.* Sir A. Burnes, in a paper on Párkar observes, as far back as 1826, that 'they had begun to look to Kachh in the hopes of finding Jáḍejá wives for their sons.' This good disposition might be fostered

that state her father 6,000 Rupees, I am informed, under this head. 2. *Súlá-Katári ki Lagat.* A sword to the father of the girl by ditto, of more or less value according to circumstances. 3. *Turan Ghoḍá.* A horse to ditto, or an equivalent in money. 4. *Virmuth.* A fee paid by the father of the bridegroom to the Chárans called Wágsundí, strictly as many korís as the one in attendance can lift with his hand from a full handkerchief or cloth. 5. *Gáum Jámpá ki Lagat.* A present given by the father of the bridegroom to the village officers, less or more as he can afford. 6. *Parwá.* This is levied from the father of the bridegroom by the Chárans, Brahmans, Bháts, Wadís or Wúms, Langá, Bhánḍ, Brahmbhâṭ and Rájdhan castes. This is the most serious tax of all. It has no limits but the supposed generosity, or ability, of the party from whom it is literally exacted. Some of the chiefs of each of these castes insist on receiving a horse, others a sum of money, cloths, or jewels. The rest fix a minimum to be paid to each individual of the castes there present.

The expences of the father of the girl are limited to the following. He has to feed the Bharát or the parties who form the marriage revenue a few days previous to, during, and after the ceremony, also all the Parwá tribes, who attend, sometimes exceeding several thousands. To the Bharát he makes a present of clothes. For his daughter he provides jewels and clothing, as he may be able to afford, and a complete outfit of furniture and essentials for house keeping.

* [The Soḍhás certainly do not themselves practise infanticide, finding it a profitable trade to sell their daughters to the Jáḍejás. It is to be feared, however, that as they make no efforts to get their grandchildren by their daughters preserved, they have little more abhorrence of the crime in its general aspects than the Jáḍejás themselves.]

and all available means employed to induce them to resort to Kachh. The Ráo's mother being herself a Soḍhí of the Thar, is a favorable circumstance. Here is a nearer and more natural outlet for the disposal of the marriageable girls than is provided in the Ráo's projected union with Jaudpur and Márwáḍ, the advantage of which may turn out, after all, to be more speculative than real."

Mr. Lumsden, in conclusion, notices the tribes "who, under the general term of *dhang* and consisting both of Jáḍejás and Muhammadans, have been guilty heretofore of systematic infanticide." "These Jáḍejás," he states, "though as the term implies, they have degenerated, yet form a great portion of the Jáḍejá population and are supposed to amount to six thousand souls; the Muhammadans to two thousand. Influenced by a genuine zeal to extinguish this national reproach, His Highneess the Ráo on the 7th of January 1841, published a notification forbidding the practice on the same penalties which are prescribed for the Jáḍejá Bháíyád. But no such stringent investigations are applied to these tribes as are used with the pure Jáḍejás. Without such we have sufficient proof in the accompanying tables,* that mere proclamations are comparatively a dead letter. Yet it would be hardly fair to call upon His Highness, without an equivalent, to go to the expense and to entertain the establishment which would be required on an enlargement of the present system. I have placed the case as it is before the Government who may consider the situation of these people as deserving of more particular attention."

The valuable information contained in Mr. Lumsden's report on the decline of infanticide in Kachh was considered by the Bombay Government, composed of Sir George Arthur and his colleagues, as truly gratifying. A copy of it was forwarded to the Court of Direc-

* These tables we omit, as the results which they indicate have been already mentioned by Mr. Lumsden.]

tors; but as Kachh had in 1843 been placed,—inconsiderately we hold,—under the Government of the newly-conquered and unsettled province of Sindh by Lord Ellenborough, it was simply put on the records of Bombay without any specific measure having been adopted respecting it.

The reports on Infanticide in Kachh presented to the Government of Sindh for the years from 1843 to 1846 were furnished by Lieutenant-Colonel H. G. Roberts, the successor of Mr. Lumsden in the political agency of that province. They bear distinct testimony to the zealous endeavours of the Ráo, and of Colonel Roberts himself, for the abolition of the dreadful crime, which, there was reason to fear, was still practised to a very considerable extent. They were declared to be "satisfactory" by Sir Charles Napier; but neither he nor the Government of India appear to have made them the subject of special consideration. A few of the incidents which they notice may be recorded.

In 1843, of 613 males between two and five years of age, 32 died; while of 318 females of the same age no fewer than 42 died, evidently showing that neglect or violence was the cause of the greatly increased rate of mortality in the latter instance. The number of marriages of Jáḍejá daughters continued to be very limited. Suspicions against various Jáḍejá villages were formed and expressed by the mehtá who analysed the returns furnished by the censors, and who proposed that a nurse and a peon should be added to the censor establishment. Colonel Roberts procured additional pay for this mehtá, who had been but poorly requited for his services, and got him an assistant Gujarátí writer. He thought that a more signal punishment than either fines or imprisonments should be inflicted on offenders; and he proposed that "a proclamation should be issued awarding death, or at least transportation for life with confiscation of property to all found guilty of this most atrocious crime." This recommendation escaped notice both on the banks of the Indus and the Ganges; but it attracted attention on the banks of the Thames. The Court of Directors, in a dispatch dated 4th June 1845, declined to sanction it, observing that what was wanted was "greater certainty of detection rather than more rigorous punishment of those who are detected." On the 25th October 1845, Colonel Roberts mentioned that only eleven marriages of Jáḍejá females had taken place. "The Government annual grant," he added, "and that of His Highness the Ráo, of Rs. 4,000 each, towards the marriage of the daughters of the poorer Jáḍejás, has not been called into operation during the year, the fund formerly accumulated on account of the suspicion of infanticide [the Fine Fund] and amounting to korís 4,175 having been sufficient; and of these 3,200 korís were paid to poorer Jáḍejás on the occasion of their daughters' marriages." Three cases of infanticide in 1845-6, were not only proved but admitted; while no fewer than eighteen others seemed to have occurred. The Ráo strenuously protested with reference to this matter with some of the Jáḍejás summoned to the Darbár and the Agency, when new engagements were exacted from them.* Colonel Roberts expressed his

* Jáḍejá Khengarjí of Sumarí Rohá writes thus. [After noticing his former agreements which were all read.] "Regarding the 2nd article of the agreement of 1839-40, I was questioned, when it appeared that it was not altogether fulfilled, when as I could not make any excuse, I requested pardon and petitioned that I would take certain measures to see that the following arrangements were duly carried out viz. 1. A skilful midwife, such as shall be approved of by the Darbár writers, I will always entertain as a servant, and she will every two months travel through all the villages belonging to my clan and come and inform me of the number of women in labour [pregnancy?] and the number of months, that she and I may be able to give an account to the Darbár writer when he comes round. 2. Whenever a premature birth shall occur, this midwife will inform me of it, so that I may keep a correct account of it, and of those who are in child-labour. 3. Thus as is written above in the 1st article the account of women in child-labour being kept, after nine months, I will cause inquiry to be made and take great care about it, and not neglect it. If after this any neglect should

opinion, in January 1847, that in order to prevent the subdivision of property, in the case of many male births, or infanticide in case of female, the use of abortive medicine was very much resorted to," thus opening up another black page of the record of Rajput crime.

The Report on Infanticide in Kachh for the year 1846-7 was presented by Col. Roberts, on the 8th January 1848, to the Bombay Government, to which the political superintendence of that country had been again judiciously restored by the Supreme Government of India. It occupied only a single leaf; but the Returns which it furnished were carefully gone over at Bombay, where it was thus acknowledged by Mr. Secretary Malet, on the 18th April of the year in which it was received.

" It would appear from the information now supplied,

be apparent on my part, the two Governments may take any measures that will satisfy them. 4. I will keep a strict register of all male and female births, with such witnesses and explanations of all deaths caused by disease etc. as will be satisfactory to the Darbár Agents. 5. From the form of the births and deaths of children which the Darbár sends annually for, the two Sirkárs observe that more deaths from disease occur amongst the female than the male children, and that sufficient care and protection is not afforded to the former, and on this account desire greater cautions; therefore I will take every possible means as above and by every other way endeavour, so that it may be certain the female infants will be carefully nourished amongst the brethren of my tribe, so that it will be apparent to the two Governments. 6. Should any of the wives of my brethren go abroad or into any other country or to the homes of their fathers, and there have female infants, and put them to death, this will not be on my head; I only answer for what may take place in my country. Thus having in view as written in the above articles together with the former engagements, I will be answerable that great care is taken, so that should any difference exist and the arrangement not be sufficient then the two Governments are masters and shall make what arrangements they choose, and such shall be binding on me.

The above in the name of my forefathers I agree to.—JA'DEJA' KHENGA'RJI' of Sumarí Rohá.

Dated 7th May 1846.

A similar agreement was entered into separately by nine of the other principal Jádejás.

compared with that furnished by Mr. Lumsden in his report for the year 1842, that a considerable increase has taken place in the Jáḍejá population since that period as shown in the following table :—

Years.	*Jáḍejá Males.*						*Jáḍejá Females.*						Proportions of Females to Males.
	Under 1 year.	From 2 to 5 years.	From 6 to 15 years.	From 16 to 25 years.	Above 25 years.	Total.	Under 1 year.	From 2 to 5 years.	From 6 to 15 years.	From 16 to 25 years.	Above 25 years.	Total.	
In 1842.	148	681	1,571	1,264	2,541	6,208	114	275	147	136	20	701	1 to 8 8-10
In 1847.	161	564	1,551	1,387	2,782	6,445	136	447	340	142	65	1,130	1 to 5 1-10
					Increase 237.						Increase 429.		

Results which the Hon'ble the Governor in Council considers to be extremely satisfactory, especially as shewing that the disproportion between the male and female children from five years old and under, is rapidly disappearing; in 1842 the number of male children of these ages having amounted to 829 to 389 females, while in 1847 the number of children of the same ages was 725 males to 583 females.

"It is also satisfactory to find, from Appendix No. 2 to your report, that the proportion of females to males in the Jáḍejá population of Kachh has during the last seven years been steadily on the increase. The number in each year from 1840-41, having been as under :—

In 1840-41........................ 1 Female................. to ... 14 ... 6 Males.
In 1841-42........................ 1 do. .... to ... 10 ... 5 do.
In 1842-43........................ 1 do. .... to ... 8 ... 8 do.
In 1843-44........................ 1 do. .... to ... 7 ... 6 do.
In 1844-45........................ 1 do. .... to ... 6 ...65 do.
In 1845-46........................ 1 do. .... to ... 6 ...00 do.
In 1846-47........................ 1 do. .... to ... 5 ... 7 do.

"His Honor in Council is much concerned to perceive from your report that no less than 15 cases of infanticide are proved to have been committed in Kachh during the year 1846. The parties who have been convicted of these murders, have, you state, been fined according to their means; but, that persons guilty of this revolting crime in Kachh are not at present visited with adequate punishment is plain from your remarks in the abstract census of the Jáḍejá population, wherein it is stated, that in no less than three of the proved cases of infanticide, the parties concerned were not visited with any punishment whatever, having been excused on account 'of poverty,' and in three of the other proved cases a fine of only 25 korís (about rupees 7) was levied, and in another a fine of 40 (about rs. 11) korís was imposed—punishments altogether inadequate and from the imposition of which it is not to be expected that the crime will ever be extinguished.

"You will perceive that the following stipulation is made in the 2nd article of the engagements into which the Jáḍejá chiefs of Kachh entered with His Highness the Ráo in the year 1840: 'Whenever a newly born child is destroyed among the Bháíyád the chief shall give information to the Darbár within the space of fifteen days, in order that the murderer may be visited with punishment by fine *or otherwise*. If the chief conceals any instance of the crime, or neglects to take such measures as are sure to prevent its concealment from himself, and information of its having been committed reaches the Darbár, from another quarter, then the chief himself shall submit to be heavily fined. It therefore behoves the chief to take good precautions; and whenever it is ascertained that the wife of a Jáḍejá has been pregnant and the child is stated to have been born prematurely, or to have died naturally, in such case, four respectable men shall take cognizance of the fact and their verdict shall be reported to the Darbár within fifteen days.' It follows, therefore, that in cases where the guilty parties are too poor to pay a fine, it could not have been intended, that they should altogether escape punishment. On the contrary the engagement above quoted, unquestionably contemplated the award of imprisonment in such cases, at first for a moderate period, and afterwards increased with reference to the magnitude of the offence as the resolution of Government to suppress the crime became more fully and certainly known. Unless His Highness the Ráo strictly enforces the provisions of the above article, and visits each proved case of Infanticide with a suitable punishment 'by fine or otherwise,' it is evident that the endeavours of the British Government for the suppression of this crime in Kachh will in a great measure be rendered abortive. You will accordingly be pleased to bring this subject to the notice of the Ráo, and strongly urge upon His Highness the propriety and necessity of his hereafter dealing with greater rigour with those who thus set at nought, not only His Highness's injunction but their own solemn engagements to abstain from, and to do all in their power for suppressing the commission of infanticide.

"His Honor in Council deems it extraordinary after such engagements had been entered into, that such leniency, as is mentioned in your report, should have been pursued by His Highness, towards parties who had been proved guilty of this dreadful crime; and I am desired to request that you will be pleased to explain what remonstrances were offered by you against this course.

"You will be pleased to report to Government the result of His Highness's investigation into the four cases of Infanticide which have happened during the year 1847.

"With reference to the 4th paragraph of your letter, in which you state 'there are also some irregularities with regard to the usual reports, directed to be made to the Darbár, immediately on the death of a child having been omitted,' I am desired to request that you will urge His Highness the Ráo to adopt effectual measures to prevent a repetition of these irregularities.

"From the statement of the Receipts and Disbursements of the Infanticide Fund, annexed to your report, it appears that the amount granted in aid of marriages is in every case the same, namely 800 korís. His Honor in Council considers the system pursued in Káṭhiáwáḍ to be preferable. In that province a careful enquiry is instituted into the circumstances of each applicant for aid; the amount granted is fixed with reference thereto, and seldom exceeds 250 Rupees, often being so low as 100 Rupees. It is, moreover, in the opinion of Government in every respect desirable that the expense of Jáḍejá marriages should be checked as much as possible, an object which would not be promoted when assistance is granted at one uniform rate.

"Your report under acknowledgment being extremely meagre, I am desired to inform you that Government will expect a much fuller report for the year 1847-48, and to furnish you with a copy of the Infanticide report for Káṭhiáwáḍ forwarded by Major Lang on the 30th December 1847, in conformity with which, you will be pleased as far as may be practicable to frame your future reports."

From the explanations given by Colonel Roberts, on the 8th June 1848, in reply to this communication, we give the following extract.

"With regard to the adequate punishment it is one of extreme difficulty. Many are the instances when the parties have positively nothing. They subsist themselves and families on the labour of their hands, and as shepherds in attending and foraging the cattle and sheep belonging to the villages at which they reside. These people are unable to make a money payment as a fine to any amount; and the alternative, imprisonment, His Highness the Ráo would be always ready to inflict, but in the case of the poor classes if the individual had a family they would, being deprived of the subsistence gained by his labour, starve, and in the case of his having no family he would consider it small punishment to be imprisoned when food is abundantly provided, and labour if awarded always light.* His Lordship in Council may rely on the cordial co-operation of His Highness the Ráo in the endeavours to suppress infanticide. His Highness proposed punishments which were considered by the Hon'ble the Court of Directors as far too great. His Highness the Ráo is prepared to inflict any punishments the Hon'ble Board may deem fit; and I have proposed to him for the future to submit the intended awards of punishment in each case for the consideration of Government. The Infanticide report for 1847-48 shall be compiled agreeable to your instructions; but the province is small compared to that of Káṭhiáwáḍ, and I believe a lengthened report, in the absence of any new matter, could only contain repetitions of my former reports and those of my predecessors."

The Government remarked, on the 10th July 1848, in reply to this representation, "that although the explanation therein afforded of the leniency hitherto exercised by His Highness the Ráo of Kachh towards persons convicted of the crime of infanticide is far from satisfactory, the Right Hon'ble the Governor in Council is of opinion that, provided His Highness agrees to the adoption of the course indicated in your 6th paragraph, the object of Government will for the future be ensured."

Some of the subsequent reports from Kachh have been very much of the same character as those now noticed, showing on the one hand a progressive increase of the Jáḍejá female population, and, on the other, the evident

* [The late excellent Archdeacon Jeffreys of Bombay was accustomed to say, that nowadays too much is heard of the "house of correction" and too little of the "rod of correction." Without here discussing the propriety or impropriety of this opinion, we would respectfully suggest to His Highness the Ráo, that it might be well to ascertain, by practical experiment, whether or not, in such cases as those here referred to, the integuments of the backs of the murderous tribes of his country are not more tender than the fibres and tissues of their unfeeling hearts.]

evasion of their engagements, and violation of the first principles of humanity, by many individuals of the Jáḍejá community.

In the report for 1848, Colonel Roberts expresses his belief that a fixed sum, as in Kachh, in aid of the marriages of poor Jáḍejá females is better than one apportioned, as in Kaṭhiáwáḍ, according to the circumstances of individuals. He founds this opinion on the liability to imposition by native authorities. But the solution of the merited preference must always depend on the course of inquiry pursued by the political agent. Colonel Roberts, in the same document, expresses his just regret that the census in Kachh is confined to the Jáḍejás, while the surveillance of the *Dhang*, and other tribes addicted to infanticide,* is comparatively neglected.

At the end of 1848, the number of Jáḍejá males in Kachh was 6,536 and of females only 1,297. At the close of 1849, they had risen to 6,629 males and 1,403 females.

The Report for 1849, a remarkably lucid document, was presented to Government by Mr. Thomas Ogilvy, of the Civil Service, the successor of Colonel Roberts in the Agency. The following items of information which it contained are worthy of notice.

There were 250 male and 211 female births, and 136 male and 95 female deaths, being rather less than 2 per cent of the former, and rather more than 6 per cent of the latter; an increase over the returns of the preceding year, of 52 Jáḍejás with one daughter alive and of 22 with two, of two with three, and of one with four daughters alive; an increase of 33 betrothed, 57 unbetrothed, and 16 married and widowed females. It appeared that of 250 male and 211 female children born in 1849, fifty-

* Of these tribes Colonel Roberts gives a list similar to that furnished by Colonel Melville. See above, p. 312. The population of such of them as are Hindús he estimates at 7,150 souls; and that of those of them who are Muhammadans at 4,500.

three of the former and sixty-five of the latter died, showing an excess of about 9 per cent of female over male deaths. Of 242 males and 251 females born in 1848, none of the former, but 45 of the latter died. The mehtás having been asked why the females of six, seven, and eight years of age were entered as more numerous than those of five, six, and seven in the corresponding statement of 1848, they explained to Mr. Ogilvy that errors had occurred in the classification of the children according to their proper ages last year, owing to the new mode of rendering the returns. The proportions of male and female deaths, from 1842 up to 1849, averaged from under 2 to nearly 4 per cent, and in the case of males; and from 6 to more than 9 per cent annually, in the case of females. The females, however, had doubled in number since the year 1842, and the disproportion between the sexes had diminished one-half.

"On examining," says Mr. Ogilvy, "the returns when first brought to me by the mehtás employed to prepare them, the great excess of female deaths in some of the villages appearing to require investigation, I addressed His Highness on the subject on the 20th October, and have the honor to annex a translation of that communication. The returns having been amended since then, some disagreement will be found with Statement V. now forwarded. His Highness replied in person, when he very fully explained his sentiments. The answer, he observed, was plain, that the measures of Government for the preservation of their daughters, met with no sympathy from the Jáḍejás, and that in numerous instances, neglect now accomplishes what more summary modes before effected. He thus, [after mentioning all the obligations of the Jáḍejás to abandon infanticide in detail] proceeded. 'Averse to the preservation of their daughters, in spite of natural affection, in spite of the precepts of their religion and of the orders of both Governments, the Jáḍejás were not slow to discover ways to evade the engagements by which they were bound.

They could represent that a child, really of full time, had died from premature delivery. They could induce sickness by unwholesome diet, and then report through the mehtás that death had ensued from natural causes. They could escape responsibility by sending their women to be delivered out of the country. The midwives employed belong to the chiefs' villages, and are therefore under their influence. If the British Government are satisfied with the progress of their measure, matters may be allowed to proceed as at present, but to extinguish the crime effectually, other means must be adopted. The time for mere warning has passed, and Government have a right, if so disposed, to revoke the guarantees, the conditions of which have been broken. The Jáḍejas may justly be assessed till the objects of both Governments have been accomplished. This is my private opinion. The chiefs, however, will remonstrate, and I shall publicly join in their remonstrance, for I cannot separate myself from their interests, or act in opposition to their advice, without risking the ruin that the enmity of the Bháíyád brought on my father Bhármaljí.' "

"The statements promised by His Highness," Mr. Ogilvy added, "giving a census of the population of other tribes suspected of practising infanticide, will be furnished in the ensuing year. In deference to the wishes of His Highness the Ráo and his chiefs, Government have fixed the amount of donations to be given to the poorer Jáḍejás, to aid them in marrying their daughters, at korís 800 (rupees 211,) and have abstained from pressing their points of difference, so long as evils are not found to follow. It occurred to me that the British Political Authorities might promote His Highness's object of encouraging intermarriages between the Jáḍejás and the Rajputs of Rajputáná, but the suggestion did not accord with His Highness's views. The Rajputs dislike all interference with their domestic affairs; and it is better, therefore, to leave them to devise a mode themselves of removing the growing difficulty of providing husbands for their daughters. His Highness is negotiating a matrimonial alliance with the family of Udépur, and hopes by that means to establish more frequent intercourse between Kachh and Rajputáná; but it appears to me somewhat doubtful whether the benefits anticipated are likely to repay the heavy expense of such an alliance."

With reference to the suggestions of the Ráo for a further interference on the part of the British Government with the Jáḍejás in the matter of the violation of their engagements, the Government requested Mr. Ogilvy to inform His Highness, that being satisfied of his sincere desire to see infanticide suppressed in his dominions, it would await the result of further experience as to the success of the measures actually in progress for the attainment of this great object.

In February 1850, the author of this work paid his second visit to Bhuj, having had occasion to pass through Kachh on a journey from the banks of the Indus to Bombay, performed along with the Rev. Dr. Duff of Calcutta making the tour of India before visiting Europe. The Ráo gave us both a very kindly welcome at his palace. On that occasion, we had a lengthened conversation with His Highness and some of his attendant Jáḍejás on the subject of Infanticide. He gave us a strong impression of his own anxious desire to see the horrid custom wholly abolished; and his brethren of the bháíyád said, "It is quite unnecessary to speak to us further on the subject. We have determined that infanticide shall be abolished. The matter is accomplished." The Ráo presented us with a table in Gujarátí, or *form*, as he called it,—a translation of which is here subjoined,—showing at one glance, the complete statistics of the whole Jáḍejá population of Kachh in 1849.

Summary of the Jáḍejá Population of Kachh for the year 1849.

A	86	85	84	83	82	81	80	79	78	77	76	75	74	73	72	71	70	69	68	67	66	65	64	63	62	61	60	59	58	57	56	55	54	53	52	51	50	49	48	47	46	45	44
B	1	1	1	4	1	1	1	2	5	6	9	4	4	8	10	11	6	8	42	12	22	13	14	36	19	26	21	18	102	35	46	31	36	45	42	59	38	30	135	47	103	42	41
C *a*	...	...	...	...	...	...	...	...	...	...	...	...	...	...	...	...	...	...	...	...	...	...	...	...	...	...	...	...	1	...	...	...	...	...	...	...	...	...	...	...	...	...	...
C *b*	...	...	...	...	...	...	...	...	...	1	...	...	...	...	...	...	...	...	1	...	...	...	1	...	1	1	...	...	1	...	...	...	1	...	...	...	1	...	...	2	...	...	...
C *c*	...	...	...	...	...	...	...	...	...	...	...	...	...	...	...	...	...	...	...	...	...	...	...	...	...	...	...	...	...	...	...	...	...	...	...	...	...	...	...	...	...	...	...
C *d*	...	...	...	...	...	...	...	...	...	...	...	...	...	...	...	...	...	...	...	...	...	...	...	...	...	...	...	...	...	...	...	...	...	...	...	...	...	...	...	...	...	...	...
D	...	...	...	...	...	...	...	...	...	1	...	...	...	...	...	...	...	...	1	...	...	...	1	...	1	1	...	...	2	...	...	...	1	...	...	...	1	...	...	2	...	...	...
E *e*	...	...	1	...	...	...	...	...	...	...	2	...	...	...	1	...	1	...	1	2	...	...	...	...	2	2	...	1	1	2	...	...	1	3	1	1	...	1	3	2	3	1	4
E *f*	...	...	...	...	...	...	...	...	...	...	...	...	...	...	...	...	...	...	...	...	...	...	...	...	...	...	...	...	...	...	...	...	...	...	...	...	...	...	...	...	...	...	...

A	43	42	41	40	39	38	37	36	35	34	33	32	31	30	29	28	27	26	25	24	23	22	21	20	19	18	17	16	15	14	13	12	11	10	9	8	7	6	5	4	3	2	1
B	85	47	72	34	54	135	63	121	46	78	113	89	125	104	77	162	85	189	104	132	144	124	128	139	125	195	99	214	131	175	170	151	162	168	143	156	165	137	159	160	150	212	197
C *a*	2	...	...	...	...	2	2	1	1	...	2	...	7	6	4	13	4	22	17	14	12	14	3	9	10	9	5	7	3	10	4	1	2	...	1	...	...	...	...	...	...	...	...
C *b*	...	...	...	...	1	1	...	1	...	...	1	...	...	1	...	2	...	...	1	2	2	1	...	...	...	...	1	...	...	...	...	...	...	...	...	...	...	...	...	...	...	...	...
C *c*	...	...	...	...	...	...	...	...	...	...	...	...	...	...	...	...	1	...	...	1	1	1	1	...	...	1	...	...	3	11	6	12	14	13	10	10	7	12	6	3	6	1	...
C *d*	...	...	...	...	...	...	...	...	...	1	...	...	1	...	1	...	...	...	2	...	1	...	...	1	4	2	4	2	3	2	13	10	20	30	48	97	79	93	113	113	101	185	146
D	2	...	...	...	1	3	2	2	1	1	3	...	8	7	5	15	5	22	20	17	16	16	4	10	14	12	10	9	9	23	23	23	36	43	59	103	85	105	119	116	106	186	146
E *e*	...	1	...	1	1	3	...	...	...	...	...	...	1	...	...	1	...	...	1	...	1	...	...	1	1	...	1	...	...	1	1	1	...	...	1	...	...	3	1	1	9	16	53
E *f*	...	...	...	...	...	...	...	...	...	...	...	...	1	...	...	...	...	...	...	...	1	1	...	...	...	...	...	...	1	...	...	...	...	...	1	...	...	...	1	3	3	18	65

A, Ages. B, Males. C, Females. *a*, betrothed; *b*, widows; *c*, married; *d*, unmarried. D, Total. E, Died in 1849:—*e*, Males; *f*, Females.

Totals: Males, 6,629; Females:—betrothed, 188; widows, 24; married, 119; unmarried, 1,072; total, 1,403. Died in 1849:—Males, 136; Females, 95.

We inspected this document with mingled emotions of pleasure and pain—of pleasure, because of the progress actually made in the preservation of 1,403 females actually alive at that time as the fruits of the merciful interference of the British Government and the Ráo with the bloody customs of the Jáḍejás; and of pain, at the manifest disproportion of these females to the 6,629 males alive at the same time, giving too palpable evidence of the perpetration of thousands of murders, even since the voice of British philanthropy was heard protesting and pleading against the awful crime. We recommended His Highness to institute such a general system of education throughout his kingdom, as would be inimical to vice of every character; but he expressed his fears that it would not be valued by his people, who, in their present social state, he held, have no peculiar need of its advantages. We especially pressed him to give a superior education to his two interesting-looking sons, who were before us, the one eleven and the other eight years of age, for their own benefit, the sake of example, and the future good of the province; but he said he was inclined to rest satisfied with the instruction which they were actually receiving, as sufficient for the particular duties which would afterwards devolve upon them. We were by no means prepared for His Highness taking this ground. When we introduced the subject of *Satí* in the Darbár, he expressed a wish to have some private conversation with us on the subject, which accordingly took place; but we shall not violate his confidence by repeating anything which he said to us which might fall under this category. On his Highness mentioning to us that Satí has the sanction of the Hindu Shástras, we admitted the conclusion as far as it recognizes only the later Shástras; but did not admit its accuracy as far as the Védas, the most ancient of the Hindu writings, are concerned.* We added that

* Referring to the genuine portions of the Védas we spoke quite confidently to His Highness on this matter. This we did from

from our point of view, which inquiry would show to be the correct one, the Shástras reveal their own character as inimical to what is good, when they do encourage Satí; and that they can be successfully quoted in bar of almost every social and national improvement which humanity could dictate, or political right and expediency suggest. The frankness and openness of His Highness we could not but admire, even though there was a great difference in our opinions on some of the matters on which we freely conversed. Every British functionary who has had to deal with him has noticed this candour and honesty. At this time, it may be added, His Highness was still seeking to exchange daughters in marriage with the family of the Udépur Rájá in Rajputáná. The expense which he would thus incur was estimated at the enormous sum of nine lakhs of rupees.

On the 29th of July of the year last mentioned, Lord Falkland addressed a kind and considerate personal letter to His Highness, strongly advising him to give a superior education to his sons. It has as yet borne no fruit. But those who fail to learn good cannot fail to learn evil. There is more than a rumour in the native community that one of them, through the influence of

our inspection of large portions of them, and our general estimate of the system of religion on which they are founded. The Bráhmans are accustomed to quote from the sixth Adhyáya of the seventh Ashṭaka of Rig-Ve'da a passage which they hold to be favourable to the burning of widows. It is thus translated by Colebrooke, in his paper on "The Duties of a Faithful Hindu Widow. Asiat. Res. iv. p. 207, 8vo. edit:—"Om. Let these women, not to be widowed, good wives adorned with collyrium, holding clarified butter, consign themselves to the fire. Immortal, not childless nor husbandless, excellent; let them pass into fire, whose original element is water." This passage, in the original Sanskrit, has lately been submitted to a critical examination by professor H. H. Wilson (Journ. Roy. As. Soc., vol. xvi. pp. 201—214), who has clearly shown that it takes for granted the conservation, and not the cremation, of the widow.

The passages in the Shástras posterior to the Ve'da favourable to Satí are numerous. Many of them have been quoted by Colebrooke.

mischievous counsellors, has already unbecomingly conducted himself in his father's palace. Of this fact, it is perhaps not yet too late to make an obvious improvement.

His Highness deserves much credit for having ultimately abolished Satí in his dominions, in deference to the repeated entreaties of the British Government, as well, as it is to be hoped, to his own ultimate convictions. Instances of religious suicide occasionally occur in his dominions, as in all the adjoining states; but they are not now countenanced by His Highness. For example, a devotee buried himself alive at Aḍisir in 1849-50; and a Cháran woman, seventy years old, lately came to her end by entombing herself along with the corpse of her husband. In punishment of the connivers at the latter offence, the Ráo, in consultation with Lieut.-Colonel Trevelyan, the acting political agent in Kachh, a gentleman well skilled in Rajput management, sentenced the son of the woman to imprisonment for twelve months in irons, and levied a fine of 150 korís from the inhabitants of the village in which it occurred.

The Kachh Infanticide Reports for 1850 and 1851 were furnished to Government by Lieutenant S. N. Raikes, acting political agent in that province. They bear good testimony to the zeal and discretion of their author. They exhibit proof, too, of continued progress in the suppression of the crime, and, like others which have preceded them, of its continued practice in individual instances, as apparent from the statistics of the population. In that for 1850, bearing the date of 11th April 1850, Mr. Raikes notices the fact that the investigations into the deaths of the Jáḍejá daughters under suspicious circumstances for the last two years had just been completed in a way calculated to show to all classes the warm interest which Government takes in the suppression of the crime and the zeal of His Highness the Ráo in the same good cause. Of the system in force for the suppression of infanticide in Kachh, Mr. Raikes gives this account in the same document. "The Ráo sends three mehtás through different parts of the province once a year, when every village is visited. A fourth mehtá remains in Bhuj to receive the reports of the births and deaths of all Jáḍejás, and grant receipts for the same." The travelling mehtás get their information from chiefs and midwives. They investigate suspicious cases on the spot, and afterwards report them to the Ráo, who, when the returns are prepared, takes them up himself, and finally reports his decision to the agency for the sanction of the British Government."

According to the information of Mr. Raikes, there seemed to be but a small inclination on the part of the Jáḍejás of Kachh to avail themselves of grants from the Infanticide Fund there formed, as presents either to those preserving their female children or those seeking their marriage. The Ráo proposed that the annual grant of Rs. 4,000 by himself, and of the same sum by the British Government, should be diminished by one half; but Mr. Raikes suggested that the censorship should be put on a more respectable footing and paid from it; and the Government recommended the use of the Fund with the same liberality that had been observed in Káṭhiáwáḍ. On the diminishment of the expences of Jáḍejá marriages, Mr. Raikes mentions that the Ráo in December 1850 sent agents to Major Lang's camp in Káṭhiáwáḍ to consult with the Jám on this point. They proposed that when the Rajputs from Káṭhiáwáḍ married daughters from Kachh, expences should be incurred only at the place of celebration, instead of both at the place of the girl's parental residence and that of her marital destination. The Jám, wishing to consult other Rajputs about such an arrangement, proposed to defer the discussion of it till the celebration of the marriage of his own daughter, when a large attendance of nobles was expected. The discussion was resumed at the close of the rains in 1854. The result, however, has not been very satisfactory; and probably little will be effected in this matter till the return of Colonel Lang and Colonel Jacob to India, who have already taken certain steps towards its accomplishment.

The report of Mr. Raikes for 1851 was presented to Government on the 4th May 1852. The returns by which it was accompanied give 6,739 as the number of male and 1,594 as the number of female Jáḍejás. During the year, 274 boys and 235 girls were born, while there had been 65 male and 67 female deaths under one year of age, and 171 male and 91 female deaths above one year of age. Only 14 males and 4 females had left the province. In the course of the year, 26 girls had been betrothed. The males under 10 years of age were 1,516, and the females 1,175. Under ten years of age, however, the death of 150 females had occurred, while only that of 128 males had taken place, a pretty significant index of the comparative want of tenderness in dealing with female life. Cases of suspicious death had been investigated without the guilt of any party having been established. Fines had been inflicted on a few Jáḍejás for failing to report the casualties of their families. At some of the investigations, conducted by the Ráo, Mr. Raikes was present; and he observed the anxiety of the Ráo to do his duty, as well as the difficulty of arriving at the truth when the parties examined were at their homes in the power of the Jáḍejá chiefs.

On the *continued existence* of the crime of infanticide Mr. Raikes thus writes:—"To show succinctly the grounds on which my suspicions rest, it is necessary to allude to a few of the villages in detail. I will take for instances:—*Mothá Bádor*, where there are 390 Jáḍejás, of whom 138 are married. Their issue during last year consists of 14 male and 17 female children; of which number, no males and 7 females died at birth. At *Dhamaḍká*, again, there are 142 Jáḍejás, of whom 57 are married: 4 female births are registered all of whom died at birth; while of eight males born, only three died. At *Bhandrá*, there are 540 Jáḍejás, of whom 184 are married. The number of births registered are 22 males, and 15 females, of which number one male, and six females, died at birth. At *Bándrésar*, there are 423 Jáḍejás, of whom 271 are married. The births registered are 21 males and 20 females, of which number 1 male, and 9 females, died at birth. The above details, together with the astounding fact of no female Jáḍejá having apparently been born at some villages for several years, form the grounds of my suspicions." "I must beg to be allowed to mention the names of a village or two, where female life appears to have been triffled with. For instance, at *Khéḍá*, there are 52 Jáḍejás of whom 29 are married; notwithstanding which no female births have been recorded for the last three years. At *Mhawá*, again, there are 19 Jáḍejás of whom 10 are married; while but one female appears to have escaped the ruthless pride of their sires; for it is utterly impossible to believe that but one daughter would under ordinary circumstances have survived during many years; while twelve sons have been reared. Lastly, at *Sutharí* there are 23 Jáḍejás of whom 8 are married; notwithstanding which, there are only two female Jáḍejás, both of whom are 5 years of age. Such instances, of what I humbly conceive to be unquestionable proof of a reckless disregard for female life, might be multiplied to a considerable extent from the detailed returns now lying before me." How painful are these statements, especially as connected with one of our latest notices of the anti-infanticide cause in Kachh!

Still, perseverance in, and the perfecting of, the measures now in operation towards the triumph, through the divine blessing, of that great philanthropic cause is the duty of our British officials. Mr. Raikes proposed that the censorship should be made more efficient by a more liberal payment of the mehtás connected with it; by securing the devotion of their whole time to its objects; by their being placed more under the control of the British agency than they formerly were; by their visiting each Jáḍejá village twice a year; by their obtaining, what is certainly greatly to be desired, a census of other tribes, for the purpose of comparison; and by getting the agency to share in the responsibility of all investigations, so as to diminish the invidiousness of the Ráo's procedure connected with them in the view of the Jáḍejá population. The propriety or impropriety of taxing the chiefs for defraying the expences of the censorship, Mr. Raikes left to the judgment of Government.

The balance of the Kachh Infanticide Fund in 1851, Mr. Raikes reported to be Rs. 23,402-12-8. Only one Jáḍejá had solicited assistance from it.

The marriage prospects of the Kachh Jáḍejá females, Captain Raikes reported as improving. "A great reduction," he wrote, "has taken place, within the last year and a half, in the expenses attending the celebration of the marriages of the female Jáḍejás, and a corresponding facility is of course experienced by the members of that tribe, in marrying off their daughters. The Jáḍejás of Kachh have within the last few years sought alliances for their daughters amongst the Soḍhá Rajputs of the Desert; and thus, since 1844 (A. D.) forty-seven Jáḍejá females have been married to Soḍhá Rajputs of the Thar and Párkar collectorate. The desert districts being temporarily in my charge, has enabled me to ascertain the number of Rajputs residing there, eligible as husbands for the Jáḍejá's daughters; and I find they amount to about two hundred and fifty. The intercourse between the other Rajputs of the Desert and Kachh has also greatly increased of late years. Since 1844, eighty-five Rajput daughters from Kachh have been married to Rajputs in the Desert, and 206 Rajput daughters from the Desert have been married to Rajputs in Kachh. This intercourse is to be attributed as much possibly to the administration of the Desert districts having been conducted from Kachh for the last seven years,* as to His Highness the Ráo being

* [These districts came under the guidance of the British Government in connexion with the conquest of Sindh.]

nearly connected by marriage with the Soḍha Rajputs of Dípalá, and distantly connected with the Rána's family in Párkar.*

The report of Mr. Raikes was submitted by Government to Lieut.-Colonel LeGrand Jacob, appointed political agent in Kachh, for the expression of his opinion, which was forwarded by him to Government on the 10th January 1853.

Colonel Jacob in this document, after repeating his views as to espionage over Jáḍejá households which we have already noticed,† thus proceeds :—"The Jáḍejá population" "generally contribute nothing towards the maintenance of the state. They are ignorant and unable to appreciate the benevolent intentions of Government with respect to their children. The tables show that human life is more respected than before, although not so much so as could be wished. His Highness the Ráo is sensible of the motives of Government and willing to co-operate in carrying them out. It is scarcely just to him, therefore, to throw on him the cost of remedying the evils done by others, when this may fairly be levied from the offenders themselves. The Jáḍejá chiefs have by their agreements rendered themselves amenable

* Captain Raikes adds :—"It is of importance to foster the intercourse between the Desert and Kachh as much as possible, with the view of gradually overcoming the repugnance that the Jáḍejá chiefs have hitherto had to marrying their daughters to the inhabitants of that district, owing both to the more lawless nature of society there, as also to the nature of the country itself, where the only means of conveyance are beasts of burthen, carts being unknown. This repugnance appears to be already yielding to the improved state of society in the Desert under British rule; and when more completely overcome, and a more extended intercourse is attained between the landed proprietors of the two provinces, I doubt not, the difficulty complained of by the Jáḍejás of being unable to obtain suitable husbands for their daughters will be greatly alleviated. It opens the road, also, for more extended intercourse with the neighbouring districts of Chachrá and Amírkoṭ in Sindh and the south-west districts of Márwáḍ."

† See above, pp. 263-265, 273.

to any punishment which the British and Kachh Governments may determine on in case of their committing infanticide. It would tend to check the crime, if a proclamation were issued that the expense of all preventive measures should for the future fall on those practising it. I agree with Mr. Raikes that better paid functionaries should be employed for the census, and I would extend their inquiries to the population generally; but I would give them no power beyond that of receiving and registering information, the expense of which should be charged to the fund. I see no objection to the Ráo's suggestion for diminishing by one-half, viz., from four to two thousand rupees, the amount now appropriated by each Government for this fund, on the understanding that the present sum might again be had recourse to whenever Government might see cause for it. The fund is rich, having 16,000 rupees invested in the 5 per cent loan, besides a balance of 15,097-5-4 standing to its credit in the general accounts; and applications for aid from it seem becoming more and more rare." "There are difficulties in the way of getting at truth in trials for infanticide as pointed out by Mr. Raikes; but I see no way of obviating them that will not give rise to more formidable difficulties and entanglements. Any way, these trials serve to check the deed, for they entail trouble, expense, and some degree of risk; although they may seldom give grounds for conviction.

"Education, the great remedy, is regarded by the Jáḍejás with supreme indifference, if not contempt. They like to adhere in everything to the ways of their forefathers, and in all matters of innovation, however beneficial or profitable, resemble the deaf adder of Scripture. I have failed to make the smallest impression on any one of them. Irresistible arguments are like light to the blind. Even His Highness, though far above all his bháiyád, is insensible to the benefit that would ensue to his country from any general system of education. He supports the [vernacular] school at Bhuj out of deference to his English advisers, not from any love for it. He tells me that he thinks his people are happier by following their own way than by learning ours. Facility in marrying their daughters is, therefore, the main remedy to be looked to; and in this point of view, I wish it may prove consonant to the views of Government to transfer the management of the Desert to the Ráo, for this would enable him to bring about many more marriages between Soḍha Rajputs of the Thar and the Jáḍejá daughters of Kachh; and now the frontier customs there are abolished, Government would be saved some 30,000 rupees a year, drawn from this treasury by the Deputy Collectorate.

"I reserve further observations on this subject till my forthcoming annual report."

The indisposition of Colonel Jacob, which has led him to leave India on leave to sea, prevented him from furnishing the report which he here expresses his hope of being able to furnish. It was stated to him in reply to his communication on the report of Mr. Raikes, "that it would doubtless be greatly preferable, if as advocated by him the object in view could be obtained 'by other measures rather than by augmenting espionage over Jáḍejá households.' As however the measures he would substitute are not detailed, his Lordship in Council hoped that he would submit to Government something more explicit in his proposed annual report, as the continued existence to a very lamentable extent of this practice in Kachh is but too apparent." The wish was expressed, that His Highness the Ráo should, by a right appropriation of the Infanticide Fund, be freed from all charge beyond the amount of his annual contribution. The opinion was also set forth that, as far as possible, the expense of the detective measures should fall on the guilty parties, as by the imposition upon them of fines when found guilty of the crime of infanticide.

On the 25th of September 1853, Colonel Jacob stated

the reasons for his not being able to furnish a report on Infanticide previously to his leaving Kachh. On this occasion he mentioned that His Highness the Ráo had assembled his bháíyád for discussing various propositions for diminishing the crime, but that ultimately nothing was agreed to by the Jáḍejás. A source of disunion amongst them and the Ráo, it was thought, consisted in his disposition to favour one class of mendicant *Chárans*, the Tumar, while Chandabhái and others wished to patronize the Máru. Major Jacob had advocated greater countenance to the censors, who went about more as wandering fakírs than accredited servants of Government; but the Jáḍejá brethren were opposed to change, and the Ráo was unwilling to draw for their support on the Infanticide Fund. The Ráo, however, ultimately agreed to increase their pay; to furnish each of them with a camel for his baggage and records; and to depute them twice, instead of once, a year on their visits of inquiry. Mr. Raikes was asked to prepare such a report as the record might admit, while Colonel Jacob could reserve his promised report till his return to his duties.

The Report solicited from Captain Raikes was presented by him to Government, as the regular document for 1852, on the 9th December 1853. The returns which it embraces, owing to certain arrangements of Colonel Jacob, are more complete and comprehensive than those wont to be furnished for Kachh. "The details of one of them," Captain Raikes remarks, "show that great progress has been made towards the entire suppression of Infanticide amongst the Jáḍejás in Kachh; the number of births of males and females therein noted are 255 and 254 respectively, while the number of deaths are 219 and 126. Again, the same form shows that the number of married Jádejás of all ages amounts to 2578, to whom were born 509 children during the year under notice.*

* ["The proportion of still-born to those of children of mature birth is nearly 6½ per cent."—Memorandum of Secretariate.]

In every point of view, indeed, this form appears the most gratifying document connected with this interesting subject that I have yet seen; and is rendered more conclusive and gratifying by the obvious inference from the collateral evidence afforded by the accompanying returns generally, that the measures adopted for the abolition of child-murder, have been successful, as far as it is possible in the absence of education to eradicate a long-standing custom from amongst an ignorant, proud, and perverse people."

But the importance of the information (overlooking clerical errors) contained in this, the latest report on Infanticide in Kachh received by the Bombay Government, will be best exhibited by an abstract of the analysis just made of it and its accompanying documents in the Bombay secretariate, and communicated to Colonel Trevelyan, the acting Political Agent at Bhuj, on the 25th November 1854.

One of the appendices to the report giving the numbers and ages of the male and female Jáḍejá population of Kachh in 1852, with the report for 1846-7, supplies details for the following contrast.

Between the ages of	*No. of males.*	*No. of females.*	*Excess of males over females.*	*Proportion* of males to females.*	*Proportion of males to females in the following years.*
1 & 10 years.	1,461	1,122	339	1·30	1840-41—14·60
10 & 20 „	1,535	396	1,139	3·87	1841-42—10·50
20 & 30 „	1,346	141	1,205	9·51	1842-43— 8·85
30 & 40 „	969	46	923	21·06	1843-44— 7·60
40 & 50 „	649	11	638	59·	1444-45— 6·65
50 & 60 „	482	4	478	120·50	1845-46— 6·00
60 & 70 „	245	1	244	245·	1846-47— 5·70
70 & 80 „	75	2	73	37·50	
80 & 90 „	8	...	8	...	Average 17 years...... } 8·41
Age 93 „	1	...	1	...	
Total......	6,771	1,723	5,048	* 3·93	

The following results are deduced from another appendix contrasted with similar returns for the previous years specified.

	Jádejás having one daughter alive.	*Jádejás having two daughters alive.*	*Jádejás having three daughters alive*	*Jádejás having four daughters alive.*	*Jádejás having five daughters alive.*
In the year 1848	727	195	49	7	1
,, 1849	779	217	51	8	1
,, 1850	779	243	62	14	1
,, 1851	789	259	70	18	1
,, 1852	809	309	70	19	2
Average of the 4 years ending 1851	768	228	58	12	1

The same appendix, contrasted with the returns for 1842 and 1847, shows that the male Jádejá population of all ages, which had increased from 6,208 in 1842 to 6,445 in 1847, numbered 6,761 in 1852; and that the female population of all ages which, in 1842, amounted to only 701, had risen to 1,130 in 1847 and in 1852 to 1,723. Another table shews the following satisfactory results :—

	10 *years and under.*		9		8		7		6		5		4		3		2		1	
	1849	1852	1849	1852	1849	1852	1849	1852	1849	1852	1849	1852	1849	1852	1849	1852	1849	1852	1849	1852
Males	168	103	143	135	156	151	105	155	137	139	159	196	160	151	150	156	212	174	197	204
Females	43	85	59	101	107	118	86	99	105	100	119	159	116	104	106	119	186	138	146	186
Excess of male and female children	125	18	84	34	49	33	19	56	32	39	40	37	44	47	44	37	26	36	51	18
Average proportion of the male to the female children	3·90	1·21	2·42	1·33	1·46	1·28	1·22	1·55	1·30	1·39	1·33	1·23	1·37	1·45	1·41	1·31	1·14	1·26	1·35	1·09

A comparative statement of the male and female Jáḍejá population in 1851 and 1852, when contrasted with previous returns, is confirmatory of the conclusion that in Kachh there is now a continued approximation of the sexes.

	MALES.		FEMALES.			
	Under 20 years of age.	*Grand Total of Males of all ages.*	*Married and Widows.*	*Betrothed.*	*Unbetrothed.*	*Grand Total of Females of all ages.*
1847	2,985	6,445	182	69	897	1,130
1848	3,655	6,536	196	86	1,015	1,297
1849	3,148	6,629	212	129	1,072	1,403
1850	3,144	6,675	216	143	1,153	1,512
1851	3,165	6,739	241	169	1,184	1,594
1852	3,083	6,761	260	200	1,263	1,723
Average of the five years ending	3,119	6,605	209	117	1,064	1,387

These statistical results, it must be acknowledged, warrant the conclusion that the cause of anti-infanticide has of late years made more progress in Kachh than could have expected. Indeed, it may be safely said, that, under the pressure of the present arrangements and supervision by the Ráo and the British political authorities, the horrid *custom* of child-murder in that province, as in Káṭhiáwáḍ, has been discontinued. Now is the time to seek for effectual appliances to prevent its return.

Only three cases had occurred in 1852 affording grounds of suspicion of Infanticide; but, on inquiry, these grounds of suspicion were found to be very slight. The cases in which the registration agreements had been infringed by Jáḍejás and Hothís amounted to twenty-nine. Their detection afforded proof of very praiseworthy attention to their duties on the part of the census mehtás.

The balance at the credit of the Infanticide Fund in 1852 amounted to rupees 31,097 5 4, exclusive of the subscription for the year of His Highness the Ráo.

The sanction of Government, on the proposal of the Ráo and Captain Raikes, was given to the extension of grants from this fund in aid of the marriage of the daughters of Grásiás or Jáḍejá landholders not in affluent circumstances, the grants formerly having been restricted to the assistance of those who had no land. The additional charge likely to fall on the fund by this measure seems to justify the resolution of Government, in August 1851, declining to reduce its subscription and that of His Highness till the available amount of the fund reaches Rs. 50,000.

The Acting Political Agent has been called on to state what proportion of the infanticide fund could, in his opinion, be properly devoted to educational purposes in Kachh, according to the suggestion of Mr. Raikes. It is not for us to anticipate the reply; though of the expediency of an appropriation of a portion of this fund to education in that province there can be no doubt.

To the report of Captain Raikes was appended an interesting memorandum from the Ráo on the reduction of the marriage expences of the Jáḍejás, especially by diminishing, by regulation, the gifts and fees to the mendicant classes attending marriages, according to the rank voluntarily assumed for the occasion by these Jáḍejás. But of the *padalás* and *parwás,—hátí* and *dnyátí,*—of these shameless mendicants, the general reader has already had a sufficient notice.* It is well that caution is observed in declining the British guarantee for them, however satisfactory on general grounds their curtailment may be to the friends of humanity and industry. They are too closely connected with Hindu superstition to merit the *sanction* on any scale of a Christian Government.

* See above, pp. 362-363.

CHAPTER XVI.

INFANTICIDE IN CHORWÁḌ AND CHÁRCHAT—INFANTICIDE AMONG THE RÁṬHORS OF THE MAHIKÁṆṬHÁ—INFANTICIDE AMONG THE KULANBÍS OF GUJARÁT.

THE labours of the Bombay Government and its officials for the suppression of infanticide have not been confined to the provinces of Káṭhiáwáḍ and Kachh. They have extended to all the districts of country under their influence or authority in which the fact of the existence of the horrid crime has been ascertained.

We have already alluded to the successful exertions of Lieutenant-Colonel Miles in getting the Jáḍejás of CHORWÁḌ and CHÁRCHAT under the Agency of Pálanpur to engage to abandon the cruel and detestable practice.* The events of the year after that on which the arrangements were completed by him, warranted him on the 16th August, 1828, to report to Government through the Resident at Baroda, that he entertained great hopes that the horrible custom would in a short time be entirely abandoned in those quarters. He certified that at the town of Sántalpur and the villages of Par, Bábará, Cháranká, Sonétí, and Limboná, thirteen Jáḍejá girls had been born and preserved.

The statistics of the Jáḍejás in the districts to which we have now referrèd were not regularly forwarded to Government for several years; but a demand for their regular transmission was made in 1845. The first

* See above, p. 153.

proceedings respecting them do not require any special notice. The returns for 1849, compared with those of the three preceding years sent in by Captain Leckie, were thus analysed by Government.

	Of all ages above 20 years.		*Under 20 years of age.*		*No. of Jádejás having 1 daughter alive.*	*Do. having 2 do.*	*Do. having 3 do.*	*Do. having 4 do.*
	Total Males.	*Total Females.*	*Total Males.*	*Total Females.*				
1846...	207	207	271	192	63	23	5	4
1847...	215	214	268	197	45	30	7	2
1848...	222	221	271	199	47	29	6	3
1849...	240	227	257	189	53	22	8	3

On these indications the Court of Directors on the 4th December 1850 made the following remarks:—"The census of the Jáḍejá population bears obvious marks of incorrectness. In each of the four years from 1846 to 1849 the number of males and females above the age of twenty as stated in the returns is nearly equal, while below that age the males are much more numerous than the females. This difference would only be explicable consistently with correctness in the returns by supposing that female infanticide had been introduced into these districts within the last twenty years. You will draw Captain Leckie's attention to these remarks."

The statistics for 1850 showed a total of 168 females less than males for the year 1849-50. To this fact, as well as to the comment of the Court on the statistics of the preceding year, the attention of Captain Keily, the successor of Captain Leckie, was directed. The Statistics forwarded by Captain Keily for 1850-51 showed that the number of females under 20 years of age less than that of males had been reduced to 84. Explanations of the discrepancy were again asked of him. In furnishing these, on the 10th May 1852, he mentioned that the mehtás employed in making the census attributed it to natural causes. "On referring, however, to the records in this office," he added, "I find that returns of the Jáḍejá population were first called for in 1845, but that the chiefs of this tribe have not been required to enter into engagements for the suppression of this crime, nor required to report the birth or death of any female child." This observation was made in ignorance of the engagement and arrangements effected by Colonel Miles.* But Major Keily acted promptly on the conclusion at which he had arrived. He issued to the Jáḍejás a proclamation pointing out the discrepancies in the proportions of their male and female population which had been observed; requiring them to report the birth and death of every female infant at the time of their occurrence, and the inspection of the body of every child before burial by four respectable persons not Jáḍejás; and enjoining them to give notice of the serious illness of children, on the penalty of their being subjected to such punishment as Government might be pleased to inflict.

The Government considered new engagements to be hardly necessary, and requested that none should be insisted on, if likely to excite dissatisfaction among those repudiating the accusation and admitting the culpability of the practice of infanticide. It called for a copy of Major Keily's proclamation.

In acknowledging the requisition of Government, Major Keily wrote as follows, showing an anxious and most laudable desire to promote the cause of philanthropy in the districts under his superintendence.

"In reply, I beg to state for the information of His Lordship in Council, that as the petty Jáḍejá chiefs under this superintendency are not bound by any engagements whatever to suppress the crime of Infanticide,

* The engagements for the suppression of infanticide entered into by the Jáḍejás of Sántalpur on the 3rd March 1827, and by those of Chárchat on the 9th June following, are given in full in the Parliamentary Papers on Infanticide ordered to be printed on the 18th July 1828. They are similar to the other engagements inserted by us. The Jáḍejás bind themselves in them to observe a regular system of reporting births for registration.

I thought,—in bringing the remarks of the Honourable the Court of Directors to their notice founded on the marked difference existing between the sexes as shewn in the various returns of population submitted since A. D. 1846,—that it would be a good opportunity to require of them to agree to certain precautionary measures to render the crime more difficult of commission, and convince all that we were as much interested in suppressing the practice here as in other districts; for I could not but admit that unbound by any engagement, and with the present amount of supervision, which required the mehtá to visit each village once a year for the purpose of taking a census of the population, and being dependent on the assertion of the parents that whatever deaths may have occurred during the year were owing to natural causes, it was in the power of any one so disposed to be guilty of the crime without much fear of detection. It is true that I have and do receive constant assurances, that the practice has been discontinued. Still the difference is suspicious; and I was anxious to ascertain by a more vigilant supervision whether there were really grounds for mistrusting the accuracy of the returns submitted. The Jáḍejás under this superintendency are so well aware of the engagements that have been entered into by their brethren in Káṭhiáwáḍ, and of the precautions taken by Government to ensure the due fulfilment of their engagements; and the detection of those who may infringe them, that I think I may venture to say that no dissatisfaction would be evinced by them in subscribing to what others have previously subscribed to."

In reply to this communication, it was observed by Government, that the holding of inquests on the death of female infants and transmission of reports on every occurrence of sickness must entail on the parents considerable trouble and annoyance, while it was considered of much importance that the preservation of daughters should involve as little burden as might be indispensable. And Major Keily was requested to ascertain the arrangements observed in Káṭhiawáḍ and to assimilate the proclamation to them as far as circumstances might admit. This was accordingly done by him in a communication addressed to Col. Lang, after the receipt of which an agreement was most willingly entered into by the Jáḍejá chiefs of Sántalpur and Chárchat, in which they not only pledged themselves to abandon infanticide but to observe the same system of reporting and dealing with births and deaths which was observed in Káṭhiáwáḍ, and which was not different in any important particular from that originally proposed by Major Keily.*

* The engagement referred to was dated the 18th June and 15th August 1853.

The following are the principal arrangements which it embraced:—

1st. "Every Jáḍejá living on Sántalpur, and Chárchat to whom a daughter may be born shall immediately give information to the kárkun belonging to his district, who will enter the child in the list kept by him from which the yearly returns are framed. The number of births which have occurred during the year will with ease be ascertained by these means.

2nd. "In the event of any Jáḍejá's daughter dying, information is to be given to the kárkun in charge of the district, who will make every proper inquiry into the cause of the death, and enter the cause of death in the list.

3rd. "Should any female infant of tender age die, its body is to be shown to four of the most respectable people of the village, but of different castes, and the cause of the death must be ascertained as far as possible, and stated in the proceedings of the inquest which must be sent to the Government kárkun, after which the body may be buried; without this precaution the body must not be buried. No Jáḍejás are to be allowed to assemble on the pancháyat.

4th. "Should any Jáḍejá's infant daughter fall ill, information must be given to the Government district kárkun, and the cause of the illness mentioned to the kárkun, that it may be noted by him in his list.

5th. "In the event of any female infant dying, and being buried without acquainting the Government kárkun, and assembling a Pancháyat to ascertain the cause of its death, then the party guilty of the infringement of this agreement shall submit to such punishment as Government may decide."

The Engagement was signed by 153 Jáḍejas. On the proposal of Mr. John Warden, copies of this Engagement were to be sent to all parts of the Pálanpur agency where infanticide might be supposed to exist.

On Major Keily's returns for 1853, the following Resolution was adopted by Lord Elphinstone's Government on the 24th February 1854. "These returns show an increase equal to 1·320 per cent in the male and a decrease equal to 0·229 per cent in the female population under the Pálanpur Superintendency; but allowing for the disparity in the births during the year the result is more favorable than might have been expected. The male births give an addition of 4·150 per cent to that sex, whilst those of females afford only 2·758 per cent, so that, taking these results into account the balance is equal to 0·301 in favor of the females. No reason appears for suspicion that infanticide has been practised in any case during the year. Resolved that these results are satisfactory."

The Political Agency or Iláká of the MA'HI'KA'ṆṬHA',—so named from the Máhí River, though the district of country which it embraces is to the north even of the Sábarmati,—lies to the south of Pálanpur and Disá. It comprehends the northern portion of the peninsular Gujarát, bounded on the west by the Raṇ, on the south by the collectorate of Ahmadábád, and the east by the range of the Aráwalí mountains and its continuation separating it from Méwáḍ. It is tributary to the Gáikawáḍ; but of late years it has been under the political management of the British Government,—rendered necessary by the disorderly and turbulent disposition of its people,—and consented to by His Highness at Baroda. Its now principal chiefs are of Rajput origin and connexion, and consist mainly of Ráṭhors who gradually entered the country from Márwáḍ, appearing first in the District, where they are called Marwáḍís, between A. D. 1724 and 1734;* though a considerable number of its Rájás are Bhumiás, Bhíls, and Kulis, of the oldest races of India. Its highest Rajput family is that of the Rájá of I'ḍar.

* See Capt. Melvill's lithographed report on Páranteʹj.

The first discovery of the custom of Infanticide in the Máhíkáṇṭha was made by Major, now Lieutenant-Colonel, William Lang, so frequently and honourably noticed in connexion with the suppression of Infanticide in Káṭhiáwáḍ. He was appointed political agent in that province in 1839. His first communication on the subject was addressed to the Bombay Government on the 1st September 1842; but it was of such a character as showed that for some considerable time he had been devoting his anxious attention to the evil which he brought to light. His report was accompanied by a preliminary engagement which he had induced all the Pattáwats and Sirdárs of the I'ḍar State to enter into for the abandonment of the crime in their own families and those of their Rajput followers and descendants. This was in the form of a *petition* addressed to the British Government, most ingeniously devised, and forming one of the most curious and interesting documents which has passed before our notice in connexion with the humane exertions of British philanthropy. It was of the following tenor.

"Petition of [various Thákurs mentioned, in behalf of themselves and connexions] showeth, that amongst us in a very few places, the lives of female infants are saved, but generally infanticide prevails amongst us, and this has been a custom handed down to us from a very long period. This is a great sin; and its having come to the sirkar's ears, we, of every degree, through our darbár of I'ḍar, assembled and listened to the advice of the sirkár as to the heinousness of the crime, and were told to make such arrangement through the I'ḍar darbár, as to ensure the lives of infants being saved of every class in the province, and any measure and any assistance we might deem necessary to the abolition of this crime, to state them to the sirkár, and the sanction of Government would be applied for. From this intimation we have derived great hope that this great sin may be removed from us. As we have been anxious to save the lives of our infants, the sirkár may depend upon our doing our best endeavours to put a stop to it; and that no infant shall be allowed to be destroyed, we have unanimously come to a strong determination about this, and to effect it, we have stated below the assistance the sirkár ought to give us. We have been from time immemorial in the habit of marrying our daughters and sisters only in Udépur, Déwaliá, Dongarpur, and Banswáḍá; but the inhabitants of these places have so enlarged their demands that the poorer people among us are unable to agree to them. We wish the sirkár to make an arrangement with them, it not appearing to come from us, by which our marriages might be contracted in the ancient manner. Besides this, we are put to great expense for Bháṭs, Chárans, mendicants, in our marriages. The sirkár should fix some limit to the largess we are called upon to give.

"After this time no one will destroy the life of a sister or daughter; but should any ignorant person be guilty of it, he should be punished by the decision of four influential sirdárs of the province through the darbár, and the sirkár should sanction the decision made in this darbár, and never reverse it. A great number of Rajputs have come from Márwáḍ, who have no estates but depend entirely for a livelihood on temporary service they may obtain. The I'ḍar darbár should be requested to employ them in their Sibandí, etc., and not to employ any one else until they are provided for. The darbár to agree to this. The places in which it has been our custom to marry our sisters and daughters have been mentioned; no inferior person ought to be allowed, for covetousness or other cause, to marry in any other place. The sirkár must give us power to prevent this.

"On a jághírdár or tálukdár dying, leaving no sons, the person who succeeds to the property should be bound to marry off the daughters and sisters of that family; any one failing in this, the darbár to have the power to enforce it. The sirkár to sanction this.

"No one will be guilty of destroying an infant. Of this we are of one mind, and will sign our agreement to this effect in our darbár; but it will be necessary for the darbár to get for us a strong paper of agreement from all the caste, and assist us in this way. Any one offending afterwards in this crime, and breaking the agreement, to be punished by us through the darbár; the sirkár to give us full authority over our dependents in this matter according to the station we possess in each tribe; and by this the crime of Infanticide may disappear from the province. We are to be allowed to live after the manner of our people in our Jághírs and Tálukás, and no innovation is to be made thereon by the sirkár. Amongst us there may be some too poor to marry their daughters and sisters. The sirkár and the darbár ought to give them assistance. The sirkár has made arrangements for the abolition of this crime in Káṭhiáwáḍ. The articles of agreement [acted on there], should we afterwards wish to adopt [them] with our own, or any part of them, the sirkár should sanction it.

"This is our petition, and we wish the sirkár to assist us in carrying it into effect." 3rd January 1842.

In explanation of the circumstances in which this petition originated, Major Lang stated to Government that most of the chiefs having attended the Samlájí fair held in November 1841, he had fallen in with them during his tour in that part of the province, and conversed with them, both privately and publicly, on the subjects to which it refers, and found no difficulty in getting them to enter into what he stated to them to be the views of the sirkár of the great business of which it treats. The only reserve they manifested in the matter, it will have been observed, was in the desire expressed by them that cases of suspicion should be investigated by the I'ḍar Darbár in the first instance, and that the punishment should be inflicted by their own chiefs, a desire which Major Lang declared to be not unreasonable, as neither the I'ḍar nor Ahmadnagar family, then in the province, was suspected of the crime. Major Lang informed the chiefs at the same time, that if this arrangement should fail to eradicate the crime, more stringent measures would be adopted by the British Government. The Ráni of I'ḍar, acting for her son a minor, having expressed a wish to confer personally with Major Lang respecting the petition, it was not forwarded to Government till some months after it was drawn up.

On the *extent* of female infanticide in the Máhí-Káṇṭhá, Major Lang thus wrote.

"The practice of female infanticide is admitted by the Márwáḍi Rajputs themselves to have prevailed very generally among all the tribes of Ráṭhors ever since they have been settled in this part of the country. It is said to have been first introduced, twelve or fifteen generations ago, by one of the ancestors of the Kumpáwat tribe, who, for some reason or other which does not appear now to be known, bound both himself and his descendants by an oath never to preserve a female child. It is now, however, almost equally prevalent among the other Ráṭhor tribes in this part of the country, the Champáwats, Jétháwats, Udáwats, Ranmaláwats, and even the Jodás (except the reigning families in I'ḍar and Ahmadnagar and their immediate relations) as among the Kumpáwats; and there is no doubt that the reason of its having become so general is the difficulty these tribes of Raṭhors have of procuring suitable matches for their daughters, and the very great expense attending their marriage. From this latter consideration alone, the practice has extended to the Sesoḍiá Rajputs who came to I'ḍar with the Márwáḍí, and who have no difficulty in disposing their female children in marriage, all the tribes I have enumerated of the Raṭhors and some others being considered good matches for them. These marriage expences are very greatly increased by the practice which prevails among the whole of the Márwáḍi Rajputs of insisting on the bridegroom coming to the house of the bride's father to be married instead of sending their daughters at once to the village of the future husbands, as is customary with all other Rajputs in this part of the country and likewise in Káṭhiáwáḍ, but by which a Márwáḍí would consider himself for ever disgraced. The Chowáns [alias, Chohâns] and Bhaṭṭís, though likewise included among the Marwáḍís and therefore obliged to follow this custom in the marriages of their daughters, form an honourable exception, and I believe they alone do, to the general prevalence of the crime. The present Thákur of Mandétá, the head of the Chowáns has three daughters living, and the Toradá chief, a Bhaṭṭí, has both a sister and a daughter; but even in their villages infanticide is not looked upon as criminal, but on the contrary is probably as commonly practised among their Rajput followers, if not indeed by the poorer classes of the Chowáns and Bhaṭṭís themselves, as in other Rajput villages. So infectious, indeed, is evil example, that even among many of the Bhumiá tribes who possessed most of this province before they were deprived of so large a portion of it by the Márwáḍís, infanticide is not unfrequently practised. Although they have no difficulty in finding suitable matches for their daughters, and being in the habit of sending them to be married to the villages of their future husbands, they are not subject to the great additional expense entailed on the Márwaḍís by having all such marriages at their own houses.

"Besides the female children of the Chowán and Bhaṭṭí tribes, who are, I hope, more generally preserved, there are, I am happy to state, a few exceptions to the almost universal practice. Infanticide is not found even among the chiefs of the Ráṭhor tribes and a good many more among their Márwáḍí dependents. Among the Champáwats, the late chiefs of Chándraṇí, Tintaví, Wánkanír, each preserved a daughter; and in the family of the Jethá-wat chief of Ghátkol two have been saved. I have not yet correctly ascertained the number of female children in the families of the inferior classes of Ráṭhor Rajputs in the I'ḍar state, but the chiefs themselves do not estimate them at more than twelve or fifteen; and the preservation even of that small number, as well as the five daughters in the families of the Ráṭhor chiefs above mentioned, is generally ascribed more to the influence which happened to be exercised with their fathers at the time of their birth either by the late Rájá of I'ḍar or other influential individuals, than to any better feeling, although there are doubtless some few instances in which parental attachment has predominated over Rajput pride. The number of Márwáḍí Rajputs in the Máhikaṇṭhá is however very limited, not probably amounting to more than six hundred families, about one-half of whom may be Ráṭhors. In addition to these, there are likewise among the Bhumiás about two hundred families of Ráṭhor Rajputs, most of whom, I fear, occasionally resort to the practice of infanticide; and when to this is added between two and three thousand other Rajput families, which at the lowest calculation the province must contain, and it is remembered that many of them likewise follow the bad example set them by the Márwáḍís, it is to be feared that the amount of crime of this description committed throughout the province must be very considerable. None of the Bhumiá Rajputs, however, admit, as the Márwáḍís do, that the custom prevails among them, and when an arrangement, therefore, has been completed with the Pattáwats and Sirdárs of the I'ḍar state for the abolition of the practice amongst themselves and dependents, it will be an easy matter to extend it to the whole of the other districts, against which any good grounds for suspicion exist; and to prevent any such imputation being wrongly made against any táluká, a return of the number of male and female children above a certain age can in the first instance be called for, and the agreement for the suppression of infanticide only be required from the chiefs in cases in which any considerable disparity may be found to exist. After the arrangements have been completed in the I'ḍar Táluká, none of the other chiefs in the province would think of objecting to entering into such engagements on this subject as Government might require of them, every assistance they might wish being of course rendered to them in taking security from any of their Bháíyád Rajput subjects who might be suspected of the crime."

In seeking for a social remedy for the evils which existed, Major Lang considered it desirable that every facility should be given to parties saving their daughters to form suitable marriage alliances in their behalf with the Rajputs of the neighbouring provinces of Méwáḍ on the east and Wágar on the west; and that with this object in view the attempt should be made to lesson the usual marriage expences and especially the exorbitant dowries demanded by the Rajputs of the districts now mentioned. The parties petitioning Major Lang desired that proposals of this tendency should appear rather to originate with the British Government than themselves; and he suggested that the political agent in Méwáḍ should advise the native authorities in that province,—particularly in Udépur, Dewaliá, Dongarpur, and Banswáḍá,—to meet in consultation with the Máhíkáṇṭhá chiefs on the matter of doweries. He recommended the institution of a fund, similar to that of Káṭhiáwáḍ, for assisting the poorer Rajputs in the marriage of their daughters, and proposed that there should be devoted to it the Mausalí and other fines of the Máhíkáṇṭhá, and a moiety of the bazar fund of Sádrá, his head-quarters.

Sir George Arthur, the Governor of Bombay, in a minute dated the 31st August 1843, in review of Major Lang's report, (to use the words of Mr. Willoughby in a narrative prepared by him for Lord Falkland), "recorded it as his opinion that the overtures which had been made by the chiefs ought to be received in such a spirit as would ensure their confidence, but observed that in order to secure the abolition of the crime, measures of vigor, tempered with prudence and conciliation should be attempted by the political agent." That functionary was on the 25th October 1843, accordingly, directed to inform, by circular, the parties to the preliminary engagament, and others suspected of the crime, of the fervent interest taken by the Government in their movement and of its readiness to co-operate with them in removing the stigma which attached itself to all the tribes practising the crime. He was also requested to follow measures of suppression similar to those pursued in Káṭhiáwáḍ, with which he was so well acquainted, and which had met the fullest approbation of the Court of Directors,* and which experience had shown to be suitable to the social circumstances of the Rajputs in general. In particular, he was to procure a census of the male and female population of the Máhikánṭhá practising infanticide ; to furnish an annual notice of its results ; to issue a proclamation expressing the determination of the Government and chiefs to put down the crime, and offering rewards and protection to informers who should bring to notice instances of its commission after this warning ; to refer probable charges of guilt to the investigation of a pancháit of chiefs, when disposed properly to discharge that duty, their award, of fine or imprisonment, being subject to his confirmation ; and to assume the investigation himself, reporting to Government and suggesting the punishment to be inflicted, when he might fear that it might not be rightly conducted by the chiefs. Copies of the Káṭhiáwáḍ docu-

* Writing to the Government of India on the 16th May 1838, the Court of Directors say, "We highly approve of Mr. Wilkinson's well-directed exertion of moral influence for the discouragement of Infanticide ; we think it desirable that you should obtain from the Bombay Government and circulate among your Political functionaries, a clear, and succint statement of the system which has now been practised for some years with considerable success by that Government for the suppression of Infanticide in Káṭhiáwáḍ and which conforms in all respects to our conception of the most efficacious means of obtaining the desired result."

ments of 1834 and 1835 were furnished to him for his information and guidance. His census tables were to correspond with those of that province. He was to be careful in selecting a censor; and he was occasionally to test the work of the censor by parties repeating his inquiries without his knowledge. He was told that it would be an important point gained by him, if he could secure an engagement for the preservation of the female issue of marriages, both among chiefs and dependents, by a clause in marriage contracts. It was intimated to him that it was thought highly expedient to establish an Infanticide Fund similar to that of Káṭhiáwáḍ, the Government making advances to it, to be afterwards repaid, till a permanent source of income was provided for it. He was empowered directly to ask from Káṭhiáwáḍ any particular information he might desire.

The Resident at Baroda, through whom Major Lang's communication had been forwarded to Government, was requested to solicit the Gáikáwáḍ to co-operate with the British Government in the abolition of infanticide in the Máhíkánṭhá, and especially to devote the Mausalí and other fines to the formation of an Anti-Infanticide Fund with the same objects in view as that of Káṭhiáwáḍ. With this proposal, however, His Highness Sayájí Ráo declined to comply, intimating that the balance in the Káṭhiáwáḍ fund might be employed in the Máhíkánṭhá. The Court of Directors, which fully approved of the plans of Major Lang, observed that all fines for breach of infanticide engagements might be applied as proposed by him independently of the Gaikawáḍ's consent.*

* It may be of use to compare the views of the Government officials in Central India with those of Western India on the subject of the suppression of Infanticide in the Máhíkánṭhá. "The late Lieut. Colonel Sutherland, the Governor General's Agent in Rajputáná," writes Mr. Willoughby, in his minute of the 4th May 1849, "was furnished with a copy of the above correspondence, and requested to favor the Government with any remarks or suggestions on the subject which the might have to offer." At the suggestion also of the Government of

Major Lang's communication to Goverment on the subject of Infanticide in the Máhíkáṇṭhá, as already mentioned by us, was received by Government in 1842. Nothing further was heard on the subject from that quarter till the 9th of June 1848, when another report was submitted by Captain R. Wallace, the able successor there of Major Lang, from which we make the following extracts.

"No Census of the Márwáḍí population had been taken; and as this was an essential step towards checking the practice, I have caused one to be made this season. It has been framed on the form used in Káṭhiáwáḍ, and exhibits all the sons of the Márwáḍís now living, and all the daughters that the heads of families have had as well as those still alive. It did not occur

India, he directed Lieutenant-Colonel Robinson, Political Agent in Me'wáḍ, to ascertain the nature of the assistance which could be obtained from the chiefs of that district in carrying out the measures contemplated by Government for the suppression of Infanticide in the Máhíkáṇṭha.

"In reply, Major Thoresby, who was officiating for Lieutenant-Colonel Sutherland as agent for the Governor General for the states of Rajputáná, on the 9th February 1844, furnished this Government with copy of a letter he had on the same day addressed to the Government of India; forwarding to that authority transcript of a communication to his address from Lieutenant Colonel Robinson (the Political Agent in Me'wáḍ,) in which that officer stated it to be his opinion, that the measures which had been suggested by Major Lang for the suppression of Infanticide in the Máhíkáṇṭhá would prove ineffectual for the attainment of the object in view, as he considered that they left too much in the hands of the chiefs, the very persons who were naturally desirous of perpetuating the evil. Lieutenant-Colonel Robinson observed, that if it were determined that the interests of humanity would justify direct interference in the part of the British Government, the least objectionable mode of exercising such interference would be, at once to denounce the practice by proclamation, under the severest penalties, a course which in his opinion, would excite no odium nor entail any loss of reputation on the British name, but on the contrary would prove equally, if not more, efficacious to the attainment of the object in view, than the more covert and conciliatory, but complicated, arrangements, which had been suggested by Major Lang.

to me, until the census was completed, that for statistical purposes the sons that have died should have been entered as well as the daughters who have died; but this omission shall be rectified in the next census which will be drawn up in the course of the present year. As far as the male part of the population is concerned, I believe this census is correct, but very much the reverse as regards females, which will be apparent enough on reference to the accompanying abstract. And by comparison of the Chowán tribe (which is happy in the freedom from this unnatural crime) with the others, it will be evident that no account has been rendered of many females that have been born, and that the causes of death assigned for many of the departed are little to be trusted.

Name of Tribe.	*Males.*					*Female Children.*							
						Alive.				*Dead.*			
	Bachelors.	*Married but childless.*	*Married with Offspring.*	*Boys.*	*Total.*	*Married.*	*Widows.*	*Unmarried.*	*Total.*	*By poison.*	*By decease.*	*Total.*	*Total females.*
Chowán	5	7	17	18	47	4	0	13	17	0	2	2	19
Udáwats	6	9	9	10	34	1	0	2	3	1	1	2	5
Jetháwats	3	11	15	21	50	0	1	6	7	0	2	2	9
Bhaṭṭí	7	14	23	39	83	2	0	11	13	0	7	7	20
Sesodiá	15	13	27	41	96	1	0	13	14	7	8	15	29
Sángará	0	1	7	9	17	0	0	5	5	0	0	0	5
Kumpáwat	13	14	30	47	104	1	0	7	8	5	2	7	15
Champáwat	30	23	36	44	133	1	0	14	15	4	6	10	25
Rammaláwat	3	6	8	16	33	0	0	2	2	0	0	0	2
Jodá	2	4	6	11	23	0	0	0	0	0	0	0	0
Miscellaneous	17	21	53	74	165	16	3	23	42	1	14	15	57
Total	101	123	231	330	785	26	4	96	126	18	42	60	186

"In forwarding Lieutenant-Colonel Robinson's letter to the Government of India, Major Thoresby observed, 'Regarding the arrangements which have been proposed as means for putting an end to the occurrence of a crime in the Mahikáṇṭhá tract, Lieutenant-Colonel Robinson has expressed his sentiments in detail in the accompanying letter, and these lead to the conclusion that they would be found in practice to be embarrassing and inefficient. But with respect to the alternative suggested in the 16th paragraph of the letter, which would

"The age of the eldest female in the above list is 33 years; so that the births and deaths enumerated in the above table are spread over that period. As it was not till November 1845 that the mass of the Márwáḍís had bound themselves to abstain from the crime, and as the chiefs who had entered into these engagements at an earlier date had not the power nor probably much good-will to check the practice among their followers of their own authority, it is only from that date that we can expect any change to have taken place with reference to the practice of infanticide. I find that since that date, therefore, there have been 38 female children, of whom 7 have died. There are also 34 boys alive who have been born since that date; but, owing to the omission which I lamented before, we do not know how many boys born in it may have died. At the same time the near equality of the sexes as they stand gives reason to hope that the mere preliminary measures that have been adopted have effected some good, for on a narrow scrutiny of the original detailed census I have every reason to believe that ten of these female children owe their lives to them.

"The I'ḍar Darbár is prepared to bear the cost of any measures that may be necessary for the extinction of this crime, both by keeping up any requisite establishment for detection, and by extending pecuniary aid to the poorer Márwáḍís in marrying off their daughters. I

seen to contemplate States under the protection merely of the British Government, I am not aware of the course that could be conveniently made available for enforcing the penalties that might be prescribed, were a proclamation of the tenor noticed to be issued. By pursuing a steady line of conduct of interdicting the practice under severe penalties wherever we have the undoubted right to enforce our orders, in exhorting chiefs and people to abstain from it themselves and to use their influence for causing others likewise to abandon it, and in reprobating and shunning these who are guilty of it, much might perhaps be effected, in due course of time, towards infusing a better tone of mind in this particular, and inducing the community in general to view the matter in a more beneficial light in parts of the country where such change is to be desired."

am inclined to believe that for the purposes of detection it will not be necessary to maintain a costly establishment. The census shows only 354 Márwáḍí families in all; and if we deduct from this number the childless and those who are not even suspected of committing the crime in question, such as the Chowáns, the Sángarás, many of the miscellaneous Rajputs, as well as many families in which there are already two or three daughters, there will remain a comparatively small number whom it will be necessary to watch. The Márwáḍís, moreover, are so thinly scattered among the rest of the population, and from their position their domestic affairs are so well known to all around them, that the absolute concealment of the birth or death of a child would be impossible. The cause of death, indeed, may be more effectually hidden and must always be difficult of proof.

"I would prefer to employ different hands from time to time in framing the population returns, and investigating the suspicious cases previous to bringing them forward for trial, arranging in such a manner that every village should be visited at least twice in the year. But I would depend in great measure on the I'ḍar Darbár for the collection of evidence to ensure conviction, as there can be no doubt of its greater opportunities for so doing, and as I have confidence in its goodwill to the cause, though it may require occasionally to be prompted to action.

"It is, however, on measures of a nature the reverse of coercive that I look with most confidence for the eradication of a crime which, being opposed to some of the best interests of human and even animal nature, may be said to commence the struggle under considerable disadvantages. In addition to the grant of six hundred rupees per annum to the Infanticide fund, and the employment of forty Márwáḍís in the Sibandí of the state, the Rájá has just evinced his sense of the heinousness of the crime and his wish to aid and encourage those who throw it off, by the employment of ten Márwáḍís who have saved their female children since 1845 as his own personal attendants. These men have been chosen from the tribes and localities where the offence has hitherto been most frequent, and being in other respects fitting, they have been placed in a position where they can earn sufficient to provide for the marriage expences of their children. The annexation of the Ahmadnagar Parganá to I'ḍar,* and the consequent increase of territory and income, will open channels for the employment of others, while it is to be understood through the principality that no favor or patronage will be bestowed on those who labour under a suspicion of being guilty of infanticide."

"We have as yet no applications for pecuniary aid in making up marriage portions, nor do I think such applications should be encouraged, for there is quite enough of the sordid in the character of these Márwaḍís to induce a run upon this fund, if the example be once given. Indeed, the tendering pecuniary aid in such matters at all is obviously open to the objection that it may encourage the seeking of higher alliances than the ordinary means of the parties could warrant; and in this view it is to be regretted that the 4th stipulation made by the chiefs was ever admitted, viz. that which allows them to put a veto on the intermarriage of the daughters of their followers with the Rajputs of the country, who though not Márwardís are, as far as purity of blood is concerned, fully their equals. I am aware however, that the chiefs were only induced to sign the bonds by Captain Lang with the greatest difficulty; and to that gentleman belongs the honor of having taken the first steps to abolish Infanticide in this province."

Much of this information, furnished by Captain Wallace, was gratifying to Government, particularly that respecting the benefits accruing from the preliminary

* [On the call to the throne of Jaudpur of Takatsingh, the Rájá of Ahmadnagar.]

engagements, and the liberality and consideration of the Rájá of I'ḍar. He was requested, however, to explain how the orders of Government in reply to the first report on Infanticide in the Máhíkáṇṭhá had not been noticed. The Government adhered to its views about a marriage fund, the propriety and benefit of which had been so well tested elsewhere. Lord Falkland, on the suggestion of Mr. Willoughby, sent a personal letter to Gaṇpatráo Gaikáwáḍ, soliciting him to give up the fines to it which his predecessor and father, Sayájí, had declined to part with for this object; and His Highness compromised the matter by granting the half of them in time to come. The plan of having a permanent censor was adhered to, as favourable to the accumulation of experience.

Another Report on infanticide in the Máhíkánthá was presented by Captain Wallace on the 26th May, 1849. The following are its principal portions.

"The arrangement effected by Major Lang in January 1842 extended only to the Rajputs of I'ḍar. Those of Ahmadnagar were not included, and the departure of the chief Takat Singh to Jaudpur in the next year, and the doubtful status of that Parganá till last June, prevented any regular measures of precaution being taken with regard to the Márwáḍis of that district, though it had been generally notified to all the country that Infanticide hereafter would be treated as a crime.

"The transfer of Ahmadnagar to I'ḍar, and the consequent increase of establishments, presented the opportunity of giving some employment to the Márwáḍí Rajputs; and forty-five of them were enrolled in the new Sibandí, principally from the Kumpáwat clan, in which the crime had hitherto been most rife. The selection was generally made of young married men, who not having yet been hardened by the perpetration of this atrocity might be supposed most likely to take the opportunity which employment offered them of saving the money necessary for the future marriage of their female children from their pay ; but it was also imperative that they should be active and able-bodied, and that it should be plainly understood that bonâ-fide service was to be performed, and not that they were merely bribed to abstain from child-murder. The Rájá of I'ḍar had offered service of a somewhat more attractive kind than the ranks of the Sibandí to ten Márwáḍís of the higher classes as his own immediate attendants ; but, as he expected them to wear a certain kind of uniform, they all refused to avail themselves of the proposal.

"In the close of the year I deputed Dhondu Shástrí, a young man whom I had received from the College at Puná in 1847, and placed on this establishment, to frame a new and more careful census of the Márwáḍí population, as I had discovered some omissions and errors in that noticed in my former Report. This young man performed his task with zeal and honesty ; and I have the honor to annex an abstract of the voluminous Returns he had framed, which include almost every particular desirable to be known of the families and connections of this tribe of Rajputs.

"Dhondu Shástrí early reported several cases of Infanticide which had occurred since the framing of the last census ; and as an immediate example seemed necessary to save children yet unborn, I directed my Assistant, Captain Keily, to assemble a Court in strict accordance with Major Lang's settlement for the trial of the offenders, as I was employed in the southern part of the Province, and it would have been inconvenient for the witnesses and others to attend at my camp. Copy of my instructions to Captain Keily is annexed, in which I requested him to lay fairly before the chiefs forming the court the inevitable consequence of their slurring over their business as they had done several years before, when they fined persons guilty of Infanticide in sums so ridiculously small as to legalize the atrocity for a trifling pecuniary consideration. Captain Keily very satisfactorily led them to admit that no punishment could be considered sufficient that did not at all events thwart the selfish pecuniary calculations of the child-murderers by taking from them, in the shape of a fine, the money which they expected to save by their crime; and as the expense of marrying off a daughter to the poorer Márwáḍís was estimated at Rs. 150, he prevailed on the court to consider that as the minimum punishment. Two Márwáḍís were immediately brought to trial, viz. Ranmaláwat Padam Singh Anar Singh, aged 20 years, and Ranmaláwat Bhárat Singh A'bjí, aged 25 years, the latter for the destruction of a female infant in November 1845, and the former for a similar crime in September 1848. Both were convicted, and sentenced to pay a fine each of 150 rupees, or to suffer two years imprisonment in irons. In the latter case, Kasan Singh Thákur of Kotrá was shown to have been privy to the murder, and to have concealed it. He, moreover, refused to give any evidence before the Court, which came to the resolution of fining him 30 rupees for his complicity and contumacy. The prisoners Padam Singh and Bhárat Singh had been employed in the ranks of the new Sibandí, but were of course immediately discharged. Subsequently, on my camp having been moved to Ahmadnagar, I superintended in person a third trial of Kumpáwat Surat Singh Zálim Sing of Báwangaḍ, who was also convicted and fined 150 rupees for the destruction of a female child in November 1847. In the course of the proceedings, it appeared that the father of the prisoner Zálim Singh had wilfully concealed, from the kárkun employed in framing the census, the birth and death of the child in question. He also grossly prevaricated on the trial; and the sirdárs agreed to fine him 15 rupees for his conduct.

"These examples have startled the Márwáḍís. I am not, however, sanguine that they will be sufficient to put a stop to the crime. Indeed, I have heard with regret that there are strong suspicions against a chief (who was most forward in recommending the adoption of the infanticide regulations to his brother chiefs and dependents) of having himself been lately guilty of the crime; but as there is no direct proof of the birth of the child, and as I am aware of much ill-will towards him, I have contented myself with directing a greater degree of watchfulness towards him. Nothing, I am aware, would more surely strike down Infanticide than the conviction and punishment of a Márwáḍí of rank; but, on the other hand, a failure in conviction would be attended with various disadvantages unnecessary to dwell upon.

"The statements of which an abstract is annexed to this report enter more fully than hitherto into the domestic circumstances of the Márwáḍís; and a new statement has been obtained of all the women enceinte when the kárkun went through the villages. This is most important, to keep up the connection between the census of one year and that following; and there seems as yet to be no great difficulty in obtaining this information; and once obtained it obviously acts as a great check on the parents, when the birth takes place. We have also information of all the alliances of the Márwáḍís, which will probably be of use hereafter in removing some of the difficulties experienced by them in obtaining suitable connexions for their daughters.

"The whole number of Márwáḍí adult males is 558, of whom 441 are married. The adult females (wives of the above, and who of course come from other tribes) are 431. There are also 49 married Márwáḍí girls, some of whom have married into Márwáḍí families of other tribes than those to which their fathers belong. On the whole, however, it seems very unusual for any one to have more than one wife, their general poverty preventing it. The 441 Márwáḍí couples appear to have 432 living male children; and the whole number of daughters confessed to, living or dead, is 276. If, however, we suppose the girls really to have been equal in number to the boys born, we have barely two children to each marriage. Out of 41 I'ḍar chiefs, 19 have no sons, and the genealogical tables of the principal families show them to have been generally saved from extinction by a single life or an adoption.

"Of the 276 female children who appear on these returns, 78 have been born since Major Lang's last arrangements in 1845; and of these only 4 are reported to have been born in that year, 1 of whom is dead. 19 births are reported for the second year, of which two are dead. 21 births are reported in the third year, of which four are dead; and 34 births in the last year, of which 14 are dead.

"It may be interesting to contrast the reported births of boys during the same time,—in the first year, 30; in the second year, 34; in the third year, 31; and in the last year, 37. We have unfortunately no information of the number of deaths, during these years, the kárkun not having made particular inquiries as in the case of females.

"It appears, however, that the last census must be not far from accurate. The reported births of females having been steadily increasing for the last four years until now, the female births are to the males only as 34 to 37. The obstacle of the concealment of births may, therefore, have been in great measure overcome.

"Of the 14 deaths of female infants born in the last year, it has been ascertained that 3 were destroyed. On this account two Márwáḍís were tried and convicted, as reported in the preceding paragraphs, and one remains untried, he being at Jaudpur in the service of Mahárájá Takat Singh. The third trial that took place in this year was for the murder of a child born in 1847, but whose birth having been concealed by the parents was not entered in the returns for that year.

"On reconsideration of the arrangements that have been carried into effect, and those yet to come for the extirpation of Infanticide, it has occurred to me, that inconvenience and inefficiency may result from not having a permanent establishment to superintend them. The trial that I have made of Dhondu Shástrí (who as I have before stated was educated and graduated at the Puná College) has been so satisfactory, that I could not expect to find another person so zealous in the work and at the same time so free from the influence which might operate on a native of Gujarát, and I have therefore with the consent of the I'ḍár Darbár, nominated him to the supervision of the infanticide arrangements on a salary of 30 rupees, which he was before in receipt of on this establishment. The Darbár also engages to pay him marching bhattá while out in the villages, and to place two or three sepoys at his disposal during his employment on these duties."

Government informed Captain Wallace that it viewed with the greatest satisfaction the zeal which he had displayed in the good cause, and the attention which he had bestowed on the various matters noticed by him. It approved of the distinct measures proposed by him, as entirely consonant with instructions already issued to the Máhíkánṭhá agency.

On the 26th November 1849, Captain Wallace,—after explaining how no proclamation against infanticide had been issued, owing principally to the non-completion of the preliminary arrangements till 1846, shortly before Major Lang left the province, though all had been warned of the consequences of practising infanticide,—proposed that it should be generally intimated, in a proclamation, that no chief in the Máhíkánṭhá has the power either judicially or otherwise of injuring life or limb, and that this declaration should be held as including infanticide. The Government, however, did not consent to the limitation of the jurisdiction of the Rájá of I'ḍar to this extent, though he was then the only chieftain in the province who had the power of life and death in his hands under the superintendence of Government.

Captain Wallace's report for 1850, presented to Government on the 8th August 1850, was declared by the

Government to be "for the most part very satisfactory, though it will be necessary for that able officer to continue to exercise the utmost vigilance in watching and enforcing the measures adopted for the extinction of the crime." It appeared from the table appended to it, that in the year 1849-50, there were born 49 females to the Márwáḍí Rajputs of the Máhíkánṭhá, of whom, however, 13 had died. Compared with the preceding year, the entire number of females noticed by it had increased from 197 to 235. It intimated various punishments of Rajputs for neglect of reporting births and deaths, according to the regulations adopted. It mentioned that there had been no demands on the infanticide fund, and that in consequence the subscription of the Rájá of I'ḍar had not been called in for the year. It noticed the attempts made by Captain Wallace to reduce the *tyága*, or marriage gifts, to Bháṭs and Chárans; but the Government doubted the propriety of the accomplishment of this through British authority, lest voluntary gifts should be converted into permanent rights. Though Captain Wallace did not think that this result would follow, and suggested some cautions calculated to prevent it, the Government finally adhered to its opinion, intimating that only general efforts should continue to be made to lessen the expences of Rajput marriages.

The reports from the Máhíkánṭhá since the year last mentioned, have continued on the whole to be of a satisfactory character, though they show sufficient reason for the continued vigilance and exertion of the British officials in that province. From the last one received,—furnished by Lieut.-Colonel H. W. Trevelyan, an officer of much experience in Rajput affairs,—on the 18th November 1853, we extract the following table of the male and female Márwáḍí Rajputs for the last five years.

	Males.	*Females.*
1848-49	991	197
1849-50	1,005	235
1850-51	1,032	268
1851-52	1,059	294
1852-53	1,074	305

The increase of five years was of males 83 and of females 108. For the year 1852-53, the mortality among the children born was 4 males and 8 females, a fact which led Lord Elphinstone's Government to observe, that although "it may not have been caused wilfully," "it is a reason why the political agent should in no wise relax his vigilance, and should endeavour by every means to awaken among the Márwáḍis a sense of the criminality of infanticide, whether caused by active means or neglect."

The systems of infanticide which we have hitherto noticed have all been connected with *Rajput* tribes claiming,—in many instances, we believe, without reason,—to be the descendants of the ancient *Kshatriya*, or warrior, class of India. Another connected with the *Kulambís*, or *Kunbís*, or cultivators, of Gujarát, who are reckoned merely *Shúdras*, or members of the servile class, remains to be mentioned.

Mr. E. G. Fawcett of the Civil Service, when collector of AHMADA'BAD, directed the attention of Government to a disproportion of males and females in the villages of the LEWA' (or REWA'*) KUNBI'S which had been brought to his notice by Thákursí Punjásháh, the native revenue officer of the Daskrohí pargaṇá of that collectorate, directly subject to the British Government. His letter was dated the 30th December 1847. The principal inhabitants of the villages referred to had admitted the existence of the crime,—perpetrated generally by parental neglect,—owing to the heavy expences of marrying their female children into good families residing at a distance, and the indisposition of the higher Kunbís to give their daughters to the families near them from which they were content to receive their wives. Mr. Fawcett had been successful in getting the heads of the caste to enter into voluntary agreements to diminish their marriage

* Re'wa, popularly corrupted into Lewá, is one of the native names of the Nirbadá, or Nirmadá river.

expences. According to these agreements, the expences were to be reduced in some instances from rupees 3,800 to about rupees 700. Mr. Fawcett feared that the custom of infanticide extended to the adjoining territories of the Gáikáwáḍ and even the city of Ahmadábád itself.

Mr. Fawcett's communication having been laid before Mr. Hutt of the Civil Service, the Judicial Commissioner for the Konkan and Gujarát, for his opinion, he made a report on it to the Court of Sadar Adálat in Bombay, on the 29th February 1848, of which the following is an extract.

"I have had a partial knowledge of the existence of this practice in this province for some years. It first forced itself on my attention at the trial of some cases of murder, while session judge of this [Ahmadábád] zillah, in 1839, which indirectly arose out of it. I have made many inquiries on the subject, during my tours as judicial commissioner, and have often found persons to admit the existence of it, in reference to other castes than those to which they belonged, and have only been withheld from bringing it to notice, from the want of that evidence which might satisfy others, and the difficulty of suggesting a remedy." "It was I who about two years since directed the attention of Ráo Sáheb Thákursí Punjásháh, mámlatdár, to it. I then pointed out the caste in which it was supposed particularly to prevail, and the evidence by which it might be inferred. He expressed surprise, which might have been real, though I should hardly have expected any person in such a position in this province, to be ignorant of it, seeing that it prevails from Daman,* northwards. He then promised me he would inquire into it, and if possible do some thing for checking it, and well has he performed his promise. In saying this I by no means desire to detract from Thákursí's merits in what he has done. Every credit is due to the magistrate and himself."

* [Daman, belonging to the Portuguese, is the southern boundary of the Gujarát province and language.]

"The measures taken by the magistrate, strike at the root of the evil, and afford a fair prospect of success, provided the penalty can be enforced summarily, of which I entertain very considerable doubt.* Yet pride, in which the practice has its origin, still operates as powerfully as ever, and may be expected to lead to violations of the engagement, which it will be very difficult to detect and punish, although well known amongst the people; or if even by great vigilance on the part of the local officers, this can be guarded against, and the agreement maintained for the present. As the actual contracting parties pass away one after another, their successors may not be disposed to hold it as binding on them. For it must not be lost sight of, that the long prevalence of the practice has rendered the people so familiar with it, that their moral feelings are blunted, and they no longer perceive the heinousness of it. Still it is so opposed to the natural feeling of parents, and especially of the mother, that if all the leading people of the caste can be brought to consent to it, there will be much room to hope. The concurrence of the families in the Chelotrá and Pitláḍ, would seem indispensable to the present arrangement, from the former being those most esteemed by the people here, as offering desirable alliances for their daughters, as those at Pitláḍ are by those in Chelotrá. This might perhaps be accomplished by the magistrate of Kaira (Khéḍá) in the latter, but the other will not be so easy, Pitláḍ being in the Gáikáwáḍ's territory."

The absolute necessity for a prompt and energetic movement in this case was sufficiently apparent from the following returns.

* [The penalty was to be five hundred rupees, for a breach of the engagements to marry daughters in the contiguous, and not distant, countries. This penalty, though sanctioned by the magistrate, could obviously not be enforced in any of the Company's Courts.]

***Return of Births and Deaths of Female children of the Lewá and Kaḍawá* Kunbís in the Ahmádabad Collectorate for* 1846, 1847, *and* 1848.**

Parganás.	1846.		1847.		1848.	
	Births.	*Deaths.*	*Births.*	*Deaths.*	*Births.*	*Deaths.*
Daskrohí	115	109	134	106	136	87
Jaitalpur	59	39	68	39	73	27
Dholká	79	7	70	15	113	22
Total......	253	155	272	160	322	136

E. G. Fawcett.

Census of the Kunbí Population, the only Caste in the Kairá (Khéḍá) Magistracy in which the crime of Female Infanticide is said to prevail.

	Tálukás.	*Kunbí Population.*			*Proportion of Males to Females per cent.*	*Remarks.*
		Males.	*Females*	*Total.*		
1	Mahunda....	10,704	7,471	18,175	70	This Census was taken on the 1st January 1849 by the different village authorities. The Kunbí population alone is exhibited in it; as from the inquiries made, the commission of the crime appears to be confined to that caste alone, especially the sect called Lewá, which forms the majority of the population in the Cherotar districts; and principally the practice is said to prevail amongst the richer portion of the community called Potídárs (portioners). The disproportion, as noted in column 6, is striking enough.
2	Mátar.........	8,519	7,921	16,440	93	
3	Nariád	18,596	13,278	31,874	71	
4	Thásrá........	6,721	4,573	11,294	68	
5	Borsad........	12,347	8,772	21,119	71	
6	Nápáḍ.........	11,433	7,462	18,895	65	
7	Kapaḍwang.	3,150	2,226	5,376	71	
	Total...	71,470	51,703	1,23,173	72	

J. Webb, *magistrate.*

Kairá, Magistrate's Office, 23*d Feb.* 1849.

* [The Kaḍawá Kunbís derive their designation from the town and district of Kaḍí, north of Ahmadábád. They celebrate their marriages only once in ten years, and then, conditionally, even of children in the womb! This extraordinary fact was first brought to the notice of the author by Major H. Aston, late assistant to the Káṭhiáwáḍ political agency. Further and indubitable testimony respecting it was obtained by himself and the Rev. J. M. Mitchell, when passing through the Kaḍí districts in 1840, especially from Jayasinghjí, the farmer of these districts

Mr. Webb, with the assistance of the munsif of Nariád, himself a Kunbí, brought the principal Kunbís of the districts of his charge under engagements for the reduction of marriage expences, similar to those recommended by Mr. Fawcett, in the Ahmadábád collectorate ; but he was not successful in inducing those in the neighbouring districts of the Gáikáwáḍ and the Nawáb of Cambay to follow this example.

The Bombay Government, alarmed by the existence of such extensive female infanticide among the cultivators of the Zillahs of Ahmadábád and Khéḍá, requested, on the 20th September 1848, the judges of the Sadar Adálat* to issue a circular to all the magistrates in the settled districts of the presidency, informing them of the alarming discovery which had been made, and requiring them to ascertain whether there were "any grounds for supposing that the same abominable practice exists in any part of their jurisdiction." The magistrates of Baroch, Surat, Tháṇá, Ratnagiri, Belgáum, Dhárwáḍ, Solápur, Puná, Ahmadnagar, Násík, and Khándesh, and the agent at Kulábá, reported that "there are no grounds for believing this inhuman practice to exist in their respective zillahs, the magistrate at Dharwáḍ, Mr. Bell, observing that the districts of the Ahmadábád, and Khéḍa collectorates, to which allusion is made, are probably those in which the Grásiás and Thákur chiefs have a proprietory right in the soil, and periodical settlements are made for the revenue at intervals of several years, so that there is little direct interference on the part of Government in the details of administration, and that

under the Gáikawáḍ. The following is an extract from the statement given by this intelligent native gentleman on that occasion. "The Kaḍawá Kunbís marry only on two days, four days intervening between them, every ten years. The exact time is fixed by ten or twelve Bráhmans, who meet at Unjá at the temple of *Mátá*, to prepare a proclamation setting it forth, to be published by the headmen of the caste."]

* Messrs. Bell, Warden, LeGeyt, and G. Grant.

while it is very possible that the practice of infanticide may have existed unobserved in such districts, he conceives it impossible that it can be carried on in districts where the administration is entirely in the hands of the servants of Government, and which are subject to constant visits from European officers."* Mr. Davies, the magistrate of Baroch, was informed, in reference to his report on the subject, that the judges were of opinion that on further inquiry he would see cause for doubting his conviction that female infanticide was not practised in his magistracy. He afterwards frankly admitted his mistake, in an able paper on the social state of the cultivators under his charge. He found that in 50 villages the disparity between Kunbí boys and girls under twelve years of age was 31 per-cent, while that of the males of the whole Kunbí population was 27 1-4 per cent, being 15 per cent in excess of the males of the whole population, which, too, exceeded the females by 11 or 12 per cent. The disparity of the Rajput population of his districts, also, was very considerable. There is reason to fear, as thought by Mr. Hutt, that even the collectorate of Surat is not altogether free from the commission of the dreadful and debasing crime of infanticide, though, as we learn from Mr. Hebbert, the present vigilant judge at that station, no case warranting imputations against any particular class of the native population there, has lately come before his court.

In the East India Company's territories, in which the collectorates now mentioned are situated, infanticide, when proved, must, according to our laws and regulations, be treated as murder. The difficulty of proving the crime, however, which is there generally effected by the parental neglect of infants, without violence, is obviously very great. To counteract the horrid custom, we have the vigilance of our British officials, directing

* Letter to Bombay Government from Mr. M. Larken, Register of the Sadar Adálat, dated the 29th January, 1851.

that of the native officials acting under their authority; a stricter system than formerly prevailed of statistical report and registration; and the conventional agreement of the castes implicated to lessen their marriage expences and to take wives from their immediate neighbours, as first arranged by Mr. Fawcett. If the crime do not immediately disappear, it must be treated emergently by special legislation. As the Government recognises certain rights of caste as a social institution, it is perfectly competent for it, in extreme circumstances, to demand from the Kunbís practising the crime, as proved by the returns of their population, a heavy fine, to be levied on them as a body, and to be raised by the caste authorities which they usually recognize. A law must be framed to authorize their being treated in this case as if they were found in our non-regulation provinces.

CHAPTER XVII.

CONCLUDING OBSERVATIONS—HEINOUS CHARACTER OF JÁDEJÁ INFANTICIDE—THE TEMPTATIONS LEADING TO ITS COMMISSION—GENERAL MORAL DEPRAVITY OF THE JÁDEJÁS—INFANTICIDE OF THE RAJPUTS IN GENERAL—ITS IMITATION BY OTHER TRIBES— BENEVOLENCE OF THE EFFORTS OF THE BRITISH GOVERNMENT FOR THE ABOLITION OF INDIAN INFANTICIDE—ENCOURAGEMENTS TO PERSEVERANCE—PROSPECTS OF ANTI-INFANTICIDE—MORAL RENOVATION OF INDIA—BRITAIN'S MISSION IN INDIA.

The reader of the preceding pages will doubtless long ere this have formed his own opinion of the Infanticide of Western India, particularly that of the Jáḍejás of Káṭhiáwáḍ and Kachh. It is in some respects probably the basest and and most atrocious as a system, if we except perhaps that of the areois of the South Sea Islands, ever known to have been perpetrated on the polluted surface of this fallen and depraved world. It proceeds not, like the sacrificial infanticide of the Canaanites, Phenicians, Carthaginians, and other peoples of ancient times, and the mountaineers of Orisá in our own, from a misinterpretation of the character and will of deity, and their belief that they were doing their gods service, and deprecating evil, and purchasing blessings, for themselves and their families, when they imbrued their hands in the blood of their own offspring, or devoted it to death and destruction by the consuming fire. It is not like the infanticide of the Spartans, who killed their weakly children by severity of discipline, or unnatural abandonment, lest an incompetency on their part to discharge the duties of the state,—which they erroneously associated too much with physical power,—should bring on them disgrace and dishonour, if not ultimate ruin. It is not like that of the Persians and others, when shrinking from the reproach of adultery and the severe punishment with which it was visited, they removed by death their illegitimate children lest they should be witnesses against them of their own incontinence and impurity. It is not like that of the Arabs, who buried their daughters under their altars, when surprized by their enemies, lest they should fall into hostile hands and be defiled and dishonoured. It is not like that of the Chinese, who apprehend that, amidst the demands of an overgrown population, they may not be able to find the means of rearing those who could perform the least service for their own support. It is not like that of the savage nations, in which the paucity of the means of sustenance and the difficulty of procuring it by the uncertain and exhausting efforts of the chase, have suggested the idea of lessening the demands for it by limiting the number of those requiring its supply. It is not the consequence of pressing famine, as on the repeated failure of a crop, or the straitness of a siege, when energetic man and tender woman have been alike driven to the most revolting extremities, from the famishing cry of their perishing children or the ravenous demands of their own unsatisfied hunger. It is not that of the mean, and ignorant, and debased outcasts of a large community, whose vice has led them to forsake the pursuits of lawful industry, and who have betaken themselves to the practice of unlawful deeds and loathsome iniquity ; but it is that of classes claiming the highest lineage from the most remote times, and demanding the privileges of nobility, and even, in many instances, of royalty itself. It has not the sanction of the prevailing religion of the country in which it is perpetrated, though it is but feebly opposed by it, and is indirectly encouraged by some of its principles and institutes. It is not approved by the majority of the population in the midst of which it occurs, though it is tolerated by its apathy in the matter of human life, which is all prevalent, notwithstanding the fanatical regard which is universally exhibited for the preservation of the life of the lowest brutes. It originates in execrable pride and selfishness, in the determination to give no daughter in marriage except to families of the highest rank and with a nuptial expenditure too great for the circumstances of those by whom it is ordered and arranged. It is the preference of murder, for the purpose of supporting a fictitious greatness, to the dictates of nature and humanity calling for the preservation and rearing of offspring according to the universal law of rational and even irrational life. Yet, the temptations to its commission are palpable and powerful, in Hindu society, especially as it appears among the Rajput race; while the moral and social impediments to its commission by that people are comparatively feeble and ineffectual. Absolute morality in any one principle is unknown to the shástra by which they profess to be guided. The degradation of woman by Hinduism, which we have noticed in the commencement of this work, more than counterbalances the pauránik injunctions for the preservation of her life. She is intrinsically, with this system of religion, of value only in so far as she may be positively needed for the purposes of marriage; and a superfluous supply of her sex, as is imagined, may be treated as a nuisance. Hinduism takes the whole responsibility of marriage from the parties most directly connected with it, whom it unites before they are able to make a rational choice for themselves; and throws it upon the parents, who order the whole of the arrangements according to their own will. The affection and love of the parties joined in marriage, which constitute its real essence, and draw parties together agreeable to recognised affinities, are unknown elements in its consummation by Hinduism.

This remarkable and heterogeneous system of faith and manners creates difficulties in the way of marriage such as nowhere exist in any other country of the globe. It tells its votaries that marriage must never be celebrated beyond the bounds of each particular caste, whatever might be the advantages of its extension to parties passing under another denomination and inhabiting the same locality and possessed of equal advantages and worth. It tells the father that his child must never be married within his own clan, or even *gotra*, or paternal lineage, though reckoned from the most distant generations. It limits the time of appropriate marriage to the period intervening between the seventh and tenth year of a girl, and sanctions even an earlier union, which is most commonly required by the customs of Indian society. It demands an ostentatious and expensive method of marriage, with numerous presents, processions, illuminations, and feastings, most impoverishing to individuals and families. It sanctions the beggary of bráhmans, bháṭs, barbers, and chárans, and other religious mendicants, representing the gifts given to them as necessary and meritorious, and attributing the greatest mischief to the satires and curses originating in their disappointed avarice. It visits conversion to any other system of faith by social and civil excommunication, which a future change of sentiment and conduct cannot altogether remedy. It has put a certain stigma, or embargo, on the Jáḍejás, in consequence of the entrance of many of them in former times, from the rigor of the Muslím arms, within the pale of Muhammadism which they try to mitigate by most lavish expenditure, and arrogant assumption, and a strict observance of its lighter ceremonies as well as its most cruel rites. It speaks of the existence of an unmarried female after she has arrived at the years of puberty as a calamity. It affords no sufficient check to the general dissoluteness of society, so that in the eyes of some parties abhorring this dissoluteness, more however from its inconveniences than immoralities, the untimely death of their daughters is preferred to their future exposure to temptation. It makes no allowance for the social difficulties of a people like the Jáḍejás removed from their ancestorial homes on the banks of the Indus to the peninsulas separated from that region of the world by deserts and seas. For murder, as well as other crimes, it offers its easy atonements. It exemplifies the liberty which in circumstances of trial may be used for the disposal of offspring by the example of Krishna, who is said to have destroyed almost the whole of the race of the Moon, to which both he and themselves are supposed to have belonged. Its Rájgurs, or princely priests, present themselves as ready to take upon themselves in behalf of their dependents, the guilt of its commission. It has its rite of *satí* for the preservation of the purity of a widow; and though it formally condemns *bálahatyá*, or child-murder, it suggests it, on principle, for the preservation of the purity of a daughter. Its most intelligible analogue to a European, is perhaps the conventual system applied to the females of the higher classes of society in the middle ages. "The same motives,"—says Colonel Tod, whose Annals of Rájasthán, notwithstanding the many errors and exaggerations which are found in them, contain a wonderful fund of information and instruction, conveyed in the most genial manner, to the student of human nature,— "which studded Europe with convents, in which youth and beauty were immured until liberated by death, first prompted the Rajput to infanticide."* In point of atrocity, however, the conventual system, bad as it was, is not to be compared to Indian infanticide.

Yet, infanticide, as practised by the Jáḍejás, is still, we are pursuaded, a grievous and aggravated sin against their consciences and moral feelings. The universal law of nature for the preservation of offspring, is written so deeply on the heart of man that it can

* Tod's Rajasthan, vol. i. p. 635 et seq.

never by conventional customs or agreements, however plausible or convenient, be altogether obscured or obliterated. It is so guarded by instincts, and affections, and the general convictions of men, that it cannot be violated without the voice of God being heard uttering condemnation. While infanticide could originate only among a people reduced to a state of great moral degradation, it must have tended to increase and confirm that reprehensible debasement. No individual sin can be habitually practised by man, without the contamination of his whole moral framework and constitution. Every sin finding its continuance in the course of life is a prolific parent, with a numerous and horrid progeny. This fact is abundantly manifest in the past and present state of society among the Jáḍejás. The more narrowly it is examined in its general developements, the more disgusting, we are persuaded, it will be found to be. Notwithstanding the anxious and laudable attempts of our political officials to avoid unnecessary offence in their dealings with them, they have sufficiently revealed their character to make it the object of abomination, mingled with pity, to every mind in a state of moral sanity. While these proud and haughty chiefs have pled poverty and purity as their motives for the destruction of their daughters, they have not restrained themselves from expensive and sensual polygamy, and disgraceful and licentious concubinage with all castes and conditions of life both bond and free. The system of *pawaiyá*, which they have especially tolerated and encouraged in their territories, is an unparalleled invention of evil, which could only be the result of their surrender, through the maturity of their apostasy from goodness, to the vilest affections. Before the merciful interference of the British Government with the districts in which they are found, they were the scene of constant disorder, rapine, and bloodshed. To the general social and educational improvement of their subjects, they are perhaps more indifferent than any of their compeers within the widely extended territory of India.

But infanticide is not a crime peculiar to the Jáḍejás originally from the banks of the Indus, though it exists among them as a people in an aggravated form. It is the besetting sin of the Rajputs in general, as long ago alleged by Colonel Walker. It has been found, by Jonathan Duncan, among the stragglers from their main body on the banks of the Ganges. By Messrs. Montgomery, Raikes, Tyler and others, it has been discovered among their offshoots on the banks of the Yamuná. By Colonel Lang it was first seen among their wanderers on the plains washed by the Sábarmatí and Máhí. Sir John Malcolm, Mr. Wilkinson, Colonel Spiers and others, brought it to notice as abounding among their colonies in Malwá and other districts of central India, and the hill-country bounding them on the west. It has been brought to light among our latest conquests in the distant region of the Panjáb, or Five-Rivers, where the A'ryan race was settled in the time of the Védas. The interior Rajputáná, has, in reference to the existence and practice of this crime, been discovered by Colonels Tod, Lockett, Sutherland, and Ludlow, and Major Richards,—some of whom have not been slow to enter into conflict with the gigantic evil,—to be little, if anything, better than most of its extremities. From the example of the Rajputs, too, other tribes, as those of the Mínas and Mhírs of Ajmír and Udepúr, the cultivators of Gujarát, and the Miánas of Máliá have not failed to learn and commit the crime. Had it not been for the merciful interposition of the British Government, there is no saying to what extent it might have spread through all the provinces of India. Even as matters stand, there is much reason to fear that the remarkable disparity between the sexes in India which all our statistics reveal, is to be attributed to the comparative neglect and ill-treatment of infant female life.

The efforts of the British Government for the suppression of infanticide in the territories referred to in this work, and in other districts of India, have been in the highest degree creditable to the Indian administration and the various officials with whom they have originated and by whom they have been carried into practical effect. They have been characterized by a wisdom, and benevolence, and ability, and perseverance rarely exemplified in the annals of philanthropy. They commenced in Káṭhiáwáḍ and Kachh with our first intercourse with these peninsulas, even before we had acquired over them any considerable influence. They form an exception, and one highly honorable and important, to the just observation of Mr. Macaulay in his telling critical essay on Warren Hastings:—"But at first English power came among them [the Hindus] unaccompanied by English morality. There was an interval between the time at which they became our subjects, and the time at which we began to reflect that we were bound to discharge towards them the duty of rulers." British compassion, indeed, rested, on these provinces long before they had any direct relations to British rule. Káṭhiáwáḍ, as we have seen, was merely tributary to our ally the Gáikawáḍ, when Colonel Walker was requested to arrange its affairs for the promotion of its peace and prosperity, and to use his best endeavours for the suppression of the horrid crime which had just been discovered as existing within its borders. Kachh was remote alike from our frontier and authority, when the call was addressed to it to stay the parental hand in its accursed work of the murder of children. The suppression of infanticide was provided for by covenant in the very first engagements made in the name of Britain with both these territories. That covenant was the fruit of most able, ingenious, anxious, and long-continued negociation, directed against rampant prejudices, and injurious customs strengthened by time and encouraged by the erroneous interpretation of family conveniences, advantages, and necessities. The implementing of its provisions has for nearly half a century demanded the utmost stretch of political and judicial sagacity. It has required a combination of vigilance, and kindness, and firmness, but seldom exhibited. It has obtained sacrifices of time, strength, labour, and money from the Government, both abroad and at home, and from its various servants in India, which have been of a most costly character. Yet, these sacrifices have not been made in vain. The moral pestilence, by which provinces interesting alike in their historical associations and natural scenery and productions were polluted and destroyed, has been stayed, or well-nigh stayed, never again, it is to be hoped, to resume its awful ravages. The equilibrium of humanity, so long disturbed and disordered among important tribes, has been recovered; and free scope has been given to the play of natural instinct and affection long restrained and suppressed. The mercy and compassion of Britain have, among large numbers of the inhabitants of India, been brought as distinctly into notice as its power and justice. Its disinterestedness in the case before us has been conspicuous. Its procedure in it, as well as in that of human sacrifice, it has been impossible for Bráhmanical craft and ingenuity to misinterpret or misrepresent. While the diffusion of enlightenment in India, the relaxation of the bonds of caste, and the material advancement of the country have all been set forth by the advocates of unmitigated Hinduism as the sure signs and omens of the advance of the *Kali Yuga*, or iron age, preparatory to the destruction of the universe, as guessed at in the curious attempts at prophecy in the Puránas which were made on the first threatenings of Muhammadan conquest. In the most philosophical of these Puránas, that dedicated to Vishnu, the following curious passage occurs in reference to the very provinces with which our present volume has had to deal:—"Men of the three tribes, but degraded, and A'bhíras and Shúdras, will occupy Shauráshtra, Avantí, Shúra, Arbuda, and Marabhúmi: and Shúdras, outcastes, and Barbarians will be masters of the banks of the Indus, Dárvika, the Chandrabhága and Kashmír. These will be contemporary monarchs, reigning over the earth; kings of churlish spirit, violent temper, and ever addicted to falsehood and wickedness. They will inflict death on women, children, and cows; they will seize upon the property of their subjects; they will be of limited power, and will for the most part rapidly rise and fall; their lives will be short, their desires insatiable, and they will display but little piety. The people of the various countries intermingling with them will follow their example, and the barbarians being powerful in the patronage of the princes, whilst purer tribes are neglected, the people will perish. Wealth and piety will decrease day by day, until the world will be wholly depraved. Then property alone will confer rank; wealth will be the only source of devotion; passion will be the sole bond of union between the sexes; falsehood will be the only means of success in litigation; and women will be objects merely of sensual gratification. Earth will be venerated but for its mineral treasures; the Bráhmanical thread will constitute a Bráhman; external types (as the staff and red garb) will be the only distinctions of the several orders of life; dishonesty will be the universal means of subsistence; weakness will be the cause of dependence; menace and presumption will be substituted for learning; liberality will be devotion; simple ablution will be purification; mutual assent will be marriage; fine clothes will be dignity; and water afar off will be esteemed a holy spring. Amidst all castes he who is the strongest will reign over a principality thus vitiated by many faults. The people unable to bear the heavy burdens imposed upon them by their avaricious sovereigns, will take refuge amongst the valleys of the mountains, and will be glad to feed upon wild honey, herbs, roots, fruits, flowers, and leaves; their only covering will be the bark of trees, and they will be exposed to the cold, and wind, and sun, and rain. No man's life will exceed three and twenty years. Thus in the Kali age shall decay constantly proceed, until the human race approaches its annihilation."* The preservation of widows and infants by the British rule, and the general advancement and improvement of the country under British administration, form as striking a contradiction of many of the particulars of this professed prophecy as can be well conceived.

The success of the measures adopted by the Bombay Government for the suppression of infanticide in Western India, as we have already remarked, has been fully as great as could have been reasonably expected; though it must be admitted that, owing to several causes which have been sufficiently explained in the course of our narrative, there have been occasionally seasons of langour, to be much regretted, in their application. The indirect influences of these measures, too, have had a most humanizing effect. These are encouragements to perseverance, which must be felt and acted upon without intermission. The work begun, the advantages obtained, the experience accumulated, and the fruits reaped, must not be lost. The plans devised, and hitherto pursued, are entirely suitable to the object which they have in view, the abolition of crime by authority and covenant. They must be persevered in, at least for the present generation. Nay, they must, we deliberately think, be extended. The whole population under the British rule and influence, with all its diversified tribes and castes, ought to be brought under an efficient system of statistical inquiry and report and registration; and the course of its increase or diminishment, with its apparent causes, ought to be regularly noted, and recorded, and considered. Measures, calculated to remove the

* Wilson's Vishnu Purána, pp. 481-482. For more matter of the same kind, with curious variations and discrepancies, see pp. 622-626. See also the 12th Skanda of the Bhágavata, and the conclusion of most of the other Puránas.

sources of the evils against which we contend ought to be multiplied and improved. Such an educational scheme as has been introduced into Káṭhiawáḍ should be made to embrace every important town of that and the neighbouring provinces, special care being taken that the families of the chiefs themselves should share in its advantages, either by the appointment of tutors or attendance at school, as in individual cases might be found expedient. Let the principles of the late noble Despatch on education of the Court of Directors of the East India Company be extended to our tributaries and allies, so far as our influence can reach them, as well as to our subjects. Let grants in aid of useful learning, and that alone, be given to all schools without exception. In connexion with education, let there be no shrinking from the inculcation of the purest and most exalted morality, founded on the recognition of the only living and true God, the great legislator, as the Witness and Judge of human thought and action, and of his revealed word as an infallible rule of faith and manners. With the sound of the law, let the tender and loving voice of the gospel be heard, revealing to man the way of reconciliation to God by the only Saviour, and that of renewal and sanctification, and heavenly elevation, by the Holy Spirit. If this hallowed work, at least for a season, cannot be overtaken by government, from a regard to native satisfaction and co-operation, let its importance be frankly admitted, and every facility given to its communication by the compassion and enterprize of the Christian Church and Christian people, who know their Lord's will in regard to the propagation of his truth. Let a patience and perseverance in that work be manifested, equal at least to that which has been exhibited in the cause of anti-infanticide, which has required so many years for its maturity. Let us remember that there is a time to enclose and break up the fallow-ground as well as to sow and gather the harvest. Let us not be weary in well-doing, for in due season we shall reap if we faint not. Let us be stedfast, unmovable, always abounding in the work of the Lord, inasmuch as we know that our labour is not in vain in the Lord.

We augur well for the destiny of the British power in India, we would say in conclusion. By most wonderful providences,unforeseen arrangements,and remarkable deliverances and extensions, it has been established and preserved in the land. It has here found its place, not so much by our own conquest of the country, as by the voluntary submission to ourselves of the country, whose sons in almost every province have rushed to our standard and fought our battles. We have granted it deliverance from violence and oppression. We have given it peace, law, order, and religious liberty, such as it never enjoyed under any of its dynasties, the traditions of which extend long beyond the times of ancient European history. We have in reality lightened the burden of its taxation, both by lessening its amount, and calling forth to meet it the resources of the country to an unwonted degree. We are giving encouragement to its agriculture by surveys and modifications of assessments, and by canals for irrigation. We have imparted security and extension to its commerce. We are joining district to district and province to province, by roads and bridges, and excavations of mountain passes, and by a system of communication by steam and lightning, by land and sea and air, which its inhabitants deem miraculous. We allow its people to share in our administration, to the full extent of their present advancement in knowledge and civilization. We are seeking to elevate all its tribes in the scale of humanity. We have quenched the funeral pyre which destroyed the widow; and we are stemming the torrents of infant blood shed by the hands of unnatural parents. We have dispersed and destroyed its bands of Thags and Ḍakaits; and Tyága and Dharaná are already terms which we have to explain to its people as well as to foreigners. Its Maryás and Poshiás are passing away. Its suicides and human sacrifices are alike interdicted and prevented as far as human law can reach them. We are giving it our literature, and our art, and our science. And, above all, we are giving it our religion, even the religion of our God in heaven above, with all its unspeakable blessings for time and eternity. The night of its darkness has passed; and its dawn has come. Its light will grow and spread, and shine, more and more unto the perfect day. And a glorious day that will be to all the diversified tribes and tongues of India scattered over her gigantic body, from "Cambay's strand" to "Ganges' golden wave;" and from the Himálaya, where she lifts her head above the clouds in the azure vault of heaven, to her Cape of Kumárí, where she bathes her feet in her own ocean.

THE END.

INDEX AND GLOSSARY.

Errata.

Page 59, in second note, for "Ráydhan" read "Khengár."

Page 299, in sheet commencing with, for "Melville" read "Melvill."